Additional Praise for
Global Fundraising

"Penelope Cagney and Bernard Ross have done our sector a great service in bringing together such a talented team of top philanthropy specialists and non-profit experts to address the big issues covered by this book and give us their insights. In times of unprecedented challenges there's much excitement and optimism here, as well as sound guidance and helpful advice. Anyone interested in fundraising and philanthropy internationally will find this book a great investment."

> **—Ken Burnett**, author, Relationship
> Fundraising and other books

"*Global Fundraising*, for an international fundraiser, is like have a Platinum Card for your favourite airline and being flown business class around the world gathering insights from some of the brightest and best fundraising practitioners on this planet. Global Giving is a must have, must read, must digest atlas for anyone taking a serious look at what is happening today in the ever globalised world of fundraising and philanthropy."

> **—Daryl Upsall**, Chief Executive,
> Daryl Upsall Consulting International

"This book is a long-overdue look at philanthropy globally. It will help every fundraiser put their fundraising program into perspective."

> **—Harvey McKinnon**, President, Harvey McKinnon
> Associates; author of 11 Questions Every Donor Asks
> and the number one international bestseller
> The Power of Giving

"Generosity always finds a way to help those in need. This extraordinary book opens our eyes to experiences from people all over the world whose remarkable vision and creativity are changing the way we look at fundraising. Without a doubt, a can´t miss read."

> **—Isabella Navarro**, former Development Director,
> Universidad de Monterrey, Mexico

A Donor Bill of Rights

PHILANTHROPY is based on voluntary action for the common good. It is a tradition of giving and sharing that is primary to the quality of life. To assure that philanthropy merits the respect and trust of the general public, and that donors and prospective donors can have full confidence in the not-for-profit organizations and causes they are asked to support, we declare that all donors have these rights:

I.
To be informed of the organization's mission, of the way the organization intends to use donated resources, and of its capacity to use donations effectively for their intended purposes.

II.
To be informed of the identity of those serving on the organization's governing board, and to expect the board to exercise prudent judgement in its stewardship responsibilities.

III.
To have access to the organization's most recent financial statements.

IV.
To be assured their gifts will be used for the purposes for which they were given.

V.
To receive appropriate acknowledgement and recognition.

VI.
To be assured that information about their donations is handled with respect and with confidentiality to the extent provided by law.

VII.
To expect that all relationships with individuals representing organizations of interest to the donor will be professional in nature.

VIII.
To be informed whether those seeking donations are volunteers, employees of the organization or hired solicitors.

IX.
To have the opportunity for their names to be deleted from mailing lists that an organization may intend to share.

X.
To feel free to ask questions when making a donation and to receive prompt, truthful and forthright answers.

DEVELOPED BY
Association for Healthcare Philanthropy (AHP)
Association of Fundraising Professionals (AFP)
Council for Advancement and Support of Education (CASE)
Giving Institute: Leading Consultants to Non-Profits

ENDORSED BY
(in formation)
Independent Sector
National Catholic Development Conference (NCDC)
National Committee on Planned Giving (NCPG)
Council for Resource Development (CRD)
United Way of America

AFP Code of Ethical Principles and Standards

ETHICAL PRINCIPLES • Adopted 1964; amended Sept. 2007

The Association of Fundraising Professionals (AFP) exists to foster the development and growth of fundraising professionals and the profession, to promote high ethical behavior in the fundraising profession and to preserve and enhance philanthropy and volunteerism. Members of AFP are motivated by an inner drive to improve the quality of life through the causes they serve. They serve the ideal of philanthropy, are committed to the preservation and enhancement of volunteerism; and hold stewardship of these concepts as the overriding direction of their professional life. They recognize their responsibility to ensure that needed resources are vigorously and ethically sought and that the intent of the donor is honestly fulfilled. To these ends, AFP members, both individual and business, embrace certain values that they strive to uphold in performing their responsibilities for generating philanthropic support. AFP business members strive to promote and protect the work and mission of their client organizations.

AFP members both individual and business aspire to:

- practice their profession with integrity, honesty, truthfulness and adherence to the absolute obligation to safeguard the public trust
- act according to the highest goals and visions of their organizations, professions, clients and consciences
- put philanthropic mission above personal gain;
- inspire others through their own sense of dedication and high purpose
- improve their professional knowledge and skills, so that their performance will better serve others
- demonstrate concern for the interests and well-being of individuals affected by their actions
- value the privacy, freedom of choice and interests of all those affected by their actions
- foster cultural diversity and pluralistic values and treat all people with dignity and respect
- affirm, through personal giving, a commitment to philanthropy and its role in society
- adhere to the spirit as well as the letter of all applicable laws and regulations
- advocate within their organizations adherence to all applicable laws and regulations
- avoid even the appearance of any criminal offense or professional misconduct
- bring credit to the fundraising profession by their public demeanor
- encourage colleagues to embrace and practice these ethical principles and standards
- be aware of the codes of ethics promulgated by other professional organizations that serve philanthropy

ETHICAL STANDARDS

Furthermore, while striving to act according to the above values, AFP members, both individual and business, agree to abide (and to ensure, to the best of their ability, that all members of their staff abide) by the AFP standards. Violation of the standards may subject the member to disciplinary sanctions, including expulsion, as provided in the AFP Ethics Enforcement Procedures.

MEMBER OBLIGATIONS

1. Members shall not engage in activities that harm the members' organizations, clients or profession.
2. Members shall not engage in activities that conflict with their fiduciary, ethical and legal obligations to their organizations, clients or profession.
3. Members shall effectively disclose all potential and actual conflicts of interest; such disclosure does not preclude or imply ethical impropriety.
4. Members shall not exploit any relationship with a donor, prospect, volunteer, client or employee for the benefit of the members or the members' organizations.
5. Members shall comply with all applicable local, state, provincial and federal civil and criminal laws.
6. Members recognize their individual boundaries of competence and are forthcoming and truthful about their professional experience and qualifications and will represent their achievements accurately and without exaggeration.
7. Members shall present and supply products and/or services honestly and without misrepresentation and will clearly identify the details of those products, such as availability of the products and/or services and other factors that may affect the suitability of the products and/or services for donors, clients or nonprofit organizations.
8. Members shall establish the nature and purpose of any contractual relationship at the outset and will be responsive and available to organizations and their employing organizations before, during and after any sale of materials and/or services. Members will comply with all fair and reasonable obligations created by the contract.

9. Members shall refrain from knowingly infringing the intellectual property rights of other parties at all times. Members shall address and rectify any inadvertent infringement that may occur.
10. Members shall protect the confidentiality of all privileged information relating to the provider/client relationships.
11. Members shall refrain from any activity designed to disparage competitors untruthfully.

SOLICITATION AND USE OF PHILANTHROPIC FUNDS

12. Members shall take care to ensure that all solicitation and communication materials are accurate and correctly reflect their organizations' mission and use of solicited funds.
13. Members shall take care to ensure that donors receive informed, accurate and ethical advice about the value and tax implications of contributions.
14. Members shall take care to ensure that contributions are used in accordance with donors' intentions.
15. Members shall take care to ensure proper stewardship of all revenue sources, including timely reports on the use and management of such funds.
16. Members shall obtain explicit consent by donors before altering the conditions of financial transactions.

PRESENTATION OF INFORMATION

17. Members shall not disclose privileged or confidential information to unauthorized parties.
18. Members shall adhere to the principle that all donor and prospect information created by, or on behalf of, an organization or a client is the property of that organization or client and shall not be transferred or utilized except on behalf of that organization or client.
19. Members shall give donors and clients the opportunity to have their names removed from lists that are sold to, rented to or exchanged with other organizations.
20. Members shall, when stating fundraising results, use accurate and consistent accounting methods that conform to the appropriate guidelines adopted by the American Institute of Certified Public Accountants (AICPA)* for the type of organization involved. (* In countries outside of the United States, comparable authority should be utilized.)

COMPENSATION AND CONTRACTS

21. Members shall not accept compensation or enter into a contract that is based on a percentage of contributions; nor shall members accept finder's fees or contingent fees. Business members must refrain from receiving compensation from third parties derived from products or services for a client without disclosing that third-party compensation to the client (for example, volume rebates from vendors to business members).
22. Members may accept performance-based compensation, such as bonuses, provided such bonuses are in accord with prevailing practices within the members' own organizations and are not based on a percentage of contributions.
23. Members shall neither offer nor accept payments or special considerations for the purpose of influencing the selection of products or services.
24. Members shall not pay finder's fees, commissions or percentage compensation based on contributions, and shall take care to discourage their organizations from making such payments.
25. Any member receiving funds on behalf of a donor or client must meet the legal requirements for the disbursement of those funds. Any interest or income earned on the funds should be fully disclosed.

The AFP Fund Development Series

The AFP Fund Development Series is intended to provide fund development professionals and volunteers, including board members (and others interested in the nonprofit sector), with top-quality publications that help advance philanthropy as voluntary action for the public good. Our goal is to provide practical, timely guidance and information on fundraising, charitable giving, and related subjects. The Association of Fundraising Professionals (AFP) and John Wiley & Sons, Inc. each bring to this innovative collaboration unique and important resources that result in a whole greater than the sum of its parts. For information on other books in the series, please visit:

http://www.afpnet.org

Global Fundraising

THE ASSOCIATION OF FUNDRAISING PROFESSIONALS

The Association of Fundraising Professionals (AFP) represents over 30,000 members in more than 207 chapters throughout the United States, Canada, Mexico, and China, working to advance philanthropy through advocacy, research, education, and certification programs.

The association fosters development and growth of fundraising professionals and promotes high ethical standards in the fundraising profession. For more information or to join the world's largest association of fundraising professionals, visit www.afpnet.org.

2012-2013 AFP PUBLISHING ADVISORY COMMITTEE

John Wiley & Sons, Inc.:
Susan McDermott
Senior Editor (Professional/Trade Division)

AFP Staff:
Jacklyn P. Boice
Editor-in-Chief, Advancing Philanthropy
Chris Griffin
Professional Advancement Coordinator
Rhonda Starr
Vice President, Education and Training
Reed Stockman
AFP Staff Support

Global Fundraising

How the World Is Changing

the Rules of Philanthropy

PENELOPE CAGNEY

BERNARD ROSS

WILEY

John Wiley & Sons, Inc.

Cover Design: Wendy Mount
Cover Image: © Andrew Johnson/Getty Images

Published by John Wiley & Sons, Inc., Hoboken, New Jersey.
Published simultaneously in Canada.

For general information on our other products and services or for technical support, please contact
our Customer Care Department within the United States at (800) 762-2974, outside the United
States at (317) 572-3993 or fax (317) 572-4002.

Wiley publishes in a variety of print and electronic formats and by print-on-demand. Some
material included with standard print versions of this book may not be included in e-books or in
print-on-demand. If this book refers to media such as a CD or DVD that is not included in the
version you purchased, you may download this material at http://booksupport.wiley.com. For more
information about Wiley products, visit www.wiley.com.

Library of Congress Cataloging-in-Publication Data:

Cagney, Penelope, 1956-
    Global fundraising: how the world is changing the rules of philanthropy / Penelope Cagney and
Bernard Ross.
    pages cm.—(The AFP/Wiley fund development series)
    Includes index.
    ISBN 978-1-118-370 70-4 (cloth); ISBN 978-1-118-41726-3 (ebk);
    ISBN 978-1-118-42052-2 (ebk); ISBN 978-1-118-57017-3 (ebk)
        1. Charities. 2. Globalization. I. Ross, Bernard, 1953- II. Title.
HV40.35.C34   2013
361.7—dc23
                                                                        2012041910
Printed in the United States of America
10 9 8 7 6 5 4 3 2 1

*Penelope Cagney dedicates this book to Nathan Newman,
for all of his support and encouragement.*

*Bernard Ross dedicates this book to George Smith, a wonderful
friend and guide to many nonprofits worldwide—
his words were his gift to us all.*

Contents

Foreword

ANDREW WATT, PRESIDENT AND CEO,
AFP INTERNATIONAL

We're inclined to talk as if globalization is a recent phenomenon. That the links we see today, from culture to culture, in global business and entrepreneurship, are something new.

Take a step back from what we read about a flat world for one moment and remember the trade routes from east to west, developing commercial links between China and Rome and all the countries in between, beginning in the pre-Christian era. Think of the way in which the influences of religion, their cultures, science and learning, from Islam, Buddhism, and Christianity, spread along those same trade routes.

Consider the origins of many of the great corporations of the twenty-first century in the global industrialization of the nineteenth—manufacturing, engineering, the exploitation of mineral resources and the operational infrastructure necessary to underpin them—we are not seeing any radical shift in approach to maximizing resources and benefits today.

The differences are differences of scale and resource. New emerging powerhouses of wealth in China, India, and Brazil—and many others besides; a generation of entrepreneurs the like of which has not been seen in more than a hundred years; population growth on an exponential scale and an equivalent growth in social need; technology-supporting connections at the click of a button; technology-supporting trades in a millionth of a second; technology-supporting lightning reactions, both good and bad.

For all the progress, all the growth, the problems that we faced in the nineteenth century of social inclusion, health, education, and political engagement are with us still. Exponential growth has not supported stability in our environment. We have seldom lived in more volatile times, economically or politically and, if ever there was such a thing as a social compact, surely governments are tearing it up as we speak?

There has never been a greater need for the impact that our community, the civil society, can bring. But we have terrifying responsibilities to ensure that our impact is a beneficial one. By its nature, civil society is unstructured, informal. Flexibility and speed of reaction are some of our strengths. But lack of structure, lack of a consistent message and a consistent approach means that our impact is far smaller than it could or should be.

We are responsible, not just for the impact of our own organizations, but for ensuring that our collective impact far outweighs the sum of its parts. We are responsible for working with partners beyond the boundaries of the NGO community—in truth, for creating and shaping a civil society inclusive of governments, the corporate sector, and giving expression to the public voice. We are the enablers—the link that binds these disparate communities together. And we have a responsibility to shape that environment to secure change and the growth of a just and fair society for all.

It's easy to forget, as we go about our daily lives, that there are essential building blocks that we have to develop.

We have to ensure that there is an enabling environment to support the work we do. Like it or not, without the partnership of government in the form of a clear, consistent, and equitable regulatory environment, we cannot begin to achieve a unified and focused community. Look to those arenas where such a thing has yet to exist. In some instances, a morass of inconsistent and diverse regulation, enforced by multiple agencies, ensures chaos and inhibits engagement from those who want to support us most. In others, the lack of clear regulation allows governments to act in an entirely arbitrary fashion, following political objectives of the moment with little or no concern for the impact on society that follows in the wake of their actions.

We can drive professionalism, we can drive awareness of good and bad practice, but without the framework of regulation and the partnership of government, we have a much reduced chance of achieving the understanding, support, and partnership of the communities in which we live.

Education, at the professional level through training and the resources to be found in books like this, yes, but also education of that greatest of our partners, our public. We have signally failed, over many years, to stand up and engage on the issue of "This is who we are; this is the impact that, with you, we achieve; and this is what it takes to secure that impact." Communication, engagement, and investment. We have failed again and again in this and yet we still pretend to be surprised at the lack of trust that is so frequently expressed in us and our work. We appear to have no understanding that it is a case of "if not us, then who?" Each of us has the responsibility of making those connections, standing up for our cause, and shouting how we have to support it.

It's for that reason that I am so glad to see the publication of this book, edited by Penelope Cagney and Bernard Ross.

The themes of the book address the strategic issues—infrastructure, strategy, regulation, and impact—in our rapidly changing and global environment. It also addresses the impact that our ever-increasing battery of tools, knowledge, and understanding has had and how it is being applied to best effect in many different environments around the world.

We can access much of that information for ourselves—using those self-same tools, but I would question whether we are able to interpret it effectively for ourselves. Penelope and Bernard have brought together a group of experts better placed than any others to help us with that interpretation and to highlight the resources that are available to us. Better yet, to highlight experiences from around the globe that we can draw on for inspiration.

More than anything else, this book highlights for me the collective strength that we have as fundraisers—a single community around the globe. We are a community dedicated to ensuring change, to ensuring impact. If there is one thing that we should take away with us, it is that, in the words of Desmond Tutu, speaking to fundraisers in Baltimore in 2010, "This is a noble profession. Yours is a noble calling."

Remember those words as you read this book and think about what they mean. Our community is more than a profession—we are the very heart of a movement for change.

Acknowledgments

The editors would like to thank the AFP Book Advisory Committee members for their recognition of the rapidly changing world of fundraising and their initiative and foresight in undertaking publication of this book. We would also like to thank our John Wiley & Sons editors, Susan McDermott, Jennifer MacDonald, and Donna Martone, for their wise guidance in this undertaking. We are also grateful to all of the authors who generously contributed their insight and knowledge of philanthropy.

A special thanks from Bernard Ross to his =mc colleagues Clare Segal, Angela Cluff, and Paula Guillet de Monthoux for their help, encouragement, and occasional glasses of wine.

P.C.
B.R.

CHAPTER 1

Introduction to Global Fundraising

PENELOPE CAGNEY AND BERNARD ROSS

Editing this book has been a humbling and exciting experience; humbling because, as two experienced—and supposedly internationally savvy—fundraisers, we were constantly impressed at the extraordinary achievements in fundraising happening outside the North American/ European bubble; and exciting because many of those developments seemed to offer innovation or developments that have implications for European and U.S. fundraisers. Just as the economic balance is changing in the world, so the balance in fundraising may be changing.

WHAT THIS BOOK IS ABOUT

This book is about global developments in philanthropy that are rocking the fundraising world and shattering conceptions about where philanthropy is strong and where fundraising innovation and creativity exist. This book presents successes from India, Brazil, Russia, Australia, Japan, and many other countries that inspire fundraisers. The book is also intended to enlighten readers about specific areas of fundraising important to the new global order—technology, innovation, and major donors. It is also about truly global nongovernmental organizations (NGOs)—the charity giants—that in relative scale are like the behemoth Jupiter is in relationship to the other planets of the solar system.

WHO THIS BOOK IS FOR

First and foremost, this book is for fundraisers, everywhere. It is also for nonprofit CEOs who are considering the philanthropic potential outside of their own country's borders. It is for other nonprofit professionals who work hand in hand with fundraisers and must understand these new global developments to most effectively carry out their own work. Those involved with grant-making and other philanthropy will learn from profiles of exemplary yet little-known international philanthropists and about general developments in the nonprofit sector worldwide. The book is for those who provide essential infrastructure for the sector—the associations, regulatory bodies, and resource organizations. Finally, this book is designed to open the eyes of anyone who still thinks that fundraising and philanthropy are the prerogative of North Americans and Europeans alone.

ABOUT THE EDITORS AND CONTRIBUTORS

Editor Bernard Ross is recognized around the world as one of the few whose fundraising, training, and management consulting expertise and experience really spans the globe. One of his company's (=mc) specialties is meeting the unique needs of international nongovernmental organizations (INGOs). He is a regular presenter at fundraising conferences around the world including the Resource Alliance's International Fundraising Congress (IFC) and AFP International's annual convening.

Editor Penelope Cagney has more than two decades of fundraising consulting experience on three continents. Early in her career she recognized the growing influence of globalization on the nonprofit sector. After graduate study of the growth of private sector funding in Great Britain, she cofounded a consulting firm there. It was then that the editors first met and had their first literary collaboration on a book about nonprofit management.

The contributors to this book are top professionals from around the world whose achievements would be recognized anywhere. Most of them are fundraising practitioners and consultants who have helped advance the work of many of the most significant NGOs on earth. All of them have been chosen not only for their success in the field, but also for their understanding, insight, and contribution to the development of philanthropy in their own region.

Seven Global Megatrends

There are some megatrends we spotted while reviewing the inputs from the skilled and experienced contributors featured in this book.

As you read this book we'd be glad to know if you pick up on the same broad issues and if they represent your view on the big trends that are happening. You may well look at the same data and think differently about it.

Trend 1: There Is a Continuing Growth of Great Wealth and Some of It Is Being Diverted to Philanthropy

Great wealth is no longer confined to the developed world—but it is still concentrated in a small number of countries. It is also concentrated in the hands of a small number of people as global inequalities increase. The inequalities exist in many nations—but they raise some significant challenges in territories like those in the Gulf or nations like Russia where there is a more limited commitment to transparency about how wealth is acquired or distributed. For fundraisers the challenge may not simply be securing funds but ensuring that the funds secured will fit with the value and ethical base of their charity.

Regardless of the ethical challenges about who really owns the money, or even how they got it, there is a growing interest among nonprofits in major donors, with increasing numbers of domestic and international NGOs making specialist appointments to improve their potential. But this organizational issue in *fundraising* is not necessarily matched by donor interest in *philanthropy*. So although the Giving Pledge has taken off in the United States, it has been less successful in engaging the rich elsewhere. And Carlos Slim—one of the world's richest men—has publicly expressed his frustration at the poor performance of NGOs in addressing the challenges in his native Mexico. Many philanthropists indeed are setting up their own operating agencies or looking for new ways to deliver change. This is a challenge to NGOs that have believed that all philanthropy should be channeled through them.

Even where NGOs are the preferred channel, the culture of philanthropy needs to take root and become more sophisticated to enable fundraisers to do their work well. In parallel we need donors to become more effective in how they invest. If not we may see more of the dreadful if well-meaning philanthropic ineptitude of Madonna in Malawi and Oprah Winfrey in South Africa.

Trend 2: Nonprofit Innovations, in Fundraising and Elsewhere, Are No Longer Coming Just from the United States or Europe

There are exciting and challenging innovations growing up in fundraising in India and China and Argentina and Kenya. These innovations are not simply technological, but may relate to recognition of how different cultures can engage in fundraising and philanthropy. By learning about these developments we may inform our own learning on fundraising.

In Argentina, for example, there are extremely high levels of online giving. This is partly a result of a poor postal system. But that lack of a postal system has driven charities to be more creative and imaginative in the way they engage with donors—moving to online engagement on a scale only dreamed of elsewhere.

In Ethiopia we're seeing some of the largest mass participation events in the world, especially marathons but also telethons—creating simple acquisition channels for charities to gain access to potential donors.

Hogar de Christo in Chile is a parish and faith-based charity that relies on the world's largest and possibly best-organized team of volunteers and door-to-door collections to deliver fundraising results. At a time when many charities are struggling to engage volunteers, this domestic NGO offers real insights into new ways of gathering and aligning supporters.

In Thailand Cabbages and Condoms[1] avoids donor-based fundraising and instead runs commercial businesses to raise cash for its social projects. (And it does so as a conscious and successful choice.) Thanks to its success as a socially engaged business it not only runs a chain of restaurants and a holiday resort but it uses the significant profits generated to pay for education, HIV work, prison reform projects, and many more.

---

[1] www.cabbagesandcondoms.com.

We see the same phenomenon in Kenya where the Red Cross Society, once financially dysfunctional, now successfully runs a chain of hotels that provide income for its relief services.

All of these experiments contain important lessons for any fundraiser anywhere in the world.

Trend 3: Indigenous NGOs/NPOs[2] Continue to Grow in Number throughout the World, But There Are Some Leviathans Emerging

As the role of the state is challenged worldwide, charities, NPOs (nonprofit organizations) and NGOs are growing in number and increasingly taking on civil society roles in health, education, and social service. So the Red Cross in Kenya has set up and runs a successful ambulance service where the government service is seen as ineffective. This growth—for example, the number of NGOs in the Philippines has grown by 50 percent in the past 10 years—is increasing pressure on fundraisers and fundraising to deliver more money for more causes.

At the same time a small number of large INGOs—Save the Children, UNICEF, World Vision, for example—have broken away in growth terms to form a *super league* of agencies able to fundraise and operate almost anywhere in the world. They have aggressive market entry strategies, significant investment funds, and teams dedicated to setting up and sustaining fundraising domestic operations. To many domestic NGOs these agencies can seem like Walmart or McDonald's—a form of unwelcome globalization.

These super league agencies can invest in developing new markets and are aggressively doing so. Some markets—Brazil, South Korea, India—represent the fundraising equivalent of BRICs. And just as

---

[2] What is commonly *nonprofits* or *not-for-profit* in the nonprofit, independent, or third sector in the United States, is called by many names in other parts of the world; for instance CSOs (civil society organizations) reside in *civil society*. There are sometimes subtle differences in meaning and application of these terms that will be explained in subsequent chapters of this book. For our purposes in this chapter, we have grouped them under two types—NPOs and NGOs.

businesses are flocking to BRICs, so INGOs are flocking to these high-growth philanthropic markets.

Most of these agencies are European or North American in origin and act in many ways like commercial multinationals. Surprisingly, perhaps, there are still only early signs of a developing world agency growing to global INGO status. Early candidates like Asia's BRAC and Grameen have grown and work in a number of countries. But both may never really grow to global status as they suffer under significant political pressure as result of their success and growth.

Trend 4: There Is Considerable Debate Worldwide about the Role of Philanthropy and the Role of the State

There is certainly a growth in adoption of the capitalist/free-market ideology worldwide generally—despite the recent global financial crisis and the challenges offered by the Occupy movement and other critics.

Philanthropy in some areas is a companion ideology to free-market capitalism. An increased role for fundraising is being accelerated by the global financial crisis—philanthropy is being asked to do more as governments have reduced funds and so seek to do less.

As noted earlier, specifically there is a perceived growing role for wealthy donors. This approach is shared in the book *Philanthrocapitalism* by Matthew Bishop. It can be summarized as "a new approach to solving social problems based on innovative partnerships between business, nonprofits, and government."[3] In practice the partnership seeks to draw in corporations and wealthy individuals to what has historically been a governmental space in many countries.

But it's important to stress that not everyone agrees with this growth in the role of philanthropy in addressing social challenges. The Gates/Buffett Giving Pledge has not played well in some European and Eastern nations where some millionaires have seen the pledge as potentially undermining the "proper" role of the state in education, in health, and in social security. In this case they may see the proper role for wealthy individuals' philanthropy as more focused in other directions like culture, medical research, and overseas aid.

The growth of philanthropy is also tied to democracy and to the promotion of civil society, home to NPOs and NGOs.

---

[3] www.philanthrocapitalism.net/about/synopsis/.

Civil society: The arena, outside of the family, the state, and the market, which is created by individual and collective actions, organizations, and institutions to advance shared interests.

Civil society encompasses civil society organizations (CSOs) and the actions of less formalized groups and individuals. *Organized civil society* refers to the independent, nonstate, and nonprivate sector associations and organizations that have some form of structure and formal rules of operating, together with the networks, infrastructure, and resources they utilize.[4]

This linkage leads to a troubling trend—as in Ethiopia, Rwanda, Russia, and elsewhere—where "anti-NGO" legislation is currently pending or recently passed at the time of this writing. Where NGOs are not banned outright, defunding through regulation is practiced in many quasi-democracies. There are about four dozen countries where civil society has been threatened over the past few years.[5] Venezuela has a new law, not yet in force at the time of this writing, putting NGOs under permanent surveillance by the state while Zimbabwe simply suspended many of them entirely.[6]

This trend appears even in parts of the world where new democracies have been formed. After the Arab Spring uprisings, a crackdown on U.S.-funded pro-democracy groups in Egypt and a bill before parliament that would further restrict nongovernmental organizations inhibited development work and activism. The move against NGOs had been accompanied by personal attacks, threats, and intimidation of activists, particularly women.[7]

This is a troubling trend because NGOs by and large seek to work alongside governments and business. But they need a license to do so.

---

[4]This definition is from the CIVICUS Civil Society Index project at http://socs.civicus.org.

[5]www.ipsnew.net/2012/08/civil-society-squeezed-on-all-sides/.

[6]www.reuters.com/article/2012/04/25/us-egypt-unun-idUSBRE83O18J20120425.

[7]Ibid.

Trend 5: Fundraising Is Becoming More Professional and Professionalized

The explosion in fundraising has fueled a demand for fundraisers with skills and experience. The reality is that there are not enough fundraisers to fill all the posts available. In turn this has led, in many countries, to significant wage inflation for skilled and able fundraisers. This can cause challenges where, for example, senior fundraisers are paid significantly more that senior service staff—or even CEOs.

Another implication has been the explosion of interest in qualifications for fundraisers—as organizations seek to "grow their own" and give fundraising stronger theoretical underpinning. In the United States, Canada, and Europe there are now professional qualifications for fundraisers to degree level offered by universities as well as extensive programs of continuous professional development offered by the main professional bodies such as AFP (the U.S.-based Association of Fundraising Professionals) and IoF (the U.K.-based Institute of Fundraising) as well as private providers.

Some recent research by the Resource Alliance suggests that there may be 20-plus countries actively involved in developing qualifications in this field with Singapore, for example, a world leader. But note that if you live in Kenya you can also secure an internationally recognized qualification as a fundraiser. And in Mexico there is a boom in courses and programs to respond to the local demand for Spanish-speaking fundraisers.

Increasingly fundraising is seen as a genuine career with a development path. This growth brings professionalization and with it regulation and codification.

Trend 6: Everyone Agrees that New and Social Technologies Are Important, But They Disagree on How

Despite many predictions of their demise, "old" technologies in direct marketing are still delivering the most income to charities. And direct mail, telephone, and especially street fundraising like face-to-face (or direct dialogue) fundraising remain the most important sources of donor acquisition for nonprofits worldwide. Some old technologies have been given new life, as when Thunderbird International Graduate School of Management conducted an alumni phonathon, but in keeping with the global nature of its alumni, had multilingual student volunteers call around the clock to connect with people in various time zones.[8] In other instances these established approaches are being combined with newer methodologies—with "telefacing," a combination of door-to-door and telephone giving, being one such idea developed in India and now growing in popularity. Tried and true methods must balance the excitement about online, social, and mobile fundraising.

Everyone agrees that these newer approaches are important and will grow in importance. But part of the challenge that is not clear is what their importance will be.

For some the big debate is about "platform" with some agencies focusing on improving their web experience for laptop users while others like Greenpeace are focusing on the mobile experience arguing that the smart phone will soon supplant even laptops, tablets, and so on.

For others there are big debates about the proper role of new and social technologies. So, are they simply a means to enhance supporter experience, or a way to link up existing supporters, or as a content-rich and flexible acquisition channel?

Many "gurus" claim to have the answer but the jury is still out in terms of results. What's clear is that some early successes are emerging. Kiva, with its online micro-credit model has become a model for social engagement in new approaches to philanthropy. Care2Give took the idea and has made it work in Europe more effectively.

Interestingly, social media use is not directly related to fundraising success. Brazil has easily the highest penetration of social media use—much greater than the United States. But it is hardly used for fundraising.

Beyond the current inconclusive data there are always inspirational anecdotal examples—many emerging from the Arab Spring.

For example, a Tunisian NGO that did a great job raising funds on Facebook, attracting not only individual givers but corporate sponsorship as well. An Australian family raised more than $600,000 with Facebook and Twitter in order to buy a large building where they could live and share their home with asylum seekers and people in desperate need.[9]

But it's not always easy to convert desire to cash. So another example is of the Jordanian family who used Facebook to raise funds to buy the license of a taxi after the driver, their primary source of support,

---

[8] www.sofii.org/node/505.

[9] http://ozphilanthropy.com/2012/09/11/hallmarks-and-next-steps-for-australias-philanthropy-coming-of-age-as-a-business-philaus12/.

died of leukemia. Seven hundred and fifty friends pledged $8,000 on the site. But these pledges couldn't be collected online because there was no platform for this. The media exists—but you need a secure and tax-efficient vehicle to convert the goodwill to cash.

This lack of a genuinely global platform for giving makes international giving more difficult. Social media expert Beth Kanter, author of Beth's blog and *The Networked Nonprofit* once sent some money (not a large sum, more of a symbolic gift of support) via Western Union to an NGO outside of the United States, discovering in the process that it cost $10 just to send it. Until a global platform emerges—probably created by Google or Facebook—the real power of global social giving will be held back. (But note that many diaspora communities—for example, in Ethiopia, Palestine, and Somalia—simply pay the price to send money to NGOs in their home country by conventional money transfer schemes.)

Our survey suggests that most nonprofits are not building social giving platforms, in large part because it is challenging to stay on top of all the technological advances, but also the cost. One exciting exception is the Red Cross and Red Crescent, which are building a portal as part of a global strategic review.

Beyond the platform is the issue of tax allowance across borders. The real barrier for most Americans to give internationally has been the expectation of a tax break for their donations to NGOs outside the United States. This will become easier. In September 2012 the Treasury and the IRS recommended significant changes to make international philanthropy easier, more cost effective, and less redundant for both U.S. grant makers and NGOs. Also under discussion is the establishment of equivalency determination repositories, like NGOsource, which would serve as clearinghouses for information on whether a non-U.S. NGO is equivalent to a U.S. public charity.

The future will bring even more change. And this change will generate new, and sometimes startling, ethical questions about the use of technology. As an example, a marketing agency in the United States outfitted 13 volunteers from a homeless shelter with mobile Wi-Fi devices, offering Internet access in exchange for donations. They were given business cards and T-shirts bearing their names: "I'm Clarence, a 4G Hotspot."[10] This sparked considerable debate about whether this exploited the homeless volunteers.

---

[10]www.nytimes.com/2012/03/13/technology/homeless-as-wi-fi-transmitters-creates-a-stir-in-austin.html.

The biggest question for fundraisers is: How can the Internet and technology be used to nurture a worldwide culture of philanthropy?

Trend 7: Philanthropy Thrives Best When There Are Codified Civil Society Structures and Regulations for Nonprofit Agencies

In order for fundraising to flourish donors have to be able to recognize and relate to the special status of NGOs/NPOs.

In some countries this special status is well established with sophisticated regulatory regimes and tax advantages. Even in these sophisticated settings these vary and there are significant distinctions between the U.K. definition of a charity and the U.S. definition of a nonprofit. There are also fiscal differences with the United States allowing 100 percent tax allowance for gifts to registered nonprofits and the United Kingdom restricting it to the tax paid. Despite these differences it is basically easier to set up and operate as a charity in the United Kingdom, the United States, or most of Europe.

But in other countries and territories such as China, the Gulf, and Russia, these charitable structures are still being developed. (In Russia and elsewhere as noted earlier, some would argue it is becoming increasingly hard to operate independently as an NGO/NPO.)

Many fundraisers and donors consider this lack of a codified approach in their country is significantly hindering the development of a genuinely transparent and sustainable philanthropic culture. Interestingly the Arab Spring, an example cited earlier, while it has opened up many structures, has not had as positive an impact on charity and NGO ability to operate.

Effective structures and regulatory policies are important to drive trust—one of the key advantages that NGOs have. Donors need to trust that the money will be spent properly—and where it is not, that some judicial process will call the NGO to account. So important is this that UNICEF internationally has a goal to be seen as the most trusted agency in key markets. The belief is that increased trust will help drive increased giving.

There also needs to be agreement about what constitutes good governance—so important to fundraising. Jon Stettner, CEO of Make-a-Wish International, has observed in his work around the world that there is little consistency about board practices and expectations. He has found, for instance, that in some cultures board rotation can be a challenge. Coming off a board suggests that one has not performed well. Remaining on indefinitely means that one is considered a valued board member. In some cultures board giving is de rigueur—and in other cultures is actively frowned on.

The key message here is that philanthropy probably can't change the world on its own. It needs to form part of a group of regulated civil society actors working toward the greater good. And those other actors—government and business—need to know their proper place. And the rules by which each operate need to be explicit.

We hope these big trends give you a taste of the excitement we felt while compiling the following chapters from our various talented contributors in philanthropy throughout the world.

THIS BOOK'S SETUP

This book includes 16 chapters organized into two parts. The first part takes us on a tour of specific regions and countries, and the second part addresses four important aspects of global fundraising—major donors, social media, innovation, and the *charity giants*. The editors acknowledge that, given the scope of the book, they have no doubt omitted important developments in philanthropy in some places. They apologize for this, and ask for the reader's understanding, given the immensity of the task undertaken. They also welcome ongoing contributions to this body of knowledge through the book's wiki (which is explained more fully at the end of this chapter).

Chapter 2 offers a look at the development of philanthropy in China, its ancient roots in culture and religion, and its integration with modern philanthropy. China's growing affluence and importance in the global order make it one to watch.

Chapter 3 discusses Japan's philanthropic history, present practices, and future trends. A new generation of technological innovators in Japan, and the growing importance of social media, foreshadow Japan's leadership role in the fundraising of tomorrow.

Chapter 4 covers Latin America, a vast region that encompasses many countries and cultures. Some of the most interesting

developments in fundraising are happening here where fundraisers have "thrown out the book" and have found their own paths to
success.

Chapter 5 looks at Western Europe, another group of diverse countries. Here face-to-face, a fundraising method that has very successfully
migrated outside of the region, was invented. Even while fundraising is well developed in this region, foundations remain a relatively
untapped source of philanthropic support.

Chapter 6 reviews the state of fundraising in North America. The
United States and to some extent Canada traditionally have depended
more on philanthropy than on government to provide a social safety
net and to enhance quality of life. Giving circles are among other
interesting things taking place here.

Chapter 7 takes us "down under" for a look at a fundraising in
Australia and New Zealand. This prosperous region's success in fundraising can be attributed to a new take on Western European charitable
traditions. Two-stepping is one of the innovations from this region.

Chapter 8 presents us with Central and Eastern Europe, the set-
ting for some of the most dramatic changes of the twentieth century.
In this chapter, two very different countries are featured—Russia and
Romania—to give us a sense of how things are developing here.

Chapter 9 shows us how Africa, previously thought of only as the
recipient of aid, is developing its own fundraising and philanthropic
prowess. The potential of this continent is enormous. In this chapter,
two countries—Kenya and South Africa—are profiled so that we can
better understand Africa's philanthropic traditions and innovations.

Chapter 10, written by one of the leaders in advancing philanthropy
in the Middle East and North Africa (MENA), provides us with an
overview of the cultural and religious origins of charity in this region,
and a sense of the region's growing recognition of its own ability to realize the potential of philanthropy for not only MENA, but the world.

Chapter 11 shows that all conversations about global philanthropy
must include Asia. This chapter features two countries—Korea and
Singapore—where philanthropy and fundraising are undergoing
rapid transformations. Individual giving in Korea is skyrocketing and
Singapore, already an international hub for business, aims to make
itself a center of philanthropy.

Chapter 12 reveals the growth of the nonprofit sector in India. Telefacing is an Indian fundraising innovation that few outside of the region know about. This immense country is also the home of one of the most important nonprofit innovations of recent times—micro-lending.

Chapter 13 chronicles the emergence of new philanthropists around the world and gives insight into their motivations and values. This chapter also advises readers on how to approach these new charitable titans.

Chapter 14 makes it clear that social media is one of the most powerful forces for change in the nonprofit sector. It is not only changing how we raise funds and how we give, it is bringing us all into a global community.

Chapter 15 tells us that the ability to innovate is the only organizational skill that is and will remain relevant; it is the only competitive advantage with staying power. The chapter details who is innovative and why; and how readers can improve the innovative capacity of their own organization.

Chapter 16 draws us into the world of the *charity giants*, the colossal INGOs that are shaping the philanthropic environment that we live in today and often are the proving grounds for new ways of raising funds. Big not only in size, but in influence, these gargantuan nonprofits cannot be ignored.

OUR GLOBAL FUNDRAISNG WIKI

Please share your views and opinions with us and a community of professionals and practitioners by logging into the special wiki we've created at http://globalfundraising.wikispaces.com. We hope that this wiki will help us all in carrying on the conversation that we and our contributors are starting with you with this book.

To kick things off, Chapter 2 visits China to see how philanthropy is being shaped to meet the demands of this dynamic nation.

PART 1

An Overview of Giving by Region

China

LU BO AND NAN FANG

This chapter introduces you to a historic review of philanthropy in China. It also gives a panorama of China's nonprofit sector—its general characteristics and the legal, administrative, and tax policies context of Chinese philanthropy. From there, it continues by identifying the major donors in China today and considers who they may be in the future. Finally, select practices of fundraising are given to showcase the new strategies of philanthropic governance brought about by a newfound public interest in nonprofit transparency and to illustrate the amazing fundraising opportunities created by rapid technology development and changes in communication.

Philanthropy in China is complex and differs greatly from what exists in other countries. The following pages provide you with a better understanding of its characteristics.

A HISTORIC REVIEW OF PHILANTHROPY IN CHINA

China was one of the first countries in the world to provide a formal public infrastructure to promote and develop philanthropy. The first government agency for relief of poverty and sickness and supervision of the distribution of aid was established in the Xi Zhou period (1046 BC–771 BC). The cultural and religious roots of Chinese philanthropy have a long-standing history. Thousands of years of Confucianism, Buddhism, and Taoism have provided a fertile ground for the rise and development of philanthropy in China's society.

Philanthropy in China has a long history and has traversed a tortuous path. It's necessary and meaningful to review it from the historical perspective.

Philanthropic Roots Found within Ancient Chinese Culture

Although each of the three cultural traditions frames philanthropy differently, the key idea is the same—to promote the general welfare and to uphold moral principles. According to the Confucian Analects, Mercy was the spirit of Confucianism. Mencius, a follower of Confucianism, thought that people should have compassion: "To love old people as your own parents; to love all children as if they were your own." Taoism teaches respect for life and emphasis on caring for the welfare of others. Taoists also place a strong emphasis in sharing wealth. Buddhism teaches its followers to care for others and protect the motherland. These powerful precepts are very much alive today in China.

The Integration of Chinese Traditional Philanthropic Culture with Western Values in the Mid-Nineteenth Century

Since the mid-nineteenth century, the Chinese have integrated Western ideas about philanthropy into Chinese traditions and modern Chinese philanthropy contains both old and new values. Churches have played a prominent role in advancing the synthesis of the two.

During the nineteenth and early twentieth centuries English and American churches were active in health care, foster care for orphans, treatment for children with disabilities, and national disaster relief. Church-based charity began in 1835 with the first church-affiliated eye hospital that was established in the Guangdong Province. In 1938, the World Statistics of the Christian Missionary Society reported 300 church-run hospitals with more than 21,000 beds as well as 600 clinics.

Another major influence in the integration of traditional Chinese and new Western philanthropy were INGOs like the Shanghai Cosmopolitan Red Cross Society, founded in 1904.

Philanthropy in the Planned Economy

Prior to the establishment of the People's Republic (PR) of China in 1949 there were about 2,000 charitable organizations funded by Chinese socialites, foreign foundations, and religious groups. In 1950, the newly formed government began to take over all kinds of charitable organizations, restructuring or closing them down. The first PR China Relief and Welfare Report in the early 1950s clearly stated that philan-thropy was "used by the ruling class to deceive the Chinese people," and in the New China, "government is the mainstay of philanthropy." This became the rationale for the government to take over all chari-table endeavors, eventually leading to the suspension of private phi-lanthropy for 30 years. Even the Red Cross Society of China lost its status as an independent international humanity organization, becom-ing instead a charitable organization supervised by the government.

There was no place for civil social charitable organizations in the new Communist social order. In the cities government was responsi-ble for the public welfare from cradle to grave. In rural communities the "five guarantees supporting system" took care of orphans, elders in need, and the extremely poor.

The Recovery Time of the 1980s and 1990s

In 1979 a period of recovery began and the Chinese government adopted policies of reform and openness that allowed for major change in many areas of Chinese life. The establishment of the China Chil-dren and Teenagers' Fund—the first public fundraising charitable organization—in 1981 signaled the reemergence of philanthropy in contemporary China. Since then, Chinese philanthropy has revived its traditions as well as welcomed new developments.

International foundations and INGOs contributed to renewal of the civil sector. The Ford Foundation, Save the Children, and Oxfam set up their China Programs in the mid-1990s and then extended their devel-opment work across the country. Many INGOs promoted philanthropy awareness and supported the capacity building efforts of the government and of many local organizations. Domestic governance of the local oper-ation and activities of INGOs disseminated modern philanthropic con-cepts and thus encouraged the advance of Chinese civil society and the establishment of China's grassroots NGOs in the following decade.

A new law created a legal context for the development of Chinese philanthropy. The Law on Donation for Public Welfare Undertak-ings, the first charity law enacted in PR China (1999), was designed to encourage donations, standardize the donation process for both donors and recipients, and protect the legitimate rights and interests of the donor, the recipient, and the ultimate beneficiary of a gift.

Early successes in this new era, like the Hope Project, also pointed the way forward. Begun in the late 1980s, by the 1990s the Hope Project had become the most widely participated charitable project, attracting supporters at home and from abroad. The Hope Project brand was embraced by the general public and set a standard of success for other NGOs.

It is important for those unfamiliar with the Chinese civil sector to understand that most domestic foundations or NGOs incorporated during the 1980s and 1990s were actually government operated. The widely used term *GONGO* stands for "government operated non-governmental organization." China's civil society was not yet mature enough for fully independent NGOs, nor did the government have the awareness and capacity to support the development of civil society organizations. GONGOs are a hybrid of government agencies and NGOs designed to address a broad spectrum of social needs.[1]

GONGOs still play a vital role in the Chinese philanthropy sector. Many GONGOs have a government mandate to provide social relief, public education, culture exchange, emergency response, and charity work. Many GONGOs also play the role of custodian agencies for grassroots NGOs unable to secure legal registration (more about this later). GONGOs receive the biggest share of domestic donations.

Booming Development in the New Millennium[2]

Chinese philanthropy really blossomed in the new millennium in terms of the amount of giving, the level of public awareness, and the number of NGOs. According to the Statistic Report on the

---

[1]The Resource Alliance, Institute of Development Studies, funded by the Rockefeller Foundation, *Philanthropy: Current Context and Future Outlook*, 90.

[2]If there is no specific attribution, all the figures in this chapter are quoted from *Giving China: Report of China Philanthropy Donation* (Chinese), issued yearly at 2007, 2008, 2009, and 2010. The 2007 Report is available at www .mca.gov.cn/article/zwgk/gzdt/200801/20080100011358.shtml. The 2008 report is available at www.mca.gov.cn/accessory/2009310160957.doc. The 2009 figures refer to: Zheng Yuanchang, Peng Jianmei, Liu Youping from Department of Social Welfare and Philanthropy Promotion of Ministry of Civil Affairs and China Charity Information Center, *Giving China: Report of China Philanthropy Donations in 2010* (Chinese), (Beijing: Chinese Society Publishing House, 2010). 2010 figures refers to Meng Zhiqiang, Peng

Development of Civil Affairs in China 2001–2010 launched by the Ministry of Civil Affairs (MoCA), the total amount of donations in 2001 was $0.19 billion.[3] The figure increased significantly to $17.01 billion in 2008 due to the Snowstorm Crisis and the Wenchuan Earthquake. Although giving was hurt by the financial crisis in 2009, 2010 brought another surprise—the total of donations climbed back up to $16.41 billion, $9.48 billion from businesses and $4.71 billion from individuals. The number of legally registered social organizations also grew quickly from 211,000 in 2001 to 440,000 in 2010.[4]

A new law played a role in the boom. The Foundation Management Ordinance, launched in 2004, broke the government monopoly on fundraising, allowing enterprises, individuals, and social organizations to establish private fundraising foundations. By 2011, the number of registered private foundations reached 1,200, exceeding the number of public foundations for the first time. Legislation dramatically boosted the number of private foundations without government.

The Internet also boosted philanthropy in the first decade of the twenty-first century. Web forums, blogs, and Weibo (Chinese Twitter) promoted greater participation in philanthropy. Public opinions could now be heard. The paths cleared by the new media make it possible for the general public to question charity organizations and request accountability.

A PANORAMA OF CHINA'S NONPROFIT SECTOR

The rapid growth of philanthropy and volunteerism in China was partly a response to the fast economic development and the strong

---

Jianmei, and Liu Youping from the Department of Social Welfare and Philanthropy Promotion of Ministry of Civil Affairs and China Charity Information Center, *Giving China: Report of China Philanthropy Donation in 2011* (Chinese) (Beijing: Chinese Society Publishing House, 2011).

[3] All donation numbers quoted in this chapter were originally calculated by CNY. For easy reference and comparison, the author converted into USD by exchange rate: 1 CNY = 0.159 USD (March 18, 2012 rate at http://fx-rate.net/).

[4] Research Center of China Philanthropy, Beijing Normal University, *Research Report of Philanthropy in China 2001–2011*, (Beijing, Beijing Normal University Publishing Group, 2012), 63.

encouragement of the government. The unbalanced regional development of philanthropy and the obstacle of registration for NGOs, however, stunt the growth of civil society organizations.

Giving Grows with Wealth

In the first decade of the new millennium, both China's GDP and the total amount of giving rocketed. The average increase rate of GDP from 2001 to 2010 was 10.4 percent[5] while the average increase rate of donation was as high as 84.74 percent.[6] China's per capita GDP exceeded $3,000 in 2008, while the number in some eastern coastal provinces gained more than $10,000, spurring giving and philanthropy development. As noted earlier, the total amount of giving increased dramatically from $0.19 billion in 2001 to $16.41 billion in 2010—more than 86 times!

China's boom created many new high-net-worth individuals (those whose net assets exceed $1 million, hereafter in this book called HNWIs). According to the Global Wealth Report released by Credit Suisse Group AG in 2011, there were more than 1 million HNWIs in China—3.4 percent of all HNWIs worldwide. The rapid growth of material wealth enables more people to act on their awareness of the needs of others and contribute to charity.

Government Influence

The government is also a major factor in this dramatic progress of philanthropy in China. The government's program, Building of a Harmonious Socialist Society, acknowledges private philanthropy as a crucial force in improving people's well-being and in supplementing the current social security system. The 11th *National Five Year Plan of Economic and Social Development* spanning 2006 to 2010[7] (FYP), and the

---

[5]Counted by the author with the increased rate of GDP annually reported by National Bureau of Statistics of China, available online at www.stats.gov.cn/tjgb/.

[6]Research Center of China Philanthropy, Beijing Normal University, *Research Report of Philanthropy in China 2001–2011*, Beijing Normal University Publishing Group, 2012, page 44.

[7]The Five-Year Plans of People's Republic of China (PRC) are a series of economic and social development initiatives. The development of the society and economy was shaped by the Communist Party of China (CPC) through

new *National Guidelines of Philanthropy Development* (2011–2015) show a government even more intent on accelerating the development and regulation of the philanthropic sector.

Major Sectors of Giving

The biased and fragmented social security system drove the demand for philanthropy development in China, making education, poverty alleviation, and disaster relief the three major categories of giving. The average portion donated to the education sector is 28.38 percent and the average portion to poverty alleviation is 10.44 percent during the period 2007–2010. More than $11.73 billion was given to disaster relief and post-disaster recovery following the Wenchuan earthquake in 2008. Even after the immediate need for relief lessened, disaster relief remained one of the three top priorities for donations.

Growth of Volunteerism

These terrible disasters raised public awareness of need. More and more individuals are volunteering their time and energy to charitable activities and community service. The number of registered volunteers increased from 20 million in 2006 to about 30.5 million in 2009.[8] A recent national research report found that the average amount of service hours for each Chinese adult is 5.95 hours per year.[9] Even with this significant growth in volunteerism, levels are still much lower than in western developed countries such as the United States, United Kingdom, and Canada.

---

the plenary sessions of the Central Committee and national congresses. Planning is a key characteristic of centralized, communist economies, and one plan established for the entire country normally contains detailed economic development guidelines for all its regions. To more accurately reflect China's transition from a Soviet-style planned economy to a socialist market economy (socialism with Chinese characteristics), the name of the 11th five-year program was changed to *guideline*. Summarized from http://en.wikipedia .org/wiki/Five-Year_Plans_of_the_People%27s_Republic_of_China.

[8]"Chinese Registered Volunteers Have Exceeded 30 Million in the Past 16 Years," *China News Net*, December 6, 2009. Available at www.chinanews .com/gn/news/2009/12-06/2002333.shtml.

[9]Zhang Wangcheng, "The Research on the Volunteer Behavior of China's Citizen," *Intellectual Property Rights Press*, Beijing, 2011, 75.

Unbalanced Regional Development

The economic and social development between eastern and western China is not equal. The development of philanthropy differs widely even across regions. In metropolises such as Beijing, Shanghai, and Shenzhen and in the eastern coastal provinces, such as Zhejiang, Jiangsu, Guangdong, philanthropy has matured in terms of the amount given, the quality and number of civil society organizations, and in public awareness. The poorer more rural central and western regions of China are more often the recipients, rather than the source of philanthropy.

Obstacle of Registration

Many INGOs and grassroots NGOs operating in China have no legal status. The difficulty of NGO registration caused by the "dual registration and management system" (which is explained in detail later in the chapter) is the reason. Figures released recently prove that there are 445,000 civil society organizations legally registered, while at least 3 million organizations remained unregistered.[10] According to a newly issued report, there are about 1,000 U.S. NGOs operating in China— and only 3 percent of them have gained legal status.[11] Without the legal status conferred by formal registration, these NGOs cannot be supervised effectively by the government and the general public, so they do not enjoy the preferential policies that registered charitable organizations do, such as tax deductibility.

Demands for Transparency

A series of scandals involving charitable organizations in 2011 led to an outbreak of suspicion and frustration with China's philanthropy sector, precipitating a significant drop in individual giving. These events taught charities the value of ethical behavior. They also informed the general

---

[10] "Three Million NGOs Have Possibility to Get Legally Registered," *Beijing Times*, July 11, 2011, available at http://news.foundationcenter.org .cn/html/2011-07/27736.html.

[11] "Less Than Three Percent of NGOs from the U.S. Are Legally Registered in China," issued on April 5, 2012, available at http://hausercenter.org/ chinanpo/2012/04/less-than-3-of-ngos-from-the-u-s-are-legally-registered -in-china/.

public about the need for NGO transparency and accountability. The public demand for greater transparency and more accountability are top priorities in the reform of Chinese charity organizations today.

FRAMEWORK FOR NONPROFIT SECTOR

China's nonprofit sector has been held back by an infrastructure that has not kept pace with all of the changes of the recent past. The framework is improving, however, and it is hoped that in the future an adequate structure will support the nonprofit sector's efforts to meet the needs of the nation.

The Administrative System

As mentioned earlier, becoming a registered social organization in China is no easy task. The duty of the Department of Civil Social Organization Administration (DCSOA), Ministry of Civil Affairs, is to promulgate regulations, manage the registration of both national and international social organizations and foundations, and supervise the local registration of social organizations and foundations. Civil Affairs bureaus take care of the registration of local social organizations and foundations according to jurisdiction. In Mainland China, all nonprofit organizations must formally register with either the DCSOA or the local civil affair bureaus. However, registration is only the part of the story.

The current administrative system for the nonprofit sector is a "dual registration and management system." To get the formal registration, a social organization (which refers to all types of organizations in the nonprofit sector mentioned previously), must obtain permits from two supervision agencies. The first agency is called a *sponsor agency*, which is a government department or another authorized social organization. With the permission of the sponsor agency, the social organization can then register with the second agency, a civil affairs bureau, which would audit the social organization for its adherence to law. The sponsor agency, the prerequisite of formal registration, however, is not easy to get. Social organizations applying for sponsorship must convince a government department or authorized branch to take on this responsibility.

The reluctance of sponsor agencies to take on nonprofits is based in the relatively heavy burden assumed in agreeing to supervise and guide the nonprofit's operations. There are associated risks (political risks in many cases). The sponsor agency has little authority and can only supervise and guide the organizations it sponsors. It cannot directly manage the finances or the operations of the social organization. Consequently the government departments prefer to sponsor those organizations that have close relationships with the government or those founded by former government officials. For grassroots organizations and other organizations founded by regular citizens, securing a sponsor agency is almost a mission impossible. Little wonder that only a small portion of the millions of NGOs operating in China have legally registered.

The current policy has been under criticism for a long time. Starting in 2009 Shenzhen and Beijing relaxed the restrictions of registration. The civil organizations in these two cities can now register under the municipal civil affairs bureau directly, and no longer have to seek a sponsor. This could be the first step in further reform.

Legal Framework

The legislation of philanthropy restarted after the reforms of the 1980s, and the current legal framework comes from four main sources.

The first source is the National People's Congress and its standing committee. Its laws include Law on Red Cross Society (1993), Law on Donation for Public Welfare Undertakings (1999), Law on Individual Income Tax (amended 2007), and Law on Corporate Income Tax (amended 2007).

The second source is the State Council. Its legislation includes National Guideline of Philanthropy Development 2011–2015 (2011), Measures for Management of Foundations (1988), Regulation for Management of the Registration of Social Organizations (1998), the Regulation on the Management of Foundations (2004), and Provisional Regulations for the Registration Administration of People-run Nonenterprise Units (1998), and the Release of Regulations on the Implementation of Enterprise Income Tax Law (2007).

The third source is various departments of central government that create laws intended to manage the different purposes of philanthropy. For instance, there is the Provisional Regulations for Disaster Relief Donation Administration (2000), and the Notice of Tax Deduction on Public Welfare Donations jointly issued by MoCA, the Ministry of Finance and the State Administration of Taxation (2008).

The fourth source is provincial governments according to their particular situation. The Ordinance of Young People Volunteering Service in Guangdong Province, and the Measure of Fund Administration in Dalian City Charity Foundations are examples.

The foundations for a legal framework for China's philanthropy have been laid, but as of yet, it is still loose and fragmented. Although more than 20 national laws and regulations and even hundreds of local regulations have been issued, they are at relatively low levels of government. There is not yet the comprehensive set of laws at the necessary high level that is needed to truly encourage and regulate the systematic development of philanthropy.[12] The law meant to regulate charity giving, the Law on Donation for Public Welfare Undertakings (1999), does not clarify the boundaries of public welfare undertakings. The law is also vague on how to protect the rights of donors if the receiving agency is inactive or abusing the donation.

CASE STUDY 2.1	YUSHU EARTHQUAKE OF 2010 UNITES FUNDRAISING OF 13 FOUNDATIONS[13]

On April 17, 2010, three days after Yushu Earthquake in Qinghai Province that killed 2,200 and destroyed billions of dollars' worth of property, MoCA issued the Notice Regarding Yushu Earthquake Relief and Donations (Notice). The Notice designated 15 national public fundraising foundations—all related to the government—as the legal recipients for all disaster relief contributions. It also stipulated that all other organizations that had already received donations must transfer funds to any of these 15 foundations. It was the first step to move giving from civil society to the government.

---

[12]Research Center of China Philanthropy, Beijing Normal University, *Research Report of Philanthropy in China 2001–2011* (Beijing: Beijing Normal University Publishing Group, 2012), 94.

[13]"Billions of Donation for Yushu Earthquake Been Asked to Remit to Qinghai Government (Chinese)," issued on August 3, 2010, available at http://news.163.com/10/0803/00/6D4EHAUA0001124J.html. "Donor Wishes Been Abused by Government Unified Arrangement of Yushu Earthquake Donation (Chinese)," issued on August 10, 2010, available at http://news.qq.com/a/20100809/001094.htm.

By July 9, 2010, $1.69 billion had been given to emergency relief and reconstruction. The 15 foundation designees had raised roughly $800 million, almost the half of the total.

The Opinion of Policy Measures on Support Post-Disaster Reconstruction in Yushu, issued by the State Council in May 2010, and the more detailed Measure of Implementation the Usage of Donation Fund for Qinghai Yushu Earthquake Relief and Reconstruct, issued by five ministries in July 2010, required 13 national public fundraising foundations (not including the China Red Cross and the China Charity Federation because their Qinghai branches were also recipients) to appropriate all the funds related to the Yushu Earthquake to the Qinghai Provincial government, Qinghai Red Cross, or Charity Federation. All funding would be pooled for postdisaster reconstruction by Qinghai Provincial government.

In addition to appropriating funding for government, the role of these public foundations is to "provide information including the total scale of the appropriated funding, total scale of the restricted funding, and the project proposals, as well as suggest how to use the unrestricted funding."

The government's "capture" of Yushu donations was just too much for the public to bear, causing another "earthquake" in the philanthropic world. The foundations that had their funds appropriated protested the Law on Donation for Public Welfare Undertakings and even claimed that contract law had been broken. China Youth Development Foundation, as an example, had signed a contract with many donors to clarify the restricted purpose of gifts. If the funds were transferred to government, it was in total violation of the contract with donors. Another critic, Professor Deng Guosheng from the NGO Research Center in Tsinghai University, argued that all property owned by the 13 designated foundations should be protected by law as they are independent legal entities. Government has no power to appropriate private property.

A few foundations complied with the August 2010 deadline and handed over their funding, but others continued to communicate with the relevant departments and try to find a better solution.

Tax Incentives

Tax incentives in China are of two main kinds: pretax deduction and tax exemption. The Law on Individual Income Tax and the Law on Corporate Income Tax concern individual and corporate donations.

Individual Income Law Article 24 states that, "Individuals who donate income to educational and other public welfare undertakings, through social organizations or government agencies in the People's Republic of China, can deduct that part of the donation which does not exceed 30 percent of the amount of taxable income declared by the individual."

Chinese law allows corporations to deduct for charitable contributions. The Law on Corporate Income Tax states that, "With regard to an enterprise's expenditures for public welfare donations, the portion that accounts for 12 percent of the total annual profits, or less, is allowed to be deducted." Although the allowable deduction for corporate donations is quite clear, the application and refund process is cumbersome.

Nonprofits have to pay tax on certain kinds of income. In November 2009 the Ministry of Finance and the State Administration of Taxation promulgated two notices devised to regulate the free tax issues and requirements of the enterprise income tax of nonprofit organizations. The Notices mandate that nonprofit organizations pay Enterprise Income Tax. The Notices also asked nonprofit organizations to distinguish between taxable income and nontaxable income. It states that only the interest of nontaxable income is tax exempt. Income from government contracts for social services also has to be taxed.

An estate tax would really help stimulate giving and academe has been calling for it for years. Based on experiences with estate taxes in the United States and in many other countries, it could efficiently promote individual giving, especially from HNWIs.

Other Legal Barriers

In addition to the limitations outlined earlier, there are at least three other legal barriers for nonprofits and donors.

Inflexible Policy

Law requires that the annual expenditure of private foundations on public benefit activities must be at least 8 percent of the surplus from the previous year. The dilemma, spending more capital funding while all investment income is being taxed, hurts the self-sufficiency and capacity of foundations. They have less money available for staffing and overhead that hampers their ability to succeed in the competitive human resource market. They have less with which to build an adequate infrastructure and to achieve financial stability. A foundation may not allocate more than 10 percent of its total annual expenditure to cover all administrative costs, including office rental, staff wages, and benefits. Nonprofit employee salaries cannot exceed twice of that of the average income of a local laborer.

The original idea behind these restrictions was to ensure the effective use of donations. Instead they have put a stranglehold on the further development of foundations.

Foreign Exchange Control

Chinese yuan (CNY) is not yet an international currency. In Mainland China strict control of foreign exchange is maintained. Regulations on the Foreign Exchange System of China (or PRC), issued in 2006 and modified in 2008, is the fundamental administrative rule to manage the foreign exchange system.

The new Management Regulation for Foreign Exchange Donated to Domestic Entity, launched by the State Administration of Foreign Exchange, causes trouble for domestic NGOs that rely on foreign funding and INGOs that seek funding from overseas. The regulation states that domestic NGOs must submit a notarized document containing a detailed budget. However, to get this kind of public notary is not easy for most grassroots NGOs, especially those not legally registered. Many of them have trouble withdrawing foreign donations from their bank accounts. The regulation requires heaps of paperwork from the overseas headquarters of INGOs. To get at donations made in a currency other than CNY becomes a time and energy consuming burden.

Strict Environment for INGOs

As previously noted, international charities have many hurdles to surmount for both registration and fundraising. They can only operate within Mainland China when formally registered under the dual registration and management system. It is difficult even for well-established INGOs to get a sponsor agency from Chinese government. Many of them have to register under the Industrial and Commercial Bureau as a corporate entity, paying tax, or they are otherwise forced to operate under the radar with no formal registration. Moreover, it is strictly forbidden for international charity organizations to raise funds in Mainland China.

CASE STUDY 2.2	HONG KONG—A FUNDRAISING HUB

With its strategic geographical location, excellent infrastructure and well-regulated banking sector, Hong Kong Special Administrative Region (Hong Kong) has developed over several decades into a dynamic financial and investment hub. There are more than 3,800 International HQs and 200 banks in Hong Kong. The city is among the highest GDP per capita economies in Asia and holds the world's eighth largest foreign exchange reserves—some $137 billion. All these factors make Hong Kong an international fundraising center.

According to the official figures released by *Giving China: Report of China Philanthropy Donation in 2011*, 24.8 percent of the total foreign giving ($0.3 billion) intended for Mainland China is funneled through Hong Kong.

It's not just the city's money and the banks that are responsible for the amount of donations coming in through the city. The civil society in Hong Kong is mature, and its nonprofit sector enjoys high transparency and accountability. Donors have sufficient information to make appropriate giving decisions. The Hong Kong government has set up public registration system reference guidelines that make the process of organizing charitable fundraising activities quite simple. All kinds of fundraising activities are allowed as long as they are in support of charitable purposes, abide by the laws, and registered three weeks prior to the proposed date.

The city does not impose restrictions on fundraising for beneficiaries outside Hong Kong. In other words, NGOs registered in Hong Kong can collect money from inside and outside of China—individuals, corporations, foundations—and the funds can be used for overseas aid. Because many multinational corporations have set up regional headquarters in Hong Kong, it is quite convenient for them to transfer funding to NGOs here, which could not access it in Mainland China. Through Hong Kong, Chinese domestic companies can even donate money to INGOs.

Therefore, most major international NGOs are already established in Hong Kong and many of them have been here a long time—Oxfam, UNICEF, Greenpeace, and Save the Children have all set up Hong Kong branches for fundraising with the aim of creating a base from which to explore the potential of the Chinese market. Funds raised from Hong Kong are not only directed to Mainland China, but also go to Africa and other regions in the world.

(Continued)

There are no enforced standards of charity and fundraising conduct in Hong Kong. There are just some best practice guidelines provided by the Social Welfare Department of the Hong Kong Government. Because of lesser restrictions, many NGOs unable to register in Mainland China moved to Hong Kong and registered there. They raise their funds in Hong Kong and operate in Mainland China as INGOs. These "offshore INGOs" exist in a gray area. No Chinese laws or regulations apply to them even if they operate for-profit businesses in Mainland China. A few complaints toward these organizations have drawn the attention of Mainland officials and may result in new regulations and greater clarity.

CURRENT FUNDRAISING TRENDS IN CHINA'S NONPROFIT SECTOR

Since 2008 donors at home have formed the bedrock of Chinese philanthropy. Business provided more than half of what has been given, and while corporate giving dropped with the recession, it has once again overtaken individual giving.

Domestic Enterprises and Domestic Individuals Are Mainstays of Giving

Figure 2.1 shows that domestic enterprise (including both public and private businesses) and domestic individuals are the two major sources of philanthropy in China. Business contributes more than half of the total amount from domestic and overseas sources. Enterprise giving declined in 2008 while individuals and foreign foundations responded to the Wenchuan Earthquake emergency. The worldwide recession hurt Chinese enterprises badly in 2009, causing both the amount and percentage of giving to plummet. Philanthropy is deeply rooted in Chinese society, however, and this factor, along with the promotion of Corporate Social Responsibility (CSR), caused business giving to overtake individual giving in 2010.

The Chinese at home contributed most of the total of domestic donations in 2008—the first time in the history of modern China's philanthropy. They gave $7.28 billion and domestic enterprises gave

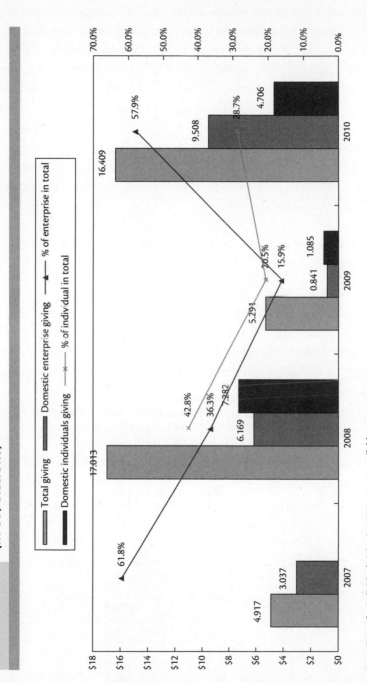

FIGURE 2.1 DOMESTIC ENTERPRISES AND DOMESTIC INDIVIDUALS ARE MAINSTAYS OF GIVING (IN US$ BILLIONS)

Legend:
— Total giving — Domestic enterprise giving —▲— % of enterprise in total
— Domestic individuals giving —✕— % of individual in total

2007: 4.917, 3.037, 61.8%
2008: 17.013, 6.169, 7.282, 36.3%, 42.8%
2009: 5.291, 0.841, 1.085, 15.9%, 20.5%
2010: 16.409, 9.508, 4.706, 28.7%, 57.9%

Note: Figure for individual giving in 2007 was not available.

Exchange rate: 1 CNY = 0.159 USD (March 18, 2012 rate at http://fx-rate.net/)

33

another $6.17 billion. Chinese authorities proclaimed a new generosity and humanitarian spirit, awakened by the 2008 Wenchuan Earthquake.

The earthquake was not the only thing that shook individual donations loose. It was also driven by several rounds of a nationwide official mobilization campaign. The campaign was advocated by different government departments and resident committees after the crisis. Official mobilization campaigns are the most common means used by the Chinese government to address emergency capital shortages caused by natural disasters.

Although government-organized mass campaigns such as this have proved an effective fundraising strategy, a truly mature philanthropic society will require more individual initiative and active participation from the general public.

The Fast Growth of Giving by Private Enterprises in Recent Years

In 2009 Chinese private enterprise grew to become the most significant among all domestic enterprises with a total contribution of $863 million, 41.3 percent of the whole domestic enterprise sector and 16.3 percent of all donations from both domestic and overseas donors. (See Figure 2.2.) Eighteen enterprises gave exceeding CNY 100 million each

| FIGURE 2.2 | AMOUNT AND PERCENTAGE OF DOMESTIC PRIVATE ENTERPRISE GIVING OF TOTAL DOMESTIC GIVING IN 2009 AND 2010 (IN US$ BILLIONS) |

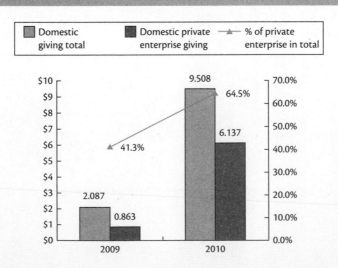

($15.9 million). Five of them were Chinese private enterprises donating a total of $330 million and five were state-owned enterprises from monopolized industries with the amount of $380 million. The role of private enterprises in philanthropy has been underestimated because of a lower reputation and less visibility compared with state-owned enterprise in China.

In 2010 giving by private enterprises surpassed expectations again, growing to 64.5 percent of all domestic enterprise and exceeding state-owned enterprises. Real estate businesses are the leaders. Eight real estate companies each donated more than $15.9 million in 2010.

Nevertheless, even with these tremendous strides forward, compared with the well-regulated and good governance of family and private foundations in a mature civil society, Chinese private enterprises and entrepreneurs have a long way to go in realizing the potential they have to change the society through philanthropy.

Most Donations Go to Government Sectors and GONGOs

Most donations go to the government sectors, GONGOs, and public fundraising foundations with strong government background while grassroots NGOs and other civil society organizations get comparatively little. The amount of donations obtained by the government has increased significantly from $810 million in 2007 to $11.79 billion in 2008 because of the Wenchuan Earthquake. It declined in 2009, but reached $4.1 billion in 2010. (See Figure 2.3.)

The Red Cross Society of China and the China Charity Federation are two major authorized public fundraising organizations and are designated recipients for donations. They have somewhat of a monopoly, receiving 44.6 percent of what was given in 2007. Their monopoly has been challenged, however, in recent years by competitors entering into the donation market. Their portion of funding declined to 16.4 percent in 2009. In 2010, they bounced back to get more than 28 percent of total donations, $3.96 billion, while all the other (about 1,000) public fundraising foundations, all together, got $4.82 billion.

In 2007 only $490 million went to grassroots NGOs and small, new, or unregistered organizations—just 13.8 percent of the total. The growth of their support has not grown steadily. From 2007 to 2010, their portion of giving declined to 3.4 percent in 2008, went back up to 7.9 percent in 2009, and declined again to 6.9 percent in 2010.

| FIGURE 2.3 | DISTRIBUTION OF DONATIONS ACROSS MAIN CHANNELS FROM 2007–2010 (IN US$ BILLIONS) |

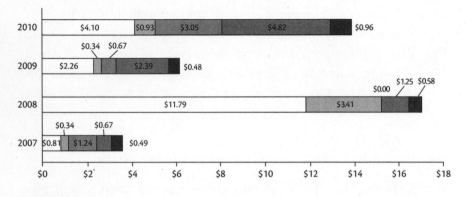

| TABLE 2.1 | DONATIONS FLOW MAINLY TO EDUCATION, DISASTER, AND POVERTY |

Field	2007	2008	2009	2010
Education	37.00%	13.60%	41.07%	21.85%
Disaster Relief	12.00	72.30	25.52	24.43
Poverty	14.00	6.37	12.13*	9.26

*Poverty alleviation in 2009 includes vulnerable group support and rural community development.

Many Chinese grassroots NGOs have to rely on funding from overseas for survival. There's a growing debate, however, among global donors about whether China, the second largest economy in the world, should be a recipient of aid at all. The Global Fund, the U.K. Department for International Development (DFID), and many others who have been generous in the past, have stopped giving to China.

Donations Flow Mainly to Education, Disaster, and Poverty

As stated earlier, in China, education, poverty alleviation, and disaster relief are the three major fields receiving donations. (See Table 2.1.)

The situation is different from the United States and other developed countries, where most donations flow to religion, education, human services, and health.

Foundations of all kinds have become the most important channel for the funding of education and they have grown quickly. In 2010, 691 foundations, 31 percent of all Chinese foundations, focused on education. Tsinghua University Foundation, Peking University Foundation, and Zhejiang University Foundation ranked as the top three private foundations in 2010 according to the China Foundation Center (CFC) Database. These university-run foundations are the primary recipients of restricted donations for educational purposes.

Discrepancies between the government benefits of medical insurance and pensions offered to urban dwellers and those offered to rural people, and the exclusion of many vulnerable groups, has led the other major thrust of philanthropy in China: to mitigate the gap between rich and poor. Poverty alleviation is one of three priorities for charitable funding allocation.

The percentage for disaster relief has increased dramatically from 12 percent in 2007 to 72.3 percent in 2008. It dropped to 24.43 percent in 2010 due to a lesser need to address natural disasters such as the snowstorm in south China, earthquakes in Sichuan and Qinghai, mudslides in Gansu, and floods in middle and south China.

FUNDRAISING PRACTICES IN CHINA

China's expanding economy, and in particular its fast growing HNWI segment, provides a significant pool of potential donors. Although China's philanthropy sector is still young, a definite upward trend in donations could be expected—especially in individual giving.

Although the newly issued regulations for philanthropy administration and new tax law haven't met all the expectations of the philanthropy sector, the positive direction of individual and private enterprise giving cannot be ignored. The vigorous debate stirred by many nonprofits and academics about restrictions and about the overall weakness of the existing system has aroused a widespread interest and more public discussion of the development of philanthropy in China. More and more individuals seek to actively participate in philanthropy and expect accountability from the nonprofits they support.

New technologies—and their adoption by society—provide more opportunities for fundraising. The Internet and new media such as online forums, blogs and micro-blogs, have fundamentally changed the ways people can participate in philanthropy. With the platforms created by the new technology, the general public can access more information on modern philanthropy. It also makes it possible for more people to express their opinions on philanthropy in a public space and demand accountability.

In addition the new technologies create even more efficient channels for raising funds. Free online video advertisements and easier online payment options decrease the cost of fundraising and reach more prospective donors.

Postdonation communication with donors, however, remains haphazard—most individual donors receive no recognition or follow-up. Insufficient financial disclosure and donor data capture methods still remain big issues for charity organizations.

The establishment of the China Foundation Center (CFC) represents a milestone for Chinese philanthropy leaders determined to improve the transparency of nonprofits and make giving a norm for the rich.[14] The CFC aims to make available financial and program details for all foundations (and nonprofits) operating in China, which will trigger a chain reaction that changes the fundamental behavior of philanthropy in China.[15]

| CASE STUDY 2.3 | RED CROSS SCANDAL SPEEDS UP PHILANTHROPY LEGISLATION AND NONPROFIT SECTOR REFORM[16] |

Guo Meimei, a 20-year-old woman claiming to be the Commercial Manager for China Red Cross Association (CRCA), flaunted her wealth and luxurious lifestyle on Weibo, the Chinese version of Twitter, in June 2011. Internet users quickly came to suspect her lavish lifestyle as a symptom of corruption in CRCA. As public pressure grew, both CRCA

---

[14]The Resource Alliance, Institute of Development Studies, funded by the Rockefeller Foundation, *Philanthropy: Current Context and Future Outlook*, 91.

[15]Ibid., 92.

[16]"China Turns against Red Cross," issued by the *Telegraph* on July 6, 2011, available at www.telegraph.co.uk/news/worldnews/asia/china/8620773/China-turns-against-Red-Cross.html. "An Online Scandal Underscores Chinese Distrust of State Charities," issued by the *New York Times* on July 3, 2011, available at www.nytimes.com/2011/07/04/world/asia/04china.html?pagewanted=all.

and Ms. Guo denied a connection with each other. However, this controversy sparked Internet users to do some digging into CRCA. They soon discovered the existence of an obscure group called the *Red Cross of the Commercial Sector*, which has vague ties to CRCA and, as some evidence shows, might have been the source of Guo Meimei's wealth. Since the scandalous posts of late June, Ms. Guo and the Red Cross have been the most talked-about subjects on the Internet in China, even gaining global notoriety as "The Scandal in Chinese Philanthropy."

Other instances of misconduct of CRCA were also found, such as a gross overpayment for equipment and an extravagant restaurant bill for an employee dinner, leading to public outcry.

As a result, many Chinese people are reluctant to donate to domestic charities. Charitable giving in China dropped significantly after the scandal. Because of the drop in giving, transparency online and elsewhere is a concern, even for government-run foundations.

Although the scandal had a strong negative impact on China's philanthropy, there is also a positive outcome. Now there is a stronger movement toward transparency. The scandal had accelerated the pace of philanthropic legislation and the reform of government-organized nonprofit organizations.

The open platforms of the Internet provided a valuable public forum for discussion about nonprofit accountability. The scandal also provided a first opportunity for many Chinese to learn about modern philanthropy and engaged them in thoughtful conversation about it. China will be better because of this incident.

CASE STUDY 2.4   NEW TECHNOLOGY BRINGS QUICK SWEEPING CHANGES FOR CIVIL SOCIETY PARTICIPATION IN PHILANTHROPY[17]

The One Foundation, begun by Kung Fu star Jet Li as a project affiliated with the China Red Cross Association, was formally registered as an independent public fundraising foundation in Shenzhen on December 3, 2010. This is the first successful case of a nongovernmental foundation registering under the Civil Affairs Bureau without

[17]"Jet Li's One Foundation Turns into Independent Public Fundraising Organization," issued by *Xinhuanet* on January 12, 2011, available at http://news .xinhuanet.com/english2010/china/2011-01/12/c_13687548.htm. The donation information about the One Foundation is available at www.onefoundation.cn/ html/cn/beneficence.html.

(Continued)

a sponsor agency after the trial project in Shenzhen. In the past, only the Ministry of Civil Affairs had this authority and only foundations sponsored by the government departments could be approved.

The slogan for One Foundation fundraising, displayed on the donation page of its official website, is, "Every one person donates one Yuan ($.159) in every one month." Taking advantage of China's huge population, this simple idea effectively mobilizes millions of people to get involved in its activities and donate massive amounts of money.

One Foundation has tried almost every available way to assess the capacity of potential donors and make it as easy as possible to make a gift. Besides the traditional methods of collection boxes and bank transfer, One Foundation employs several newer strategies: online donation by credit card and PayPal; cooperating with commercial banks for direct debit monthly; partnering with the owners and operators of Automatic Teller Machines to create donation platforms; and mobile phone fundraising.

One of its most ingenious strategies has been to work in cooperation with the biggest online shopping site, Taobao, to create a new brand for its fundraising. Taobao customers can donate money or donate goods they buy online.

Its fundraising success speaks to the effectiveness of its multiple methodologies. One Foundation raised $1.2 million in the first quarter of 2012.

In Summary

To summarize, here are the major features of Chinese philanthropy today:

- **China has a long-standing history of philanthropy**.

   China was one of the first countries in the world to provide a formal public infrastructure to promote and develop philanthropy. Thousands of years of culture and religion have provided a fertile ground for the rise and development of philanthropy in modern China.

- **China's philanthropy has been booming since the new millennium**.

    China's total amount of donations in 2001 was $0.19 billion, then increased significantly to $17.01 billion in 2008, and then $16.41 billion in 2010. The number of legally registered social organizations grew quickly from 211,000 in 2001 to 440,000 in 2010.

- **Philanthropy in China is complex and differs from that of other countries**.

    China has many features and limitations in terms of the administrative system, unbalanced regional development, legal framework, foreign exchange control, and so on. Those may become barriers for donors and fundraisers.

- **A great leap in giving could be expected**.

    China's expanding economy and fast-growing number of HNWIs provides a significant pool of potential donors. Although China's philanthropy sector is still in an initial development stage, a definite upward trend in giving could be expected—especially for domestic enterprises and individuals.

- **Two donors and three fields are worthy of attention**.

    Domestic enterprises and domestic individuals are becoming two major giving sources in China. Education, poverty alleviation, and disaster relief are the three major fields receiving donations.

- **New technologies provide more opportunities for fundraising**.

    The amazing development of the Internet and new media, such as mobile phone, QQ, and MSN (instant messaging systems), Weibo (a Twitter-style micro-blogging service) has fundamentally changed the ways of giving and raising funds.

Japan

MASATAKA UO

In 2010, Japan had the 10th largest population in the world with about 126 million people and the third highest GDP in the world. Japan is the world's fastest aging society, where people aged 65 or over accounted for 23.1 percent of the total population in 2010 (Population Census 2010). Meanwhile, the birthrate in 2010 was just 1.39 percent. The trend of "declining birthrate and aging population" can be said to be one of the current biggest issues in Japan. Some say that the declining birthrate and aging population are responsible for an increase in government expenditures, including social security costs and medical costs, and are preventing the reduction of the government budget deficit.

During the high-growth period between the end of World War II and the 1990s, Japan had a successful economic development model founded on a strong partnership between the government and the business sector. However, since the 1990s, the inefficiency of government agencies has grown and the development of the business sector has slowed. This situation has caused Japan's current budget deficit, most of it the result of government bonds, to balloon to approximately $12.5 trillion. While most government bonds are purchased by domestic savers, the budget deficit is recognized as a very serious social issue. Against this background, the private nonprofit sector is increasingly looked to as an alternative to government providing for social welfare.

Personal financial assets (excluding real estate) reached 1,439 trillion Japanese Yen ($17.9 trillion), 60 percent of which is said to belong to people aged 60 or over. As a result there are now more bequests being made and they are attracting attention as a vehicle for giving. According to the whitepaper *Giving Japan*, published by the Japan Fundraising Association, 21 percent of people aged 40 or over view bequests positively and so these are expected to increase in the future.

JAPAN: OVERVIEW OF AN ISLAND NATION

Japan is an island nation located in Eastern Asia and geographically vulnerable to many natural disasters. Sixty-seven percent of Japan is forested, and areas suitable for agriculture and human habitation are limited. As a result, the Japanese have learned to coexist with nature and cooperate with neighbors. They know the importance of mutual cooperation and the power of community. Japan, which started on the road to a modern state after the Meiji Restoration in 1868, achieved economic growth by means of technological innovation mainly in the manufacturing industry and remained the world's second largest economy until the 1990s. More than 80 percent of the populace believes in Buddhism and Shinto and about 1 percent is Christian. Confucian philosophy has also influenced Japanese thought.

From 1955 until 2010 when the Democratic Party of Japan took control of the Japanese government, the Liberal Democratic Party or coalition governments headed by the Liberal Democratic Party had been in power (excepting eight months when an opposition coalition government had control). While this political structure provided adequately for social welfare and encouraged economic growth up until the early 1990s, the development of the nonprofit sector and promotion of giving from the private sector, such as a favorable tax system for donations, was neglected.

The Nonprofit Sector

There are many different legal forms that Japanese nonprofits can assume, including special nonprofit corporations (tokutei hieiri katudo hojin), public interest corporations (koeki hojin), social welfare corporations (shakai fukushi hojin), religious organizations (syukyo hojin), incorporated educational institutions (gakko hojin), medical corporations (iryo hojin), and labor unions (rodo kumiai). They differ in the government agency that is responsible for supervising them, how they are certified, and the criteria by which they are monitored. There are 374,648 corporations in the nonprofit sector.[1] This includes:

- 38,997 special nonprofit corporations
- 26,014 public interest corporations
- 18,688 social welfare corporations
- 182,709 religious organizations
- 1,339 incorporated educational institutions
- 45,901 medical corporations
- 61,000 labor unions

Although the Japanese people have been actively engaged in mutual support and private philanthropy throughout their history, an adequate legal structure for them did not exist in the past. During the past 15 years this situation changed dramatically. The typical legal form assumed by nonprofit organizations was a public interest corporation (PIC) until the mid-1990s, but it was difficult to obtain the necessary approval of incorporation from ministries and agencies responsible for this. There was a time when private nonprofit organizations led by the private sector could not easily obtain this legal status even though many government-led PICs were created. Many private sector nonprofit organizations were only granted status as a voluntary group (nin'i dantai).

Public awareness and legal changes made it easier for nonprofits to be independent of government. Increasing public recognition of volunteering and nonprofits after the Great Hanshin-Awaji Earthquake in 1995 and the establishment of the Special Nonprofit Corporation Law in 1997 created an environment in which nonprofits could flourish. The Public Interest Corporation Reform Act of 2007 enabled individuals and businesses to establish PICs. They are authorized by the Public Interest Corporation Commission, consisting of knowledgeable private citizens (not government ministries and agencies).

Influences on Philanthropy

The Japanese people admire Intoku-no-bi—a Confucian concept that encourages donors to refuse recognition and sometimes to donate anonymously. Recently, however, more people have been willing to

---

[1]Japanese Nonprofit Almanac 2010.

be more public in their giving, indicating a change in social attitudes. Another historic influence, dating back to Buddhist temples in medieval times, is the promotion of charitable activities for the poor, the disabled, and other disadvantaged persons. Philanthropic merchants constructed bridges and managed of schools for their communities. The imperial family and other elite members of society were also philanthropic.

The Edo Shogunate (1600–1868) had an isolationist policy for 260 years. It was not until the Meiji Restoration in 1868 that Japan started down the road to becoming a modern nation. Although there were education and welfare activities undertaken by the private sector before the Restoration, the Japanese government's newly adopted "increasing wealth and military power" policy—an initiative designed to help Japan catch up with foreign countries and stimulate socioeconomic development—set the stage for philanthropic growth.

With the nation's commitment to an efficient centralized economic development model—supported by the government and corporations—Japan rose to become the world's second largest economy. However, new government-provided social services increased *amakudari* (meaning "descent from heaven," is the institutionalized practice where Japanese shift retired bureaucrats to executive positions in the private and public sectors) and government spending. As a result, Japan, facing an era of low growth since the bubble burst in the early 1990s, saw its social structure shift toward another model for providing social services, one more reliant on the private nonprofit sector and the philanthropy that supports it.

Sector Infrastructure

Until recently tax deductions for donations were minimal and attaining tax exemption status was difficult because of strict eligibility requirements. In June 2011 both were significantly improved. Specifically, the deduction for giving was increased to approximately 50 percent (i.e., when you donate $1,000, about $500 can be deducted from income tax). The criteria for becoming an organization that is eligible for tax deduction (approved Special Nonprofit Corporation) were significantly relaxed and most organizations are now eligible for at least temporary approval. These changes dramatically improved the fundraising environment.

The creation of organizations devoted to building the capacity of the nonprofit sector also helped to improve the environment. The Japan Fund-raising Association (JFRA) was established in 2008 with the support of 580 founding members from all 47 prefectures in Japan. Its purpose is to promote philanthropic giving, elevate best practices and teach fundraising skills. It is accomplishing this through a conference, publishing, and certification.

- More than 800 delegates attended the third annual JFRA conference in February 2012—double the number of delegates in 2010—and a significant increase from the 550 attending in 2011.
- In 2011 JFRA published the first edition of *Giving Japan 2010* in both Japanese and English. This annual survey of the nonprofit sector provides insight into donors, new trends, and relevant statistics.
- The Certified Fundraiser program began in 2012 and the first certificate exam was conducted in June 2012. This program provides comprehensive educational opportunities and is the first systematic effort to establish standards for professional fundraisers in Japan.

There are other educational opportunities offered elsewhere but as of yet they are somewhat limited. There are many college and graduate level courses on nonprofits, volunteers, social innovation; there are only a few graduate-level programs specializing in nonprofit management and fundraising. The Japan Nonprofit Research Association, an academic conference of the nonprofit sector established in 1999, provides a forum for nonprofit research exchange.

Significant Nonprofits

UNICEF and the Red Cross are INGOs that are successful raising funds in Japan. Other major INGOs here include World Vision, Save the Children, Médecins Sans Frontières, Plan International, Peace Winds, and World Wildlife Fund (WWF). Domestic fundraising organizations, universities, as well as *Ashinaga* (educational and emotional support for orphans worldwide) and Community Chests (a national federation) have also been achieving great results.

Significant NGOs include the Japan Platform, a disaster aid funding platform having as participants the Keidanren (Japan Business Federation) Ministry of Foreign Affairs of Japan, and other powerful influencers.

Philanthropy and Other Support

More than a third of the adult population gives in Japan and they favor projects with clear deliverables. There are at least 4,000 foundations. Ten percent of Japanese corporations give, but their contribution is equal to what is given by individuals. Government remains an important source of nonprofit support.

Individuals

Giving Japan 2010 estimated the total amount of 2009 individual giving as $6.8 billion (545.5 billion yen)—equivalent to 0.12 percent of the national real GDP. In Japan, membership support is another common means of individual support. The total estimated amount of membership fees paid to nonprofits was $4.7 billion (375.5 billion yen) in 2009.

The total number of individuals who donated was estimated as 37.66 million people, equivalent to approximately 34 percent of the total Japanese population ages 15 or over. See Figure 3.1.

The amount of giving for religious organizations accounted for the highest percentage of donations (44.2 percent), followed by giving for international cooperation activities (12.1 percent), and then for the government (9.6 percent—in Japan, donors sometimes give to local

| FIGURE 3.1 | PERCENTAGE OF DONOR BY SEX AND AGE |

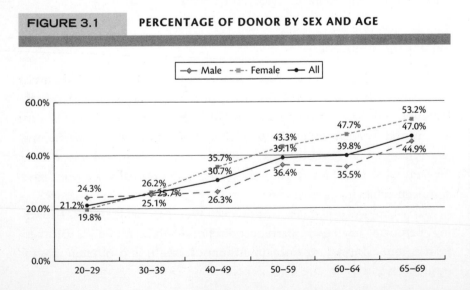

government), for education (7.8 percent), for emergency assistance and disaster relief (4.3 percent), and for the Community Chest (3.4 percent).

Projects with clear deliverables (establishing libraries and schools in developing countries and disaster aid) tend to be more successful than causes with less readily understood objectives.

Foundations

Although there are no accurate statistics on the number of grant-making foundations, the total number of incorporated foundations and incorporated associations that are engaged in grant programs is estimated at approximately 4,000 organizations. *Josei Zaidan Yoran* (directory of grant-making foundations) published annually by Japan Foundation Center, contains information on around 1,000 of them, including grant policies and details of grants made. Many corporate foundations were established in the late 1980s with Japan's corporate success and with low-interest rates, but the number of newly established grant-making foundations has declined since the 1990s.

In 2011 the Japan Foundation Center reported that 483 foundations of the 1,657 surveyed were engaged in educational grant programs. Other fields of grant programs included the health and medical field (264 organizations), social welfare (165 organizations), and culture and art (143 organizations). The total grant-in-aid amount of 754 organizations surveyed was $750 million (60 billion yen).

Corporations

The total amount of corporate giving was $6.2 billion (494 billion yen) in 2009, equivalent to 1.4 percent of the total amount of corporate annual income. In Japan the ratio of total individual giving to total corporate giving is nearly fifty-fifty. Although corporate profits have drastically decreased due to the worldwide economic depression, their giving has actually slightly increased.

Nearly 10 percent (9.8 percent or 256,000 corporations) of all corporations made contributions, mostly for education (30.5 percent), culture and entertainment (sports clubs, recreation facilities, arts) (24 percent), and environmental protection (13.5 percent). Construction, chemical industry, financial insurance, and transport and communications utilities are the most generous businesses.

Government

Although complete statistics on government funding are not available, outsourcing to nonprofits, subsidies, and support programs has been increasing due to the government budget deficit and the growth of nonprofits in recent years. This is especially the case for the designated manager system (where nonprofits and corporations are entrusted with operation and management of government facilities through open-tendered contracts for government-owned sports clubs, community centers, and libraries). This began in 2003 and has rapidly increased government subsidies to Japanese nonprofits.

The New Public Commons, a 2010 initiative by the Hatoyama Government, clarified the role of nonprofits in fostering community leadership. It proposed a comprehensive strategy for leadership development. In 2011, under the proposal, the Cabinet Office embarked on a plan for strengthening nonprofit fundraising ability and consequently raising levels of private support in all 47 prefectures with a budget of $96 million in 2011 to 2012. Such a widespread national government-led initiative in fundraising is the first in Japan's history.

Efforts are regional as well as national. Private community foundations have been established in regions throughout the country. At the same time, many local governments have launched nonprofit funds, a system to mediate donations from local residents. The number of these funds has been increasing over the past decade.

GIVING PRACTICES

Figure 3.2 shows a few different ways of giving. In Japan the largest percentage of donors make their gifts via giving boxes (53.1 percent); followed by face-to-face fundraising (32.2 percent); donation of reward points via credit cards, online shopping, and so on (14.8 percent); click-to-donate sites (14.7 percent); postal bank transfer (14.5 percent); bank transfer (10.4 percent); and donation of goods (9.4 percent). Although giving boxes and street donations are the most popular, donations are relatively small, and it is hard to obtain even the most basic information on donors—such as names. More effective methods include direct mail (house lists and acquisition), online giving, cause branding, and membership.

FIGURE 3.2 **WAYS OF GIVING (%)**

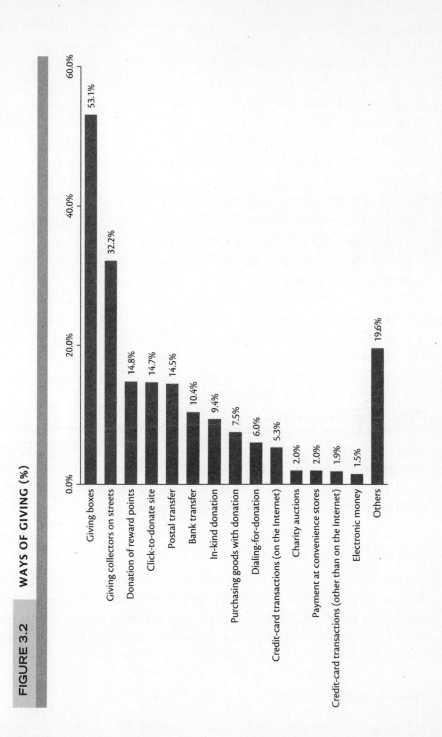

Donors are most responsive to requests for emergency disaster aid and to large-scale efforts like university capital campaigns. Generally speaking there are not many large donations made. Bequests are on the rise and hold great potential for the future. Although there are no actual statistical data on bequests, in recent years larger organizations have attracted the most.

Figure 3.3 shows a few motivations for giving. Japanese donors cite their motivations as: "I donate every year" (33.1 percent); followed by "I want to contribute for others and the society" (30.9 percent); "monetary giving is the most suitable way to make contributions" (28.0 percent); "I want to compensate for my lack of time for volunteer activities" (26.7 percent); and "giving is a part of my socialization" (23.6 percent).

Figure 3.4 shows triggers for giving. The most common reason given for making a donation was, "Because I was asked to donate on the street" (31.7 percent). Other significant triggers are: "Because neighbors came by and asked me to donate" (30.8 percent); "because I was interested in making donations" (19.4 percent); "because there were postings on websites asking for donations" (16.5 percent); and "because family members, acquaintances, or organizations asked me to donate" (14.0 percent).

FUNDRAISING PRACTICES

While the Japanese use the common fundraising methods, they also have some unique approaches, including Mottainai giving. In addition to all the latest practices, traditions, like giving to mark important events like funerals and weddings, are also in use.

Direct Mail

Although many Japanese nonprofits adopt a fundraising strategy of direct mail using house lists, they may not necessarily be familiar with acquisition-type direct mail approach. On the other hand some major INGOs have used direct mail for acquisition since the mid-1990s and achieved highly cost-effective results.

Cause-Related Marketing

While cause-related marketing (CRM) has existed in Japan since the 1990s, the approach was not commonly used. Since the late 2000s,

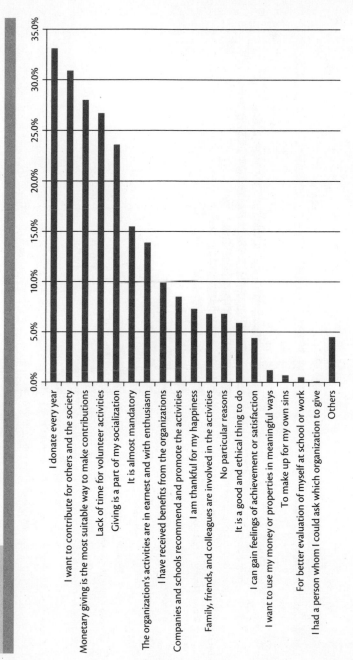

FIGURE 3.3   MOTIVATIONS FOR GIVING (%)

FIGURE 3.4   TRIGGERS FOR GIVING (%)

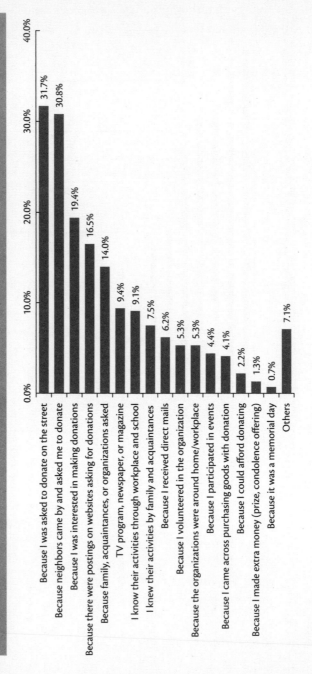

Trigger	%
Because I was asked to donate on the street	31.7%
Because neighbors came by and asked me to donate	30.8%
Because I was interested in making donations	19.4%
Because there were postings on websites asking for donations	16.5%
Because family, acquaintances, or organizations asked	14.0%
TV program, newspaper, or magazine	9.4%
I know their activities through workplace and school	9.1%
I knew their activities by family and acquaintances	7.5%
Because I received direct mails	6.2%
Because I volunteered in the organization	5.3%
Because the organizations were around home/workplace	5.3%
Because I participated in events	4.4%
Because I came across purchasing goods with donation	4.1%
Because I could afford donating	2.2%
Because I made extra money (prize, condolence offering)	1.3%
Because it was a memorial day	0.7%
Others	7.1%

however, it has rapidly gained in popularity. This is because so many, approximately 70 percent, of the public have started to think about contributing to society, and businesses are more interested because in many instances CRM has led to a large increase in sales of corporate products.

Mottainai Giving (Recycle Giving)

Mottainai giving (*Mottainai* is a traditional expression of respect for irreplaceable earth resources) has been spreading widely. Corporations and individuals give away goods, such as books, postcards, precious metals, and CDs, to nonprofits that then convert the goods to cash. This way of giving is an easy introduction for those new to philanthropy. One popular example is the donation of used books to libraries in developing countries.

Online Giving (JustGiving/Click to Donate)

Only 5 percent of donors make use of online credit card giving, less than donation boxes (53.1 percent), street donations (32.2 percent), postal transfer (14.5 percent), and bank transfer (10.4 percent). On the other hand, there are successes like JustGiving Japan, a rapidly growing foundation that has collected more than $10 million in the two years since it was established in 2009. Click-to-donate sites are proliferating and online giving has been becoming popular among the young. Also popular is donation of points obtained by purchasing products (14.8 percent).

Monthly Donation (Regular Gift)

Credit for nonprofits used to be tight and introducing a credit card donation system was difficult. In recent years, however, the situation has improved dramatically. Automatic monthly donations (donation system by monthly automatic withdrawal) have been become commonplace in the international cooperation field.

Ceremonial Gift (Funeral, Wedding)

The tradition of making a donation to mark the occasion of a funeral or a wedding offering instead of sending a gift is on the increase.

One-on-One Support

Programs like child sponsorships and scholarships for children that give donors the opportunity to provide one-on-one support are easily accepted and popular in Japan.

Planned Giving (Bank Trusts)

A 2011 tax revision introduced tax breaks for planned giving trusts offered by financial institutions in Japan. Although the tax benefits are small relative to those in some other countries at this time, it is expected that they will improve in the future.

Donation Boxes and Street Solicitation

Donation boxes located at supermarkets and restaurants and street solicitations get many small gifts. Donation boxes attract 54.1 percent of all donors and street solicitation attracts 32.2 percent. Although the amounts are not large, these are the most common means of making a gift in Japan.

AC Japan (Advertising Council Japan)

Every year, AC Japan selects some lucky nonprofits to receive free advertising campaign support. Those chosen get free TV commercials and "free" (production costs borne by the nonprofits) advertisements such as those found on trains and in stations. Being selected by AC Japan can mean a lot in terms of fundraising.

CHALLENGES AND INNOVATION

Japanese leadership in technological innovation holds promise for fundraising. Bequest giving, because of the concentration of older people, is another area where the Japanese may take the lead, and the nation is already on the cutting edge in education on giving.

Innovation in Online and Mobile Giving

Japan is the world's leader in process innovation, mainly in the manufacturing field. This has been the driving force behind Japanese economic development. In recent years Japan has sought to apply this know-how to creating a new nonprofit fundraising model. Online fundraising and mobile phones have a huge potential for future development. A new generation of technology entrepreneurs is leading the way.[2]

Increased Bequest Giving

Ten percent of the Japanese people make a will. For the remaining 90 percent who don't, inheritance is allocated among family members in accordance with the law. If there is no family, it is claimed by local government. Given that the individual financial assets of people aged 60 or over are expected to exceed $11 trillion, and that 21 percent of people aged 40 are favorably inclined to donate their inheritance, bequest giving is expected to increase along with the number of people making a will.

Education on Giving

Although volunteer education has been adopted by many junior high schools and high schools, education on donating is not provided in most schools. Therefore, adults do not understand philanthropy and distrust the process. In response to this, the Japan Fundraising Association has been developing model programs of "donation education" and has started to promote them throughout the country in recent years.

CASE STUDY 3.1	GENEROUS RESPONSE TO NATURAL DISASTERS

The Japanese volunteered time and money to help provide relief to the victims of a large-scale earthquake that struck Kobe in 1995, killing more than 6,000 people and wreaking devastation. More than 1.3 million volunteers gathered in Kobe. That year came to be called the *First Year of Volunteering* in Japan. In fact, volunteering has spread even more widely since the Kobe Earthquake.

The Great Eastern Japan Earthquake on March 11, 2011, also claimed many human lives. The unprecedented level of generosity shown by the Japanese was one positive development out of that

---

[2] www.nytimes.com/2012/10/04/technology/a-new-tech-generation-defies-the-odds-in-japan.html?_r=0.

terrible tragedy. According to *Giving Japan 2010*, while ordinarily about one out of three Japanese people make a donation, 76 percent gave for disaster relief during that dark time. The total amount donated for relief exceeded $600 billion. The Great Eastern Japan Earthquake has already begun to be viewed as a turning point in Japanese philanthropy and 2011 was dubbed the *First Year of Donation* by the media.

Many other countries offered aid to Japan after the earthquakes and Japan realized its place as part of a larger international mutual aid network. The nation's consciousness of philanthropy grew tremendously. The Red Cross and Community Chest raised large amounts of funding for the Great Eastern Japan Earthquake, and disaster aid platforms such as Japan Platform, based on a unique prior agreement among the business world, NGOs, and the government, was also a significant fundraiser. Japan Platform was established in 2000 as a cooperation platform of the government, corporations, NGOs, media, universities, and so on, to provide mainly disaster aid in foreign countries (domestic aid in some cases). This disaster aid platform has provided funds totaling more than $315 million to many NGOs.

In Summary

Japanese generosity has its origins in ancient Confucianism and Buddhism. Recently the awareness and practice of philanthropy has blossomed due to response to large-scale natural disasters, and also because of an improved infrastructure, including better tax incentives and support organizations like JFRA. In addition to common fundraising methodologies like direct mail, online giving, donation boxes, and street fundraising, there are also uniquely Japanese methods like Mottainai or recycle giving.

The Japanese are known for embracing technological innovation, and this extends to fundraising. Mobile phone, social media, and other promising developments are being explored. There is significant potential for increasing bequest giving because of the aging population. Although still more formal educational opportunities in philanthropy and fundraising are needed in Japan, the growth of philanthropy is being helped along by such efforts as JFRA's public education program.

Latin America

NORMA GALAFASSI

Latin America is a region with a great array of diversity, creativity, and passion. Describing the fundraising scene is a challenging task, as Latin America is a wonderfully diverse group of countries, as well as a growing political and economic force with its own contradictions. Fundraising in this context is as varied as the people; it ranges from conventional strategies such as gala dinners to the most innovative online approaches.

Statistics on giving and fundraising are quite poor in this part of the world. There is no reliable official data resource that provides an accurate idea of the number of existing NGOs, their source of funds, or information about their annual revenue. Statistics on NGOs are only available for some countries where private studies were conducted. For this reason, this chapter provides you with insight from experts in the region including examples and cases, and my own experiences from my years as the first Fundraising Manager for UNICEF in Argentina, founding member of the Argentinean Fundraisers Association, and as a consultant.

AN OVERVIEW OF LATIN AMERICA

Let's get started by defining what exactly is considered Latin America. Latin America encompasses more than 40 countries and territories including the Caribbean, where Romance languages (i.e., those derived from Latin)—particularly Spanish and Portuguese, and variably French—are primarily spoken. It extends from south of the

Mexican–U.S. border to Tierra del Fuego in Argentina, comprising an area of approximately 21,069,500 km[1] (7,880,000 square miles), almost 14.1 percent of the Earth's land surface area.

As of 2010, its population was estimated at more than 590 million[2] and its combined GDP at \$5.16 trillion (\$6.27 trillion at the International Monetary Fund's PPP [purchasing-power-parity] per capita calculation, which is the value of all final goods and services produced within a country in a given year divided by the average [or mid-year] population for the same year). According to World Bank studies, the region was expected to continue its growth of 3.5 to 4.5 percent of GDP in 2011[3] on account of the region's commodity export boom and strong domestic demand. As a result, unemployment has hit new lows in many countries and is about 7 percent in most of Latin America—significantly less than in wealthier European and North American nations. It is a region that still shows socioeconomic disparities, but for the first time in 2012, the inequality gap shrank and about 60 million people were lifted out of moderate poverty.

Although Latin America is a huge region with many countries, languages, and cultures, certain areas share common traits, which helps to explain the fundraising culture in that region.

- Going from north to south we find Mexico, the second-largest economy in Latin America, which has a well-established media and a strong corporate sector. Like many Latin American countries, a wide socioeconomic gap between classes still exists.
- Below Mexico lies the group of Central American countries that because of their history and proximity are strongly linked to the U.S. economy. There is a mixture of indigenous and Spanish

---

[1]World Bank information: http://web.worldbank.org/WBSITE/EXTERNAL /COUNTRIES/LACEXT/0,,contentMDK:20340156~menuPK:258561 ~pagePK:146736~piPK:146830~theSitePK:258554,00.html.

[2]*CIA World Factbook.*

[3]World Bank information: http://web.worldbank.org/WBSITE/EXTERNAL /COUNTRIES/LACEXT/0,,contentMDK:20340156~menuPK:258561~pa gePK:146736~piPK:146830~theSitePK:258554,00.html.

culture, it is predominately Catholic, and subscribes, however, to U.S. business models and ideas.

- Caribbean countries also have diverse cultural influences from countries such as the United Kingdom and France, as well as an important percentage of its population being of African descent. It is a region of islands with paradisiacal landscapes and great vacation resorts and sharply contrasting social and economic disparities. Haiti, for example, is the poorest nation in the Americas. Bordering the Caribbean is Venezuela, a country that like many of its neighbors, struggles with social and economic problems. Venezuela does, however, have many natural resources, including some of the world's largest proven oil deposits, as well as huge quantities of coal, iron ore, bauxite, and gold.

- Seven out of 10 people in Latin America live in the four largest countries: Brazil, Mexico, Argentina, and Colombia. Brazil is the largest country in the region with more than 200 million inhabitants, and is one of the rising economic world powers. Brazil, one of the BRIC[4] countries, presents a culture unique in Latin America, as it was primarily colonized by Portuguese explorers and has a large population of African immigrants. Over the past few years it has made major strides in its efforts to raise millions of its citizens out of poverty. Although there is a wide socioeconomic gap, the World Bank has praised the country for its progress in reducing this gap and creating a stronger middle class. Brazil includes much of the world's largest rain forest around the Amazon, where exploitation of the environment has become a major concern. It possesses one-third of the Earth's biodiversity and it is the world's largest source of fresh water.

- The Andean countries include Colombia, Ecuador, Peru, Bolivia, and Chile that, like the Central American countries, also have a mixture of indigenous and Spanish cultures and strong Catholic traditions. Colombia has significant natural resources, a diverse culture, but it has also been ravaged by a decade-long

---

[4]BRIC countries are Brazil, Russia, India, and China, all considered to be in accelerating stages of economic development.

violent conflict, which has only improved in recent years. Chile is a multiethnic society, with a history of European immigration as well as indigenous ancestry. Although Chile struggles with socioeconomic disproportion within its society, it has seen a lot of growth in the corporate sector. Bolivia has been historically one of the poorest countries in South America with the largest proportion of indigenous inhabitants, who make up around two-thirds of the population.

• Finally there is the Southern Cone, comprised of Argentina, Paraguay, and Uruguay. Argentina, a country rich in natural resources, with a well-educated workforce, is one of South America's largest economies. Argentina has had one of the largest and most recent influxes of European immigration compared to other Latin American countries. In 2001 Argentina suffered an economic crisis and has since struggled with poverty, socioeconomic disparities, and governmental corruption. Uruguay and Paraguay are smaller nations with economies that primarily revolve around agriculture and livestock. The whole sub-region has well-developed media and corporate markets.

Latin America has some of the largest cities in the world, which house a high percentage of the population. In terms of fundraising, this is an important and beneficial trait as it makes it easier for organizations to concentrate their fundraising efforts.

Latino culture is a rich melting pot with many diverse influences: indigenous cultures, Western civilization, and more specifically Spanish, Portuguese, and Italian and also African culture. Some of history's greatest writers, thinkers, musicians, and artists have come from Latin America. Although Latin culture is impossible to describe or define in a few short words, certain traits do stand out in the context of fundraising. It is a culture where people are warmhearted, passionate, creative, communicative, and have a strong sense of community, which is why there is tremendous potential for fundraising success. On the downside, they often have a hard time organizing themselves and planning for the long term. This could be linked to years of economic instability and social and political turmoil.

Most of the countries have been through recent periods of dictatorship, from both the left and right. Democracy is relatively young in Latin America; many Latin American countries did not achieve or restore democratic governments until the 1980s and early 1990s. Today, Cuba is the only remaining Latin American country still under dictatorship. Culture and the arts flourished after military governments were replaced by democratic ones. So did the nonprofit sector—80 percent of Brazil's nonprofits were created during and after the 1990s.

Nongovernment organizations (NGOs) in the region generally work in a wide-reaching geographical area. They have suffered from political and economic instability, high levels of corruption, lack of transparency, and social disparities. Accountability is a new concept to most of them, while at the same time most NGOs exist in a context of highly developed corporate and media markets.

Although official statistics on the number of nonprofit organizations in the region are not reliable, different data suggest that Mexico has more than 22,000[5] organizations, Brazil has more than 338,000[6] nonprofit organizations, and Argentina has more than 100,000.[7]

Generally, the third sector consists of thousands of very small organizations, some of them with only one employee. There is also a small group of large NGOs in which are concentrated most of the sector's employees and revenue. Another characteristic of these nonprofit institutions is the high participation of religious entities, as well as community-based associations, schools, universities, hospitals, and even sports clubs.

A common problem in these organizations is the lack of professional human resources to effectively develop all aspects of their work, including fundraising or resource mobilization jobs. Many are unaccustomed to planning ahead, not only in resource mobilization, but

---

[5] According to CEMEFI Mexican Center for Philantropy (www.cemefi.org).

[6] According to research conducted by IBGE—Instituto Brasileiro de Geografia e Estatística, IPEA Instituto de Pesquisa Econômicas e Aplicadas—Associação Brasileira de ONGs—ABONG e o Grupo de Institutos, Fundações e Empresas—GIFE.

[7] According to data by Argentinean CENOC, Centro Nacional de Organizaciones de la Comunicad (www.cenoc.org.ar).

also in program areas. They may struggle with aspects of budget formulation, strategic planning, and proposal writing.

Most of the NGOs are unaware of the wide variety of resource
mobilization methods available to them, and thus only utilize certain strategies (e.g., applying for government funding or to international agencies). Many organizations share the prejudice that certain
fundraising techniques work only in countries where fundraising is
already developed. Furthermore, many believe that they will not be
able to raise funds and that their best option is to ask for in-kind
donations rather than money. Despite this perception, there are a
growing number of organizations that are testing and putting into
action various fundraising strategies with great success. It is a matter of finding the right combination for each organization in its own
specific context.

According to expert opinions and past studies undertaken in several
countries of the region, it is possible to affirm that most revenue of the
civil society organizations historically is in the form of fees for services.
There is also a high percentage of revenue received from public funds
and international donor agencies and foundations.

Most of the techniques used by organizations are pretty traditional
and include:

- Special events
- Lotteries and raffles; gala events
- Corporate partnership campaigns
- Strong board fundraising activities

Several organizations conduct street collection campaigns, with the
support of TV networks or high-ranking government officials.

Professional fundraising is in its infancy, but is growing rapidly. Top
NGOs and international charities currently conducting private sector fundraising campaigns (most notably Greenpeace, UNICEF, SOS
Children's Villages, World Vision) have been highly successful. Many
of them have developed advanced online fundraising capabilities, and
they are showing success with face-to-face, the use of mass media, and
online appeals. Others have been using traditional techniques, such as
direct mail and telemarketing with good response rates.

A good indicator of the level of professionalization in fundraising is
the figures provided by national fundraising associations. There are

few fundraising associations in the region: AEDROS[8] (Argentinean Fundraisers Association) has more than 270 active members; ABCR[9] (Brazil) close to 350 active members; the seven Mexican Chapters of AFP[10] have in total 120 members. Chile has a small group of fundraisers that gather informally. Other countries might not have a formal association yet. Comparing these figures with the total number of nonprofits just mentioned shows that, in most cases, the number of professionals dedicated to fundraising is 10 times lower than 1 percent of the total number of NGOs. The startup of these associations has been possible thanks to the personal effort and support of different fundraisers who are committed to working together for the advancement of the sector—investing long working hours, in-kind resources, and their own money. This has been the case in Argentina, where the association finally consolidated and managed to have a separate office and a paid staff.

It is important to mention that tax systems in the region offer little incentive to give. In Brazil, for example, donors can write off a maximum of 6 percent of taxable income as donations to officially registered nonprofit organizations. In Argentina, grant-makers can write off 5 percent of taxable income, while in Mexico the limit is 7 percent. Conversely, Colombia's relatively generous rules allow write-offs of up to 30 percent. According to different sources, the weak tax incentives for private philanthropy are related in part to the cultural legacy that views social welfare chiefly as the responsibility of the church and the state, rather than private individuals. In addition, the notion of willing private wealth to public or private charity foundations is largely absent in Latin America. Most legislation is consistent with Roman law, where the family is the natural heir and only a small percentage can be left to a charity by means of a will or bequest.

Having said that, there is good news as well. The trend is positive, as year after year, civil society organizations are working more actively in the management of resources and creating strategies for achieving financial support. They acknowledge it is key for successfully implementing their programs, fulfilling their missions, and especially achieving

---

[8] AEDROS www.aedros.org.

[9] ABCR www.captacao.org.

[10] AFP Mexican and Puerto Rican Chapters, www.afpnet.org/content.cfm? ItemNumber=4170.

sustainability in the long run. Most organizations feel more comfortable with the term *resource mobilization* rather than fundraising, as it encompasses mobilizing people who will in turn mobilize others, their own resources (financial, time, in kind, influence).

A major advantage for many NGOs is that they can approach fundraising, a relatively new area to them, without preconceived ideas about it. They test and implement techniques available easily, without prejudice as to what will and will not work. Most successful NGOs have done fundraising "without the book" and in fact, many NGOs in Latin America have been successful due to fundraising creativity and implementation of new funding models (especially entrepreneurial models, as in the case of NGOs funded by Ashoka or AVINA). In more mature fundraising markets some organizations rely on the same techniques year after year without integrating or attempting new approaches.

A good example of the above is when in 2001 Argentina declared bankruptcy, which severely affected the economy and the entire population. The social work of most NGOs was desperately needed but, at the same time, organizations were challenged financially as the economy was collapsing. Important decisions had to be made. The winners were the ones who, despite the crisis, continued their fundraising efforts by creatively adjusting their strategies. When some of its donor members called to stop their direct debits, Greenpeace, for example, made an interesting proposition. They offered their donors a three-month holiday break where they did not extract donor funds through automatic debit. After that period donors were contacted to set up the direct debit again. The strategy to keep donors worked well, as people felt the organization understood their current situations and they could begin helping Greenpeace again when their personal finances were somehow balanced.

Some newer and smaller local or national NGOs in Latin America have been able to grasp fundraising concepts quickly and have even improved them. As a consequence, some leading fundraisers within the region are invited to give seminars on fundraising at international workshops in more developed fundraising markets to share their success stories.

INCOME FROM SERVICES

Income from services is the top revenue source for nonprofits in Latin America. In most cases, fees relate to services provided by hospitals, health-care facilities, schools, and so on. Some of the services are also funded by governmental subsidies. In the case of Brazil, nearly three-quarters[11] (73.8 percent) of all nonprofit revenue came in the form of services. In contrast, private philanthropy—from individuals, corporations, and foundations combined—accounted for 10.7 percent of nonprofit income in Brazil, while public sector payments accounted for 15.5 percent.

Linked to the income from fees for services are new entrepreneurial models in which organizations develop a commercial enterprise by selling a product or service linked (or not) to the core mission of the NGO. The Brazilian NGO Canto Cidadao, which works to promote citizenship as a way of strengthening democracy, has a number of activities. For instance, they've created a network of more than 1,000 volunteers who dress up as clowns and help out at hospitals (like Patch Adams). One of their income generation activities is performing lessons in drama and clowning targeted to individuals as well as a number of services for companies such as consulting in CSR issues and advice on organizing corporate volunteers, among others. The Argentinean organization La Usina,[12] which works to integrate people with disabilities into society, has launched two social enterprises. One, Redactivos,[13] is a network that distributes and markets different products made by a network of producers who employ workers with disabilities, under a specific criteria of social justice and an ethical code. The second social enterprise launched will produce and distribute specially designed clothes for people with disabilities.

Costa Rica Red Cross, for example, has one of the most diverse funding strategies in the region. They mobilize $44 million in a country of more than four million inhabitants. Not only do they rely on the income of governmental funds, but they also have a number of different corporate partnerships and the development of different product lines and services. Their income generation activities include the provision of ambulance services to transfer patients to hospitals, a network of payment points where people can pay cash for more

---

[11] The Johns Hopkins Comparative Nonprofit Sector Project, Brazil (1999).

[12] www.lausina.org.

[13] www.redactivos.org.ar.

than 200 different services (including gas, telephone bills, electricity), the provision of funeral services, training in first aid, and the selling of uniforms and Red Cross–branded products (even bottled water). According to Rodolfo Parra Fernández, National Director for Resource Mobilization of Costa Rica Red Cross, the success of the strategy relied on the adoption of a resource mobilization philosophy within the National Society. This philosophy includes full support from the governing body and management; investment in infrastructure (budget and human resources); good follow-up; accountability and transparency; and ensuring sustainable social programs. Interestingly, the National Society receives 37 percent of its income from the public sector through six unusual laws. They get a fixed percentage on different taxes or income sources including: 15 percent of every transit ticket, 6 percent of tax to cigarettes and alcohol beverages, and 1 percent of overall telephone billings.

Giving by Individuals

Individual giving is growing at a good pace in the region, from traditional appeals to wealthy individuals to innovative campaigns for recruiting regular givers. Historically, individual giving has been channeled through special events, from gala dinners to sporting events such as golf tournaments. As might be expected of a region with large social and economic gaps, giving by wealthy individuals in some countries has greatly impacted revenues. Conversely, some international organizations have been pioneers in recruiting small individual givers with success (especially in Argentina) and throughout the region there are examples of strong campaigns addressed to the general public by religious organizations. The trends toward individual giving becoming a bigger piece of the whole philanthropy pie is evident in every country.

Major Individual Donors

Traditionally and historically, individual giving in the region has been primarily promoted among the wealthy. There was a belief that a donor had to be a wealthy person.

Boards are key to major donor gifts. Major donors in the region are either part of a governing board or are approached by a board of trustees. The use of boards is particularly successful in countries like Mexico, Colombia, and Argentina, where boards are based on peer relationship and tradition. Many successful businesspeople belong to various boards, to which they contribute financially and assist by sharing their contacts. As a result of this tradition in philanthropy, organizations like UNICEF have a board or an advisory council in its Mexican office, unlike elsewhere in the world. Businesspeople, leading figures, and top management of advertising agencies or media are among its members.

The main fundraising activities organized by boards are gala dinners. Boards or patrons provide their contacts for the event. Seats for these events range from $70 to more than $10,000 in some cases, and even to $1 million.

There are a number of very wealthy families in the region (see Table 4.1). Thirteen of the top 100 on the *Forbes* magazine list of billionaires are Latin Americans. Number one in the world, Carlos Slim, the telecom magnate, is from Mexico. The list comprises fortunes made from mining and other primary industries—banking, telecom, or retail. It is difficult to study major donors, as most of the personal giving information of wealthy families is not public. Most of the rich in the region prefer to give through their own companies (under CSR) or they create their own private foundations to channel their gifts. There are a number of factors that contribute to this: Some families may not have their assets in the country they live in due to past and present economic and political instability and also for tax reasons; others are hesitant to disclose their philanthropic activities due to safety and crime issues (targeted kidnapping is present in many areas). In addition, some believe that the government should be solving the problems that NGOs aim to fix, and that by paying taxes, one is already contributing. It is well known that Carlos Slim even argues that the whole principle of charity is flawed and that investment in job creation is what is needed to solve the region's problem. This is his focus in creating jobs through his companies.

Several countries have successfully organized capital campaigns. In Mexico the market has grown considerably in the past decade. According to Annette Candanedo, Mexican fundraising consultant, Mexican hospitals and universities have been built with the support of highly committed local donors. Some of those donors sit on the boards

TABLE 4.1   TOP BILLIONAIRES IN LATIN AMERICA RANKING IN FORBES TOP 100 BILLIONAIRES LIST

Ranking	Family	Net Worth in Billions	Source	Associated Company/ Foundation	Country
1	Carlos Slim and family	$69	Telecom	TELMEX, America Movil, Carlos Slim Foundation, TELMEX Foundation	Mexico
7	Eike Batista	30	Mining, oil	OGX Petroleo e Gas	Brazil
32	Iris Fontbona and family	17.8	Mining	Antofagasta, Quinenco, playa Laguna	Chile
37	Ricardo Salunas Pliego and family	17.4	Retail, media	TV Azteca, Grupo Elektra, Azteca Foundation	Mexico
38	Alberto Bailleres González and family	16.5	Mining	Industrias Penoles	Mexico
48	Germán Larrea Mota Velasco and family	14.2	Mining	Grupo Mexico	Mexico
52	Joseph Safra	13.8	Banking	Grupo Safra	Brazil
64	Luis Carlos Sarmiento	12.4	Banking	Grupo Aval Acciones y Valores	Brazil
67	Antonio Ermirio de Moraes and family	12.2	Diversified	Grupo Votorantim	Brazil
69	Jorge Paulo Leman	12	Beer	Stake in Anheuser-Busch in Bev. Burger King	Brazil
86	Eliodoro, Bernardo, and Patricia Matte	10	Paper	Grupo and Empresas CMPC	Chile
97	Alejandro Santo Domingo Davila	9.5	Beer	SAP Miller, Santo Domingo Group, Valorem SA, Caracol TV	Colombia
98	Horst Paulmann and family	9.1	Retail	Cencosud, Jumbo Supermarkets	Chile

Source: www.forbes.com/billionaires/list/.

of these organizations and become regular major givers outside of the specific objectives of a campaign. According to Annette, the campaigns have all been successful because donors understood the need for investment and infrastructure.

One of the pioneers was the University of Monterrey (UDEM).[14] They had a crazy dream of launching a capital campaign in 1995, with no donors or databases, or even a proper fundraising department. UDEM was not the principal university of the area, did not have a powerful board, and probably was not an attractive brand compared to its main competitor Tecnológico de Monterrey. UDEM's managing team, under the leadership of Adalberto Viesca, and driven by determination and passion, launched and developed the first capital campaign for the university, "An Investment in Values." Their key message to the public was that "people are naturally generous, but philanthropy must be taught," as the country was just awakening to professional fundraising campaigns. And they succeeded. Not only did they manage to raise more than $27 million on an initial goal of $25 million in their first campaign, but also they mobilized 2,000 benefactors and more than 90 key committed volunteers. One of the keys to their success was their unique and innovative strategy to engage and acknowledge their donors. Donor care was always central in the campaigns. Each person, each donation, each volunteer effort, was treated as the most important one by a highly motivated team of professionals.

After their first success, they conducted two more capital campaigns producing similar results. Several other Mexican universities have also organized major donor appeals, including Tecnólogico de Monterrey, Universidad de las Américas, and Iberoamericana, Puebla. Organizations in other countries in the region such as Argentina, Colombia, and Brazil, have also successfully organized capital campaigns.

GETTING MONEY FROM THE BOTTOM OF THE PYRAMID

Medium- and small-size gifts from individuals have been slowly growing in importance. While individual giving has been consistently

---

[14] www.udem.edu.mx/.

a significant income source for religious organizations in Brazil and Chile, for example, most experts agree that direct response techniques introduced in the late 1980s and early 1990s by INGOs like UNICEF, Greenpeace, SOS Children's Villages, in their local branches in Argentina, Brazil, Mexico, Ecuador, and elsewhere, were largely responsible for shifting strategies toward more sustainable funding from the bottom of the pyramid. Domestic organizations adopted their methodologies. Still, the total amount raised from small individual donors is not at the level of the U.S. and European third sectors.

The size of donor bases ranges considerably across the countries. Several INGOs and NGOs in Argentina have bases of more than 50,000 and 100,000 donors, most of them on automatic debit to credit cards. In the case of Brazil, Chile, Colombia, and some other countries, INGOs do not reach those figures. Religious organizations, however, may have more than 600,000 donors, and some of them even over a million (i.e., Cancaonova and Comunidade Catolica Sagrada Familia in Brazil, Hogar de Cristo in Chile).

The region rapidly adopted regular giving through automatic debit, especially to credit cards. In most countries the payment process is relatively easy (Mexico, Paraguay, Colombia) while others may face challenges. Automatic debit to credit cards in Chile, for example, cannot be made unless the donor stamps his or her signature, so attempts to get regular donors via online or telemarketing are not very effective. What works well is face-to-face recruitment for direct debit donors. The case for Brazil is different, as people prefer automatic debit to their bank accounts, which in practice means that the NGO has to get an agreement with each bank where their direct debit donations are made.

If we analyze each technique involved in direct response, we can conclude that all of them are working in the region, but each country may face slightly different challenges and each organization has to find its own mix. "Organizations need to find their own models and break their own prejudice," says Alejandro Ferraez, Fund Development and Communications Advisor for Central America & Caribbean at SOS Children's Villages. She says:

> We are having amazing results in unexpected markets. Take for
> example Nicaragua, where we have managed to put together a very

successful face-to-face program for the first time and now we are planning to go for telemarketing; or Venezuela where we are successfully recruiting donors with new media appeals. People react positively to our campaigns, despite the beliefs that the economy is not going well or there is insecurity or corruption. People give everywhere. It is just the challenge of the NGOs to find the right combination of techniques to appeal to that market.

Direct mail was used for fundraising appeals in the 1990s, especially by UNICEF and Greenpeace, among others, as earlier noted. Some organizations are still using it, but a lack of databases in some places proves an obstacle for succeeding with this technique. There are also organizations that develop corporate partnerships (with banks, credit cards, or other service-oriented companies) where the company facilitates access to their customer's database so that the NGO may send out direct mail packs for recruitment. Once organizations have built their own donor bases, cultivation strategies include direct mail packs for continuing the relationship with the donor apart from online communications.

Telemarketing is probably the most often used technique in Latin America. Cold calling or calls to warmer databases can provide a good return on investment in most countries. Some organizations testing recruitment with cold lists (telephone book) are able to recover the costs in less than 12 months. Telemarketing is currently being used in everywhere in the region. Some organizations manage to access the client lists of their corporate partners and in that way get access to new databases.

There are a number of alternative strategies developed by organizations trying to adjust a technique for a particular environment. UNICEF Uruguay managed to launch automatic monthly debit to the telephone bill as an option for its donors. In Brazil, several organizations receive individual donations debited to the electricity bill, opening up yet another new payment method. These methods offer solutions to markets where the percentage of the population with a bank account might be still low compared to other regions of the world.

Face-to-face was tested in the region some years after its launch in Europe. Certain countries were able to adopt it more quickly than others. Greenpeace, for example, was able to implement it with success in the late 1990s in Mexico, Chile, and Brazil, but not in Argentina. The use of this technique is growing across the region by Greenpeace, Doctors Without Borders/Médecins Sans Frontières (MSF), SOS Children's Villages, and Amnesty International, among other international organizations.

The use of mass media, including Direct Response Television (DRTV), is also working well. UNICEF fundraising strategies in the region have been based on combining communication campaigns aimed at creating a clear positioning concept and activities involving individual giving integrated with corporate partnerships. Through cause-related marketing partnerships, UNICEF has been able to reach new audiences and acquire new individual donors. According to Juan Ignacio Calvo, UNICEF Regional Fundraising Specialist at the Americas & the Caribbean Regional Office, the secret for success resides in the capacity of the organization to sustain long-term investment and consolidate its fundraising tools. UNICEF has fundraising operations in nine countries in the region, with Argentina leading in individual donors (more than 120,000 regular donors), because of its coherent and mature fundraising strategy. Brazil, Mexico, and Colombia also show great potential, the latter currently with 25,000 donors.

Online giving is widely used in the region as several Latin American countries have good Internet usage penetration percentages, the average for the region being around 39 percent (Argentina 67 percent, Chile 59 percent, Colombia and Uruguay 56 percent, and several Caribbean countries and territories even higher than that: Antigua 80 percent, Barbados 66 percent, etc.).[15] Greenpeace Argentina has historically been the leader, promoting its website as a natural response mechanism for all its campaigns. It got started with online giving or online donations in 1996, having at that time less than 2 percent of its new donors from the web (total of 1,700 donors). Today its donor base contains more than 85,000 regular donors, and directly and indirectly, 90 percent of them are recruited through the website. They either donate directly or they become cyber activists first, who are

---

[15] According to internetworldstats.com, 2011.

then cultivated and converted to donors with subsequent telemarketing and online appeals. Martin Tinghitella, Greenpeace Fundraising Director for the South Cone, explains that its campaigns are successful because it manages to change the way the organization thinks, and campaigns are at the center of its communications. Greenpeace manages to tell the general public what it does in a simple and engaging way. Its program activities become stories where the main character is the donor.

Social media networks are also being adopted quickly in the region, and social networks like Facebook are booming. Three of the top 15 Facebook countries in the world are in Latin America (mainly Brazil, Mexico, and Argentina, see Table 4.2). Brazil grew 57 percent in the past six months while Argentina has a penetration close to that of the United Kingdom's. Organizations are quickly adopting social networks not only to disseminate their messages and campaigns, but

TABLE 4.2	TOP FACEBOOK USERS WORLDWIDE AND PERCENTAGE CHANGE—JULY 2012			
Ranking	Country	Users	Change	% Change
1	United States	156,830,580	+ 849,120	+ 0.54%
3	Brazil	48,041,640	+ 17,588,380	+ 57.76
4	India	46,307,580	+ 8,262,580	+ 21.72
5	Indonesia	42,586,260	+ 1,756,540	+ 4.30
6	Mexico	33,579,520	+ 3,458,120	+ 11.48
7	United Kingdom	31,114,800	+ 633,500	+ 2.08
8	Turkey	30,666,980	+ 193,700	+ 0.64
9	Philippines	27,102,380	+ 350,380	+ 1.31
10	France	24,436,340	+ 1,188,000	+ 5.11
11	Germany	23,686,860	+ 2,052,480	+ 9.49
12	Italy	21,678,020	+ 1,101,320	+ 5.35
13	Argentina	18,481,100	+ 1,216,720	+ 7.05
14	Canada	18,246,980	+ 1,338,600	+ 7.92
15	Colombia	16,478,180	+ 889,300	+ 5.70
16	Spain	16,399,020	+ 1,109,580	+ 7.26

Source: www.socialbakers.com/Facebook-statistics/?interval=last-6-months.

also to implement other integrated approaches. The use of click-to-call is highly successful. Also known as *click-to-talk, click-to-chat*, and *click-to-text*, this is a form of web-based communication in which a person clicks an object (e.g., button, image, or text) to request an immediate connection with another person in real time either by phone call, Voice-over-Internet-Protocol (VoIP), or text. Click-to-call requests are most commonly made on websites but can also be initiated by hyperlinks placed in email, blogs, wikis, flash animations or video, and other Internet-based object or user interfaces.[16] NGOs will place ads on Facebook and other online media, prompting people to fill in a form requesting to be called later by the organization. The landing page has a simple form where prospective donors leave their name, email, and phone number and fill in the desired times to be called. Telemarketing completes the cycle and conversion to regular givers is successful.

Most direct response techniques are effective and several organizations work them into integrated strategies. Two years ago, MSF launched its fundraising operations in Argentina. They managed to acquire more than 13,000 monthly donors by using a combination of mass media appeals (including DRTV, radio, and press ads), mailing packs, a successful face-to-face campaign and integrated telemarketing, and online appeals. The key for Jonas Beccar Varela, fundraising director of the organization in Argentina, is a well-crafted plan and a decision to invest. He adds: "Many NGOs in my country do not understand the importance of investing in order to generate new revenue. When our program was created we knew we had to invest at least for two years and at the same time that we needed a solid strategy and a good team of engaged professionals."

Other colleagues who work on a regional basis agree with this idea. Juan Cruz Mones Cazón, SOS Children's Villages Director of Fund Development and Communication for Latin America and Caribbean, oversees the fundraising operations of 18 countries in the region. He agrees that NGOs in the region do not understand the importance of investing to raise funds, and thus the concept of return on investment.

---

[16]http://en.wikipedia.org/wiki/Click-to-call23.89%.

TABLE 4.3	SUMMARY OF AVERAGE MONTHLY DONATIONS

Country	National Currency	U.S. Equivalent
Argentina	AR $30 to $50	$5.66 to $9.43
Brazil	Reais 25 to 50	$13.99 to $27.78
Chile	Chilean Peso $3,000	$6
Colombia	Colombian Peso $24,050	$13
Mexico	Mexican Peso $100 to 150	$7.31 to $10.96

Source: in2action, Fundraising & Communication.

However, at the same time he explains, "Whenever an organization understands and invests, it definitely pays off."

A last item to consider on fundraising from individuals is the great opportunity presented by diaspora giving. Latin America and the Caribbean is the region with the largest estimated diaspora savings ($116 billion)[17] followed by East Asia and Pacific ($84 billion), Europe and Central Asia ($73 billion), and South Asia ($53 billion). One of the reasons why the Latin America region has the largest diaspora savings is that its migrants are mostly in the United States and Western Europe, and have relatively higher incomes on average than migrants elsewhere. The Latin American diaspora community living in the United States is estimated to have the largest diaspora savings due to the relatively higher incomes of migrants in the United States compared to other corridors. Comparing all countries, Mexico is estimated to have the largest diaspora savings ($47 billion) while in terms of remittances inflows, it is estimated to be in third place worldwide after India and China. Although there are no important fundraising campaigns addressed to diaspora yet, it represents a target audience with great potential for NGOs in the region.

---

[17]From the *Bellagio Report* issued by the Institute of Development Studies (IDS) and the Resource Alliance, with support from the Rockefeller Foundation. www.resource-alliance.org/pages/en/bellagio-initiative.html.

CASE STUDY 4.1   BEHIND THE HOGAR DE CRISTO
SUCCESS STORY

One cannot discuss individual giving in Latin America without mentioning the Hogar de Cristo Foundation in Chile.

Hogar de Cristo has established itself as the leading institution in Chile on issues of poverty, currently serving more than 73,200 people per month in more than 800 programs throughout the country. Hogar de Cristo was founded in 1944 by Jesuit Alberto Hurtado, who was canonized by the Vatican for his work in Chile. Since its inception, it has improved the lives of people who suffer mostly from social exclusion and material poverty. Their efforts concentrate on the promotion, repair, and restoration of basic needs—such as education, an adequate standard of living (relative to food, clothing, shelter, medical care, and basic social services), citizenship, equal opportunity, physical and mental health, integration of persons with disabilities, and dignified work.

Since the beginning Father Hurtado stressed the importance of the donors and volunteers in the Foundation, praising them for their efforts and crediting the success of Hogar de Cristo to those who supported and carried out its mission. Today, it is one of the largest organizations made up of individual donors in Latin America, with more than 600,000 active donors in 2012. Out of the 600,000, two-thirds donate on a monthly basis. In addition there are another 600,000 donors from past years who are not currently active. The total donor base number is impressive, given the total population of the country (16 million inhabitants). More than 50 percent of the foundation's revenue historically has been collected door-to-door by about 1,000 female members of the Church. In the process of collection donors were updated on the foundation's activities. The system is still in place, although more modern methods are also used nowadays. In the early 1990s payment by credit card was established and today more than a third of the regular members donate via debit or credit card.

Individual donation is not the sole strategy of the foundation. They also have a program for companies and their employees to sponsor a specific project. Also they raise funds through the sales of religious items in shops throughout the country, as well as through fees for services (including funeral services), corporate partnerships, and governmental funds.

(Continued)

TABLE 4.4	HOGAR DE CRISTO NET INCOME COMPOSITION (PERCENT)

Income Source	1990	1995	2000	2005	2010	2011
Program for Companies and Individual Givers	35%	38%	54%	52%	55%	54%
Income from Religious Products	18%	13	10	7	5	5
Licenses (Cinerario)	7%	7	9	7	14	11
Donations	28%	23	19	14	1	5
Services	9%	11	7	18	18	18
Governmental Funds	3%	8	1	2	7	7

Source: Hogar de Cristo Marketing Department.

TABLE 4.5	HOGAR DE CRISTO ANNUAL NET INCOME (IN MILLIONS OF DOLLARS AS OF 12/31/2011)

1990	1995	2000	2005	2010	2011
$30.6	$24.7	$53.2	$52.7	$74.1	$70.2

Source: Hogar de Cristo Marketing Department.

In the past 21 years, the composition of the net income of the foundation has changed. Five percent of income is now generated primarily by regular monthly $5 donors.

The total net income from 1990 to 2011 has doubled. This was achieved by an important change of philosophy within the organization. Marketing Director, Francisco Vallejo Giubergia stated, "The key to success has been the professional management of fundraising within the organization. In Chile, organizations are afraid to professionalize their efforts, but we knew we had to invest in technology including the purchase of a CRM[18] and managing with a Balanced Scorecard,[19] among other things. We managed to convince the

(Continued)

---

[18]CRM (customer relationship management) is a technological model for managing a company's interactions with customers, clients, and sales prospects. http://en.wikipedia.org/wiki/Customer_relationship_management.

[19]Balanced Scorecard is a strategic performance management tool.

board of our organization that having a professional fundraising operation was an investment. That was the key."

In addition, every year they hold a month-long televised campaign where they aim to attract 50,000 new donors. According to Giubergia, thinking big is key to achieving big.

INSTITUTIONAL GIVERS: GOVERNMENTS, FOUNDATIONS, AND CORPORATIONS

Although institutional donors are present in Latin America, large international agencies are less active in this part of the world. According to cooperative data compiled by the Organisation for Economic Co-operation and Development (OECD), in 2008 the region received $5.66 billion, less than a fifth of what Asia or Africa received in the same period. With the exception of the recent earthquake emergencies in Haiti and Chile, Latin America seems to have less than equal access to funds from some of the large international cooperation agencies. The main international cooperation agencies that are investing in the region are either from North America or Europe including USAID, Europe Aid (European Union), AECID (Spain), International Development Association, or the Canadian International Development Agency.

To explore the characteristics and trends of institutional givers in the region, the AVINA Foundation in partnership with the Office of Outreach and Partnerships of the Inter-American Development Bank (IDB), created the Latin America Donor Index.[20] This index includes data on major donors in Latin America. Donors are consulted annually about where their funds are allocated. They recognize four donor types: development agencies, NGOs, private donors (foundations), and corporate donors (Social Corporate Responsibility Initiatives). In 2008, with the data provided by 283 organizations, the study concluded that the region received more than 7.5 billion, 45 percent of

---

[20] www.lacdonors.org/.

which came from international cooperation, 30 percent from NGOs (Transparency International, UNICEF, etc.), 15.3 percent from foundations, and 9.4 percent from corporate donors.[21]

Donors have slightly altered their focus in the past years. Previously, donors tended to address issues such as poverty or crisis relief, whereas now they have shifted more toward economic development and support of democratic causes.

The Bill and Melinda Gates Foundation (U.S.), Ford Foundation (U.S.), Gordon and Betty Moore Foundation (U.S.), Telefonica Foundation (Spain), and Repsol Foundation (Spain) are among the main international private foundations donating to the region.

There are, however, several Latin American foundations and corporate donors active within the region such as Fundacion Bradesco (Brazil), Fundacion Perez Companc (Argentina), Grupo Santander (Brazil), Fundacion Televisa (Mexico), Fundación Azteca (Mexico), Fundación Telmex (Mexico), among many others. Donations by private foundations are linked to contributions made by wealthy families. As described earlier in this chapter, many individuals of higher socioeconomic levels channel their own donations through privately owned foundations under the name of the initial company or family or through CSR by the companies directly.

CSR has been on the rise in most countries. Brazil has been a major developer in this. In fact, Ethos Institute,[22] a leading CSR organization in Brazil and a globally respected expert on CSR, has more than a thousand affiliated companies. Ethos Institute was conceived by businesspeople from the private sector, and it is a center for mobilization, organization of knowledge, exchange of experiences, and development of tools that can help companies to analyze their management practices and deepen their commitment with corporate responsibility. There are a number of organizations that promote philanthropy within each country, for example, the Mexican Centre for Philanthropy CEMEFI, GIFE (Brazil), IARSE (Argentina), the Social Enterprise

---

[21] Augustina Budani, Maximiliano Luft, and Carmen Lopez, "Report: Main Philanthropy Trends in Latin America," Avina and IDB, 2010.

[22] www.ethos.org.br.

Knowledge Network (Latin America), the Alliance for Social Responsibility (Mexico), Acción RSE (Chile), Consorcio Ecuatoriano para la Responsabilidad Social CERES (Ecuador), DERES Desarrollo de la Responsabilidad Social (Uruguay), Fundación Hondureña de Responsabilidad Social Empresarial (FUNDAHRSE Honduras), Fundacion Pro Humana (Chile), and several others. These organizations are sometimes composed of companies or company foundations. In Brazil GIFE[23] (Group of Institutes, Foundations, and Enterprises) is reportedly the first South American association of grant-makers, uniting privately held organizations that fund or operate social, cultural, and environmental projects of public interest. Ninety-five percent of its members, however, are corporations.[24]

There are also companies working with organizations from a cause-related marketing perspective. This ranges from the rounding up of grocery bills at supermarkets and other retail outlets (extra change being donated), to joint communication campaigns, and to typical sales promotions where a percentage of the sale of specific product goes to a given charity. CRM partnerships work well for organizations with some brand recognition, but it is less applicable to smaller NGOs. UNICEF is quite active in the region, creating and promoting different strategic partnerships. In addition, there are some strong national NGOs such as SOS Mata Atlantica in Brazil, Fundacion Cimientos and LALCEC in Argentina, Minuto de Dios in Colombia, and Fundacion Peluffo Gigens in Uruguay.

SOS Mata Atlantica is a Brazilian environmental NGO, created in 1986, with the mission to restore and protect the Atlantic biome. SOS has a large number of members due to several cause-related partnerships. One of the main partnerships is with Bradesco, a top Brazilian bank, which transfers 50 percent of the issuing fee of new credit cardholders to SOS. In addition, every new cardholder is automatically made a member of the organization and receives newsletters and appeals. After the first year, the cardholders may decide to renew

---

[23] www.gife.org.br.

[24] From the *Bellagio Report* issued by the Institute of Development Studies (IDS) and the Resource Alliance, with support from the Rockefeller Foundation. www.resource-alliance.org/pages/en/bellagio-initiative.html.

their credit card, in which case the renewal fee is transferred again to SOS Mata Atlantica, so the cardholder remains a member. Bradesco and SOS Mata Atlantica have also launched other products, including certificates of deposit. Bradesco issues certificates of deposit on behalf of SOS Mata Atlantica. People make a monthly payment and certificates are due to pay after five years. For each certificate issued, SOS Mata Atlantica receives a percentage and customers are also entitled to a money draw on specific dates. The organization has also successfully organized the click-tree initiative,[25] a website where the participation of people (clicks) corresponds to corporate sponsor donations of seedlings to reforest the biome of the Atlantic. From August 2000 to April 2010, web visitors and sponsors of Clickarvore helped to donate 22 million seedlings and contributed to the restoration of more than 13,000 hectares of forest.

Special events are another important collaborative strategy for companies and NGOs. These range from typical gala dinners to sports events, music concerts, and telethons. Companies advertise in the program book or have a specific brand presence at the event site. Sports or music events often attract good media partnerships. Sponsorship of gala dinners is largely connected to a major donors strategy.

Even organizations in smaller countries manage to have successful events. The Jamaican Red Cross, for example, holds an annual gala dinner addressed to HNWIs. They manage to get on board a good number of corporate sponsors that advertise in the evening's program as well as promote their products during the event.

Telethons are definitely among the successful fundraising initiatives in the region.

UNICEF also has a number of telethons in the region. One of the oldest ones is "A Sun for Children" (Un Sol para los chicos), a partnership with Argentina Chanel 13 that combines individual donations by credit cards through the telephone with online appeals and a strong strategy of corporate sponsors. Uruguay and Peru UNICEF offices have also organized fundraising telethons adapted to the local markets, and, for example, managed to negotiate donations through monthly debit to the telephone bill.

---

[25] clickarvore.com.br.

CASE STUDY 4.2   BRAZIL TELETHON CRIANCA
ESPERANCA (CHILDREN'S HOPE)

Brazil Telethon Crianca Esperanca (Children's Hope) started in 1986 as a partnership between Red Globo, the largest multimedia Group in Brazil, and UNICEF. The partnership lasted until 2003 when the media group changed the beneficiary organization to UNESCO. The aim of the show is to raise funds to help educate Brazilian children. Although the main event is a telethon, Crianca Esperanca is basically a 30-day campaign, with the telethon taking place halfway through. During that time every TV show broadcasted by this mega network references the telethon and invites people to make a financial contribution. Donations are made by calling three different telephone lines that enables automatic debit donations to the telephone bill of either R$7, R$15, or R$40 ($3.46, $7.42, $19.78). People can also make online donations[26] and pay by credit card, debit from bank account, check, or bank deposit. In 2003 the show raised R$9.5 million ($4.5 million), in 2005 R$16.5 million ($7.17 million), while in 2012 over R$18 million ($9 million) was raised.

A major player in the telethon business is the International Organization of Telethons (ORITEL), a group that oversees charity broadcasts in Chile, Mexico, and 11 other Latin American countries. Oritel raises tens of millions of dollars annually to benefit children with disabilities. The head of Oritel, Mario Kreutzberger, who hosts programs on Univision under the name Don Francisco, launched the first telethon in his native Chile in the 1970s with the guidance of Jerry Lewis, longtime former host of the Muscular Dystrophy Association telethon. The Chilean Telethon has a robust corporate sponsorship strategy involving different cause-related marketing promotions. It raised more than $40 million in 2011 and the beneficiary organization is Fundacion Teletón.

In August 1998, with thanks to the success achieved by Teletón in Chile and to the constant support and consultancy given to other

---

[26] http://criancaesperanca.globo.com.

countries interested in starting their own Teletón Foundations, Mario Kreutzberger decided to join the countries of the continent in the earlier-mentioned ORITEL, with the purpose of opening opportunities for those with disability.

In Summary

In a region with more than 40 countries and territories that for many might look the same, each country's geography and history has produced its own traditions, socioeconomic, and cultural differences. After years of nondemocratic governments, NGOs have grown in number and in quality. Professional fundraising is in its infancy, but is growing rapidly. It is a road under construction, which will soon become a great highway.

Nonprofit organizations in Latin America are mobilizing resources successfully and professionally, using all available techniques. The trend is positive and the potential is enormous. Every technique analyzed is working in different parts of the region; from direct mail to telemarketing and face-to-face, from individual donors to corporate and institutional givers.

The recent earthquakes of Haiti and Chile in 2010 are probably the best proof of the power of giving in the region. Most of the countries in Latin America had different organizations collecting funds for both tragedies. The International Federation of National Societies of the Red Cross and Red Crescent reported that 20 different National Societies from Latin America mobilized resources for Haiti, even in small countries or territories. Resources were mobilized from companies, foundations, governments, and individuals.

It is a fact that different target audiences respond in a positive way to well-planned and executed campaigns, especially those that are presented in creative and compelling ways. Undoubtedly regular giving by individuals is the rising star in the region. The usage of off-line and online media and social networks and the development of creative corporate partnerships are key ingredients for any organization aiming to expand their individual giving potential. Social enterprise models are also on the rise and have a long way to go as well. The corporate sector and institutional givers are becoming more sophisticated donors and want better-equipped NGOs and carefully considered proposals.

Most experts here agree that the challenge is to find the right combination of techniques for each organization in a given country or place, which is likely true in many other parts of the world. One of the major challenges is probably the need for most NGOs to understand the concept of investment, both in human resources and in their own fundraising budgets. Many organizations still develop their fundraising appeals with volunteers who cannot dedicate the needed time and energy, and with almost no budget.

The second challenge is within the NGOs themselves, as they either lack knowledge of the wide variety of resource mobilization methods available to them, or share the prejudice that certain fundraising techniques work only in countries where fundraising is already developed.

Having said that, successful organizations in Latin America might be said to share common aspects:

- NGOs that have strong institutional policies and programs are better prepared to start their fundraising efforts.
- Many organizations are finally understanding the need of asking professionally for the funds and also the need of having the right people for the job, both at the professional level but also at the governing body levels, where there are still many prejudices to be taken down.
- They know the importance of investing their resources to obtain the desired income objectives in reasonable periods of time.
- They acknowledge the need of having a consistent image across the time and the importance of transparency and accountability.

As the nonprofit sector strengthens after many years of authoritarian governments, more qualified and dedicated people will ensure a stronger fundraising profession. Professional fundraising associations such as AEDROS, ABCR, and AFP chapters are key to that development. Future efforts should aim at having a fundraisers' association in every country and helping organizations to identify, recruit, and train competent professionals. The experts point the way forward.

Flavia Lang and Ader Assis from the Brazilian consulting agency Ader & Lang, agree that the future belongs to organizations that communicate their results in a transparent way. Sooner than expected, many NGOs, especially INGOs, that were recipients of outside aid, will be collecting funds not only to sustain themselves but to help other countries as well.

Juan Cruz Mones Cazon, from SOS Children's Villages, shares that the secret for success might be how long each organization is able to sustain its long-term investment efforts for testing and consolidating all the different fundraising tools available.

The future will find NGOs making larger efforts to integrate all their communication appeals using the power of new media, social networks, and any new communication or technological improvement that the general public might quickly adopt.

Using innovative fundraising techniques has been a great approach for many Latin American NGOs. Out of necessity, they forged new strategies with their own creativity and passion. With the wide scope of global communication, and especially in an online environment, this can even be amplified as ideas come from all over the world, easily, to the desk of any fundraiser. The challenge is whether NGOs in the region will invest and put certain ideas into practice to start thinking big and achieve big results.

CHAPTER 5

Western Europe

CHRIS CARNIE

Western Europe—509 million people, 23 official languages, and the cradle of Classical civilizations—is, as I write, in the throes of an economic seismic shift, an enforced evolution, in which the dinosaurs of State are being wiped out by the high-impact meteorite of the financial sector crisis, leaving private, and associational, initiatives to take their place.

So you will have to forgive me if I avoid predictions and projections of how things will be. I focus on how they are, how they have been, how we have got here, and what forces are at play. The countries broadly accepted as forming Western Europe are the 27 members of the political and economic European Union (EU) that are not former Iron Curtain countries, as well as Norway, which is still, surprisingly, holding out against joining the EU, and Switzerland. I do not dwell on the tax or philanthropic intricacies of tiny states like Andorra, Liechtenstein, Monaco, or the Vatican City. Despite being a Scot, I will not be drawn into arguments of whether Scotland, Catalonia, Val d'Aosta, or Cornwall should be treated as separate countries; I stick with the political states as they are currently defined.

In this chapter, you find a briefing note on each country, followed by an overview of the nonprofit sector across the region, a look at how philanthropy is changing the rules, and a review of fundraising including examples. There are links to relevant sites for further information at the book's wiki site, http://globalfundraising.wikispaces.com.

THE NONPROFIT SECTOR IN WESTERN EUROPE

The nonprofit sector in Europe defies clear definition. It is a mess of contradictions, cultures, histories, and arcane legalities. It is relatively easy to say, as the European Foundation Centre (EFC) says, that foundations are "purpose-driven, asset-based, independent and separately constituted, nonprofit bodies," but you could throw a stone from the Brussels offices of the EFC and hit a foundation that does not meet that definition. Admittedly, a long throw, but the point is that Europe's active nonprofit sector is very, very hard to tie down. (Also see Table 5.1 for various data for countries in Western Europe.)

In part this is because Western Europe has had two major legal traditions to follow—the common law traditions of England, and the civil law systems, such as the Napoleonic laws of much of Southern Europe. The key distinction between the two traditions that is relevant here is that common law is uncodified—essentially you are free to do anything you like so long as it is not illegal. Civil law systems are codified, meaning, very roughly, that you are free to do anything that the law says you can do. This is one reason why in the United Kingdom there is a single type of charitable foundation, called a *charitable trust* while in France there are currently seven, each for different, defined, purposes.

For purposes of this book, we include in our definition of the nonprofit charitable sector all of Europe's *public utility* foundations, all of the charitable trusts registered with the Charity Commission for England and Wales, and the charities registered with the Office of the Scottish Charity Regulator. We include some of Europe's associations—a legal form that is different from a foundation—although we also exclude many; the Barcelona Football Club, for example (a wonderful association but not really a charity). We also include foundations that do good while doing other things—Sandoz Fondation de Famille, for example, which states that its primary aim is to "encourage entrepreneurial commitment through long-term holdings in companies in a variety of sectors"[1] but which also makes substantial contributions to the arts.

---

[1] www.sandozfondation.ch.

TABLE 5.1   COUNTRY DATA

Country	Population in millions (2009/2010)*	Official development aid assistance US$ millions 2010	Private development aid assistance US$ millions 2010*	GDP, constant prices, PPPs, reference year 2005, US$ millions*	% of total population age 65 and over 2010*	Is religion an important part of your daily life? Those answering YES (%)**	Estimated 2010 Catholic population**	Estimated 2010 Protestant population**
Austria	8.4	$1,208	$3,608	$296,832	22.4	N/a	6.3 M	430,000
Belgium	10.8	3,003	4,530	357,476	22.7	N/a	6.6 M	150,000
Denmark	5.5	2,871	1,778	178,810	20.7	19	40,000	4.5 M
Finland	5.4	1,333	2,921	168,927	22	N/a	10,000	4.3 M
France	63.0	12,915	22,855	1,923,456	22	30	37.9 M	1.1 M
Greece	11.3	508	243	273,918	23.5	71	80,000	30,000
Iceland	0.3	28.7	N/a	10,424	15.5	N/a	10,000	290,000
Ireland	4.5	895	1,500	161,045	14.2	54	3.95 M	230,000
Italy	60.1	2,996	6,612	1,641,306	26.5	72	50.25 M	800,000
Luxembourg	0.5	402	N/a	34,852	17.6	39	330,000	20,000
Netherlands	16.6	6,357	5,999	614,724	19.4	N/a	4.83 M	3.63 M
Norway	4.9	4,580	9	229,334	19.5	N/a	100,000	4 M
Portugal	10.6	649	–492	230,420	22.5	N/a	98.6 M	170,000
Spain	46.1	5,950	4,391	1,242,462	22	49	34.67 M	460,000

(Continued)

91

TABLE 5.1 COUNTRY DATA (CONTINUED)

Country	Population in millions (2009/2010)*	Official development aid assistance US$ millions 2010	Private development aid assistance US$ millions 2010*	GDP, constant prices, PPPs, reference year 2005, US$ millions*	% of total population age 65 and over 2010*	Is religion an important part of your daily life? Those answering YES (%)**	Estimated 2010 Catholic population**	Estimated 2010 Protestant population**
Sweden	9.4	4,534	372	318,761	23.6	17	110,000	6 M
Switzerland	7.7	2,300	19,254	294,123	22.6	41	3.3 M	2.8 M
Turkey	71.9	967	670	912,795	8.6	82	50,000	80,000
United Kingdom	60.9	13,053	12,246	2,020,830	20.2	27	10 M	33.8 M
United States	309	30,353	161,234	13,017,000	16.9	65	74 M	159.9 M

*OECD

**Pew Research

Source: Factary.

The hidden giant in most definitions of the nonprofit sector in Europe is the Church (or rather, the churches, the synagogues, and the mosques). The Catholic Church, predominant throughout Southern Europe apart from Greece (Orthodox) and Turkey (Muslim) is generally excluded from definitions of nonprofit. And yet it owns land and buildings that far outweigh the assets of even the largest foundations in Europe. Why is it not counted in? There are two principal reasons: the first is that the law in Southern Europe treats Catholic Church foundations differently from their lay equivalents—for example, in Spain, Catholic Church foundations are held in a separate register, the Registro de Entidades Religiosas. These differences exempt Catholic Church foundations from normal reporting requirements—so we simply do not know what their assets or income are, who controls them, or what they control. The second is that the Church is not one entity. It is tens, or possibly hundreds of thousands, of entities loosely but not legally bound together by one set of belief and practice. Impossible to measure.

There is one final, critical caveat in attempting a definition of the sector—the use of the word *foundation*. This word can cover many different types of entity. In France alone a foundation may be:

- A *public utility* foundation
  - Legally created only with a specific authorization, decreed jointly by the Prime Minister and the Minister of the Interior, on the advice of the Council of State. Must have a permanent endowment sufficient to meet their needs.
  - The Board includes a representative of government—since 2003 this may be as an observer only.
- An endowed foundation
  - May be created by an individual or a company, after registration with the Prefect, and with any level of endowment.
  - May earn revenue from services offered, but may not accept public (State) funding.
- A corporate foundation
  - First recognized in 1990, this is a foundation with a flow of funds from the company to which it is linked; its lifespan is linked to the parent company, with a minimum of five years. Created by decree from the regional (*department*) government.
  - A donor-directed fund within an umbrella foundation.

- Created when an individual or company irrevocably donates an asset (normally, money) to a public utility foundation, for the public good.
- Has the legal right to call itself a *foundation*.
- A scientific cooperation foundation
  - May carry out any activity relevant to research or higher education.
  - Created by decree, their structure must include a government representative.
- A partnership foundation
  - May be created by any public body that is scientific, cultural, or professional, and may mix universities with research centers and companies.
- A university foundation
  - A form of donor-directed fund within public universities.

Beyond the borders of France, confusion around what constitutes charity deepens. There are some very strange creatures stalking the foundation landscape of Europe. Austria, for example, has around 1,200 foundations. All but a tiny minority were established to take advantage of legislation that allowed wealthy Austrians to enjoy tax-free assets so long as they invested via a foundation in their own country. The Netherlands has as many as an estimated 220,000 foundations called *stichting* in Dutch. A foundation might be charitable, but equally it might simply be a vehicle for holding, and to some degree hiding, an asset. Thus one of Europe's leading furniture retail concerns (IKEA) is ultimately controlled by an almost unknown Dutch foundation, the Stichting Ingka. In Germany, the Robert Bosch Stiftung (*stiftung* being German for foundation) owns one of Europe's largest car spare parts manufacturers . . . and two large hospitals. And in Britain there are two sets of laws, and two different registration bodies depending on whether you are sitting in Penrith (England) or Pitlochry (Scotland.)

The Charities Aid Foundation *World Giving Index 2011* (CAF, London, 2011) is a report based on Gallup's *WorldView World Poll*[2] research project across 153 countries and surveying a representative sample of 1,000 individuals living in urban areas, using telephone or

---

[2]worldview.gallup.com.

in-person data gathering. Gallup asks respondents whether in the last month they have:

- Donated money to an organization?[3]
- Volunteered time to an organization?
- Helped a stranger, or someone they didn't know who needed help?

Across Western Europe, 49 percent of people give money (versus 65 percent in the United States) and 24 percent give time (versus 43 percent in the United States). The United Kingdom is in the lead with 79 percent of the population giving money.[4] In joint second place are the Netherlands and Ireland, with 75 percent of the population as donors. There are some truly remarkable fundraising programs in the Netherlands that are responsible for this success, such as:

- WWF in the Netherlands, with 960,000 regular donors[5]
- The Dutch Cancer Society with 880,000 regular donors
- Greenpeace International with 495,000 donors
- Doctors Without Borders/Médecins San Frontières (MSF) with 460,317 donors

There are five countries in Western Europe where a percentage of the population over the age of 15 gives equal or greater than the 65 percent who donate in the United States. They are Iceland (67 percent), Ireland (75 percent), Malta (65 percent), the Netherlands (75 percent), and the United Kingdom (79 percent). Two of these countries—the Netherlands and the United Kingdom—are attracting the interest of global fundraising organizations. Some have either opened organizations there or have active visit and fundraising programs in operation.

The number of nonprofit organizations in Europe is unknown. We do know how many foundations—or at least 273,000 organizations that are termed *foundations*—exist in the main EU states (24 states, excluding Lithuania, Malta, and Romania). More than a third of them (around 95,000) are public-benefit foundations.[6]

---

[3]Giving money or time to an organization could include political parties/ organizations as well as registered charities, community organizations, and places of worship.

[4]Charities Aid *World Giving Index 2011*.

[5]CBF Netherlands.

[6]EU Foundations Facts and Figures, EFC, Brussels, 2008.

How Western Europe Is Changing the Rules of Philanthropy

Individual giving has a long tradition in Europe. Foundations, perhaps because of their complex diverse forms, are an overlooked source of funding. Corporate giving is especially popular in some countries like France.

Individuals

Walk through almost any city center in Europe and you can see evidence of Europe's long history of philanthropy. Stop at a cathedral—like Winchester Cathedral—based perhaps on a seventh-century church built from the philanthropy of a local king. Visit an art gallery, perhaps built in the nineteenth century with merchants' donations. Spend the evening at the opera, perhaps built by popular subscription in the nineteenth century and then rebuilt, with a fresh round of subscribers, in the twentieth century. My favorite is Sant Joan de les Abadesses, a ninth-century nunnery in the Pyrenees built by the Catalan ruler Guifré el Pelos (Wilfred the Hairy) and to which he donated a substantial parcel of land.[7]

Philanthropy—in its simplest sense of helping another human being—has been around since we first chipped flint. But large-scale, lasting philanthropy in this region appeared in three stages: linked initially to royalty, then to merchants, and finally to consumers. Alongside this rulers-to-commoners axis there appears to be a second historic axis, from the religiously motivated to a more secular philanthropy.

First there were devout members of the aristocracy who erected houses of prayer and also gave alms for the poor—a tradition dating back, in the United Kingdom, to the thirteenth century and continued on today when the Queen (or King) of England gives a purse of Maundy money to pensioners.

Second came wealthy merchants, patrons of the arts who created some of our great museums. Later, with the Industrial Revolution, a new class of socially conscious factory owners emerged. A few of them—such as Richard Cadbury in nineteenth-century England—became significant

---

[7]J. Jarrett, "Power Over Past and Future: Abbess Emma and the Nunnery of Sant Joan de les Abadesses" in *Early Mediaeval Europe*, 2003, e, 12.

philanthropists, founding schools and early social service programs for their community of workers. My compatriot Andrew Carnegie, one of the wealthiest men of the late nineteenth century, focused on education and public knowledge with his philanthropic program of library building. At around the same time (1854) Florence Nightingale was appealing for a hospital for victims of the Crimean War and Henry Dunant (1863) was founding the Red Cross in Geneva, reversing out the Swiss flag to create one of the world's most recognized brands.

The third stage of development introduced the democratization of philanthropy in the twentieth century, when two World Wars inspired millions to knit blankets for the troops or to cut down the iron railings around their gardens so they could be smelted into munitions (arguably an act of patriotism rather than one of philanthropy).

And then there is a lull. After the end of the World Wars, the Welfare State was constructed across Europe. The state would take care of us, in Beveridge's hackneyed phrase, "from cradle to grave." Through taxes we would rid ourselves of Want, Disease, Ignorance, Squalor, and Idleness. Philanthropy, at least for our hospitals and our poor, was old fashioned, unnecessary, and maybe even patronizing.

A few kept on fundraising. The arts, never fully subsumed into the State, carried on soliciting donations. The human rights and ecology movements of the 1960s and 1970s relied on fundraising. Hence the strength in Europe of Greenpeace (known in Germany, as *The Money Machine* for its fundraising prowess), Friends of the Earth, and Amnesty International. Development cooperation NGOs such as Oxfam were also outside of the welfare net and were dependent on fundraising for their survival.

This explains in part why in Europe it is the NGO sector that has led the way into professional fundraising, not our (state-funded) universities or hospitals. The state-funded bodies—in the United Kingdom at least—were pushed toward fundraising during the premiership of Margaret Thatcher (1979–1990), a period that saw the state dismantled and private initiative encouraged. Universities thus entered the fray relatively recently, with the United Kingdom in the vanguard in the 1980s. This is simply a repeat of what happened before the welfare gap-years—Balliol College, Oxford, for example, ran its first fundraising appeal in 1670.

The current picture of philanthropy in Europe is intimately linked to the current picture of professional fundraising. Of all the factors that appear to influence philanthropy (taxation regimes, religiosity, the existence of wealth, etc.), this appears to be the most significant. When asked, people give.

Professional fundraising is developing across Europe, broadly from West to East. The largest and oldest professional association of fundraisers is in the United Kingdom. The Institute of Fundraising has 5,000 members and was founded in 1983. It encompasses a series of special interest groups including the Black Fundraisers Network, Corporate Fundraisers, Legacy Marketing, Trusts and Statutory, and my own specialty, prospect research. This many professional fundraisers in a market of 62 million people explains, in part, why philanthropy in the United Kingdom is a £11 billion ($17 million) market with between 58 percent, 29.5 million adults, and 79 percent, 40 million adults,[8] giving.

Giving and fundraising in Europe take many forms. In the United Kingdom[9] donating cash is the most frequently used method of giving, with almost half of all donors (47 percent) using this method in 2010 to 2011. Direct debit is the next most common method, used by 32 percent of donors, followed by buying goods (27 percent) and buying raffle tickets (21 percent). Donations through membership fees/ subscriptions and payroll giving were much less popular, used by 5 percent and 3 percent of donors, respectively. In the United Kingdom there is a slow but steady trend away from cash giving and toward direct debit, reflecting in part the efforts of fundraisers to move cash donors to direct debits, and in part the growth of street-based face-to-face fundraising, a technique first created by Greenpeace in Austria and which is now being used in almost every country in Europe.

New Media and Fundraising

New fundraising techniques reflect the inventiveness of the new breed of European professional fundraiser. In continental Europe direct mail is still queen, but myriad forms of direct marketing—DRTV appeals, telephone, email, web, face-to-face, and social media programs—are now in use. In some places these techniques are modified by local

---

[8] Charities Aid *World Giving Index* 2011.
[9] UK Giving 2011, NCVO and CAF, London.

circumstance and tradition—for example, in Italy, where giving usually involves visiting your bank or post office to complete a Giro payment in favor of the charity.

New fundraising techniques are not changing giving behaviors as fast as some expected. In 2010 to 2011 just 7 percent of those who gave to charity in the United Kingdom made at least one online donation.[10] Although this figure almost doubled (from 4 percent to 7 percent) between 2008–2009 and 2009–2010, it is still small compared with the proportion of donors who donate by other means. Three times as many people give by raffle, for example, than give online. People aged 25 to 44 and people in managerial and professional occupations were the most common online donors. The same survey indicated that only 2 percent gave by phone, and a negligible less than 1 percent by SMS messaging. These figures belie the hype that sometimes surrounds these techniques. But as these new media grow, and as fundraisers develop their skills in using them, these numbers will change.

In Spain and in Italy people can also give via their tax. Italians can allocate 0.5 percent of their tax payment (*cinque per mille* in Italian) to a social cause; charities compete to win a share of these funds.

And then there are the trendsetters of Europe. Sometimes these are special people, like Jean-Marie Destrée of Secours Catholique in Paris, a member of the Caritas Internationalis Confederation (see Case Study 5.1). Sometimes these are movements, like the *new* philanthropy. This encompasses a range of innovative approaches to giving embraced by large-scale philanthropists (*major donors* or *strategic donors*) characterized by a high degree of engagement in programs or projects, careful measurement of the social impact of the program, and the use of new or different vehicles for giving.

One facet of the new philanthropy is venture philanthropy. In Europe, as in the United States, it started with venture capitalists applying their investment savvy to philanthropy (the first venture philanthropy fund in Europe, Impetus Trust, was created in the United Kingdom in 2002). It has also been adopted in France (read *La Nouvelle Philanthropie*, Virginie Seghers, ADMICAL, Paris, 2009, or get a friend to translate it), in the Netherlands (visit the website of Noaber Stichting for example,[11] or read

---

[10] Ibid.

[11] www.noaber.com.

Secours Catholique (a member of the Caritas Internationalis Confederation) was for much of its long existence a quiet, conservative organization supporting social need in France. Then along came Jean-Marie Destrée—a Belgian national with a mission. Jean-Marie developed Secours' first major donor program. Then, in 2009 he and colleagues created the Fondation Caritas France, the first fundraising charity offering donor-directed funds in France. Donor-directed funds have a long history in France, led by the Fondation de France and the Academie Française. But no one in a fundraising charity had tried the technique. Destrée and his team have recruited 20 donor directed funds in the short life of the foundation, and in 2010 funded $4.2 million in national and international projects. Five family funds have been created, and the foundation has also attracted a number of associations, as well as three religious congregations, to set up funds.

Part of the attraction of the foundation is that the donor-directed funds are precisely that. This is not a covert fundraising program for Secours Catholique; donor-directed funds are permitted to put their money wherever, within the law and reason, they wish to. Donors are thus fully engaged in their philanthropy.

Die Nieuwe Mecenas by Renée Steenbergen), in Switzerland (see the activities of LGT Venture Philanthropy Foundation, created by the Princely family of Liechtenstein), and in Italy, where one of the country's largest and oldest foundations, Cariplo, sponsored the annual conference of the European Venture Philanthropy Association in 2011. Fundraisers are slowly realizing the potential in this area and innovators such as Scope, the U.K. organization for people with disabilities, have created special vehicles to attract venture and new philanthropy.

Foundations

If you are a fundraiser at, say, the University of New Orleans, Louisiana, then your colleagues probably include one or more foundation fundraisers and a grant-writer or two. At a university in (old) Orléans, France, you might not have such colleagues. Foundation fundraising is not in its infancy in continental Europe. It has yet to be conceived. There are almost no, zero, foundation fundraisers in continental Europe.

Why is this, when we know that the foundation sector in Europe is large and growing fast? I have no clear answer. It simply appears to have been overlooked by the nonprofit sector's enthusiasm for direct marketing. The inevitable corollary is that grant-making by European foundations is limited, many preferring to run their own projects and programs.

There are variations in where foundations put their money, depending on where the foundation is located. In the United Kingdom and France, education is in first place, with immigration in second. In Italy, Spain, and Greece, second place is occupied by culture, reflecting the enormous programs of the large Italian foundations. In Scandinavia, science and technology is the most frequent grant-making or program area, while in Eastern Europe education is popular (84 percent of foundations give grants or have program in this area) and community development comes second.

Measured in euro or dollar terms, these top priority areas barely shift. Education remains the most popular cause overall, with 76 percent of the charitable expenditure of Europe's largest foundations (those with expenditures of $6 million or more) being directed there. Arts and culture is in second place when measured in Euros or dollars with 74 percent of spend—but the bias created by a small number of very large Italian foundations that have traditionally favored this area has to be taken into consideration. Target populations for foundations include children and youth (74 percent of foundations in the survey stated that they were most likely to specify this population group in grant-making or programs), followed by the economically disadvantaged (50 percent of foundations), people with disabilities (48 percent), and the aging or elderly (48 percent). Note this key, and depressing, statistic from this study: "Most of the surveyed foundations devoted less than 10 percent of their expenditures in support of women and girls . . . [and] the median percentage of total grant monies that were allocated in support of women and girls was 4.8 percent."[12]

---

[12]Source for all of these figures: *The Foundation Center, Untapped Potential: European Foundation Funding for Women & Girls*, 2011.

Foundations in Europe are in the midst of a revolution, in part because of a rapid growth in numbers. The European Foundation Centre[13] reported a 15 percent growth in the number of public-benefit foundations in 2001 through 2005. The normally sober EFC describes the growth in some places as *dramatic*[14] with a growth of 6,574 new foundations in Germany 1994 to 2004 and 3,968 in Spain in the same period. Factary, my own company, measures the creation of new grant-making foundations in the United Kingdom, and in 2011 identified 214 new funds—almost exactly the same number as in the previous year (213).

But it is not just growth in numbers. European foundations are evolving in other ways, too. They are, finally, becoming more transparent. Today, it is relatively easy to obtain the financial accounts of most of the leading 236 foundations in membership of the European Foundation Centre. All of the foundations in England and Wales (but not, yet, those in Scotland) have their annual financial reports on the web, thanks to the sterling efforts of the Charity Commission.[15] Foundations in Germany, Italy, and France are becoming more visible—with at least their governance structures and board membership available on websites. There is still a long way to go in this direction—most public-benefit foundations in continental Europe still refuse to publish or make available their accounts—but the trend is set.

Foundations are also becoming more professional—with full-time paid staff managing grant-making and programs. And the distinction between foundation and company, philanthropy and business, is becoming blurred with the emergence of a spectrum of entities including social enterprises (the Big Issue in the United Kingdom, for example) taking up a middle ground between the purely nonprofit and the purely for-profit.

For more information on the European foundation sector, see the resources section at http://globalgiving.wikispaces.com, or visit the European Foundation Centre at www.efc.bel.

---

[13] EU Foundations Facts and Figures 2008.

[14] Ibid.

[15] www.charity-commission.gov.uk.

Corporations

Europe's companies, like companies around the globe, love a bit of CSR. But the big fundraising question is whether this is true love, or a marriage of convenience.

It is certainly popular in France where the national association to promote sponsorship by companies—ADMICAL—provides a detailed analysis. In 2012, 31 percent of companies with more than 20 employees were involved in sponsorship[16] in France, with a total budget of $2.5 billion. ADMICAL encompasses social, sport, and cultural sponsorship and notes that social is the largest with 43 percent of the budget. Culture comes in second place, with 26 percent of the budget—($652 million) and sport in third place with 6 percent of the budget. Eighty-three percent of companies sponsor in their local geographic area.[17] Among the larger firms (more than 200 staff) the average sponsorship per project is $13,200 representing, for three quarters of all large firms, less than 0.1 percent of turnover.[18]

We can see the contrast in styles in CSR when we review ADMICAL's sister organization in Ireland, Business to Arts.[19] Their latest figures (from 2006 to 2007, sadly) show total business sponsorship of the arts as $17 million—less than 3 percent of the 2012 figure from France.[20]

Follow this trail to Belgium and you can see that corporate sponsorship totaled $499 million in 2012.[21] Of this, 40 percent went to sport, 24 percent or $119 million to humanitarian and social projects, 20 percent or $100 million to culture and arts, and 4 percent or $20 million each to education and scientific or medical research.

---

[16] The word in French is *mécénat*, which does not translate perfectly as *sponsorship* in English, where we associate sponsorship with sports. Mécénat includes sports, arts, and social activities.

[17] Le Mécénat d'Entreprise en France, ADMICAL-CSA, Paris, April 2012.

[18] Mieux Comprendre les Flux Financiers du Mécénat d'Entreprise, ADMICAL, Paris, December 2011.

[19] www.businesstoarts.ie.

[20] Private Investment in Arts and Culture Survey Report, Business to Arts and Deloitte, 2008.

[21] Enquête Prométhéa-IPSOS 2012, Prométhéa, Brussels, June 2012.

Fundraising reflects these figures. Corporate fundraising is healthily alive in France—review the lists of large donors to campaigns there and you can see companies (rather than individuals or foundations) featured most prominently.

Government

Researching the state contribution to European nonprofits is like taking a cold reality shower. According to a Johns Hopkins University Comparative Philanthropy study, 53.7 cents in every dollar raised in Europe comes from government, and a further 40.2 cents comes from fees—largely paid by local, regional, and national governments. In other words, 93.9 percent of funding for nonprofit sector comes from the state. Fundraising from companies, foundations, and the rest of the private sector, brings just 6 cents on the dollar.

Governments—at the three typical levels of nation, region, and city/town/village—are deeply engaged in nonprofit funding. They directly fund "private" trust hospitals, museums owned by foundations, and charities' social service provision for people with disabilities. They fund community centers run by nonprofit associations, employment projects, and medical research foundations. They also fund intermediaries—Germany's GIZ,[22] for example—the nation's development aid organization that in turn funds nonprofits. And they fund the tax breaks that some public utility nonprofits enjoy in some European countries.

Above the state apparatus there is also a raft of pan-governmental institutions. The most important of these is the European Union (EU), a constant target for fundraising. There are also the UN organizations, many headquartered in Geneva, Switzerland, which channel some funding to nonprofits. And even NATO, the North Atlantic Treaty Organization, provides some funding for academics and universities.

WHERE WE ARE AND WHERE WE ARE GOING

We promised at the start of this chapter to avoid predictions, but we can draw together a summary of what is happening, starting with the key fundraising techniques.

---

[22] www.giz.de.

Fundraising Techniques

Fundraisers in Europe are using the same, wide array of fundraising tools to encourage donors to participate.

Direct Marketing

Fundraising by direct marketing remains the leading technique employed by nonprofits across Europe. In some markets this has become a highly sophisticated mix of social media, telephone, and direct mail. In others it remains an old standby, providing a reliable stream of steady funding. Although direct debit payment systems have become the norm (and the focus of much fundraising effort) in other European countries, Italy remains stubbornly stuck to its paper Giro slips.

Social Media

Social media is a subject of fundraising interest in Europe, as it is else-where. NSPCC, the U.K. charity was one of the first to use social media, setting up a Facebook application in 2007. Some organizations, such as the Dutch Cancer Foundation have built social networks around sporting events—in their case the Alpe d'Huez contest.

Face-to-Face

Face-to-face fundraising was invented in Europe—in Vienna, Austria, where Greenpeace wanted to find a way of attracting and securing younger donors while conveying a campaigning message. It has spread rapidly across Europe, thanks to private agencies offering face-to-face fundraising services to nonprofits. Some organizations chose to run their own face-to-face teams—España con ACNUR, for example, Spain's committee for UNHCR. They run a highly successful face-to-face program from its offices in Madrid.

Middle Donor Programs

"Middle donor" programs—for donors in the range of $500 to $10,000 (what constitutes a middle donor varies from organization to organization)—are growing in popularity in Europe and a number of organizations—UNICEF and Greenpeace, for example, have success-fully developed them.

Legacies

There is still some resistance to the development of legacies programs in Europe. Sensitivity about discussing death with donors, and the belief that supporters would not appreciate a legacies approach, have held them up. My company Factary was part of a group of nonprofits and consultancies that carried out the first study of legacy-giving potential in Spain in 2006. We found that older donors did not, in general, object to being approached about legacies but they did not know about the opportunities available and were leery of the legalities involved in leaving gifts of estate. In part this confusion arises from the complexities of the legal system in much of continental Europe; in Spain two-thirds of an individual's estate by law belongs to one's spouse and immediate family. A charity legacy can only receive, under normal circumstances, the other third.

Lottery

Fundraising by lottery has a long history in Europe. These are often long established and, to one degree or another, state regulated or state inspired. The painful 1936 to 1939 Civil War left many Spaniards blind, so the government permitted a charitable foundation, the Spanish National Organization for the Blind or ONCE, to run a national lottery. Lottery ticket sellers are themselves people with a disability. This brings in $2.5 billion[23] per annum to the charity. Other large European lotteries such as the Big Lottery Fund established by the British Government in 2004, and the Dutch National Postcode Lottery are substantial contributors to charitable and community activity. The Dutch National Postcode Lottery distributed $356 million in 2010 to good causes.

Challenges and Innovation

American fundraisers are sometimes surprised by the degree of control that state and nonstate bodies impose on the nonprofit sector. Regulation comes from three main sources—the European Union (EU), national governments, and charity control bodies in individual countries. Personal data is a particular focus of EU regulation, with a Europe-wide Data Protection Directive providing the framework for a set of national regulations that are tighter in some countries (France) and

---

[23] ONCE annual report 2010.

looser in others (the United Kingdom, for example). Fundraisers, and their boards of management, are very conscious of the limitations on handling personal information, and this can hinder developments in data analysis that are possible in markets with lighter regulation.

Charity control bodies may be statutory—such as the Charity Commission for England and Wales—or voluntary, such as the Centraal Bureau Fondsenwerving (CBF, in the Netherlands) or the Deutsches Zentralinstitut fuer soziale Fragen (DZI) in Germany. These voluntary bodies typically issue a seal of approval for organizations that match their criteria, a seal that is displayed on the mailings, websites, and publicity of the approved organizations. DZI currently certifies 262 organizations, raising $1.5 billion annually. There is some discontent in the fundraising community about some aspects of this process—particularly the fact that by strictly controlling expenditure on fundraising to a set percentage, the voluntary regulators stifle investment in innovation and risk.

Another challenge to the development of fundraising in continental Europe is the lack of skilled fundraisers. Recruitment of people with experience in France, the Netherlands, Italy, and Spain is difficult, with many organizations recruiting and training people who are new to the profession. This situation will ease with time, and initiatives such as Germany's Fundraising Academy[24] will help. But start-up and new market entrants are still reporting difficulties in this area.

In spite of these all of these challenges, Europeans are finding creative ways to cope with the challenges. Some fundraisers—like the Greenpeace team that created face-to-face fundraising (they called it *Direct Dialogue*) in Austria—invent whole new ways of working. Others take a successful project from A and adapt it to B. The creativity is in the adaptation.

In Summary

Western Europe is, finally, on the fast track in fundraising. It is humming with new ideas and new people at a time when governments are realizing that they must rely yet more on the nonprofit sector to provide social and other services. Despite the difficult economic conditions, now is a good time to be a fundraiser in Europe.

---

[24] www.fundraising-akademie.de.

North America

PENELOPE CAGNEY AND ANDREA MACMANUS,
WITH A CASE STUDY BY R. F. SHANGRAW JR.

Occupying the same continent as much of Latin America, North America is distinguished less by geography from its neighbors to the south than by language, culture, customs, and history. The United States and Canada have the English language in common, although many Canadians speak French as their first language. These are relatively new nations sharing a colonial history and democratic governments.

There are important differences in the nonprofit sectors. In Canada, the nonprofit sector is a mix of the "welfare partnership model" of civil society development (found in the Netherlands, Belgium, France, Germany, and Ireland), with an "Anglo-Saxon model" (found in Australia, the United States, and the United Kingdom) having a higher level of private philanthropic support. Although there are distinct differences in philanthropy and fundraising, there are also similarities between Canada and the United States.

THE UNITED STATES OF AMERICA

Long considered a leader in philanthropy, the United States of America is rethinking its role here, as it is elsewhere on the world stage. Although some countries have benefited from its international aid, it is also true that the United States has sometimes exported democracy and free market capitalism under the guise of philanthropy, a sort of unofficial policy, as was the case with Eastern Europe after the Berlin Wall came down.

The United States has learned that its intervention in the affairs of other nations through the nonprofit sector is not always welcome. In 2012 Egypt denied U.S. nonprofits and some local civil society organizations with ties to the United States, the right to operate on the basis that they would interfere in Egypt's internal affairs.[1] That same year Russian clampdowns on "foreign agents" included the nonprofit organization Golos, which has been monitoring Russian elections for 11 years and is financed by two U.S. agencies, the National Endowment for Democracy and the United States Agency for International Development[2] (and for more on this subject, see the chapter on Eastern Europe).

The U.S. economy is the world's largest, although China's economy seems destined to overtake it by 2025 and some other national economies follow fast on its heels. With wealth spread more widely and with a larger, increasingly sophisticated NGO sector around the globe, other nations are also emerging as powerful and creative philanthropic forces.

The United States' strong philanthropic tradition dates back to its beginnings. Early visitors to its shores remarked on the tendency of U.S. citizens to band together to address concerns rather than leaving it to the government to resolve them. Alexis de Tocqueville, a French political thinker and historian, observed about eighteenth-century America: "In the United States, as soon as several inhabitants have taken an opinion or an idea they wish to promote in society, they seek each other out and unite together once they have made contact. From that moment, they are no longer isolated but have become a power seen from afar whose activities serve as an example and whose words are heeded."[3]

Four factors have contributed to the strength of philanthropy in the United States:

1. **The Constitution**. Philanthropy is actually grounded in the Constitution:[4] The First Amendment makes freedom of assembly

---

[1] www.nytimes.com/2011/12/30/world/middleeast/egypts-forces-raid -offices-of-us-and-other-civil-groups.html?pagewanted=all.

[2] www.nytimes.com/2012/07/03/world/europe/russia-introduces-law -limiting-aid-for-nonprofits.html?emc=eta1.

[3] Tocqueville 1840, *Democracy in America*, 599.

[4] http://paytonpapers.org.

a fundamental right and the Tenth Amendment states that everything that is not explicitly reserved to the federal government is
left to the States and "to the people."

2. **Capitalism**. Although charity is innate in every society, modern philanthropy is the necessary companion to capitalism,
providing the social infrastructure that is the responsibility of
the government in other societies. Philanthropy is needed as
a counterweight to less attractive features of U.S. culture—
individualism, materialism, and commercialism.

3. **Immigration**. Generations of immigrants, beginning with the
British and other European settlers, brought with them charitable traditions from home, periodically infusing U.S. philanthropy
with new perspectives and methodologies. For example, in 1907
fundraiser Emily Bissell started a new fundraising scheme in the
U.S. based on one that had worked in her native Demark, and
thus the American Lung Association's Christmas Seals were born.

4. **Sector size**. The strength of U.S. philanthropy lies in the
very size and scope of the sector itself and its infrastructure. Its
diversity provides a fertile ground for innovation. The United
States' nonprofit sector grew tremendously especially in the last
few decades, with the Internal Revenue Service (IRS) reporting 1,494,882 registered nonprofit organizations in the United
States in 2011.[5]

The juggernaut of the sector may, however, be slowing. The number of nonprofits, which had grown dramatically (25 percent from
2001 to 2011 and contributing 5.4 percent of the GDP in 2010), has
declined. The number of applications for tax-exempt status declined
by about 7 percent in 2011 compared to 2010. This is due in part to
the Great Recession, which pushed some organizations under, forced
others to merge, and discouraged the formation of new ones; due in
part to a funder focus on collaboration and avoidance of duplication
of effort; and due to the fact that in 2011 the IRS eliminated many
smaller nonactive nonprofits—18 percent of the 1,821,824 charities
that were registered in 2010.

---

[5] *IRS Data Book for 2011*, Department of the Treasury Internal Revenue
Service, March 2012.

Historical, Geographical, and Economic Isolation of the United States

The size and diversity of the U.S. economy has historically enabled it to be independent of from other countries. Bordered only by Canada and Mexico, in the past outside influences have been limited. In comparison, for instance, the close geographic proximity of members of the European Union have for many years encouraged them to work together, share a common currency, and to learn one another's languages and cultures.

Technology has brought everyone closer together. The ability to work collaboratively—across borders and across sectors—is crucial to non-profit success as technological advancements, multinational companies, an increasingly global economy, and large-scale problems like global warming, famine, and disease, have changed the nature of philanthropy.

And global affairs are getting more attention. According to *Giving USA 2012*,[6] in 2011 giving to international affairs gained 7.6 percent in donations to total more than $22 billion. In the past decade it has been the fastest growing in the 11 categories covered in the annual report.

The U.S. Population Is More Diverse and Older

There are more minority births today in the United States and the predominantly Caucasian (63.3 percent) population of 308.7 million is a "minority majority." The two other largest race/ethnicities are Hispanic/Latino (16.7 percent) and Black/African American (12.3 percent). The Asian population, however, grew faster than any other major race group between 2000 and 2010 (5.8 percent).[7]

In the prior decade, 2000 to 2010, more than half of the growth in the total population of the United States was due to the increase in the Hispanic population. The trend has reversed for a number of reasons including the economic downturn in the United States, increased deportation and border enforcement by U.S. authorities, and increased economic opportunities and declining birthrates in Mexico.[8] Ethnicity is not the only demographic factor that is

---

[6]http://store.givingusareports.org/2012-Full-Report-P44.aspx.

[7]www.pewsocialtrends.org/2012/06/19/the-rise-of-asian-americans/.

[8]Ibid.

changing. This United States is graying (13 percent of the population).[9] More people were 65 years and over in 2010 than in any previous census (taken every 10 years).

This influences both what will be supported and the types of fundraising that is effective. U.S. fundraisers seek to incorporate the different philanthropic traditions of new donors into their strategies. Also they increasingly turn to planned giving as a strategy as the population ages.

The U.S.'s International Nonprofits

Washington, DC, is home to most U.S.-based INGOs—only London, England, has more. Some INGOs like UNICEF and CARE International got their start with relief programs in World War II, but their relationship with the government changed during the 1984 Ethiopian famine. The charities disagreed with U.S. aid policies. The government would only give food relief to intermediaries that distinguished between relief and development. INGOs, however, saw their responsibility not only to give short-term aid, but also to support long-term economic and social gains, *regardless of the political ideologies* of the countries needing aid.

Foundations emerging after the end of the Cold War emphasized cross-border, global programs.[10] George Soros, an immigrant, came to play a role in Eastern European development. The Bill and Melinda Gates Foundation arrived in 1994. In 1997 media mogul Ted Turner gave $1 billion to the United Nations.

Fundraising in the United States

Two important trends in U.S. fundraising today are an increasing degree of professionalism in a more complex environment and a reevaluation of the costs of fundraising.

---

[9]U.S. Census 2010 at http://2010.census.gov/2010census/.

[10]Peterson, Anne C. and Gail D. Mclure, "Trends in Global Philanthropy Among US Foundations: A Brief Review of Data and Issues." Johnson Center for Philanthropy at Grand Valley State University. *Foundation Review* 2, no. 4 (2011): 88–100(13).

CASE STUDY 6.1	WORLD VISION PARTNERSHIP: AN ICONIC INGO

Although World Vision got its start in the United States, its international success makes it difficult to claim it solely as a U.S. case study today. In fact, its name often crops up in other chapters of this book, including being the subject of another case study in Chapter 16 "The Charity Giants." It is considered one of great success stories in the INGO world because of its longevity, adaptability, and commitment to mission.

World Vision is a Christian humanitarian organization with a broad programmatic mandate, which includes programming for water, sanitation, and hygiene, hunger, education, basic health, economic development, and child protection. Its approach is community-based, with a focus on the children in its program communities.

Funding—in the form of cash and product donations—for World Vision's work comes largely (almost 80 percent) from private sources, including individuals, corporations, and foundations.

Joan Mussa, senior vice president of mobilization at World Vision's U.S. office, attributes their success to prayer and to the organization's unwavering dedication to working with children, families, and communities to overcome poverty and injustice. Joan also points to the trust of donors that World Vision has earned through consistent delivery on commitments; to knowing their donors well; and to a self-critical culture and openness to better ways of doing things.

THE WORLD VISION PARTNERSHIP

World Vision got its start in the 1950s with a child sponsorship program designed to meet the needs of orphans at the end of the Korean War. Over time World Vision reorganized itself to more effectively fulfill its global mission. Originally headquartered in Monrovia, California, World Vision's international executive office moved to the United Kingdom in 2010, after it became apparent that this would be a better location for a global organization. As noted earlier, London is home to more INGOs than any other city.

World Vision is organized as a federation. It consists of numerous national entities around the world, grouped in what is informally referred to as the World Vision "partnership." World Vision International (WVI), established as the international coordinating body in 1977, provides global coordination for the partnership, and ensures

(Continued)

that global standards and policies are pursued. Offices in London, Geneva, Bangkok, Singapore, Johannesburg, Nairobi, Dakar, Cyprus, New York, Los Angeles, and San José, Costa Rica coordinate the strategic operations of the organization and represent World Vision in international forums. Its board of directors (the International Board) oversees the partnership, and its body of members (the Council) is the highest governing authority for certain fundamental decisions. Nearly two-thirds of World Vision's offices (56 of 90 offices at the time of writing) have their own governing boards or advisory councils. World Vision's international president has a seat on every board and council, and has the power to intervene in local affairs if necessary.

World Vision's staff also reflects its global nature—more than 90 percent work in their country of origin. This contributes to the well-being of staff and also ensures that workers thoroughly know the culture, language, and other aspects of the environment.

FUNDRAISING

Joan Mussa leads World Vision's U.S.-based fundraising operation, overseeing some 500 staff. They meet with the marketing staff at World Vision offices around the globe once a year to share best practices. The largest six offices meet once or twice a year, and in between, Skype and other means are used to maintain communication. "We don't have a lot of turnover within the U.S. office," says Joan, "so we don't have to cover the same ground repeatedly with new employees."

Each support office has fundraising staff and some of their field offices do as well. Several offices in Asia and Latin America, notably, India and Colombia, do substantial fundraising within their general populations as well as community development programming. Becoming a support office doesn't change an office's status in any legal or procedural way, but when an office begins raising enough money on its own not only to fund its own programs, but also to send funds to other field countries, it does attain this status. Several offices serve as both field and support—raising funds as well as administering programs. World Vision draws no hard line between national and support offices. In fact, although the U.S. office is considered a support office and raises about 40 percent of the Partnership's funding (60 percent of the $2.61 billion that World Vision raised in 2010 came from outside of the United States), it is also a

(Continued)

field office in the sense that it oversees U.S.-based programming in inner-city communities as well as rural communities in Appalachia.

In considering World Vision's fundraising successes, Joan particularly noted child sponsorship. "Sponsorship has been the primary way we've raised funding for 60 years," she said. "Very few products have that kind of longevity." She credited the relational nature of sponsorship and its ability to connect donors to children benefiting from World Vision's work—even as it raised funding for program efforts.

Other successes include World Vision's gift catalog, which more than tripled its revenue over five years. According to Joan, the gift catalog provides donors with a snapshot of World Vision's work and allows them to connect to often complex development programming in simple and easy-to-understand ways.

The organization is also seeing success with relatively new initiatives including:

- Team World Vision, which allows donors to raise funds through participation in athletic events like marathons and long-distance cycling events.
- World Vision ACTs, which coordinates, equips, and empowers young people who engage in advocacy efforts to address poverty-related issues.

World Vision magazine has a readership of 600,000; their Facebook page boasts more than 900,000 fans; and the organization enjoys regular favorable news coverage by top media outlets and various Christian media outlets.

As a partnership, World Vision has clearly succeeded in garnering support outside of the United States. Some of the newer donors come from Asia, where not only economies are flourishing, but where, in Korea, World Vision first got its start.

World Vision is relentless in its quest for improvement. "Innovation is in our DNA. We don't claim to be Apple or Google, but we do embrace the new. We tend to be incremental innovators," she says. At the time of this writing she was in the process of hiring a director of innovation for revenue generation to help the organization improve its "game-changing" innovation. "We've just concluded a season of becoming more efficient and effective and have the foundation set for meaningful change."

(Continued)

At the same time, what's old sometimes becomes new again at World Vision. The fundraising team tries fresh approaches with traditional fundraising methods. Many will remember the hour-long World Vision television shows in the 1970s through the 1990s. They ended television promotion because of the cost, but they are taking another look at it as part of a mix with other fundraising channels. "It may be the right vehicle for some products, like World Vision Micro, our microfinance product," says Joan.

World Vision's donors give more online than most donors do. "Our Facebook page is the most 'liked' among nonprofits after PBS. But then who can compete with Big Bird?" Joan gently jokes. Still, they have also found that newer technological methodologies have limitations as well as promise. For instance, text-to-give via mobile phone, doesn't identify much about the giver and so the opportunity to build a relationship is lost.

One of the new products Joan is excited about is World Vision Micro. This nonprofit microfinance instrument was first introduced in the United States. "One of the most interesting things about World Vision Micro is that 44 percent of the contributors to this were new to us, younger, and gave more initially than is the norm for new donors."

In fact, reaching out to youth and young adults is a particular passion of Joan's. She's speaks enthusiastically about the generational differences she sees. She observes, "Donors under 30 have more of a global mind-set. They travel more than their parents did and have seen poverty firsthand. Many of them are connected to the people they've met around the world through Facebook and other social networking sites. These relationships make every issue, from drought to political unrest, very personal for them." This generational interest in international issues has helped World Vision and many of its peer organizations get the word out about many of the issues facing its development program communities.

"My generation didn't have a sense about the need for clean water," she says. "Not the way that today's twentysomethings do. More than just acknowledging that people are poor, they have a greater understanding about specific poverty issues like clean water and human trafficking." As a result, Joan sees this greater awareness trickling down to affecting organizational name awareness. "When we first tested for awareness about international child-focused poverty organizations in 1996, more than 60 percent could not name a

(Continued)

single organization. In 2005, however, that had been reduced to just 19 percent. More people know about us and our peer organizations across the country."

With a generation that increasingly longs to engage personally in relief and development work, Joan acknowledges a challenge to balance the desire for engagement with what's best for the communities where World Vision works. "Facilitating deep relationships between our donors and the communities we serve has always been a critical part of our work," she says. "But development work is incredibly complex. It should be done by professionals—experts in their field—and it's best when those experts are from the communities where they serve."

At the same time, she says, the organization will continue to seek ways to make those global connections in ways that respect everyone involved. "We are honored to help in molding the worldview of this new generation," she says. "We love their passion for others and we want to help them fully understand how best to empower their friends around the world."

Growing Professionalism

The need for ethical and professional fundraisers became apparent in the last century and gave rise to AFP, founded in 1960. AFP was the first association of its kind, although today there are many similar such associations in other parts of the world. (Please see the Global Fundraisng wiki for the listing at http://globalfundraising.wikispaces.com.) There are also other associations for fundraisers like CASE (the Council for the Advancement and Support of Education) and AHP (Association for Healthcare Philanthropy). Today there are also 142 certificate, 317 master's, and 44 doctorate programs in nonprofit management administration and fundraising[11] that contribute to an increasing level of professionalism.

In addition to association and formal education, fundraisers also strive to improve themselves and demonstrate their commitment through certification. CFRE (Certified Fundraising Executive International) was begun by AFP and AHP in 1981 and in 2001 became an

---

[11] www.gradschools.com/search-programs/non-profit-administration.

independent entity. In recent years this certification has become available outside of North America—in Australia, Great Britain, and New Zealand. The ACFRE (Advanced Certified Fundraising Executive) certification is conferred by AFP.

Fundraising Costs

The cost of nonprofit operations in general has been much discussed in recent years, and not just in the United States. (See the forthcoming chapter on Australia and New Zealand.) Some argue that cost as a primary measurement of organizational value is inadequate. What is most important about nonprofits—their impact—is often difficult to measure while costs are relatively easier to track.

Opinion about nonprofit administrative expenses as a key measure of organizational success, however, is beginning to change. After all, if a food bank spends more than another but obtains greater value, that is, more nutritious food, more qualified staff, more clients served, the expenditure is justified. Some industry leaders have come to modify their nonprofit rating systems as a result.

Most Americans believe that spending 23 cents out of every dollar raised on fundraising and administrative costs is reasonable, but also believe that charities actually spend 37 cents, according to a 2012 research report by Grey Matter Research.[12] A 23 percent cost is close to what nonprofits actually do spend, which is 20 to 28 percent.[13] Interestingly, according to the study, 18 percent of donors think that 9 percent is too much to spend on fundraising and administration, and another 18 percent think 40 percent is acceptable. What is alarming is that more than a third believe that nonprofits spend more than half of their donations on fundraising and administrative costs and 62 percent believe that what charities spend on fundraising and administrative costs is unreasonable.

As an alternative to using costs to evaluate fundraising success, the AFP Fundraising Effectiveness Project (FEP) was begun in 2007 to provide nonprofits with tools for tracking and evaluating their annual *growth in giving*. Growth in giving is the *net* of *gains* in giving minus

---

[12] www.greymatterresearch.com/index_files/Nonprofit_Overhead.htm.

[13] http://nccsdataweb.urban.org/knowledgebase/index.php?category=40.

losses in giving. The FEP is focused on "effectiveness" (maximizing growth in giving) rather than "efficiency" (minimizing costs). FEP conducts an annual survey and publishes gain (loss) statistics in a yearly report through a partnership between AFP, the Urban Institute, and AFP's Donor Software Workgroup.

Philanthropy in the United States

Individual giving dominates the giving landscape in the U.S. A growing divide between the wealthy and the rest of the population has implications for philanthropy.

Individuals

In 2011 total giving to charitable causes was $298.4 billion (*Giving USA 2012*). Most of it came from individuals. The living gave $217.8 billion or 73 percent and $24.4 billion came by bequest, a total percentage of 82 percent of all contributions. Corporations gave $14.6 billion (5 percent) and foundations gave $41.7 billion (14 percent). Really, if you add individual giving, bequests, and family foundation giving, the percentage coming from individuals is 88 percent and this is the focus of the following paragraphs.

Individual donors in the United States can loosely be grouped into two important groups. At one end of the spectrum are the mega- (major donor) philanthropists, like Bill Gates, and at the other end are the micro- (mass) philanthropists, whose collective impact through many small gifts is growing.

Occupy Wall Street and Inequity

A widening gap between the rich and the poor has caused tension in U.S. society in recent years and inevitably this becomes part of the context of philanthropy. U.S. citizens have long cherished the notion of themselves as a classless society, a meritocracy. Today they are no longer certain that opportunities like good education are truly available to all and that it is possible to advance one's status in life solely through one's own efforts. They no longer believe, as their parents did, that each successive generation will enjoy greater prosperity than the last.

Wealth has become concentrated at the top of the income scale. The media describes the majority of U.S. wage earners as the *99 Percent* and the fortunate few atop the economic pyramid as the *One Percent*. To illustrate the disparity: In 2010 additional income created an average single year pay increase of:

- 32.5 percent for the .01 percent (15,000 households with average incomes of $23.8 million).
- 11.6 percent for the 1 percent (average income is $1,019,089).
- $80 increase per person after adjusting for inflation for the 99 percent.[14]

This disparity has been fueled by the exponential growth of CEO salaries and bonuses untied to company performance. And not just for CEOs. Even the lower average bonus of $121,000 for Wall Street workers is larger than the annual salaries of the vast majority of non-profit executive directors.[15] The public is angered that Wall Street bankers and investment firms were bailed out after the financial debacle of 2008, while individuals were left to struggle along on their own. This tension culminated in the backlash movement Occupy Wall Street.[16]

This problem is not likely to be resolved any time soon. This matters to fundraising because it colors the way that the rich and philanthropists are perceived. But this is not the first time hugely successful U.S. tycoons have had to battle a negative public perception.

Mega-Philanthropists

Technology and the stock market have created vast new fortunes, leading to what some have called a second *Gilded Age*.[17] The newly rich are comparable to the *robber barons*—entrepreneurs who built their wealth on industries like steel and railroad in the late 1900s. Like today's *One Percent*, the robber barons were unpopular with the public.

---

[14] Steven Ratner, "The Rich Get Even Richer," *New York Times*, March 25, 2012. www.nytimes.com/2012/03/26/opinion/the-rich-get-even-richer.html.

[15] Rick Cohen, "Wall Street Bonuses Larger Than Most Nonprofit Executive Director Salaries," *Nonprofit Quarterly*, March 1, 2012.

[16] http://occupywallst.org/.

[17] http://en.wikipedia.org/wiki/Gilded_Age.

Some of them, responding to criticism such as John D. Rockefeller and Andrew Carnegie did, became exemplary philanthropists, creating foundations that would propel some of the great social developments of the past century. The mega-philanthropists of this new millennium could be as influential as those of the past.

The new mega-philanthropists, however, differ in some respects from their predecessors. Some donors today want to give their wealth during their lifetime rather than leaving it to their heirs to give away. Idaho businessman T. Denny Sandford, honored as AFP's 2012 Philanthropist of the Year, for example, intends to give away his $400 million fortune before he dies.

Other trends: Today's mega-philanthropists are more proactive and better informed; they seek to shape the work of nonprofits; they have a tendency to give to causes rather than to organizations; they demand evidence of impact to justify their philanthropic investments; and they seek to leverage their resources.

Bill Gates is first among today's U.S. philanthropists not only because his is the largest foundation in the world, or because of the global ambitiousness of his programs, but because of his efforts to influence others with affluence to devote half of their wealth to charity. Bill and Melinda Gates and Warren Buffet started the Giving Pledge in 2010. At the time of this writing 81 individuals had joined them in pledging more than half of their fortunes to charity. They have a combined net worth of roughly $400 billion and the commitments made by the current 92 participants could bring an estimated $200 billion or more to charity over time.[18]

They're not just giving their money to charity. Many like Bill Gates intend to apply the knowledge and skills acquired in business to solve complex global problems. They are the philanthrocapitalists.

Philanthrocapitalism

Philanthrocapitalism,[19] a term coined by Matthew Bishop and Michael Green, is just one label applied to these kinds of donors. Some operate

---

[18] www.probonoaustralia.com.au/news/2012/08/website-keeps-eye-us -giving-pledge#.

[19] www.philanthrocapitalism.net/about/about-the-authors/matthew-bishop/.

as relatively hands-off, diversified social investors, and others as more proactive venture philanthropists, the nonprofit equivalents of mainstream venture capitalists.

It's good to remember that this kind of business-like purposefulness is not really new. The Carnegie and Rockefeller foundations not only made grants, but also ran programs. The Rockefeller Foundation, for example, found a cure for yellow fever. Carnegie built thousands of public libraries. (For more on mega-philanthropists, see the section on major donors in Chapter 13.)

Micro-Philanthropists

On the other end of the donor spectrum are the micro-philanthropists who have recently been empowered in their giving by technology. There has been an explosion of websites—not dedicated to a particular charity or cause—but designed to enable individual givers, no matter the size of the gift, to make a difference. Some sites are targeted to local giving and others are global in scope. There are 138 in the United States at the time of this writing.[20]

Micro-patronage has a lot of potential. New York–based Kickstarter, begun in 2009, announced in February 2012 that it would distribute more than $150 million to the arts that year—more than the entire National Endowment for the Arts' fiscal year 2012 budget![21] Kickstarter, like some of the other sites, is not a charity itself, and donations are not tax deductible. Promoting itself as "a new form of commerce and patronage," this company charges a 5 percent fee to anyone who lists with it.

There are other for-profit ventures, like Crowdrise, which was launched by actor Edward Norton. He came up with the idea after taking part in New York City's marathon to raise money for the Maasai Wilderness Conservation Trust.

Nonprofit sites focus on different causes (Donorchoose for classroom needs), or different populations (Modest Needs for the low-income but

---

[20]Katie Morell, "How Crowdfunding Is Reshaping Philanthropy," *Crains Chicago Business*, March 19, 2012.

[21]Patricia Cohen, "Artists Find Benefactors in Web Crowd," *New York Times*, March 16, 2012.

generally self-sufficient), or on different opportunities—micro-lending (Kiva.org), involving one's social network (Citizen Effect)—or even to give directly to individuals (USA Projects and Benevolent.net). EveryoneGives is not an organization, but a two-week giving event.

Giving Circles

Although micro-patronage has benefited from the possibilities of the Internet, it need not necessarily depend on it. A giving circle is a group of individuals who pool their resources (money and/or talent) and donate to a common charitable cause. Donors usually contribute financial resources, but some donate their skills as well. The size, structure, and charitable focus of a circle can vary—from friends meeting over coffee and choosing a local nonprofit to support—to hundreds of individuals governed by a board. Members may donate anywhere from $100 to $1,000 and more per year.

Giving circle donors educate each other about a specific nonprofit, the philanthropy sector, the needs of their community, or the cause they wish to support. Giving circles tend to appeal to those who wish to meet with others with similar interests and beliefs.

In 2009 there were more than 600 giving circles in the United States made up of more than 12,000 people. They gave $100 million to various causes. (There isn't yet comprehensive data on giving circles throughout the world, although this trend is gaining momentum outside of the United States.)[22]

Cash Mobs

Like "flash mobs," convening strangers via social media to converge in some public action like a choreographed dance, "cash mobs"[23] bring people together in a concentrated shopping effort. First organized to help financially strapped small businesses, they are now also helping nonprofits. Some cash mobs assist both business and charities in a community. Nonprofits such as a Habitat for Humanity's resale shop and even a food drive are benefitting from this novel approach. While

---

[22] www.currencyofgiving.com/post/giving-circles-what-they-are-and-why -they-matter/.

[23] http://philanthropy.com/article/Cash-Mobs-Give-Charities-a/135356/.

the amounts of money these impromptu events raise vary, there are additional benefits like increased virtual visibility and sometimes bringing people on site where they can learn more about the mission.

Challenges and Innovation in the United States

One of the more dramatic new developments in the United States are hybrid alternatives to the traditional nonprofit model, such as Benefit Corporations and Certified B Corporations, which share much in common and have a few important differences. Certified B Corporation is a certification conferred by the nonprofit B Lab. Benefit Corporation is a legal status administered by the individual state. Benefit Corporations do *not* need to be certified. They are a new type of corporation that use the power of business to solve social and environmental problems.

An L3C (Low-Profit Limited Liability Company) is a new kind of organization that combines low profits with a social mission. Many questions surround these new organizations including how to frame the case for support, what constitutes proper composition of boards of directors, and the role of professional fundraisers in these new models.

Universities have been engaged in international fundraising for some time because of the global nature of much of higher education. In Case Study 6.2, the head of fundraising for the largest one, Arizona State, offers advice for those who wish to expand their fundraising efforts outside of their own country. For more on university fundraising, see the case study "Oxford Thinking" in Chapter 13.

CASE STUDY 6.2	GLOBAL GIVING TO UNIVERSITIES— THE NEXT FRONTIER

Most large universities are reaching out to alumni and parents living across the globe to expand their development efforts. But global giving is much more than individual philanthropy. Universities are engaging with international foundations, international corporations headquartered in other countries, and even unaffiliated individual donors. In 2009, for example, more than $200 million in monetary gifts were raised from international sources by U.S. universities (U.S. Department of Education, 2011). Table 6.1 shows the distribution of all monetary gifts from international sources to U.S. universities in 2009.

(Continued)

TABLE 6.1	DISTRIBUTION OF MONETARY GIFTS FROM INTERNATIONAL SOURCES TO U.S. UNIVERSITIES IN 2009
Europe	48%
Middle East	18%
Asia	19%
North America	11%
South America	1%
United Nations	1%
Australia	1%
Africa	1%

Source: U.S. Department of Education, *Records on Foreign Gifts to American Institutions of Higher Education,* 2011.

A number of universities, and not just those in the United States, have built a strong reputation around raising funds outside of their national boundaries. For example, Oxford University raised over half of their gifts in their last campaign from international sources. A number of U.S. universities have established campuses and offices in foreign countries to extend their global education and research activities but also to serve as a foreign base for philanthropic engagement.

Universities are encountering some interesting findings as they pursue international prospects. First, international students with the means to attend a university are often supported by parents with significant giving capacity. Second, international students who graduated from universities more than 20 years ago often hold senior government or corporate positions if they return to their home country. And, to the surprise of many development officers and even some university administrators, most large universities have a diverse and rich set of experiences across the globe through individual faculty relationships.

However, fundraising outside of your home country has some special challenges. There is a high degree of variability across the globe in terms of giving behavior. The *CAF World Giving Index 2011* highlights the wide range of giving behavior across the globe. Some countries do not have a culture of or place a high value on giving regardless of affluence. This perspective extends to foreign companies. Equally important, many donors are interested in funding programs that benefit both their home country as well as their beloved alma mater. Collaborative programs, although difficult to execute, are more appealing to many international investors. For foreign corporations

(Continued)

and foundations, collaboration between the United States and the host country is generally a requirement of the grant-making process.

More practically, prospect identification techniques designed for domestic donors are frequently ineffective for international audiences. International alumni records are not as easy to maintain and information about financial capacity is much more difficult to ascertain. Data-based screening methods are often of little help. And although email and social media are proving to be useful tools for connecting with international prospects, development officers are more successful if they have a good command of the local language and a set of trusted volunteers to open doors.

Finally, building a strong relationship with an international donor can be expensive. In-country education programs or collaborative research programs can minimize some of the costs of international fundraising. Local alumni networks also are useful in maintaining connections with international students. However, universities often need to commit to several international visits a year by senior university officials to build a robust relationship with international prospects. Social media is becoming a lower cost alternative to traditional media in the number of visits and many countries have very active social media platforms. Once again, language skills are important.

Once international prospects are identified, fundraising staff should consider the following:

- What is the culture of giving in the foreign country? Are there any cultural norms to observe when meeting with the donors (exchanging gifts, table seating arrangements, etc.)?
- While international alumni have a good command of your home language, should you translate any key collateral into their native language for stakeholders (parents, advisors)? Do you need a translator when you travel to the foreign country?
- What current programs (student exchange, research, recruitment) are currently active in the foreign country? Are there any faculty members on sabbatical in the foreign country?
- Are there any specific tax, currency exchange, or other regulatory issues regarding gifting from a foreign country to your home country? It may be necessary to establish a local foundation to receive gifts to overcome country-specific gifting restrictions.
- Are there any alumni volunteers living in your home country from the foreign country that can help with introductions, cultural considerations, and relationship building?

(Continued)

Global fundraising can complement a strong domestic program but it should be done thoughtfully. As global wealth continues to shift, more universities will be exploring or expanding their international development efforts to cultivate this growing donor base.

By R. F. Shangraw Jr., PhD, Chief Executive Officer, Arizona State University Foundation for a New American University

Additional Sources

John McLoughlin and Jane Joo Park, eds., *Across Frontiers: New International Perspectives on Educational Fundraising*, CASE, 2010.

Susan Buck Sutton and Daniel Obst, eds., *Developing Strategic International Partnerships: Models for Initiating and Sustaining Innovative Institutional Linkages*, Institute of International Education, 2011.

U.S. Department of Education, *Records on Foreign Gifts to American Institutions of Higher Education*, 2011.

CANADA

Canada is the second largest country in the world in terms of land mass, slightly smaller than Russia but larger than the United States, the only country with which it shares a border. However, by population comparison the United States outstrips Canada 10:1 (approximately 300 million to 33 million). Where this is particularly evident is in terms of population density. For example, Canada's population by square kilometer is 3.3 whereas the United States has a density of 31.6 per square kilometer (80.9 per square mile). Canada's geographical diversity, with a small population spread out over a large country, influences the culture of its organizations and its people and is evident in the emergence and growth of the Canadian nonprofit sector.

The Economy in Canada

Canada is one of the world's wealthiest nations with the 10th largest economy. The service industry dominates the Canadian economy and employs about three quarters of Canadians. However, it is also a country of regionally diverse industries, for example, logging in British Columbia, oil and gas in western provinces, and manufacturing in central

Canada. Canada closely resembles its southern neighbor in its market-oriented economic system and its economic freedoms. Overall, its total government debt is the lowest in the G8 countries. And while Canada and Canadians definitely felt the impact of the 2007 to 2010 global financial crisis, it suffered less than the United States and other countries around the world because of its more tightly regulated banking system.

The Nonprofit Sector in Canada

Canada has more than 240,000 charities and nonprofits that report more than $112 billion in annual revenues and employ more than 2 million Canadians. It has one of the largest and most diverse sectors in the world that encompass education, social services, community benefit, health, religion, environment, arts and culture, sports, and civic betterment.

It is also a significant contributor to the Canadian economy, accounting for 7 percent of the country's GDP and if the value of volunteer time is included this rises to more than 8.5 percent. Even without the "institutional" organizations (sometimes referred to as *QUANGO*—quasi-nongovernment organizations) such as hospitals, universities, and other postsecondaries, the core sector still contributes 2.5 percent ($36.6 billion) to the nation's total economy.[24]

According to *The Canadian Nonprofit and Voluntary Sector in Comparative Perspective*[25] the Canadian nonprofit sector has a number of unique features:[26]

- Canada's nonprofit sector is the second largest in the world as a share of the economically active population, employing up to 12 percent of the population and relying more on the efforts of paid employees than sectors in other countries.
- Excluding the one-third of paid employees who work for hospitals and universities, this number is still as high as 9 percent and,

---

[24] "Statistics Canada, Satellite Account of Nonprofit Institutions and Volunteering," 2007.

[25] http://library.imaginecanada.ca/files/nonprofitscan/en/misc/jhu_report_en.pdf.

[26] "The Canadian Nonprofit and Voluntary Sector in Comparative Perspective," Imagine Canada and Johns Hopkins University, 2005.

in fact, engages nearly as many full-time equivalent workers as all branches of manufacturing in the country.

- Service activities dominate nonprofit activity more in Canada than in other countries and about 74 percent of all nonprofit workers (paid and volunteer) are engaged in direct service delivery in education, health, and housing (compared to 64 percent internationally). Health organizations in particular employ a much larger percentage of workers than in other countries while fewer individuals are involved with the more expressive activities of culture, arts, sports, recreation, and religion.

The Nonprofit Sector's Relationship with Government in Canada

Canada has a long history of voluntary activity that began in its aboriginal roots, carried through with the introduction of the Elizabethan Poor Law of 1601 (to this day the basis of the definition of charity), the role of the Roman Catholic Church, fueled by western expansion and influenced heavily by the arrival of various immigrant populations from around the world, particularly over the last century. Although the influx of immigrant populations began in the late eighteenth century, one-fifth of whom arrived destitute,[27] the numbers increased in the latter half of the twentieth century and specifically since 1971, when Canada became the first country in the world to adopt an official multiculturalism policy. The involvement of the federal government in the economic activity and development related to all of these factors also heavily influenced the development of the nonprofit sector.

Overall, the Canadian nonprofit sector is a mix of the "welfare partnership model" of civil society development found in the Netherlands, Belgium, France, Germany, and Ireland, which has a high level of government funding and a predominance of service activities with countries that have more of an Anglo-Saxon model of development, such as Australia, the United States, and the United Kingdom, which enjoy a higher level of private philanthropic support.[28] In November 2012

---

[27] P. Elson, "High Ideals and Noble Intentions," *Civil Sector Press*, 5. 2011.

[28] Imagine Canada.

the Canadian Parliament passed into law Bill S-201, which formally recognizes November 15th as National Philanthropy Day. Canada is the first and only country that has taken such a step.

Canadian nonprofits also receive more government funding than in other countries and this is mostly due to the role of hospitals and postsecondary institutions, the funding for which grew rapidly from the 1960s to the 1980s[29] but with service delivery staying in the hands of the nonprofit organizations. By the early 1990s it became apparent that the funding from all three levels of government (municipal, provincial, federal) in the sector was unsustainable and the resulting retrenchment had profound impact on sector organizations, the growth of fundraising, and the spreading of philanthropic investment.

Tax and Regulatory Environment

There are important legal distinctions between the 150,000 or so nonprofit organizations and the 84,000 or so registered charities. Registered charities are formally registered as charitable organizations with the Canada Revenue Agency. In order to be eligible for registered charity status an organization's major purpose must fall into one of four areas: the relief of poverty, the advancement of education, the advancement of religion, or other purposes of a charitable nature beneficial to the community as a whole, including health. Charitable status provides two main advantages for organizations. It gives their donors access to tax incentives for the donations they make and enables organizations to access funding from charitable foundations that are restricted by law to registered charities and a small number of other "qualified donees."[30]

The Charities Directorate, a division within CRA, is responsible for monitoring and regulating charitable applications and activity and does so within the terms and conditions of the Income Tax Act of Canada. Over the past decade several important changes have occurred within the ITA that have had major impact on fundraising and philanthropy. In the mid- to early 2000s the government reduced the capital gains on gifts of registered securities to charitable organizations. After

---

[29] *Imagine Canada*, 23.

[30] Vic Murray, *The Management of Nonprofit and Charitable Organizations in Canada*, 2nd ed. (Toronto: Civil Sector Press, 2009), 28.

several subsequent reductions the capital gains were eliminated in their entirety in 2008, which resulted in a significant rise in gifts of stock to charities.

In 2009 CRA introduced a Fundraising Guidance to provide a reporting framework for charities. The Directorate worked closely with nonprofit umbrella organizations such as Imagine Canada and the Association of Fundraising Professionals to design and implement a policy that was educational to the public and equitable to diverse charities.

Composition of the Nonprofit Sector in Canada

Outside of the historical roots and government involvement the Canadian nonprofit sector is very similar to the United States, with two broad categories of functions:

1. Service functions involving the delivery of direct services such as education, health, housing, community, and economic development promotion, animal welfare, and social services.
2. Expressive functions involving activities that enable the expression of cultural, spiritual, professional, and other interests and beliefs. Organizations service expressive functions include sports and recreation groups, religious organizations, arts and cultural organizations, labor and professional associations, advocacy groups, and those working on environment issues.[31]

Within these two areas there are small, medium, and large nonprofits, institutional organizations such as universities, colleges, and hospitals (QUANGOs) and foundations, both private (family) and public (community and parallel to a specific organization). Large international organizations are present in Canada but these offices are mostly located in Central Canada (Toronto, Montreal, and Ottawa) with a few very small satellite functions in Western Canada.

There are a number of umbrella organizations in Canada but this is an area that is generally lacking as compared to the United States.

---

[31] Dr. Lester M. Salamon, Dr. Helmut K. Anheier, eds., *Defining the Nonprofit Sector: A Cross National Analysis* (Manchester, NY: Manchester University Press, 1997).

Imagine Canada is a national organization with the mandate to be a voice for the sector. Community Foundations of Canada represents all of the municipal funding foundations. The Association of Fundraising Professionals is the largest of the professional associations and has 16 chapters and more than 3,500 members from coast to coast. The Association of Healthcare Philanthropy, the Canadian Association of Gift Planners, and CASE are all active to varying degrees. One of the downsides of having so few umbrella organizations is the lack of research that is available for fundraising, philanthropy, and nonprofit work in general.

Philanthropy in Canada

Philanthropy in Canada is similar to the United States if, however, on a smaller scale reflective of a smaller population. Canadians in general give about 0.64 percent of their aggregate income[32] to charity compared to 1.32 percent given by Americans. Further, 26.6 percent of Americans claim charitable tax receipts each year as compared to 23.3 percent of Canadians.[33] This is reflective, however, of the welfare state and has been increasing steadily over the past two decades as government funding has declined and charities have had to reach out to other funding sources.

Fundraising in Canada

The growth in philanthropy is inextricably linked to the growth and maturation of the fundraising profession. As more charities needed new revenue sources they turned to fundraising. This required professional staff to find and work with donors. With the advent of the Internet donors were able to access more information and became more discerning in their giving. This fueled a more professional approach by fundraisers and their fundraising organizations. The result has been an emergence of a *philanthropic culture*.

The donor population includes individuals, foundations, corporations, service clubs, other groups, and government grants. Casinos,

---

[32] Fraser Institute, *The Generosity Index*, 2011.

[33] Ibid.

lotteries, and other gaming activities are also staples of many fundraising programs. Like the United States, individuals account for upward of 82 to 85 percent of all tax receipted gifts with corporations somewhere around 10 percent to 12 percent. According to CRA, Canadians gave $9.2 billion in 2010 but anecdotal research indicates the true number to be in the $15 billion range.[34]

Fundraising practices are also similar to the United States. Most organizations will employ up to 10 different methodologies including direct response, telephone solicitation, events, gaming, major gifts, social media, door-to-door, and on-street fundraising. The latter, however, is less prevalent than in other parts of the world and largely concentrated in Toronto and Montreal. Although there is some in Western Canada the fact that Canada is a northern country doubtless plays a role in limiting the growth of this methodology.

Capital campaigns play a significant role in philanthropic revenue and there is a steady rise across the country in individual campaign dollar goals and the sheer number of very large campaigns.

In Summary

A major challenge for Canada and the United States is to redefine and develop their role in relationship to the worldwide civil sector. North American fundraisers need to open themselves to innovation from abroad and continue to be willing to share their own with other nations.

---

[34]Convio/Cygnus study, 2010.

CHAPTER 7

Australia and New Zealand

SEAN TRINER

The average person might mistakenly lump the two nations of Australia and New Zealand together, but they would be wrong. What the two nations share are similar accents, a high proportion of English-speaking Caucasian people in the population, and having the Queen of England as head of state (like Canada). They are both notoriously less formal than other developed countries in dress, as well. They also share some common history and natural resources, which we review, among many other things, in this chapter.

The revolution and formation of the United States in the eighteenth century forced the United Kingdom to find another place for its undesirables (usually convicts, for instance) and Australia was chosen as a new penal colony of sorts for the Crown. The British government established several new colonies on the continent of Australia and islands now known as New Zealand.

Both countries grew up with enormous natural assets and in the past agriculture has been the economic mainstay. New Zealand was the third richest nation in the world (GDP/Capita) in 1950 and Australia the fifth—despite their small populations. But agriculture wasn't enough to ensure prosperity. Australia was blessed by mind-blowing amounts of resources—an entire continental hoard of valuable stuff underground (and more recently, offshore). Gold, uranium, copper, coal, gas—everything the world wanted. These resources are not the only reason the region is so rich, but they certainly contribute to its wealth.[1]

The Australians are richer than the New Zealanders. According to the 2012 Credit Suisse global wealth report, only the Swiss have more wealth per person than do Australians. The average Australian has 60 percent more wealth than the average American and earns 30 percent more.

Across the Tasman Sea, New Zealand has not fared quite as well. It is now down to number 23 in terms of wealth—with New Zealanders GDP per capita just over half their Australian neighbors. For context, the average American produces 40 percent more wealth than New Zealanders.

Low wages and limited opportunities are creating a chronic brain drain. A 2012 campaign run by a New Zealand trade union featured a picture of Australia and complained that unless wages were put up and public sector jobs protected "the only job opportunities for Kiwis are in Australia."

The differences in the degree of wealth enjoyed in New Zealand and Australia inevitably affects fundraising.

Despite differences in economy, the average Australian and average New Zealander are pretty generous. According to one report they are first and second in the world in percentage that donate. But this report is from polling, and people can say they give, even if it is just putting one dollar in a collecting tin.

There is not much difference in motivations and giving between Australian/New Zealanders and other wealthy, Anglophone countries. There is a tendency to be more charitable when people do well.

A little bit more Catholic than England and less Catholic than Ireland—Christianity has had the most dominant role of all the world religions in building up what is New Zealand and Australian British–centric culture. Wave upon wave of immigrants—China and Afghanistan in the nineteenth century, then World War II refugees from all over Europe, more British, Greeks, Italians, Vietnamese, and then the Chinese again—have moved to their shores, but both nations are still dominated by their British colonial roots.

---

[1] www.google.com/fusiontables/DataSource?docid=1YDlqQzZHVMPxSadc t1u5cBBiN341xOCMcO6kSkU.

Consequently the basis of the charity system is similar to that in the United Kingdom and many British expatriates living in the region are involved in raising funds. In fact, it is still full of new British immigrants (such as myself). Within my company, Pareto, a third of our staff were born and educated in the United Kingdom and about a third of the staff within our charity clients are British or Irish. The pattern is similar in New Zealand. We joke that Australia seems to have more New Zealand fundraisers than does New Zealand.

In terms of fundraising tactics, the collecting tin, sponsoring friends, local fundraising drives (such as *sausage sizzles* and *cake stalls*) are as prevalent in New Zealand and Australia as any U.S. or British town or village.

NEW ZEALAND

A 2008 report, *The New Zealand Non-Profit Sector in Comparative Perspective* by Johns Hopkins University, concluded that the sector contributed $5.5 billion,[2] or 4.9 percent of GDP. They attributed $1.25 billion of that to donations.

The more recent *Giving New Zealand Philanthropic Funding 2011* report estimates that New Zealanders donated about $2 billion in 2011—twice what they donated five years previously, and representing 60 percent growth since the Johns Hopkins report. More than half of this (58 percent) came from individuals, another 36 percent from trusts and foundations, and the balance of 6 percent from corporations.

The largest fundraising success in 2011 was the New Zealand Red Cross. (See Table 7.1.) A devastating earthquake in New Zealand rallied $80 million in contributions toward disaster relief. Without the earthquake, the Red Cross would have otherwise fallen in the middle in the ranking of fundraising performance shown in Table 7.1.

AUSTRALIA

A 2010 Government Productivity Commission report, *Contribution of the Not-for-Profit Sector*, attributed more than 4 percent of GDP to the sector (just below $43 billion) with an additional 5 million volunteers contributing $14.6 billion of value in unpaid labor.

---

[2]http://www.ocvs.govt.nz/documents/publications/papers-and-reports/the-new-zealand-non-profit-sector-in-comparative-perspective.pdf.

TABLE 7.1	TOP NEW ZEALAND CHARITIES BY FUNDRAISING INCOME (EXCLUDING ANIMAL HEALTH BOARD)[3]

Name	Fundraising Income
NZ Red Cross	$73,820,773
World Vision NZ	$30,129,346
Salvation Army NZ	$27,086,372
Order of St. John	$16,091,721
Royal NZ Foundation for the Blind	$10,457,254
Child Fund NZ	$ 8,527,120
Medical Council NZ	$ 6,179,015
IHC NZ	$ 6,172,202
St. John Northern Region	$ 5,769,783
Cancer Society NZ Auckland	$ 5,575,712

Source: creative commons©

The report estimated that there were 600,000 nonprofit organizations, 59,000 of which were "economically significant" and that they employed 8 percent of the population. Thirty-five thousand of these nonprofits do not employ staff. Another 26,500 qualify as DGRs (Deductible Gift Receipts). Their donors can claim a charitable contribution deduction.

Another government report, *Giving Australia*, coordinated by the Australian Council of Social Service, reported in 2005 that individuals donated around $7.7 billion. On top of the $1.9 billion in corporate contributions, gifts in kind, sponsorship, and community business projects amounted to another $1.4 billion, for a total of $3.3 billion from this sector.

Interestingly, the report attributed $2 billion to "charity gambling"—usually lotteries and raffles.

---

[3] The Animal Health Board manages the National Pest Management Strategy and is funded by "members," including government and organizations with farming interests. It is not a fundraising charity in the traditional sense. It reports fundraising income of more than $7 million but is excluded because this does not represent fundraising in the same context as this book.

According to Givewell[4] (not to be confused with the U.S. organization of the same name), government accounts for nearly half of all nonprofit income, with fundraising and bequests accounting for about 21 percent and the rest coming from fees, sales, services, and investment income.

Australia is a federation of states and territories, and many organizations are state-based. Fundraising legislation is quite different in each state and territory, and this variegated state system is not helpful for the sector's growth. The Australian Charities and Not for Profit Commission are attempting to harmonize regulation, initially through a task force advised by representatives of the Charity Commission of England and Wales.

In terms of top fundraising performance, Givewell reports that World Vision dominates other charities by an extraordinary amount, raising $325 million in 2010, with $200 million of it coming from child sponsorship. To give an idea of the scale of World Vision's dominance, the charity would likely need to acquire more than $20 million in *new* donors every year just to maintain its present position. Only 30 charities raised more than $20 million in 2010. The Salvation Army is second, raising $178 million across its regional divisions. Both charities are well known and well established in Australia.

The third charity by fundraising income, Compassion, however, is not well known. Although there is a huge drop from $178 million to $54 million for third place, Compassion proves that solid hard work focused on a clearly defined audience is key to fundraising growth. The charity has zoomed up the charts with superb fundraising and marketing of child sponsorship into Christian communities. See Table 7.2.

The top 50 fundraising charities raise around $1.7 billion. With the $1.6 billion earned from fees for services, sales, and contracts, their total income was $3.3 billion.

When ranked by total income, only two of the top 10 fundraising charities (Salvation Army and World Vision) feature in the top 10 by total income. See Table 7.3.

In terms of brand awareness, unprompted awareness surveys, in which researchers ask members of the public to name five charities, are often used. These surveys have returned the same six or seven charities "scoring" over 10 percent quite consistently over the years. The Red Cross (between 40 and 65 percent) tends to win, followed by Salvation Army (25 to 40 percent) with the Cancer Councils, World

[4] www.givewell.com.au/.

TABLE 7.2	TOP 10 AUSTRALIAN CHARITIES BY INCOME

Organization	Unearned Income
World Vision Australia	$325,457,675
Salvation Army	$178,418,000
Compassion Australia	$ 54,106,148
Cancer Council, NSW	$ 48,796,000
National Heart Foundation	$ 48,070,000
Australian Red Cross Society	$ 44,477,000
Médecins Sans Frontières Australia	$ 43,551,736
Boys Town	$ 43,394,000
Oxfam Australia	$ 42,724,162
Save the Children Australia	$ 39,708,304

Source: Compiled from annual reports.

TABLE 7.3	TOP 10 AUSTRALIAN CHARITIES BY TOTAL INCOME 2010

Organization	Total Income
Australian Red Cross Society	$1,027,511,000
Salvation Army	$ 637,023,000
World Vision Australia	$ 346,578,459
The Children's Hospital at Westmead	$ 333,775,000
Mission Australia	$ 309,684,866
Royal Flying Doctor Service of Australia	$ 273,311,627
Peter MacCallum Cancer Centre	$ 239,760,000
St. Vincent de Paul Society NSW	$ 107,203,171
The Walter and Eliza Hall Institute of Medical Research	$ 104,984,000
Multiple Sclerosis Ltd.	$ 85,489,552

Source: Compiled from annual reports.

Vision, St. Vincent de Paul, and the various brands that make up Vision Australia dominating unprompted recollection of charities.

Infrastructure in Australia

Australian fundraising is governed by the States and Territories rather than nationally. This causes some problems for most fundraising activites.

Authorities

The Fundraising Institute of Australia[5] (FIA) is the best source for information about regulation, law, and more. Givewell compiles lots of useful data taken from charities' annual reports. The federal government is establishing a new, national body for charities known as the Australian Charities and Not-for-Profits Commission (ACNC).

Across the Tasman Sea, the New Zealand Charities Commission[6] is still in its infancy, but has conveniently made all of their data available and searchable on their website. At time of writing there are still some key flaws (for example, a "sponsorship" search calls up both corporate sponsorship and child sponsorship, which have absolutely nothing in common) but it has already proved an invaluable resource for those who seek information about the sector.

Suppliers

There is a healthy variety of suppliers to nonprofits in Australia and New Zealand, although the size of the markets means there are few of each kind. It is simply too small to sustain lots of competing agencies. Some professionals, like John Burns, Fundraising Director at Médecins Sans Frontières Australia, said in 2012 that the lack of healthy competition between talented vendors can be a problem in terms of quality of services and products and also cost to nonprofits.

New Zealand has a few locally based suppliers for telemarketing, direct mail, face-to-face, database, and online peer fundraising, but many of the services provided are through New Zealand branches of Australian companies.

Australia has a dozen or so face-to-face providers, two or three donation processing companies, a few large (15-plus staff) full-service charity-specific direct marketing agencies, and a dozen or so smaller, charity direct marketing agencies. There are plenty of printers, some of whom offer creative and design services. There are three regular giving specialist telemarketing firms, and five or six much larger, but more broadly focused telemarketing firms (covering lotteries and appeal calling, too).

---

[5] www.fia.org.au.

[6] www.register.charities.govt.nz/CharitiesRegister/OpenData.aspx.

There are roughly 100 specialist fundraising consultants[7] of various sizes, some with specialists in areas such as bequest and major donor training as well as trust and corporate fundraising. Some of these also offer copywriting, production, and branding services. Finally, there are two or three established capital campaign companies with proven track records of helping charities raise very substantial sums for capital campaigns.

Philanthropy in Australia

Traditional philanthropy is nowhere near as well established as in other nations.

Major Donors

Rich Australians and New Zealanders give much less than their U.S. counterparts. Despite 200 Australians having wealth over $200 million and thousands with seven-figure incomes, the greatest donor to Australia is a foreigner, Chuck Feeney. New Zealand has fewer superwealthy, but suffers from the same problem. In both countries there are no big commitments by people such as those made by Bill Gates and Warren Buffet. When interviewed for this book, Carl Young, fundraising director of the Peter MacCallum Cancer Centre in Australia, said in 2012:

> Fundraising in Australia had a strong Christian background, similar to Europe and America, but Aussie giving follows "mateship"—I am doing alright and want to look after my mate. However, people don't want the same level of recognition as in the United States. This is not helpful, as is there is no social pressure to give. Two major philanthropists, Dame Elizabeth Murdoch and Lady Southey (former president of Philanthropy Australia and a Myer family member) have been vocal for some years about encouraging wealthy people to give, and more importantly to give publicly in order to encourage a culture of philanthropic giving amongst high net value individuals.

And John Burns, fundraising director of Médecins Sans Frontières, said in 2012:

> Mateship and egalitarianism is probably bull; our giving culture is no different to others. People help people who are in need; it is a human

---

[7]The FIA has a list of a few of these providers on its website, www.fia.org.au; go to Resources and Suppliers.

thing not a national thing. The latest BRW Rich List shows how little our wealthy give; it is embarrassing and there are no excuses.

Corporations

Corporate giving in Australia and New Zealand is on par with that of the United States and the United Kingdom. Data on corporate giving from CAF (United Kingdom) and Giving USA are comparable to Australia and New Zealand, with corporations giving a dismal average of less than 1 percent of their profit to charity. The *Giving New Zealand* report shows just 6 percent of charity donations are from companies. The *Giving Australia* report had that figure closer to 20 percent. Just as is the case in many other places, corporations here tend to like funding the big, sexy brands like Breast Cancer Network Australia, the Heart Foundation, and UNICEF.

According to Hailey Cavill in 2012, an expert in corporate fundraising, the best approach is not "fundraising" at all, "My experience is they are *donating* less, but are *investing* more through marketing, sponsorship, CSR, human resource budgets."

Up-to-date information on corporate giving is scarce, but a breakdown of the fundraising income in the top charities is telling. Clearly the largest source of income for Australian nonprofits is from individuals giving through automatic payments, appeals, and bequests. Corporate donations are a less significant source. A workplace-giving scheme is in place in Australia, with more than 100,000 employees contributing, but it is not a significant income stream, generating just $23 million in the 2009 to 2010 financial year.

Trusts and Foundations

There are a few decent-size trusts, but nothing on the scale of the British-based Wellcome Foundation and the U.S.-based Bill and Melinda Gates Foundation. Nearly all trusts demand that charities have DGR. The best course for raising funds from trusts and foundations is probably to use a specialist consultant.

Over the past decade, it became easy to create personal private trusts—donors put money into them and then the trusts distribute the funds. Most of the thousand or so of these are for the purpose of making discretionary contributions to any tax-deductible charity. A few have a formal application process. These trusts are called *private ancillary funds* or PAFs.

There is no mandatory reporting for trusts and foundations, so little information is available. Philanthropy Australia, a national association that represents Australia's leading grant-making private, family, and corporate trusts and foundations, however, estimates that there are 5,000 foundations including the 1,000 or so PAFS (see Table 7.4.) Giving is estimated as being between $500 million and $1 billion from assets of around $10 billion. In context, all of the Australian trusts and foundations added together would probably not sneak into the top 10 individual global trusts. The Bill and Melinda Gates Foundation (with nearly $40 billion in assets) is around four times bigger than the entire Australian trust and foundation market.

New Zealand trust and foundation giving is more important to the sector than in the United States—according to *Giving USA 2011*, trusts account for 14 percent of total income whereas in New Zealand it is 36 percent.

Trust and foundation expert Jo Garner said in 2012 that the biggest challenge facing charities trying to raise funds from trusts and foundations is ensuring that they don't employ "hope" as one of their strategies to achieve grant revenue targets! "All too often charities in Australia (and elsewhere) adopt the, 'you've got to be in it to win it

TABLE 7.4	LARGEST (REPORTED) DISBURSEMENTS FROM AUSTRALIAN FOUNDATIONS IN 2010–2011

Organization	Disbursement
Macquarie Group Foundation	$17,000,000
The Ian Potter Foundation	12,400,000
The Sidney Myer Fund and The Myer Foundation	11,000,000
Lord Mayor's Charitable Foundation	7,700,000
Geoffrey Gardiner Dairy Foundation	7,200,000
AMP Foundation (2010 figures)	6,200,000
Colonial Foundation	5,600,000
Helen Macpherson Smith Trust	5,500,000
R. E. Ross Trust	5,300,000
The William Buckland Foundation	3,300,000

Source: © Philanthropy Australia 2012. www.philanthropy.org.au/research/fast.html.

approach.' But with some funders only granting 2 percent of the applications they receive, for grant seeking to remain cost effective in such a highly competitive environment, the process needs to be based on solid prospect research, targeted donor communications and excellent stewardship," she says.

Individuals

By far and away the largest growth area, individual giving also provides us with the most data about giving patterns in Australia. The ATO (Australia Tax Office) releases statistics on giving based on tax deductions. It reported that giving was down in 2009 to 2010 (per the most recent data) from the year before by 6 percent.

Although charities report fundraising in different ways, nearly 50 of them have come together to look at giving trends and "harmonize" how they measure donor gifts, retention, and stated legacy intentions for a report is compiled by Pareto Fundraising. The ninth version of this benchmarking report, looking at data 2002 to 2011, is known as the *BM9 Report*.

The *BM9 Report*'s strength is that it is based on actual transactional data, not opinion or survey. Each charity must hand over its donation transaction records that are then labeled for consistency with the other charities. Its weakness is that the type of charity that understands the benefit of such an exercise and chooses to participate tends to have trained fundraisers and enlightened management (two ingredients for fundraising success)—and this skews the results.

The year 2011 to 2012 was probably the best year in fundraising for Australia ever for most of the benchmarking charities in the *BM9*. This goes against a general "feeling" that things are not so good. A 2012 forum for nonprofits run by the 3 Pillars Network, sponsored by Givewell, was downbeat, with many charity staff participants fearing what was ahead for them and incredulous about the growth of organizations such as Compassion, the Heart Foundation, Peter MacCallum Cancer Centre, Médecins Sans Frontières, and the Cerebral Palsy Association. These five enjoyed growth well into double figures from 2009 to 2011.

Benchmarking Study Key Findings

The following data is based on 48 charities from New Zealand and Australia. (Of the 48, New Zealand has 8 and Australia has 40.)

It is indicative of fundraising trends from direct marketing activities (including mail, phone, online, and face-to-face.)

Regular Giving

Scott Palmer, national face-to-face manager of World Vision, New Zealand, said in 2012:

> Regular giving is really big even though most charities don't do it. It is the big ones that drive it and are getting the money. Face-to-face is the biggest source of sponsors for World Vision. Sixty-five percent of new sponsors came through that channel.

When we look for growth drivers for fundraising in Australia, we see that regular giving is the biggest driver, and in turn, that growth is driven by face-to-face—the process of asking strangers, cold, for monthly commitments on the street, door-to-door, in shopping malls, and at events. See Figure 7.1.

FIGURE 7.1	*BM9 REPORT* SHOWING CHARITIES INCOME BY TYPE OF TRANSACTION

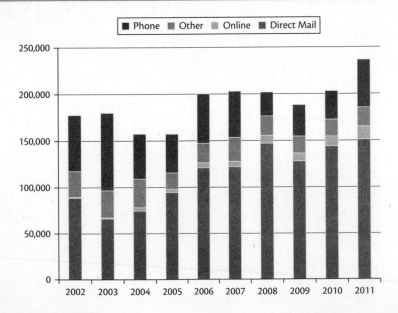

Source: Pareto Fundraising.

The charities in the study have steadily increased income from individuals from around $130 million in 2002 to just short of $350 million in 2011. Back in 2002, nearly half of the $130 million came from bequests, 40 percent from appeals and general donations and less than 10 percent from regular giving (automatic debits from bank accounts and credit cards). By 2011, regular giving had overtaken one-off donations and bequests.

Although regular giving contributions from people acquired by direct mail have increased from $6.5 million in 2002 to $22.4 million in 2011, by far and away the biggest growth has been face-to-face—from just $3.4 million in 2002 to more than $71 million in 2011. In the meantime, online advertising and cold email solicitation has increased from $228,000 in 2002 to $5.7 million 10 years later. Online acquisition of regular givers has risen close to what direct mail was achieving a decade ago. Interestingly the *rate* of growth in online acquisition during this digital decade has actually been *less* than the rate of growth in old-fashioned direct mail. Like everyone everywhere else in the world, we believe that at some point growth in acquisition of regular givers from digital sources will overtake direct mail, but that looks to be at least another decade away.

An innovative approach used in other countries known here as *two-step*, a process that is providing growth for advocacy organizations. Two-step involves face-to-face canvassers stopping people, conversing, and collecting their details for follow-up by phone, digital media, and sometimes mail. It is the opposite of the *telefacing* strategies described in Chapter 12 on India. Two-step has grown from nothing in 2007, to generating $383,000 of income in 2010, and reaching just short of $1 million in 2011. This method of fundraising tends to be more expensive than straight face-to-face acquisition, but is great for advocacy organizations as it is used not only to persuade people to give, but also to take action, like signing online petitions.

Although face-to-face delivers on volume, it has the worst attrition rates. In the six years from 2005 to 2011, the benchmarked charities acquired 360,356 donors in this way. Nearly 41 percent of these donors were no longer giving after 12 months. However, there is considerable variance in success: The best performer lost only 33 percent and the worst lost 60 percent within the first year. At an average monthly donation of $29.82, this is a massive income stream for the charities.

Regular givers acquired by using alternatives to face-to-face, techniques such as phone, mail, and online, numbered just 34,975 in the same period. Even though only 14 percent had stopped within a year, these more "loyal" donors contributed a fraction of what the face-to-face donors did.

Face-to-face fundraising has revolutionized fundraising—and has added tens of millions of dollars to charity income. It provided the single biggest revenue growth driver in Australia and New Zealand. It has opened an entirely new market—face-to-face donors tend to be much younger than traditional donors—almost half of the new recruits in the benchmarking study were under 35 years old, and 95 percent under 65.

One-Time Donations

For nonemergency, nonautomatic donations (where the donors contact details are captured), such as gifts in response to an appeal, by far the biggest source is direct mail. Direct mail in Australia has been growing considerably, with improving response rates over the past years beginning to overcome the incredibly prohibitive and inflexible postage and print costs.

The direct mail renaissance can be attributed to more charities worrying about poor results from new innovations, potential economy insecurity, and so are putting their money into established and proven acquisition methods.

Still, direct mail is expensive, even more expensive here than it may be elsewhere. Let's compare Australian mailing rates with those of the United States. To mail a package in Australia averages around 39 cents minimum in contrast to 14 cents in the United States, and mailing a premium package (e.g., containing key-rings) costs around 74 cents—double what it would cost in the United States. Charity mail discounts apply only to standard letters. New Zealand post is not much more affordable, and its rules differ on size and weight, so trying to produce a direct mail pack that will work in both countries can be challenging. Not only is postage expensive, print per package in both countries also tends to cost around double what it would be in the United States. Some nonprofits get around this by manufacturing and shipping packages from China for distribution through Australia Post.

Cold telemarketing is legal in Australia and New Zealand, and both countries have well-established programs, often including incentives such as lottery tickets or gifts such as teddy bears.

Gambling is tightly regulated, but both Australia and New Zealand have a history of both illegal and legal gambling. Gambling gaming machines fund many nonprofit clubs such as surf lifesavers, football clubs, and more. Charities use charity lotteries, mailing, and calling intra- and interstate to sell lottery tickets. The more enlightened charities try "converting" these gambling givers to other forms of giving, and regular giving programs including automated entry into lotteries.

Legacies

As in Europe, nonprofits seeking cures or treatment for terminal diseases like cancer, other health causes, and animal welfare do best with legacies. However, well-thought-through marketing programs have made this a viable option for many other kinds of organizations.

Legacy income accounts for nearly one-third of individual donations from all of the benchmarked charities in the *BM9 Report*. According to New Zealand Charity Commission open data, the top 50 fundraising organizations declare 15 percent of their unearned income comes from legacies.

Steps are being taken to encourage legacy giving in Australia. Include a Charity is an industry-wide organization, cofunded by many charities, dedicated to increasing the rate at which Australians mention charities in their will.

Challenges in Australian Giving

Three senior fundraisers working within charities that have grown considerably over the past 10 years were interviewed in preparation for writing this chapter. They all agree that the challenges for fundraisers in both countries were mostly internal, not external—hiring the right people and finding the right strategies being more important than outside factors such as the economy. These two factors are intrinsically linked.

When interviewed, Scott Palmer, national face-to-face manager at World Vision New Zealand, said:

> World Vision New Zealand income growth is flat at the moment and has been for two years. Mainly because of internal things, such as community projects, coming to an end. The projects of 18,000 of our 80,000 sponsors will come to completion in the near future. We

know that when we try to transfer them, we will lose 15 percent of those 18,000 sponsors, on top of normal cancellation. . . .

It is not the economy causing the flat line in our income growth. It is a factor but not a top reason. We reckon we need to refresh sponsorship product income (which accounts for two-thirds of our income), in particular improving the experience between donors and their children. This is not unique to New Zealand, but we have reached saturation because of our small population.

Lack of Skilled and Experienced Fundraisers

The first factor is the shallow talent pool. The markets are small, wages are relatively low, and fundraising is still not an established career choice for new graduates. Many of the heads of fundraising of top charities did not come from fundraising backgrounds. Instead they may have marketing backgrounds, occasionally direct marketing, but otherwise arrive in the job with nothing but their passion for the cause and the willingness to work hard.

They know little about the field they have just entered. When 50 fundraisers at a conference were asked to identify the top five fundraising charities in Australia, not one person could name them all, and few knew where they could find this information. Raising money is no easy task and without the background and skills needed, they become frustrated, quit, and then the cycle continues.

Some charities have circumvented this issue by outsourcing much of their fundraising to outside agencies and many of the larger ones (more than $20 million in Australia, $10 million in New Zealand) that have achieved the greatest growth do so. They combine internal and external talent in order to maximize returns in regular giving, including face-to-face.

Cost of Fundraising

The second factor, a consequence of the lack of talent, is ignorance. Few know what works, what doesn't, have or can produce good data, and don't know what to do with it when they have it. There is a naive belief that people will give just because it is a good cause.

Because there is a lack of good information about the sector, lazy media and government officials fall back on the cost of fundraising and other administrative expenses as a measure of success for charities, even though it bears no reflection on the impact an organization may have. Here is an example of just how misleading cost of fundraising can be: A charity with a 40 percent cost of fundraising, growing at 50 percent each year, would be judged as "worse" than an otherwise identical charity spending 10 percent on fundraising, yet not growing.

Nonprofits face a dilemma. Although growth is in itself not success, some must grow to achieve their missions. And it is difficult to grow without spending more on fundraising, which can leave nonprofits open to undeserved criticism by the uninformed.

Scott Palmer of World Vision New Zealand thinks this is a problem in his country. Lawmakers are reforming a piece of legislation that could make cost of fundraising an element for regulation in the country:

> The Reform of the Fair Trading Act could directly affect us. At the moment it looks like it will mostly impact tele-fundraising, but it could also harm face-to-face. World Vision is arguing that regulation of cost of fundraising will fuel the false interpretation of what makes a good charity.

For more on fundraising costs on North America, see Chapter 6 on North America.

IN SUMMARY

The giving cultures in New Zealand and Australia are similar to those found in the United States, Canada, and the United Kingdom. Over-arching laws and definitions of *charity* are similar and attitudes to giving and reasons for not giving are also similar. The main differences are:

- Religious giving is important, but nowhere near the proportion seen in the United States. Australia and New Zealand are more like the United Kingdom with the majority of donations not given to overtly religious organizations.
- The rich don't give enough; proportionally much, much less than the United States, Canada, and the United Kingdom.
- People (mostly in the 40-to-65-year-old bracket) are much more comfortable with direct debits from their credit cards and bank accounts.
- Proportionally, more young people (40-to-65-year-old) give than in the United States, mostly due to face-to-face fundraising.

When it comes to fundraising there are no techniques known to this author that are unique to Australia and New Zealand. However, both nations seem to pick the best from abroad—with U.S.-style direct mail leading the acquisition of older (65-plus) donors and U.K.-style face-to-face acquiring younger donors.

In governance, New Zealand has the one governing body (like England and Wales) whereas Australia still suffers the curse of multi-state legislation (like the United States).

Although New Zealand's economy is not on fire at the time of this writing, Australia's is one of the best performing in the world—out-stripping the United States, Canada, and every EU country with its resources boom. Australia seems like an ideal market for charities looking to expand internationally, and—relative to its small scale—it is.

CHAPTER 8

Central and Eastern Europe

MATT IDE, MAIR BOSWORTH, ANCA ZAHARIA, WITH AN INTRODUCTION BY CHRIS CARNIE

At midnight on November 9, 1989, East Germany's Communist rulers gave permission for gates along the Berlin Wall to be opened. Crowds surged through, and over, the Wall.

Five years earlier, George Soros had established his first non-U.S. foundation, in Hungary. He began to supply photocopiers to universities, libraries, and civil society groups, breaking the Communist Party's grip on information. By the fall of the Berlin Wall, Soros had established two more foundations, in Poland and Russia. Philanthropy was part of the change in Central and Eastern Europe (and Soros central to that philanthropy).

The example of the Trust for Civil Society in Central and Eastern Europe illustrates this. The Trust, created in 2000 by five large U.S. foundations including Soros' Open Society Institute, was "founded on the assumption that democratic transition was nearing its successful completion and that . . . civil society . . . was more or less fully (re)-established.)"[1] Note the "(re)-established" civil society; giving, and thus fundraising, existed prior to the emergence of the Communist super-state. For example, St. John's Hospital in Budapest (Szt. János Kórház) was founded in the eighteenth century as a poor house supported by wealthy locals. It was expanded in 1903 following the donation of a building by a wealthy entrepreneur, Wodiáner Albert.[2]

---

[1] *Global Philanthropy*, edited by Norime MacDonald and Luc Tayart de Borms (London: MF Publishing).

[2] www.janoskorhaz.hu.

In the 23 years since the Wall went down, Central and Eastern Europe has become a place for fundraising. Fundraisers there have successfully imported funds and techniques to the region. Lawmakers have established the grounds on which philanthropy can exist.

THE LEGAL GROUNDS FOR PHILANTHROPY

The basic legal elements for philanthropy exist in all of the Central and Eastern European states:

- Foundations—All of the states have foundations written into their law. In most cases this is relatively recent—Romania's foundation law[3] dates from 2000, for example. As in other European countries there is a legal basis for both foundations (which may be public benefit, or not) and associations in all of these countries.
- Taxation—In most countries foundations are exempt from taxes. In some cases this only applies to foundations that are classed as being of public benefit. In Lithuania foundations win tax exemption after clearance from the tax office.
- Donations and tax—Slovenia is the only country in Central and Eastern Europe that does not offer some form of tax deductibility for donations. All of the others offer either deductibility or, as in the case of Hungary, a system of tax credits. Thresholds on deductibility are sometimes low; Slovenia allows deductions up to only 0.3 percent of income, for example.[4]
- Donations from tax—A number of countries in the region have a system like Italy's *cinque per mille* under which taxpayers allocate a percentage of their income tax to causes. Hungary, Lithuania, Poland, and Slovakia all offer this system. The Hungarian League Against Cancer (Magyar Rákellenes Liga),[5] for example, runs a series of YouTube videos to promote their fundraising from a 1 percent tax donation. Romania also has a 1 percent tax provision.

---

[3] Foundations' Legal and Fiscal Environments, EFC, Brussels, 2007.

[4] www.givingineurope.org.

[5] www.rakliga.hu.

FUNDRAISING IN CENTRAL AND EASTERN EUROPE

Fundraising is alive and well in Central and Eastern Europe. Medical, environmental, social, and cultural organizations are all raising funds. SOS Children's Villages, World Wildlife Fund, and UNICEF, as three examples, are all active in the region.

There are bright sparks like the Copernicus Science Centre[6] in Poland, which has an active and successful corporate sponsorship program run by a professional staff. Plamienok, a children's hospice in Bratislava, Slovakia, has a large donation button on its front website page, and a list of the individuals who have donated each year; other nonprofits in Western Europe could learn from Plamienok's transparency. Tulip Foundation[7] in Bulgaria runs an annual "marketplace" for projects, marrying local companies with civil society projects in a form of speed-dating; in one hour in July 2012 they signed 41 deals with a value of $15,000.

Fundraisers have come together to share experience—the Polish Fundraising Association, for example,[8] was founded in 2006 and now runs a substantial annual conference. Slovakia has a fundraising center and club[9] with a regular program of meetings, as does Ukraine—and there are other groupings in Armenia, Czech Republic, Georgia, Hungary, Moldova, Romania, and Serbia.[10] There is still a long way to go in Central and Eastern Europe. Critics point to the wide variety of legal definitions of organizations across the region—a criticism that could equally be leveled at Western Europe. There is also a great deal of variation in the level of professionalization of the sector. The full transition from dependence on external funding—from U.S. and European states and private funders—to national or internal funding, has yet to occur. And the economies of much of Central and Eastern Europe have been badly hit by global recession.

---

[6] www.kopernik.org.pl.

[7] www.tulipfoundation.net.

[8] www.fundraising.org.pl.

[9] www.fundraising.sk.

[10] European Fundraising Association.

But the portents—the growing cadre of professional fundraisers, the increasing transparency, the networks, and fundraising associations—are good. They point to an innovative, growing sector with a strong future.

To give readers a better sense of what is happening in the region, we have profiled the evolving nonprofit sector in two different countries: Russia and Romania. The section on Russia includes two case studies, one on SOS Children's Villages Russia, and the other on WWF Russia. The Romanian Red Cross is featured as a case study in the other section.

RUSSIA BY MATT IDE AND MAIR BOSWORTH

Fundraisers in Russia today have their work cut out for them. They are fighting on two fronts: Faced on one side with the restrictive and obstructive red tape of a government paranoid about foreign intervention and anxious to control the development of civil society and—on the other hand—the skepticism of a public worn down by the post-Soviet scandals of "foundations" that turned out to be none too charitable and by "charities" that promised to channel donations to the children of Chernobyl, but which instead transformed public gifts into shining Bentleys.

Yet the fall of the Soviet Union has ignited a blossoming of civil society in Russia, with hundreds of charitable organizations working to cure society's ills. Over the past 20 years we have seen the rebirth and evolution of philanthropy in Russia. Although the market is still relatively immature for fundraising, philanthropy has been growing along with the economy, and a culture of giving that had been all but lost under the Soviet regime has begun to re-emerge.

To instigate tangible reform, Russia's civil society sector and Russian donors have to begin to influence the restrictive and discriminatory regulation system of nonprofit organizations created in recent years by the Putin Government. Russian donors, with the support of membership and intermediary organizations, should also develop a dialogue with the wider charitable sector and make their funds more accessible to Russian NGOs, which struggle to raise funds and sustain their often much more effective and innovative programs.

Despite the pressures and limitations that Russian NGOs and INGOs seeking to raise money in Russia face, fundraisers are optimistic about the potential for growth in the market and are working to win public trust, to lobby government for a more favorable legal framework in which to operate, and to build a culture of giving in Russia.

This section explores the philanthropic landscape in today's Russia: what the potential of the market is, who is giving, and how, and what are the challenges that fundraisers face and how might they be overcome.

Russia Today: A Very Big Bear

Measuring any phenomenon in Russia is complicated by the country's size, a lack of comprehensive data covering its people and institutions, and the complex, often dichotomous nature of its social and economic trends.

At almost twice the size of China or the United States, and more than 70 times the size of the United Kingdom, the Russian Federation (its official title) is the largest country on earth in terms of surface area.[11] Reaching from Norway and Finland in the West to Mongolia and North Korea in the East, Russia borders 14 countries and spans nine time zones—but has a population of just 142.9 million.[12]

Only a quarter of the population lives in urban areas and, with just 8.4 people per square kilometer,[13] Russia is one of the most sparsely populated countries in the world. The Russian Federation boasts a high literacy rate (99.5 percent) but its citizens have a life expectancy rate of just 68.8 years.

Russia has emerged from a decade of post-Soviet economic and political turmoil to reassert itself as a world power, moving from a

---

[11] CIA World Factbook, www.cia.gov/library/publications/the-world-factbook/geos/rs.html.

[12] UN World Population Prospects 2010, http://esa.un.org/unpd/wpp/unpp/p2k0data.asp.

[13] The fourth lowest of all developed nations on the globe. Those with a lower population density are Australia (2.9); Iceland (3.1); and Canada (3.4)—UN World Population Prospects 2010, http://esa.un.org/unpd/wpp/unpp/p2k0data.asp.

centrally planned to a more market-based and globally integrated economy. In 2011, Russia's economy was the ninth biggest in the world, with a GDP of more than $1.5 trillion, placing the country in the upper-middle income level.[14] Between 2005 and 2010, the per capita GDP of Russia doubled to approximately $10,360 and continues to rise as Russia strives to move to a high-income status.

The Russian economy has grown at an average rate of 7 percent annually in recent years and unemployment has been falling. An abundance of natural gas, oil, coal, and precious metals has helped Russia to continue growing economically and withstand economic pressures and fluctuations from around the world. Russia has a robust and autonomous economy, which—despite experiencing a deep but brief recession in 2008 and 2009—recovered quickly compared to most of Europe.

However, despite Russia's sizable budget surplus, it still faces short-term challenges. It remains vulnerable to a prolonged recession in Europe, which is putting renewed pressure on Russia's banking sector. In the medium- and long-term, Russia's growth depends on the success of establishing a new competitive model of economic diversification and a strategy to address Russia's declining and aging population. Although this population is well educated and skilled, it is largely mismatched to the rapidly changing needs of the Russian economy.

Russian society has become increasingly stratified but the middle class is growing. The rich have doubled their wealth in the past 20 years, while almost two-thirds of the population is no better off, and the poor are barely half as wealthy as they were when the Soviet Union fell.[15] One estimate suggests that 25 percent of the Russian population could now be deemed middle class, accounting for nearly 40 percent of the workforce. There has been a change not just in household income but in lifestyles: car ownership, Internet use, and IKEA-visits have all boomed over the past decade.[16]

---

[14] World Bank Data, 2011.

[15] Higher School of Economics (HSE), Moscow.

[16] www.economist.com/comment/1298849.

Civil Society in Russia: One Step Forward, One Step Back

There are more than 114,000 voluntary organizations in Russia, made up of more than 52,000 active NGOs,[17] of which just 3 percent (1,665) are classed by the authorities as charities,[18] although definitions of what constitutes an NGO or indeed a charity are not explicit. Branches and representative offices of international organizations and foreign NGOs number just 240, of which only 10 were newly registered in 2010. This perhaps reflects the difficulty that foreign NGOs in particular experience in establishing a presence in Russia.

Significant economic, social, and political changes over the past 20 years have transformed Russian civil society, taking it from a barren wasteland with virtually no NGO activity, to a developing wilderness with much potential. Prior to the 1990s, if people saw a problem they tried to address it as individual citizens or by forming small groups. The post-Soviet era has seen civil society evolve into a more organized sector, with the help of the overseas organizations that flooded to Russia to set up offices, providing along the way free training and funding for both projects and local NGOs. In Russia today, nonprofit organizations are now predominantly owned and managed by Russian nationals, meeting national needs directly.

Yet despite this transformation, civil society in Russia continues to suffer from dysfunction; caused partly by government legislation and partly by the lack of self-definition and adequate assessment of the status of civil society within the country.

In 2010, the CIVICUS Civil Society Index (CSI)—which aims to assess the state of civil society across a wide range of countries—rated the level of organization of civil society in Russia as relatively high, with a fairly established, institutionalized, and stable infrastructure that offers civil society a reasonable platform on which to conduct its work. However, the Index also suggests that NGOs do not achieve a high degree of impact or significantly contribute to sociopolitical change in

---

[17]This number is lower than figures provided by the Higher School of Economics, which estimates there are 70,000 to 80,000 active NGOs. www .blago.ru/about/faq/russiannko/.

[18]Federal State Statistics Service/Russian Ministry of Justice, www.gks.ru/ bgd/regl/b11_13/IssWWW.exe/Stg/d1/02-12.htm.

TABLE 8.1	CSI CIVIL SOCIETY DIAMOND SCORES FOR SELECTED COUNTRIES				

	Russia	Slovenia	Italy	Argentina	Japan
Civic Engagement	33.7	46.5	48.3	38.8	44.5
Practice of Values	39.8	42.5	42.1	39.6	41.3
Level of Organization	51.4	60.2	63.2	52.6	62.3
Perception of Impact	34.4	31.8	41.6	47.6	55.2
Environment	53.3	64.9	71.8	64.4	75.8

Source: CIVICUS Civil Society Index Shortened Assessment Tool.

Russia (civic engagement), not least because of the lack of systematic interaction with authorities.

The study also found that civic participation in Russia is also limited and there are low levels of trust in NGOs. This suggests that to strengthen civil society there are significant investments needed, including utilizing modern methods of encouraging participation, promoting civil society work more widely, and raising awareness of the best practices of NGO activities.[19]

To put the CIVICUS findings into context, Russia scored lower on most counts than several other countries, which also recently had their civil societies assessed, as shown in Table 8.1.

Russia scores lower than the other four countries recently assessed for its "Civic Engagement" (the level of individual participation in social and political organizations), "Level of Organization" (the degree of institutionalization that characterizes civil society and environment— the status of socioeconomic, sociopolitical, and sociocultural conditions that influence the scope of activity of civil society). For "Practice of Values" (i.e., the extent to which civil society is seen to internalize and model positive values) it scored only slightly higher than Argentina and only marginally higher than Slovenia for "Perception of Impact." Although this may seem surprising for a country of its size and status, it does highlight the relative immaturity of Russian civil society.

---

[19]"Civil Society in Modernising Russia," CIVICUS, 2010.

The freedom and impact of NGOs to influence societal change is partly down to the legal framework in which NGOs operate in the country. For example, establishing and running an NGO in Russia is not an easy process. In 2006 the Russian Federation Law (Russian NGO Law) was introduced, which made it difficult for NGOs to register (or re-register), providing prohibitive reporting requirements accompanied by severe penalties for noncompliance. The law also gave new broad powers of registration bodies to audit the activities of NGOs, particularly those engaged in human rights for example.

The legislation caused widespread concern in civil society circles because it allowed for broad and restrictive interpretation of the law. In addition, some reporting requirements are not only difficult and costly to comply with, but can be hard to understand, leaving room for discretion in determining whom to target when enforcing these rules.

Recently, the growing hope for positive civil society reform has been dealt a huge blow after the Russian parliament passed a bill requiring NGOs engaging in "political activity" and receiving foreign funding to register as "foreign agents."[20]

Under the new bill foreign-funded NGOs involved in political activities must undergo financial audits and issue biannual reports on their activities. Failure to comply is punishable by heavy fines or even a two-year prison sentence. Critics argue that the bill is written in such a way as to be able to regard almost any NGO as a foreign agent and therefore be subjected to harassment from the authorities. Similarly, for foreign or international organizations wishing to make tax-exempt grants to Russian citizens or NGOs, they must be on a list of organizations approved by the Russian Government, with access to this list severely limited.

Yet even before the bill was approved in 2013, evidence of political pressure on NGOs was evident. In 2010 the Moscow City Prosecutor's office summoned some of Russia's most well-known human rights groups, including the Moscow Helsinki Group, Memorial, Public Verdict, and Transparency International, to inform them of the upcoming audits and demand documents. Auditing such organizations is common means of exerting official pressure on them, following a 2006 law that restricted their activities.

---

[20]www.bbc.co.uk/news/world-europe-18732949.

Other organizations could also fall under the bill, including universities and research institutes; even the Russian Geographical Society or the State Hermitage Museum. Some even argue that the Supreme Court may be considered a foreign agent in its financing of judicial reform in Russia involving the World Bank.[21] For the majority of INGOs in Russia, receiving money from abroad, even from inside its own organization, could make them a target for the authorities. It's not hard to see why, in a recent survey of NGOs in Russia, some 40 percent said they do their job while trying not to engage in unnecessary contact with the Russian authorities.[22] This number could rise dramatically.

Despite wide spread protest from civil society and without the fundamental backing of public opinion, more legislation, the "Dima Yakovlev Law" imposing further restrictions on NGOs has received preliminary approval and will likely go into effect in 2013.

One has to wonder what effect this will have on nonprofit organizations operating in Russia and their ability to effect positive change in the country.

Philanthropy in Russia

Finding up-to-date data on giving in Russia is difficult, due largely to the lack of a central focal point for fundraising in the country. Although organizations like CAF Russia and the Russian Donors Forum do exist, there is no "Institute of Fundraising" or "Association of Fundraising Professionals," nor any centralized body through which to conduct detailed analyses of philanthropic activity in the country.

Research on philanthropy is largely carried out by the Center for Studies of Civil Society and Non-Profit Sector "Higher School of Economics" at the Moscow State University. Fundraising as a profession does appear to be growing, however, and the first books on fundraising in the Russian language began to appear in 2009, published by the NGO School Fundraising Master Class.

---

[21] http://philanthropy.ru/analysis/2012/07/10/8086.

[22] Monitoring the State of Civil Society, National Research University "Higher School of Economics." www.hse.ru/org/hse/monitoring/mcs/grans2.

The most recent data available suggests that giving in Russia totaled $10 billion in 2007. Although this is a tiny fraction when compared to the United States (at around $295 billion for the same period),[23] it reflects a huge rise from the $1 million reportedly donated in 1992, when the idea of private philanthropy, after decades of communism and reliance on the state, was completely alien.[24]

In Russia today philanthropy is undertaken predominantly by companies, and supported by oligarch foundations, some mass individual giving, and government subsidies. Money from overseas is also very visible, coming from international governments, bilateral donors, and some international foundations. Following is a look at the status of philanthropy within Russia as well as consideration on how far it still has to go.

Charitable Engagement

According to the *CAF World Giving Index 2011*,[25] which looks at charitable giving behavior across the world, Russia is rated 130 (out of 153 countries) for its charitable giving. The data suggests that only 5 percent of Russians give money, while 23 percent volunteer and 36 percent "help a stranger." Compare that to 2010 and we see a 3 percent growth in volunteering and 7 percent growth in helping a stranger, while giving money to charity fell by 1 percent. Charitable giving is particularly poor among the younger generation of Russians, under the age of 35. Although Russia has moved up eight places from the previous year, this does offer some indication of the challenges faced by NGOs when raising money from the public in Russia.

Of all the countries in Central and Eastern Europe, only Georgia had a lower percentage of the population giving money (4 percent). Even more worrying, however, is that according to the *Index*, Russia has the second lowest percentage of people giving to charity in the entire world. Even poorer countries in Africa and Asia like Madagascar and Vietnam manage to give more.

---

[23] Giving USA Foundation.

[24] www.washingtonpost.com/wp-adv/advertisers/russia/articles/society/20090325/the_state_of_giving.html.

[25] www.cafonline.org/publications/2011-publications/world-giving-index-2011.aspx.

Other research carried out by the Center for Studies of Civil Society and Non-Profit Sector[26] found that only 16 percent of the Russian population participates in any activities of NGOs, and only half of those were members of an NGO.

Major Donors

Russia is home to 96 of the world's billionaires and more than 136,000 HNWIs.[27] Among many ordinary Russian citizens there is an enduring resentment toward those who made their fortunes during the Yeltsin era by buying up Russia's natural resources, oil and gas. Those who didn't get as lucky as the oligarchs during the turbulent 1990s feel that the oligarchs have a duty to give something back to Russian society.[28]

Today, there are few Russian oligarchs[29] without their own private foundation, with most providing significant support for education, culture, and the arts, as well as social needs. Yet many argue that the majority of newly wealthy donors struggle to identify a long-term focus in their giving despite aspiring to embrace strategic philanthropy. Although both the Russian Donors Forum and CAF Russia are trying to help private donors "find themselves" in their private giving and make HNWI philanthropy more effective and accountable, more still needs to be done. Many also argue that it is the responsibility of these wealthy philanthropists to help educate the population about philanthropy (to include wider charitable causes for example), but until they begin to "practice what they preach," fundraising from HNWIs will in reality only be a pipe dream.

Russia's philanthropic revival has been most visibly led by a small number of these wealthy individuals. In 1999, Vladimir Potanin, one of Russia's wealthiest men, established the Vladimir Potanin Foundation,[30] which now spends more than $10 million per year on

---

[26] www.hse.ru/org/hse/monitoring/mcs/ustmcs.

[27] World Wealth Report 2012, Capgemini.

[28] http://russianow.washingtonpost.com/2009/03/the-state-of-giving.php.

[29] http://en.wikipedia.org/wiki/Russian_oligarch.

[30] www.fondpotanin.ru.

education and heritage projects in Russia. Potanin has also been the first to pledge his entire fortune to charity, following in the footsteps of Bill Gates and others equally committed to philanthropy. Many in Russia believe this reflects a broader shift on the part of Russia's business elite away from the "robber baron" mentality of the turbulent 1990s, when many of them earned their fortunes. As Vladimir Potanin said in an *Alliance Magazine* interview in 2007:

> Nowadays we have in Russia a class of people who have become rich and self-sufficient. They feel a natural need to do something good for the others, to share their success, to create a favorable image. We have learnt how to help, but we still face the need to institutionalize philanthropy, to make it compatible with international standards.

In 2006, Potanin also established the Potanin Foundation as a U.K.-registered charity designed purely to make grants to its sister organization, VPF in Russia. It is unclear whether this is for tax purposes, to safeguard wealth, or to enable funds to be raised in the United Kingdom, but with assets of more than $89 million, it provides an interesting approach to Russian philanthropy.

In 2002 Dmitry Zimin, co-creator of major communications firm Vimplecom Inc., founded the Dynasty Foundation,[31] claiming to be the first family charitable foundation in post-Soviet Russia. The Foundation seeks out talented scientists, scholars, and educators, supporting their ideas and projects in the natural and social sciences. Even Russian celebrities have been getting in on the act; like the Russian supermodel Natalia Vodianova, who founded the Naked Heart Foundation[32] in 2004, which is building playgrounds across Russia.

The third highest paid supermodel in the world, worth an estimated $25 million, Vodianova's gone from a poverty-stricken childhood to making a name for herself as a philanthropist. Although she lives in the United Kingdom she is still regarded as one of Russia's most prominent philanthropists. She is also an ambassador for "Hear the World," a global campaign that seeks to raise awareness of hearing and hearing

---

[31] www.dynastyfdn.com.

[32] www.nakedheart.org.

loss around the world. She is a spokesperson for the Tiger Trade Campaign and was a model for Bugaboo's partnership with (RED), the campaign to help eliminate AIDS in Africa. In honor of her philanthropic achievements, *Harper's Bazaar* awarded Vodianova the award for "Inspiration of the Year" in November 2010.

Individuals

Research carried out by the Center for Studies of Civil Society and Non-Profit Sector[33] showed that in terms of philanthropic activity, more than half of respondents they surveyed (51 percent) made charitable donations during the past two or three years, although this includes giving money to individuals (i.e., someone on the street), as well as to a charity. Of those, around 33 percent said they donated rarely or only a few times. The value of donations varies, with around 43 percent of people giving up to 500 Rubles (around $15), 15 percent between 500 and 2,000 rubles ($15–$60) and just 7 percent giving more than 2,000 rubles.

Although giving by the middle classes is growing, the problem is that by and large it bypasses registered charities. The level of suspicion and distrust towards the voluntary sector is very high in Russia due to scandals in the mid-1990s, and the majority of middle class donors prefer to give directly to individuals, for example, in the form of paying for treatment of a seriously ill child, or donating funds to government institutions such as schools or orphanages.

From the comfort of a mature fundraising market like the United Kingdom, it's easy to be downbeat about the situation in Russia. We must recognize that the general philanthropic trend is upward and civil society engagement is rising, albeit very slowly. The real frustration comes from seeing the vast potential for civic engagement in a growing market like Russia being underutilized, undervalued, and undermined.

Corporations

Today, corporate giving in Russia represents around 70 percent of all domestic philanthropy (in comparison with around 5 percent in the

---

[33] www.hse.ru/org/hse/monitoring/mcs/ustmcs.

United States),[34] but is tightly bound by regional obligations inherited from the Soviet past.[35] Often struggling to cope with past and present social obligations, a large percentage of corporate donations are tightly linked to specific towns and communities surrounding companies' production sites, thus making corporate giving less accessible to the wider charitable sector.

Prior to 2000, 98 percent of all charitable giving by Russians was corporate and few companies had any strategy or policy to guide their philanthropy, with no opportunity or mechanism to monitor the results.[36] Few companies established priorities for funding and procedures for choosing the most effective proposals and most simply responded to emergency appeals from communities, petitioners, or local authorities.

Fraud was also a problem. After Russia entered the market economy in the mid-1990s, legal chaos prevailed. Tax incentives for charitable foundations were widely abused with numerous organizations calling themselves *foundations* or *funds* providing cover for shady business activities, money laundering, and currency operations. This resulted in sapping public confidence in foundations and philanthropy, which the sector is still trying to turn around to this day.

Today the situation is markedly different as companies have come to understand how social investments can help them maintain a positive image in communities. Strategic philanthropy has also begun to emerge with many companies realizing that the long-term societal impact of their philanthropy on beneficiaries and society is more important than espousing the amount of funding they give. Some Russians view corporate philanthropy as a form of social compensation for unfair privatization and now that the businesses are thriving, the society expects repayment.

Fundraising in Russia

Today Russian nonprofit organizations primarily raise funds through events that are sponsored by companies promoting their products (and

---

[34] Giving USA Foundation.

[35] www.philanthropyuk.org/quarterly/articles/russia-historic-growth-private -giving.

[36] www.icnl.org/research/journal/vol8iss3/special_3.htm.

often running their own charities) and are supported by individual philanthropists, who increasingly use private foundations to distribute some of their wealth to the masses. Although individual donations from the public have—thus far—lagged behind other income streams, some international and domestic charities are succeeding with a variety of fundraising methodologies such as online and payroll giving.

To date, perhaps Russia's greatest success in public fundraising has been seen via the recent explosive growth of so-called assistance funds—fundraising platforms, mostly online, that are usually initiated by middle-class volunteers, but also sometimes by companies. These funds raise money from the middle class typically to pay for operations of seriously ill children and to help state orphanages or animal shelters—three causes that apparently attract the most interest and funding from new donors in the Russian middle class. Most assistance funds are built on a strong position that they give money "directly" to individuals in need rather than through charities. Despite clearly helping to increase overall giving in Russia, this approach resulted in more than 80 percent of the Russian middle class giving to only two or three causes.

The most notable example is Rusfond, which more than doubled its budget due to a joint fundraising campaign with the first TV channel.[37] The reason for the success of assistance funds is their method of marketing to individual beneficiaries by showing their photographs, giving names and stories, as opposed to raising money for a cause. *The World Giving Index* shows that many of those people giving money to assistance funds believed they were helping a stranger rather than giving money to a charity, in which case philanthropy is perhaps more widespread than usually thought. Yet, arguably these assistance funds do nothing to help with educating the public about how broader active NGOs operate or the widespread opportunities and potential benefits to society that exist beyond funding merely one individual.

INGO Fundraising

Despite the potential fallout from recent moves by the Russian authority to maintain a stranglehold on civil society and keep it apart from

---

[37] http://philanthropynews.alliancemagazine.org/the-new-year-has-started-what's-in-it-for-giving-in-russia/.

CASE STUDY 8.1	SOS CHILDREN'S VILLAGES RUSSIA

SOS Children's Villages—an international charity caring for orphans and abandoned children in more than 130 countries worldwide—is one of a handful of international NGOs currently actively fundraising in Russia. Now with a team of fundraisers in Moscow and St. Petersburg, the charity is raising more than $12 million each year.

Twenty percent of its income comes from the efforts of the fundraising team in Russia, with around half ($1.2 million) coming from Russian government subsidies and the other half being raised from individuals, corporations, and a few major gifts from Russians, as well as a handful of international foundations.

Dmitry Daushev, SOS-Russia's head of fundraising and communications, sees corporate giving as one of the income streams with the greatest potential for growth over the next few years.

"Last year we raised around $368,000 from companies, but I think we can raise much more. There are still many international companies that still don't give enough to charities—or at all—and we as a big international organization have a chance to access this money, perhaps more so than the domestic charities."

Although SOS-Russia has had some success fundraising from wealthy individuals, this is not seen as a priority fundraising area for the charity.

"If we think of the classic donor pyramid, at the top we have a small number of major donors giving perhaps 20,000 or 50,000 euros ($24,792 or $66,798). Many oligarchs decided some years ago what they will support and there is a long queue of people waiting for their money, so accessing this sort of cash is difficult. It's much easier to grow lower level major donors and develop existing, smaller donors."

According to Daushev, one of the biggest challenges is in developing a culture of giving where there has been none and overcoming public skepticism about the role of charities.

"With Russians and charity there has traditionally been a culture of 'doing' rather than 'giving' and a preference for giving directly to individuals in need. The public have a lack of confidence in charities' ability to make a difference. Sometimes people try you out with a 200 euro donation, not because they don't have more money but because they want to see if they will receive good communications and good reports . . . they can then go on to donate much more. We

(Continued)

have a lot of work to do to change public opinion and get public trust. It's changing, but slowly."

Despite the challenges of the regulatory climate for NGOs in Russia, Daushev has great hope for growing income from mass individual giving and is placing an emphasis on securing repeat (ideally regular) donations from the public. Improvements to the infrastructure for charitable giving in the next two to three years, such as the recent availability of direct debit, are desperately needed so that organizations like SOS can develop this income stream.

For developing its individual giving programs, SOS Russia will be focusing on Internet giving, mailings to warm lists, cooperation with the media (inserts in magazines, ads, and so on). Farther down the road, SOS Russia plans to undertake telemarketing as an upgrade tool and, if and when direct debit becomes available as a payment mechanism, some face-to-face activity to recruit new individual donors.

Daushev's advice for any other INGOs looking to enter the Russian market is to concentrate on local programs. Setting up a fundraising office purely to fundraise for projects in other countries is a long way off yet.

outside influence, there are a number of large international NGOs successfully navigating the political storms and reaching into the heart of Russian society. Case studies 8.1 and 8.2 look at two such organizations—SOS Children's Villages Russia and WWF Russia.

Challenges in Russian Philanthropy

To summarize and recap, there are a number of key issues and challenges for those seeking to fundraise in Russia, namely:

- An underdeveloped culture of giving: Following 70 years of state reliance, the concept of charitable giving by average citizens is still fairly new.
- An underdeveloped infrastructure for regular giving: Most of the millions of charitable donations by Russians are one-off donations and while some payment mechanisms such as

CASE STUDY 8.2   WWF RUSSIA

WWF projects in Russia began in 1988, and six years later, in 1994, the organization established the first official Russian WWF office. In 2004, WWF became a Russian national organization and has successfully implemented more than 200 field projects in over 40 regions of Russia, investing more than $50 million in projects in the country. Today, WWF Russia has 145 staff members working in Moscow and in six regional offices, and is widely regarded as one of the most successful INGOs fundraising in Russia today.

WWF Russia's income is predominantly made up of foreign donations, including other WWF organizations, governments in Europe, and U.S. foundations. The largest source of funding comes from the international WWF network ($5.5 million). International and governmental aid agencies, such as the German Federal Ministry for the Environment, World Bank, USAID, Royal Norwegian Ministry of Foreign Affairs, and others, provided a further $2.4 million for WWF's work in Russia.

With regard to fundraising in Russia itself, WWF actively involves Russia's private sector and individuals in nature conservation activities. In 2011, Russian donations contributed some $2.2 million or about 20 percent of the total income for WWF Russia. This was made up of corporate sponsorship and donations of $1.1 million and donations from individuals of $1 million (coming from a total of 16,500 WWF Russia supporters). What these figures don't show, however, is that WWF is leading the way in the relatively new concept of regular giving in Russia.

As a Russian charity receiving funding from overseas, every year WWF Russia is subjected to an independent financial audit. The audit's conclusions are made public through its website, which WWF claims "proves that the organization's financial practices and statements are valid and comply with Russian law." Similarly, "regular internal and independent checks ensure that funds received from our supporters, corporate partners, and international donors are invested in the future of our planet." These statements, taken from the charity's annual report, show, on the one hand that it is complying with stringent government regulation, while on the other attempting to use this as a means of convincing the Russian public that its money is (and would be) properly spent.

(Continued)

Yet despite these pressures to conform, WWF is attempting to remain optimistic in the face of overwhelming pessimism. Igor Chestin, the head of WWF in Russia, commenting on the recent legislation, said:

> I'll try to get the word *foreign agent* to become a sign of quality. We will write our publications using these words. We are not crooks and thieves. We are foreign agents. Therefore, we do not give bribes or kickbacks nor plunder the Russian budget. You can trust us! And this is the image of the country we will create: showing Russians that hundreds of thousands of people support our organization around the world. I think if we act in this way, then after a very short time, the foreign agent is going to sound like Dior sounded compared to the factory *Bolshevik*.

standing orders and payroll giving are available to donors, these are underutilized; and Russia does not—at present—have direct debit systems in place for use by charities. Until 2012, direct debit didn't exist in Russia at all. It has now been approved for use and if the insurance companies, mobile phone companies, and banks start using direct debit, it is hoped people will begin using the system for making donations.

- State policies: Complex and unfriendly tax laws, which tax both the donor and the recipient, along with restrictive policies around foreign funding for NGOs and regulations such as Federal Law 103, which states that only banks—not companies—can transfer donations to charities.
- Public mistrust of charities: Charities are often seen as corrupt or inefficient from the days when individuals abused the concept of charity for their own personal gain.
- Widespread poverty outside affluent places like Moscow and St. Petersburg, in a country with a small urban population.
- Preference for giving directly to individuals in need is fueled by a lack of confidence in charities' ability to really make a difference.
- A culture of doing rather than giving: Many Russians are willing to volunteer their time but charities have struggled to translate this desire to help into a desire to give.

Conclusion

Despite continued efforts to restrict outside influence on Russia via civil society, there have been some developments that have encouraged philanthropy to mature. In 2009, under President Medvedev, who promoted democratic reforms during his term of office, made various amendments to the legal framework for civil society gave some hope for a fairer system of governance including:

- Small NGOs that do not receive foreign funding and have no foreign founders are exempt from formal reporting of annual revenue totaling less than RUB 3 million (approximately $91,000).
- All NGOs may make required reports on their activities publicly available by either posting the reports on their website or publishing the report in selected media.
- Mandatory government audits of NGOs no longer take place annually, but rather every three years—the same as for commercial enterprises.

In 2011 tax law changes made giving to NGOs easier. Previously, when a charity paid for specialized care for children battling ongoing health issues, such as cancer, their families owed taxes on all services following the first treatment because the contribution was treated as personal income. Volunteers who donated time to NGOs had their reimbursed expenses taxed as income and NGOs accepting free advertising were required to pay taxes on the fair-market value of the donated services. The elimination of these rather harsh taxes were partly aimed at reducing the tax burden on NGOs so they could become more self-sustaining, as well as more competitive when competing with public institutions for government contracts.

A subsequent change now offers tax deductions to individuals who donate to registered charities, religious organizations, and other public-benefit NGOs. Russians can now deduct donations that do not exceed 25 percent of their total taxable annual income—even when the money is earmarked for building endowments. But the tax deductions do not apply to all Russians with high incomes as those who generate money from interest and dividends instead of a regular wage are ineligible. Similarly, most of the July 2011 tax law changes do not apply to businesses either. Maria Chertok, director of The Charities Aid Foundation Russia (CAF Russia 2011), said:

> For many years, nothing changed in the legislation and it seemed so hopeless. But here we are now seeing results, so there is progress. By changing several tax laws, some of which already are in effect, the government has formally recognized the important role NGOs play in Russian society.

The latest recent development could really help to transform public giving in Russia. Traditionally Russians don't have checkbooks and donating to a charity required the tedious process of making a bank transfer. In 2012, direct debit was legalized, which many charities hope will encourage donors to move from one-off givers to regular donors. In the past, charities that undertook a fundraising campaign did it often to collect a single donation from each donor it attracted, which is a very expensive way of fundraising and only really affordable for very large charities. This system has also pushed charities into asking for much higher donations, which some argue is unrealistic and obviously unsustainable.[38]

Reducing the amount donors are asked to give, by utilizing facilities like direct debit, may not only help to promote strategic giving, but begin to allow charities to educate donors about the myriad of worthy causes and not just individual cases of need.

ROMANIA BY ANCA ZAHARIA

This section is a snapshot of the fundraising situation in Romania, showing how the country is slowly changing from dependence on external aid for charities and NGOs to greater internal sustainability.

Romania is on the eastern border of the European Union. It is the ninth largest country in the Union, with a population of 19 million. GDP per capita is low at $6,900. The unemployment rate is 7.6 percent, with an average monthly income of $862 and an average pension of $206.

---

[38]http://philanthropynews.alliancemagazine.org/a-suggestion-to-improve -fundraising-in-emerging-markets-just-a-technical-issue/.

Romania hosts a varied population. It is home to 6.5 percent Hungarians, 3.2 percent Gypsies, and also Ukrainians, Turks, Germans, and Greeks.

Although officially a secular state, 86.7 percent of Romanians declare themselves Christian Orthodox.

The Road to Philanthropy in Romania

Romania's road to a modern philanthropic culture has not been a straight one. As long ago as 1924 the country adopted progressive laws—for the time—allowing associations and foundations to operate. In 1945, however, the ruling Communist party suspended these laws—so reducing the independence of NGOs. (Communist regimes throughout Eastern Europe were all nervous about NGOs, seeing them as infringing on the state's role.) Then, in 1990, the government reestablished the original 1924 law. Although this was positive, the resuscitated legislation was not really suitable for contemporary society.

Sadly it wasn't until 2000 to 2004 that a new piece of legislation to encourage NGOs was introduced. This established the National Register of NGOs[39] and allowed them to carry out fundraising activities directly. (There is, however, still much to do. Only in 2012, for example, did direct debits for donations start.)

As a result of these positive changes we currently have 62,680 established NGOs,[40] placing Romania among leading countries[41] in the European Union for number of NGOs by head of population. According to the annual Barometer of NGO Leaders,[42] the main areas of activity for NGOs are social welfare, health care, counseling, education,

---

[39] The social sector in Romania intentionally adopted the term *Nongovernmental organizations* rather than charities or nonprofits.

[40] Ibid., quoting the Romanian Ministry of Justice, www.just.ro/MeniuS tanga/PersonnelInformation/tabid/91/Default.aspx.

[41] Ibid., associative indicator is calculated as number of associations per 1,000 inhabitants.

[42] FDCS, *Barometrul de opinie al liderilor ONG—sondaj national online in randul reprezentantilor ONG din Romania*, 2011.

and training, followed closely by awareness-raising activities, research, advocacy, and monitoring of public policies.

A recent study shows that 63 percent of the organizations have paid staff, a similar percentage to past years. But in the economic downturn, 39 percent of NGOs didn't hire any new personnel. If staff is not growing, volunteering is. And volunteers in Romania are young— many students and young professionals.[43] This compares to Northern Europe where volunteers tend to be older active people.

Fundraising Practices in Romania

The prevailing attitude of NGOs in recent years has been caution with only a few predicting income growth. And in 2013 many NGOs are openly pessimistic.

The main income source for NGOs currently is European Union Structural Funds. Growing sources of income are individual giving, company sponsorships, and grants from international foundations and organizations.[44] But this change in sources is slow and not easy.

Still in its infancy, fundraising in Romania is open to experimentation and is trying out all methods traditionally used in other parts of the world, including:

- Texting has become popular. In parallel, individual giving through SMS with a fixed amount of $2.50 to $6 has also grown. It has proved highly successful for very specific causes: natural disasters, building a children's hospital, purchasing equipment for schools, and so on. However, SMS is really only suitable for large organizations, because one of the criteria for granting a short SMS number is to have a well-planned promotional campaign with a mix of channels—TV, radio, outdoor posters, and print.

---

[43] The communist regime used to force people to work "voluntarily" outside the scope of their profession. It was called *patriotic work*—for example, engineers were made to crop potatoes for two weeks every year. This is why middle-aged people tend to refrain from volunteering.

[44] FDCS, *Barometrul de opinie al liderilor ONG—sondaj national online in randul reprezentantilor ONG din Romania*, 2011.

- Face-to-face fundraising, however, is practically nonexistent in Romania. It was on the rise, but due to a wave of fraudulent practices in the 1990s has fallen out of favor. It remains to be seen if it will rise again.
- Employee giving has been growing steadily in the past few years. Companies have encouraged their staff to give by matching donations. Corporate volunteering is also on the rise among more progressive companies.
- Commercial activities such as thrift shops or sale of goods are not a reliable income source for the third sector in Romania. According to official statistics they actually decreased from 2007. This was from a low base compared to other EU countries.
- Individual giving has benefited from a 2 percent provision, which means that people can now redirect 2 percent of their annual taxes toward a nonprofit cause. This tax break has encouraged individual giving to a point where almost 10 percent of NGOs now count on it. It has also been the catalyst for many creative campaigns.
- Currently on the rise are the micro-loans to organizations or private persons, but they will need more support and time to become fully functional and popular.
- Yet, it's not all good news. One specific concern at present is the growth of mass media–owned foundations. They promote their own causes. A concern is that they shrink the "space" of more professional NGOs.

Conclusion

Romania is a country still facing many social challenges. The terrible orphanages of the 1980s that attracted so much Western attention are gone—many are now efficiently run by the state. But there are many more issues to tackle. Philanthropy is one way to address them, and the good news is that fundraising is becoming more professional and growing.

IN SUMMARY

The philanthropic sector in Central and Eastern Europe is in a state of flux, although clearly there are successes emerging and some encouraging signs of progress in establishing a solid civil sector. Russia's

CASE STUDY 8.3 ROMANIAN RED CROSS

The first social assistance institution in Romania—*Domnita Balasa* Women's Asylum—was established in the capital in 1751. In 1876 Prince Carol I signed a decree establishing the Romanian Red Cross.[45] The organization today is the largest NGO in Romania with more than 6,000 volunteers, 50,000 members, and 400,000 beneficiaries.

These are challenging times for the Society. The income of the Red Cross has fallen dramatically in the past three years. Twenty years after the fall of Communism, the Red Cross National Societies of the West have mostly withdrawn their financial or material support. Romania's needs are not as dire as they were.

As is the case everywhere in the world, the Romanian Red Cross has seen a decline in government funding of its programs and projects.

International aid instead has gone to countries seen as more in need: Sahel, Pakistan, Afghanistan. The Romanian Red Cross needs to shift its mentality from an assisted National Society to an agency able to raise funds by itself.

For us the most sustainable source of income is the One Percent Law. This law obliges entities organizing public shows, be it sports, dance, music, cinema events, to donate to the Romanian Red Cross 1 percent of the value of the tickets sold.

More unusually we have seen a rise in corporate support. CSR activities are growing as the public demands more quality and transparency from corporate agencies. Companies are moving away from a simple public relations approach toward substantial support for the communities where they are engaged.

middle class, for example, is showing surprising strength in its giving, and in Romania, newer fundraising methods like texting are popular. It will be interesting to see how nonprofits in the region respond to the challenges in front of them.

---

[45]Saulean Daniel and Carmen Epure, Defining the Nonprofit Sector: Romania, Working Papers of the Johns Hopkins Comparative Nonprofit Sector Project, no. 32, edited by Lester M. Salamon and Helmut K. Anheier, 1998.

Africa

MIKE MUCHILWA

Africa is the least understood continent when it comes to philanthropy and giving. Few understand African giving patterns and philanthropic motivations. To gain some insight into these patterns and motivations, this chapter first presents an overview of philanthropy and some the forces driving change. Two countries with well-developed nonprofit sectors are then presented, Kenya and South Africa.

Many consider South Africa to be the only bright spot for philanthropy on the continent. Other countries are seen as beneficiaries only, but nothing could be further from the truth. All Africans have a great tradition of giving and sharing what they have. They often give on the spur of the moment. This spontaneity may actually result in giving proportionally more than what their Western counterparts do. Africans do not give based on the amount of wealth they possess—they feel a responsibility for those in need. It is what the South Africans call *Ubuntu*.

Africans give to a wide range of causes. They give to mark social events such as weddings and funerals and to help individuals with health care (hospital bills and surgery) and with education (fees). Africans also give for organizational purposes such as the building of schools, health centers, and water projects. They also look after the less fortunate in the community—the widows and orphans.

GIVING TO NGOS IN AFRICA

Outside of South Africa, people are less likely to support NGOs than is the case in other parts of the world. The community in general does not believe that they need their money. To the contrary, they feel that they need not support the NGOs because they are believed to be literally swimming in money! The NGOs have acquired an image of having highly paid staff driving huge fuel-guzzling cars and working in sleek modern offices. Although this makes them attractive as employers and business customers, it also makes it harder for them to raise funds from individuals. They raise most of their funding from institutions: bilateral and multilateral donors, foundations, and the government.

There have been some exceptions, however. The Red Cross has managed to mobilize significant funds from both individual and corporate entities for its disaster work during famine. The 2011 Kenyan's for Kenya campaign for drought victims in the country raised a record $7,951,350 or (671,784,062 shillings KES), against an initial target of $5,895,000 (500 million KES). An additional $336,615 in in-kind materials and $2,962,500 in in-kind services was raised. The campaign was successful because the Red Cross worked with a consortium of organizations, including the media telecommunications companies, banks, and other businesses. The Red Cross had built a strong brand in the local market by its presence during disasters and therefore many Kenyans feel that their money is well used. Although the success of this campaign is remarkable, Kenyans have shown great generosity at other times in the face of tragedies like famine. Their generosity is now being extended to other nations, with Kenyans donating $23,580 following the tsunami in Japan in 2011 and the earthquake in Haiti in 2010. The same level of generosity is common elsewhere in Africa.

CASE STUDY 9.1   DAR-ES-SALAAM GOAT RACE

The first goat race in East Africa was introduced in 2001 by Paul Joynson-Hicks, and was modeled on a pig race held in Zimbabwe in 1991 for the 50th birthday of a well-known horse breeder. Members of Uganda's business community, including Joynson-Hicks, decided that this novel type of race would help raise charitable funds. Goats were preferable to pigs, as goats were more available and easier to handle. Joynson-Hicks brought the concept to Tanzania in 2001.

(Continued)

The Dar-es-Salaam goat race is the biggest event of its kind in Tanzania. The charitable fundraising event is held at the Leaders Club in Dar-es-Salaam. The Goat Races are a fun day out for all of the family. More than 3,000 people attend, encouraged by a low entrance fee of about $2. Tickets usually sell out in two weeks and in 2011, the event raised $280,000.

Money is raised through:

- Sponsorship of races
- Ticket sales
- Goat buying
- Betting
- Generous donations from companies and individuals

Other income-generating activities include:

- A special children's play area with a $1.28 entrance fee. Entertainments include jumping castle, face painting, organized games, and much more
- Raffle prizes
- Food and drinks
- Fancy dress and hat competitions

Nearly 50 of Tanzania's biggest companies have sponsored the event including Holiday Inn, British Airways, Tigo, Tanzania Breweries Limited, Safmarine, Oryx, Tanzania Printers, and Monier.

GIVING FOR RELIGIOUS PURPOSES

Churches and their charitable work attract far more money than do NGOs. After giving unto "Caesar what is Caesar's," Africans willingly give to "God what is God's," and some churches raise large amounts of money during regular Sunday collections and for special projects. They can collect so much that specialized security is needed to transport this money to the bank. Those churches that have adapted sophisticated fundraising strategies may have huge resources at their disposal. On the other hand, those less strategic in their fundraising efforts are struggling to make ends meet.

Some churches have set up development arms that manage their philanthropic work. An example of this is the Anglican Development

Services (ADS) that is based in Kenya. The ADS raises funds not only from churches but also from bilateral sources, foundations, and trusts. Churches engage in a variety of charitable work. The Nairobi Chapel and its sister churches, for example, provide health care services for the very poor. The fundraising success of some of the churches demonstrate the huge potential that exists to raise funds on the continent as long as an organization has a clear strategy, a mission that Africans can identify with, and the right image.

THE LACK OF INFORMATION ON AFRICAN PHILANTHROPY

The dearth of information on the continent about philanthropy in general must be addressed. If philanthropy is to be promoted, its growth must be measurable.

Volunteering in Africa

In Africa, helping others is a simply part of your responsibility as a member of the community. The time spent organizing community events or projects, giving advice, working with CBOs (community-based organizations) or short-term NGO work is not considered volunteering. Few consider community policing, environmental clean-ups, and tree planting as volunteer work. Nor is organizing fundraisers for funerals, weddings, or the health care or educational needs of individuals thought of as volunteer work. Time spent on boards or committees is not counted as such.

Some do volunteer for NGOs and other development organizations. These volunteers may be motivated by a desire to make a difference, but are also often seeking valuable work experience. Many will happily work for free if it will improve their employment prospects. Most of the NGOs are tracking the contributions of their volunteer workers.

In many small, grassroots organizations the tracking of volunteer time is irregular and its valuation is inconsistent. For instance, the volunteer time of a small women-based CBO that is looking after orphans will not be considered monetarily as valuable as volunteer time for a more professional nonprofit in part because the CBO will not be tracking the time volunteers spend managing its operations, looking after the orphans on a daily basis in their homes—or the value of the food, accommodation, clothing, and other support that the women will provide. There may be millions of CBOs on the continent, and the lack of information about them is a largely uncaptured aspect of African philanthropy.

Until recently no one saw a need to track this kind of activity. Although the attitude of "it's free time anyway, so why put a price on it?" lingers, there is a growing recognition of the value of voluntary time and volunteering in a more formal sense is on the rise. VSO Jitolee[1] is playing a big role in formalizing volunteerism within East Africa. It has been able to get professionals from the region to volunteer their skills not only within East Africa, but in other countries—Asia especially. Some companies, such as General Motors in East Africa, allow their employees to volunteer on company time. In the 1990s, employees of the Kenya Management Assistance Program volunteered their time to help small and medium-size businesses. This kind of volunteering is likely to become more popular as part of CSR and Corporate Social Investment (CSI) activities.

Foreign Influences

A heavy reliance on foreign funding also tends to distort the picture of African philanthropy. NGOs, trusts, foundations, and the manner in which they operate are alien to Africa's culture. Paid staff work because they are paid to and not out of Ubuntu. Huge overheads and budgets, complex vision and mission statements, are not part of the Ubuntu philosophy. It is therefore not surprising that Africans consider these development actors as vehicles through which wealth from the rich West is channeled to the poor South. It mirrors the common colonially inspired belief in many African communities about the wealth of the *Mzungu* (white man).

---

[1]VSO is the world's leading independent international development organization that works through volunteers to fight poverty in developing countries. VSO Jitolee recruits skilled volunteers, from Kenya and Uganda, with relevant professional qualifications and a minimum of two years' work experience from a range of disciplines to live and work in local communities (in Africa and Asia), sharing skills and changing lives for periods between six months and two years.

The close association between nonprofits with the West rein-forces the belief that NGOs are rich. It is therefore not surprising that many Africans in the continent do not understand why NGOs would require money from them. The grandiose lifestyle of some NGOs—huge cars, large salaries, and lavish offices—do not help. Africans are selective about whom they share their limited resources with and non-profits are not high on the list.

PHILANTHROPY AND OTHER SUPPORT

Major Donors

Africa's wealth is growing. According to consultants Merrill Lynch and Capgemini, there are now 100,000 Africans with at least $1 million to invest in for-profit as well as nonprofit enterprises. Newly rich indi-viduals in Africa are now giving away more money than ever before, either directly or through foundations. For example, 73-year-old The-ophilus Yakubu Danjuma, the magnate of South Atlantic Petroleum, which is an indigenous oil exploration and production company, granted $100 million to his charity, the TY Danjuma Foundation.[2] He is Nigeria's biggest philanthropist and his charity is one of the larg-est in Africa. He says: "This was extra money I did not know what to do with. I did not just want to leave the money in the bank. At some point, I thought about saving the money for my children, but I decided against it. I realized that they could fight over the money after I'm dead. So, I decided, why not give back to my people." Based in Abuja, Nigeria, the Foundation grant-making focus is education, free health care, policy advocacy, and poverty alleviation.

He is not alone. Other large-scale philanthropists include Francois van Niekerk ($170 million), Allan Gray ($150 million), Donald Gordon ($50 million), Mark Shuttleworth ($20 million), Jay Naidoo, Cyril Ramaphosa, Tokyo Sexwale, and Patrice Motsepe. These new philan-thropists are influenced not only by local traditions of giving, but also by the actions of well-known philanthropists such as Bill Gates, George Soros, and Ted Turner. Not all major philanthropists set up a founda-tion. They include successful businesspeople such as Manu Chandaria of Kenya and Reginald Mengi of Tanzania.

---

[2] www.tydanjumafoundation.org.

Growing Middle Class

The growing African middle class is having a profound effect on philanthropic practices. According to the African Development Bank, Africa's middle class had 313 million people as of 2010. This represented 34 percent of the continent's population and it is predicted to grow to 42 percent of the population or 1.1 billion people by 2060.

This growing urban middle class has weaker links with its rural roots and extended family. They are more likely to give to wider philanthropic causes than Africans who have stronger links with their rural origins (and are more likely to channel more resources home). Members of the middle class are more likely to give to the NGOs they have seen in action—those they believe can be entrusted to deliver support to those in need. Growing media coverage of disasters coupled with more appeals for aid encourage the middle class to give. Peer pressure, especially from friends and work colleagues, also motivates middle class citizens to give. It is not uncommon for friends and working colleagues to ask each other for support, for example, to sponsor their participation in fundraising competitive events. Eventually this growing middle class and its disposable income will result in more and greater donations to the charities that know how to reach them.

Corporations

African companies, largely from South Africa, West Africa (Nigeria and Ghana), and East Africa (Kenya) are spreading their wings across the continent in banking, retail, insurance, fast foods, and manufacturing, some growing into African multinationals. These include KCB, Equity, ECO, and UBA Banks, Nakumatt, Uchumi, and Tuskies supermarkets, East African Breweries, Castle Breweries, MTN, Nandos, and Steers, among others. Some are donating funds in these countries to insinuate themselves in these new markets. Many of them have established foundations to support their work and are changing the social investment face of the continent. These include the Safaricom Foundation, East African Breweries Foundation, and KCB Foundations.

However, it's not just corporate entities and rich individuals establishing foundations. Politicians have also stepped in. This includes the Nelson Mandela Foundation, Julius Nyerere Foundation, and Moi Foundation. These foundations attract both national and international donors—individuals, companies, foundations, as well as institutional donors.

CASE STUDY 9.2   THE SAFARICOM FOUNDATION

The Safaricom Foundation was established in August 2003. It is funded by Safaricom Limited and the Vodafone Group Foundation. Its vision is "a prosperous Kenya, where people's lives are positively transformed." Its mission is "to partner with local communities to address social, economic, and environmental issues to foster positive and lasting change." Its focus is strengthening the social fabric of communities and contributing toward changing lives in a sustainable way. Safaricom Foundations strategic direction is based on:

- Making a sustainable contribution toward the provision of health care, education, and water for the people of Kenya.
- Providing sustainable support for the preservation of the Kenyan environment and the management of its natural resources.
- Driving forward the economic empowerment of the Kenyan nation.
- The preservation and promotion of Kenya's national heritage in terms of sports, music, arts, and culture.
- Providing timely responses to any national emergencies that may occur.
- Providing a forum whereby Safaricom employees may interact with, be inspired by, and provide support for the many community initiatives identified by the Foundation.
- Influencing innovation and best practice in the broader Corporate Social Responsibility agenda.

The Foundation supports initiatives and projects that provide sustainable solutions to the most pressing social challenges. Its areas of focus are education, health, economic empowerment, environmental conservation, arts and culture, music and sports, disasters and humanitarian emergencies. It aims to support Kenya's development agenda as well as the Millennium Development Goals. The Foundation supports projects that have potential to achieve positive, long-term, social, economic, and environmental impact without jeopardizing the needs of future generations. The Foundation funds projects that are to be implemented in Kenya by legally constituted and registered community groups and NGOs.

The Foundation provides Safaricom with a formal process for charitable contributions to communities, community groups, and

(Continued)

NGOs in Kenya, which are key partners in responding to social and economic development issues in the country. It supports philanthropy through financial and technical support and with the participation of Safaricom Limited staff. The participation of Safaricom staff is meant to make a sustainable difference in communities, as it believes that volunteerism is at the heart of sustainable CSI partnerships. Safaricom actively promotes staff involvement in the foundations activities. This is not limited to payroll giving, fundraising, matching grants, and the Staff Sponsors program. Each member of the staff is entitled to four CSI leave days per year where they can work with or in any of the Foundation's projects or activities. The staff fundraising program motivates staff members to actively participate in building their communities through the *Pamoja* (meaning *oneness* in Kiswahili) scheme. Under the scheme, Safaricom provides 90 percent to match the 10 percent raised by individual employees or teams for projects of their choice.

Through the Safaricom Foundation, Safaricom goes beyond the old CSI model of occasional donations. The foundation makes all-year investments in its engagement with local communities. The foundation shares its expertise, financial and human resources to support community initiatives that aim to bring economic, social, and environmental benefits to local communities targeting the marginalized, vulnerable, and less privileged in particular. It works in partnership with community groups, civil society organizations, NGOs, and other corporate organizations whose objectives are consistent with the Foundation's vision, mission, and values. Since its establishment, the organization has grown to become the largest local foundation in Kenya providing $2.39 million per year.

Africa's NGOs

The continent is beginning to see the growth of African NGOs. Greater financial demands on people's incomes, urbanization, and changing lifestyles are weakening the traditional extended family and community structures. More responsibility for welfare will be shifted to the state and with that, the threat of many in need falling between the cracks will also grow. As Western support becomes less reliable, philanthropy will play an increasingly important role in supporting social development in Africa. More NGOs will be needed to deliver support.

One such NGO is AMREF that not only has operations in Tanzania and Uganda in addition to its Kenya operations, but also has fundraising offices in several Western countries. It is only a matter of time before more African NGOs follow the example of successful fundraising churches like the Winners Chapel and establish their own fundraising operations in Africa and the West. Not only are NGOs springing up in Africa, international NGOs are increasingly registering their local offices independent of their mother organizations. Organizations that have followed this route include Action Aid, Care International, Plan International, and Christoffel Blindenmission International (CBM).

FAIR TRADE AND SOCIAL ENTERPRISE IN AFRICA

The Fair Trade movement has witnessed substantial growth in the continent in recent years. Even though it has existed in Africa for the past three decades, it is only in the past 10 years that African Fair Trade Networks have emerged that have revitalized the global Fair Trade movement. Networks such as the Confederation of Fair Trade in Africa (COFTA), the Kenya Federation of Alternative Trade (KEFAT), and Tanzania Federation of Alternative Trade (TAFAT) and others, are now influencing the development of the movement within and outside the continent. Food-oriented Fair Trade organizations include Mpanga Tea, Gikanda, and Iriaini cooperatives in Kenya; KNCU and KCU coffee cooperatives in Tanzania; and Eswathini in Swaziland.

In addition to food cooperatives and plantations, a host of social enterprises that access small producers to markets in the West have entered the market. Some of the nonfood social enterprises include Kazuri Beads, Undugu Fair Trade, KICK Trading, Smolart, KISAC Fair Trade, and Bombolulu in Kenya; Kwanza Trading, Mavelous Boutique, and Mikono in Tanzania; Gone Rural in Swaziland; and Streetwise in South Africa. They have capitalized on local resources to support marginalized producers through improved market access. Fair Trade organizations are blazing the path of social enterprises and may provide viable alternative models to meet some of the development challenges facing the continent.

A FOCUS ON TWO COUNTRIES

The rest of this chapter focuses on Kenya and South Africa, the biggest economies in East Africa and Southern Africa respectively. They also have the best-developed nonprofit sectors and so provide some valuable insights into philanthropy in Africa.

Kenya

Kenya has one of the most vibrant philanthropic environments in Africa. The country is home to the East African Association of Grant Makers as well as the Kenya Association of Fundraising Professionals—the first association of its kind in Africa.

Kenya's population of 40 million is young with just under half (42.2 percent) being aged between 0 and 14 years, 55.5 percent ranging from 16 to 64 years in age with a paltry 2.7 percent aged above 65 years. There are slightly more men than women within the 0 to 64 age bracket, but the reverse is true for those aged above 65 years. Thirty percent of the population lives in urban areas with the rate of urbanization growing at 4.2 percent annually. It has an unemployment rate of 40 percent as of 2010. Half of its population earns less than $2 per day. Kenya's youthful population and the high unemployment rate keep the average disposable income low and this affects philanthropy negatively.

The life expectancy for women is 60 years while it is 58.9 years for men. One and a half million people, 6.3 percent of the population, were living with AIDS and HIV in 2009 and 80,000 Kenyans succumb to the disease annually. AIDS and HIV have exacted an enormous toll on families, often taking the life of one or both breadwinners. Huge resources have been dedicated to containing the pandemic and thus there is less available for other needs such as small enterprise development, agriculture, and water.

Kenya covers an area of 362,039 miles (582,646 square kilometers), making it slightly bigger than France. It's a beautiful country with a long coast straddling the Indian Ocean. Its strategic location on the equator and the East African coast has increased its importance in the region, especially to investors. Part of its appeal is accessibility—the relatively short flying time from key locations—8 to 10 hours from major European cities and about 16 to 20 hours from North American cities. Kenya Airways flies to most of the important cities in Africa, Asia, and Europe.

The diversity of wildlife and varied natural beauty of the landscape and the fascinating Kenyans themselves, including the famous Maasai, have made the country one of the world's favorite filming locations. Kenya is a product that is easy to sell to potential donors and the country has a longer list of institutional donors than any other in Africa. Many of Kenya's hotels and other businesses related to tourism support philanthropy to local communities.

Some areas of Kenya, however, suffer from famine and high levels of poverty. The northern, northeastern, and parts of the eastern regions are arid and semi-arid. Pastoralism and limited amounts of agriculture are practiced here. These areas have high numbers of NGOs and relief organizations and are often the target of high-profile fundraising events such as the Kenyans for Kenya Campaign (see Case Study 9.1 in this chapter).

Kenya is the largest nonmineral-based economy on the continent with a GDP of $66 billion as of 2011. It has a population of 40 million people and a GDP of $66 billion as of 2011. The service sector is the largest, contributing 62 percent to the GDP, followed by agriculture (22 percent) and industry (16 percent). Tourism, horticulture, tea and coffee, as well as financial services, construction, and transport are also key income earners.

Kenya is emerging as a fast-growing key information, communication, and technology (ICT) hub within the region. The country pioneered mobile phone–based money transfer and payment solutions through the award-winning MPESA that is now in 70 other countries. Twenty-five to 30 percent of Kenya's GDP is transferred through MPESA annually. Other mobile phone platforms such as YuCash, Airtel Money, and Orange Cash also do well. The presence of three undersea cables has supported the rapid growth of ICT-based services and increased the rapid adoption of Internet and social websites such as Twitter and Facebook. The country is now in the process of developing a "Silicon Savannah" city at Konza in Machakos.

ICTs have been crucial to fundraising efforts such as the Kenyans for Kenya Campaigns. Most of the contributions by individuals were made through mobile money transfer services such as MPESA, Airtel Money, and YuCash. Kenyan innovations in this area—such as Ushahidi, a nonprofit company offering free and open source software—have also been critical in coordinating aid efforts in Haiti and elsewhere.

Recent discoveries of valuable minerals and oil are expected to significantly change Kenya's economy in the coming decade and hasten its development into a middle-income country. Currently Kenyans earn $800 annually, but by 2020 their annual earnings will rise to $1,000, the middle-income country threshold. As South Africa has already experienced, improvement in earning power will reduce the number of outside donors. Kenya will have to rely on its own philanthropy and its own government to support social development and nonprofits.

The country has 44 ethnic groupings, with non-Africans (Asian, European, and Arab) accounting for just 1 percent of the population. The official languages are English and Kiswahili. The familiarity with English has made it easier for Kenyans to raise funds from English-speaking countries. Kenya's literacy levels are 79.7 percent. Its well-educated workforce rivals South Africa's as Africa's best.

Nearly half the population is Protestant (45 percent), 33 percent Roman Catholic, 10 percent Muslim, 10 percent indigenous believers, and 2 percent other. All of these religions have strong philanthropic traditions.

Kenya's Nonprofit Sector
Regulation of Nonprofits

There are many forms of nonprofits in Kenya. These include NGOs, nonprofit companies, trusts, faith-based organizations, societies, community-based organizations, and self-help groups. They are regulated by the following entities:

- NGO Coordination Board for NGOs
- Registrar of Companies for companies limited by guarantee without share capital
- Registrar of Societies for voluntary associations
- Ministry of Lands for Trusts
- Ministry of Culture and Social Services for CBOs

The NGO Coordination Board is responsible for registering national and international NGOs. According to the NGO Coordination Act (1990) an NGO is "a private voluntary grouping of individuals or associations, not operated for profit or for other commercial purposes but which have organized themselves nationally or internationally for the benefit of the public at large and for the promotion of social welfare, development, charity, or research in the areas inclusive of, but not restricted to, health, relief, agriculture, education, industry, and the supply of amenities and services."

Kenya has 8,500 registered NGOs. On registration, NGOs automatically become members of the NGO Council. The 1995 NGO Act establishes the responsibilities and functions of the NGO Council, a self-regulatory body. The Council has a Code of Conduct that its members are meant to observe. NGOs are required to submit annual returns each year so that the NGO Council's Board can get a general picture of the sector and identify areas requiring attention. Anyone can purchase these reports. If an organization does not provide reports and the NGO Council's Board has reason to believe that it is no longer operational, it can be deregistered after placing a notice in the *Kenya Gazette*, during which the NGO has 30 days to provide proof of its operations and existence.

The NGO Council has a regulatory committee responsible for disciplining errant NGOs. The committee has the power to hear complaints and recommend disciplinary action to the NGO Council Board including the cancellation and suspension of registration. (Unfortunately the Council has been bogged down in leadership squabbles over the past decade and few NGOs take it seriously.)

There are several other ways for nonprofit organizations to register. Prior to 1990 when the NGO Act was passed, many nonprofits registered under the Companies Act of 1959, which allows nonprofits to register with the Registrar of Companies. Nonprofit societies and associations can also register with the Registrar of Societies under the Societies Act of 1968. Trusts are registered with the Ministry of Lands under the Trustees Perpetual Succession Act of 1982. The Ministry of Culture and Social Services is responsible for the registration of community-based organizations. There are more than 200,000 CBOs registered in Kenya.

Size of Sector

The nonprofit sector (NGOs, CBOs, associations) was comprised of at least 220,000 organizations in 2002 and the annual income of NGOs alone was $1 billion, approximately 3 percent of GDP. In 2011 NGOs reporting to the NGO Coordination Board earned $1.88 billion. This did not include the incomes of NGOs that failed to report to the NGO Board or nonprofits falling under other regulators. The bulk of this money, however, was from foreign donors making Kenyan NGOs very vulnerable to changes in funding. NGOs employ 50,000 people. Four hundred of the 8,000 registered NGOs are INGOs.

Influences in Giving

Harambee is a Kenyan tradition of community fundraising. Harambee literally means *all pull together* in Kiswahili, and is also the official motto of Kenya and appears on its coat of arms.

Following Kenya's independence in 1963, the first prime minister, and later first president of Kenya, Jomo Kenyatta, adopted harambee as a concept of pulling the country together to build a new nation. He encouraged communities to work together to raise funds for all sorts of local projects. Individual harambees have been raised as more than $10 million. Harambees are governed by the Public Collections Act but not many organizers are aware of this.

Harambees are used for varied purposes. They raise funds for education, health, and water projects. They raise funds to construct buildings (including churches), to buy school buses, and to purchase equipment. Harambees are used to support national teams so that they can participate in international sporting events. They are used to raise money for the education of individuals and for their health treatment, weddings, and funerals. NGOs are not key beneficiaries of the harambee system, although NGOs that care for orphans, and CBOs have better luck with it.

Harambee events may range from informal affairs lasting a few hours, in which invitations are spread by word of mouth, to formal, multiday events advertised in newspapers. Technology is also used— money transfer systems such as MPESA, Airtel Money, and Yu Cash have made it easy and economical to give, and Facebook has made it easy to connect people with various causes. Harambee events can include auctions and raffles.

This traditional fundraising approach may have had its day as the harambee market has become oversaturated. High inflation and other economic challenges have led to more and more harambees to be organized to keep up with social needs. The overgrowth has negatively affected the success of the whole. Organizers have to be careful in planning the events if they hope meet their fundraising targets.

Although there is no information available on how much is collected by religious institutions in Kenya, there is no doubt that religion plays a key role in philanthropy. Ten percent of Kenya's population, 4 million people as previously noted, is Muslim. Many of them regularly give to philanthropy. This is based on Zakat and Sadaqah. Zakat is one of the personal obligations of Islam (for more on Islamic giving, see Chapter 10 on MENA). Considered a wealth tax, it is said to cover 2.5 percent of incomes. There is also Sadaqah that is based on voluntary charitable giving. The poor will surround mosques during Friday prayers where they are given money by worshippers. Muslims give to NGOs, CBOs, and projects usually linked to the Islamic faith.

Christians tithe for church-related work such as missions and operations. However, with churches taking a more prominent role in development, targeted fundraising has become more common. Special collections during church service and harambees are used for particular projects like buying real estate, building churches, schools, and broadcasting facilities. Churches will also fundraise to help the less fortunate during times of famine and other disasters.

Kenyans in general are generous for emergency relief and have been known to contribute large amounts of cash and in-kind resources to help out during natural disasters like droughts, and man-made disasters like the U.S. Embassy terrorist bombing of 1998 killing 81 persons and the 2011 pipeline explosion in the Sinai slums that killed 75 and injured many more people. (This clearly demonstrates the potential to raise funds at home, but NGOs remain fixated on Western donors.)

Infrastructure

Donated income to NGOs is not taxed. NGOs, however, need to apply for tax exemptions for import taxes and VAT (value added tax). To be exempt from tax, the NGO must have been established for public benefit such as poverty reduction, education, or religious purposes. The Commissioner of Income Tax must be convinced that the income benefits the residents of Kenya and is spent within the country.

In addition, the earned income of nonprofits is exempt if it meets one of the following requirements:

- The business is carried on in the course of advancing the organization's stipulated purposes.
- The business is conducted mainly by beneficiaries of those purposes.

- The gains or profits consist of rents (including premiums or similar consideration in the nature of rent) received from leasing land and attendant chattels.

In addition businesses and individuals can deduct cash donations made to registered and tax exempt NGOs from their income tax.

Projects approved by the Minister of Finance such as building public schools, hospitals, or roads and approved scientific research by universities and research institutes are also tax exempt.

NGOs seeking tax exemptions from VAT need to apply though the NGO Council's Board to the Minister of Finance. However, to qualify it must not only be registered under the NGO or Societies Acts (or exempted from doing so) but also must be exempt from tax under the Income Tax Act. The VAT Act also exempts services to members performed by professional, trade, and labor associations, as well as educational, political, religious, welfare, and other philanthropic associations. INGOs in Kenya include:

- Action Aid International
- Care International
- Concern Worldwide
- Médecins Sans Frontières/Doctors Without Borders (MSF)
- Oxfam International
- Plan International
- Save the Children International
- Family Health International
- ACT International
- International Committee of the Red Cross
- World Vision International
- Practical Action
- Catholic Relief Services
- World Neighbors

Umbrella Organizations
In addition to the NGO Council, Kenya has several umbrella bodies and networks. These include:

- The National Civil Society Congress, a voluntary umbrella body whose objectives include supporting interaction and exchange of information.

- National Community-Based Organization Council, representing community-based organizations.
- Kenya AIDS NGOs Consortium (KANCO), representing civil society organizations involved in HIV, AIDS, and TB activities.
- Constitutional and Reform Education Consortium, a national organization that supports the coordination and capacity building of civil society.
- PeaceNet Kenya involves civil society organizations involved in peace and reconciliation, justice and conflict resolution in Kenya.

Philanthropy and Other Support in Kenya
Individuals

Kenyans, like other Africans, give for all kinds of initiatives. Giving to help the community is ingrained in their psyche. Unfortunately, most NGOs have not been able to tap into this. One reason is that NGOs have traditionally been focused on institutional donors and consider individual gifts too small to matter and the tedious process of collecting them not worth the effort.

Technology

Technology has been a real a game changer for nonprofits in Kenya. Although the traditional harambees are still the best way in Kenya to raise funds from individuals, technology is creating some viable alternatives. The availability of mobile money transfer platforms makes giving economical and convenient. Kenyans can contribute as little as 12 cents (KES 10)—the rich and poor alike can support causes of national interest. Without these platforms, the Red Cross, Kenyans for Kenya campaign would not have been as successful as it was. Social sites such as Facebook and Twitter are also transforming Kenyan giving. For example, people have raised funds quickly from individuals for costly medical procedures.

Diaspora Giving

The media has become extremely powerful across East Africa in influencing the public on various issues including philanthropy. The Kenyans for Kenya campaign would not have been as successful without the full support of the media. The media is not only influential at home, its influence extends outside of the country.

Many Kenyan newspapers and TV and radio stations are available now on the Internet and the diaspora is much better informed of social and political issues back home. More expatriates are contributing to initiatives such as Kenyans for Kenya. This is still a largely untapped market. Given that they sent home more than an estimated $900 million in 2011, up from $609 million in 2009, it is a market that non-profits cannot afford to ignore.

Credit Cards

Not many Kenyans use or trust credit cards. They prefer to make a one-time contribution rather than regular pledged payments. This is due in part to uncertainty about their future economic security.

ATMs

In May 2010, the Imperial Bank, Kenya, partnered with UNICEF to launch the first ATM fundraising campaign in the region. It was called the *Key in Your Donation* campaign. To make a donation, donors simply had to visit any Pesa Point ATM in 120 locations countrywide, select the payment tab on the screen and choose the UNICEF option. There is no information on how much money was actually raised.

Special Events

Special events have also gained currency as a great tool to fundraise from individuals. In fact Africa boasts some of the most innovative events in the world. Events like the Rhino Charge, Safaricom Marathon, and Standard Chartered Marathon raise significant amounts.

Foundations

Significant foundations that have a strong presence in the country include U.S. foundations like the Bill and Melinda Gates Foundation, Ford Foundation, Rockefeller Foundation, and the Open Society Initiative. Others include Aga Khan Foundation and Hans Seidel Foundation. There are several other foundations and trusts that have funded activities in the country but have no presence. These include Stephen Lewis Foundation and Richard Gere Foundation. The international foundations supporting local initiatives include:

- Ford Foundation
- Rockefeller Foundation

- Welcome Trust
- Kleinwort Charitable Trust
- Aga Khan Foundation
- Bill and Melinda Gates Foundation
- Hans Seidel Foundation
- Friedrich Neumann Foundation for Freedom
- Richard Gere Foundation
- Japan Trust
- Netherland Trust Fund
- Packard Foundation
- Stephen Lewis Foundation
- Elton John Foundation

And various Kenyan foundations include:

- Safaricom Foundation
- East African Breweries Foundation
- East African Portland Foundation
- Bamburi Foundation
- Rattansi Trust
- House of Manji Foundation

Corporations

More Kenyan companies are engaging in CSR and CSI than ever before. This trend mirrors those happening in many other African countries. There is pressure on multinationals and their subsidiaries, especially in Europe, to support CSR and CSI activities. The intense competition for market share coupled with corporate leadership that believes in the need to invest in their communities, has also contributed positively to CSR and CSI in Kenya and Africa in general. There are still relatively few companies currently engaged in CSR and CSI, but the number is increasing.

In Kenya, companies involved in CSR and CSI include Safaricom, Airtel, Kenya Airways, East African Breweries (EABL), East African Portland Cement, Brookside Dairies, Citizen, Equity, Kenya Commercial Bank, Barclays, Standard Chartered, Equity Bank, Bamburi Cement (Lefarge), Kenya Re-insurance, Glaxo Smithkline Beecham, Coca Cola, Mumias Sugar and Chandaria, and many others.

The picture is not entirely a bright one. Many corporations will not fund NGOs that their competitors are funding. Few companies give any reasonable amounts of money that are worth the time spent in mobilizing it. Fewer than 30 companies in Kenya can be considered to be serious partners for nonprofits.

The reality is that not many companies are interested in long-term relationships and partnerships. Many prefer the short term. This tends to undermine the long-term fundraising strategies that are favored by nonprofits. Working with companies requires a different approach and set of skills that many nonprofits do not have. Typically, companies will require very short proposals and reports and do not want to be bogged down with too many implementation issues. Nonprofits therefore have to undergo a paradigm shift if they want to work with the for-profit sector.

The country has a number of organizations that support Corporate Social Responsibility. This includes *Ufadhili* (which means philanthropy in Kiswahili), which pioneered CSR and CSI in Kenya. Ufadhili conducted a Corporate Social Responsibility Initiatives in East Africa survey in 2008. The report found that those sampled spent the following on an annual basis:

- 16 percent spent $1,179 to $5,895
- 14 percent spent $ 5,895 to $11,790
- 14 percent spent $ 11,790 to $58,950

Table 9.1 shows the major causes the companies supported.

TABLE 9.1 CAUSES SUPPORTED BY COMPANIES

Cause	Percentage
Environmental Conservation	48
Education	46
Sponsoring NGOS/CBOS	34
Sports	19
Famine/Hunger Relief	15
Health Care Support	10
Temple/Mosque/Church Support	5
Art/Music/Culture	3
Disability	2

Most companies surveyed tend to go for causes that they can engage in with ease. These include visiting or supporting children's homes, tree planting, donations to schools, marathons, and walks. The values and principles adhered to are integrity, helping the community, satisfying the community, the addition of value where it will generate growth, and being a good corporate citizen.

As previously mentioned, there is a trend to establish corporate foundations to support nonprofit activities. Examples of companies that have done so include Safaricom, Equity Bank, and EABL. These foundations sometimes receive funds from international partners or investors. For example, the Safaricom Foundation receives money from Vodacom, a partial owner of the company.

Individual companies are increasingly focusing on sectors of interest. Popular sectors include education, water, environment, and sports. Equity, for example, has focused on education while East African Breweries is strong in water. Safaricom has been a leading supporter of education and the environment.

There is an increasing interest in sports such as athletics, soccer, and rugby. Soccer has attracted great interest from companies following its coverage by SuperSports and the greater enthusiasm from fans. Companies supporting soccer include Mumias Sugar, Brookside (through Tuzo), and East Africa Breweries. Kenya Airways has been a great sponsor of the Kenya Rugby Sevens team while East African Breweries also supports the game. This has diverted funds from other development activities as sports are seen to provide much better visibility.

Although NGOs see the potential of corporate funding, they also realize that they may not be the "knight in shining armor." They are unwilling to meet organizational overheads such as salaries, office, and transport costs, forcing NGOs to use funds from other donors or self-generated activities to meet the difference. This has greatly reduced the appeal of funds from corporate sources.

The small amounts given by most companies also make the funding less attractive to larger organizations. Some companies give as little as $250 while many others give nothing at all. Corporations are therefore more attractive to small NGOs and CBOs. However, this changes with large relief initiatives that involve powerful brands such as the Red Cross. In this case, they give large grants and compete with one another for the public's attention.

Companies provide support both in cash and in-kind. However, some of the support is indirect. Some companies, like Barclays Bank, have used their branches to raise funds from their clients for a particular cause such as Girl Child Network. They even have matching programs that triple the amounts of money raised by staff for approved philanthropic activities. KCB Bank has used its branch networks to raise funds in support of various relief efforts while media companies like the Nation and Standard Groups have provided free publicity. Telecommunication companies such as Safaricom, Airtel, and YuCash have used their mobile phone networks to enable individuals contribute to particular causes. Other companies support special events that allow them to provide cash and in-kind support. Some companies get their staff involved in special events as part of their CSR and CSI activities. There are therefore many ways in which nonprofits can engage with corporate companies.

Follow-up with corporate donors tends to be more intensive than with others. One advantage though is that they ordinarily provide funding within a shorter time frame. It is usually much easier reporting to companies once the funding is received.

Government

The Kenyan government is not a key donor to nonprofit organizations. However, it has given small amounts of funds to CBOs in the recent past. This has been through the Department of Social Services under the Ministry of Culture and Social Services. Some CBOs have also accessed funds through the Constituency Development Fund (CDF), which is provided to all the constituencies in the country. The funds have also been used by CDF Committees to build schools, health centers, roads, and for water initiatives. Currently 2.5 percent of the national budget is invested in CDF activities. In the 2011 to 2012 financial year, the CDF funds amounted to $226,730.

The adoption of a new constitution in 2009 has led to a devolved system of government and the establishment of 47 counties that will share not less than 15 percent of the national budget. It is estimated that $2.358 billion will be provided for the 2013 to 2014 financial year. Some of this money may support NGOs under public-private partnerships (PPP) initiatives and used for education, health, agriculture, environment, water, and infrastructure. Smart NGOs see this as a means of replacing some of their dwindling foreign support.

> ### CASE STUDY 9.3   KENYA ASSOCIATION OF FUNDRAISING PROFESSIONALS (KAFP)
>
> The Kenya Association of Fundraising Professionals (KAFP) is a non-profit, voluntary membership association. Its main purpose is "to encourage people involved in fundraising and resource mobilization to adopt and promote high standards of ethical practice and inject professionalism." Launched in 2004, KAFP has its roots in the desire of Kenyan professionals for a fundraising forum that would bring them together. They wanted a forum that would facilitate their continued professional development, sharing of ideas, experiences, and new product innovations. They wanted workshops and other training. Professionals also desired relaxing social networking opportunities.
>
> KAFP aims to give fundraising professionals in Kenya a voice commensurate with the important role they play in mobilizing or providing the resources required for national development. It gives them the resources they need to push for a more favorable fundraising environment backed by appropriate national policies. The Association's activities include certification of professional fundraisers; promoting, stimulating, and enabling cooperation and exchange of information between its members in the field of resource mobilization; and supporting research and learning in fundraising practice. There are individual and associate members. Among them are chief executives, project managers, and fundraising professionals.
>
> KAFP intends to make its presence known in the whole resource mobilization arena in Kenya by positively influencing the way resources are raised and used. It seeks to ensure that Kenyan fundraising professionals are not only among the best in the world, but are leaders in best fundraising practices.
>
> Some of its activities include:
>
> - Eastern Africa Resource Mobilization Workshops: KAFP organizes the Eastern Africa Resource Mobilization Workshop that attracts fundraising professionals from as many as 14 countries. These are held annually in Mombasa in November/ December and present global trends and best practices. The event was started by Resource Alliance two decades ago and the KAFP has been organizing it since 2005.
> - Short courses: KAFP organizes short one- to two-day courses using both local and international speakers focusing on particular areas of interest.
>
> *(Continued)*

- Coffee Talks: Since 2005 Coffee Talks have been held on the last Thursday of every month in Nairobi, Kenya. These are popular three-hour forums in which selected speakers engage with participants on specific themes.
- CFRE (Certified Fundraising Executive): The Association has partnered with the Association of Fundraising Professionals in the United States for certification by CFRE International.
- Course development: KAFP has offered support to educational institutions interested in introducing courses on resource mobilization.
- Capacity building: KAFP supports development organizations to strengthen their resource mobilization capacity through tailored training workshops and advisory services.
- Global representation: KAFP represents Africa in global forums that bring resource mobilization networks from various countries together. It was involved in the development of a code of practice that underpins fundraising ethics globally.

Following the success of KAFP, a sister organization has been launched in Uganda. They remain the only organizations of their kind in Africa outside of the Southern Africa Institute of Fundraising (SAIF).

Fundraising Practices in Kenya

As noted earlier, most nonprofits look to the large institutional donors like foundations and trusts for funding and grant writing as a primary means of access. However, many donors require nonprofits to raise 10 to 50 percent of a project's cost from other sources like other institutional donors, social enterprise activities, and individuals to match these contributions. Some donors allow nonprofits to count in-kind contributions such as office space, labor, and transport.

While the potential of social enterprises has generated a lot of excitement among nonprofits, not many have the capacity or expertise to run profitable ventures. However, Fair Trade organizations such as KICK Trading, Smolart, KISAC, and Kazuri Beads have demonstrated that it's possible to survive on earned income. Popular options include investment in property or real estate, consultancy and training, health services and trading.

Strategies used to raise funds include:

- Proposals
- Project concept notes
- Special events
- Training and consultancy
- Social enterprise
- Competitive bidding

Training and consultancy offer good opportunities for raising funds for organizations that have the skills and expertise to sell. With regard to individuals, special events, harambees, and collection cards are the most commonly used strategies.

Challenges and Innovation in Kenya

The biggest challenge remains the overwhelming reliance of NGOs on institutional funding. Some are burdened with huge overhead structures that are hard to sustain on funding from philanthropic sources alone. They haven't yet learned to raise smaller amounts of money from more donors. While social enterprise offers prospects for sustainability, few organizations have the capacity to run a business well. With funds from bilateral donors declining, there are major fears that some NGOs will collapse or will be forced to significantly downscale their activities.

As far as innovation goes, Kenya is the heart of special events in Africa and in this it has no equal! Though Kenya has its share of the usual walks and golf tournaments, it also has some very unique events.

Rhino Charge

The Rhino Charge is one of the most dynamic fundraising events anywhere. It mobilizes a million dollars every year for environmental causes and is organized by the Rhino Ark Charitable Trust, the Kenyan conservation charity. It is an annual off-road motorsport competition that requiring a high level of skill in off-road driving and navigation from participants, and is designed not to adversely impact the environment in which the events take place.

The Rhino Charge was launched in 1989 to raise funds for the building and maintenance of a 250-mile electrified fence around the Aberdare ecosystem over a number of years. This objective was achieved and in 2010, its conservation mandate was expanded to include the Mau Mt. Eburu and Mt. Kenya.

The event is open to four-wheel-drive cars. Modifications are allowed, including the use of winches, sand ladders, and ropes. Each car can have between two and six occupants. Competitors can help each other, but planning such teamwork in advance is forbidden.

The concept is simple. The competitors must visit 13 points over 62 square miles of rough terrain within a 10-hour period. All the competitors are provided with a map of the area and coordinates of the 13 Control Points the night before the event. The cars must visit all Guard Posts within 10 hours to complete the course. The winner of the event is the car that completes the course in the shortest possible distance . . . not the fastest one. The drivers must be very skilled and contend with swamps, cliffs, bush, and wildlife. It's a crazy challenge and is great for those who love the African wilderness.

Entrants must raise a minimum amount in sponsorship (and most raise more). The record amount raised to date is $137,175 in 2011. Entries are limited to 60 cars to limit environmental damage. The event always attracts far more applicants than available places. It also attracts considerable corporate sponsorship.

Rhino Charge enthusiasts include adventurers from all over the world, both young and old. Teams come in from Kenya, South Africa, the United Kingdom, and elsewhere. There is a lot of fun and entertainment alongside the event.

In 2012, the Rhino Charge raised $1,043,000 million. In 2011 it raised $907,830. Sixty-five cars entered the race and 22 finished. Each participating team has to raise a minimum of $5,895. Most raised more than twice that amount, with the highest setting a record of $135,585.

Safaricom Lewa Marathon

The Safaricom Lewa Marathon was launched in 2000. It is hosted by Lewa Downs, a private ranch and rhino conservation area in Northern Kenya. The event raises money in particular for rhinos, and also for community development, education, health, and wildlife conservation projects around Samburu, Isiolo, Laikipia, and Meru areas. It is run by Tusks and Safaricom.

The half-marathon is a grueling and unique 13-mile loop through a wildlife conservancy. The race is run over a bush course of dirt roads that wind across open plains, rough terrain, through forest and hills and under harsh climatic conditions. It is the only race of its kind (with the exception of the recently launched Maasai Mara Marathon) where people race while the animals watch them!

The popular event attracts competitors from all over the world—many from the United States and United Kingdom but also runners from Australia, India, Europe, Canada, Spain, and South Africa. Teams from major U.K. and U.S. international companies including Black Rock, Deutsche Bank, Elephant.co.uk, Investec, and Artemis Investment Management participate. Sponsors of the event in 2010 included Safaricom, LG Electronics, Hewlett-Packard, Nokia Siemens, Standard Chartered, Broadband Communications, Andy Forwarders, Ericsson, Atos Origin, Linksoft Communications, DHL, Red Sky, Huawei, Pesa Point, Seven Seas Technologies, General Motors, Braeburn Schools, Highlands Water, Safarilink, British Airways, Radio Africa, Land Rover, and GSK.

More than 1,000 runners participated in 2011, raising $442,125. Since 2000 the event has raised $3.25 million.

Cricket in the Wilderness

The Cricket in the Wilderness event is held in the Ol Pejeta Wildlife Sanctuary with a stunning view of the majestic Mount Kenya. It provides cricket fans a good opportunity to enjoy their favorite sport in a magnificent outdoor setting. The first Ol Pejeta Cricket in the Wilderness tournament was held in 2006 and raised $120,000. Seven teams from Kenya, South Africa, and England played.

Ol Pejeta works to conserve wildlife and provides a sanctuary for great apes, at the same time generating income through tourism that is invested in conservation and community development. Every team that enters the game is required to raise funds for specific projects related to Ol Pejeta's community-assistance program, supporting the local needs for health and education services, and water and road infrastructure. Each team raises a minimum of $2,900, usually in sponsorship. Trophies and prizes awarded for the winners, runners-up, and the most successful fundraising team. To keep the event lighthearted, the organizers award a crate of Tusker, a Kenyan beer, to the most humorous player.

The inaugural trophy was an elephant head carved by a community member.

The event attracts a range of institutional, corporate, and individual sponsors including the Driftwood Beach Club (Larby's), Serena Hotels, Rhino Ark, Lewa Wildlife Conservancy, Lewa Ceramics, Wines of the World, the Glass Gallery, One Way, Sandra and Brendan Hill, East African Women's League's Nanyuki branch, Nanyuki Cottage Hospital, Rhino Porini Camp, Sarova Hotels, Fly 540, Callum Looman, Kingfisher, Aqua Ventures, Farmers Choice, and the Kenya Wine Agency Limited (KWAL).

Maralal International Camel Derby

The Maralal International Camel Derby was initiated in 1990 and is held annually at the Yare Camel Club and Camp. Maralal is 217 miles from Nairobi, in Kenya's wild and arid North. Maralal is a haven for adventurers, nomads, and camels. The derby raises awareness on desertification in Kenya. It also promotes camel husbandry and its importance for the nomadic people of Kenya.

The Camel Derby is Africa's best known, most prestigious and competitive camel race. Locals and internationals come for the action and excitement as the finest camels and riders in the North gather for the big race.

Other competitive events at the derby include cycling races and donkey rides for children, and spectacular local dancing displays. The cycle racing is serious business and incorporates an intermediate-level competition covering about 18 miles and an elite, marathon-length race for the fit. The cycle races are recognized by *Union Cycliste Internationale* (Geneva). The diverse events get even more of the spectators involved in the fun while raising funds for philanthropy.

A wide audience from 28 different countries including Australia, America, New Zealand, Canada, England, France, Spain, Japan, and South Africa come. The mix includes ranchers, farmers, adventurers, spectators, racers, the local and international press, and school groups from Kenya and abroad.

Special events have virtually minted money for some NGOs. Still, nonprofits have to be careful. There are more sad tales than successful ones like those just described.

CASE STUDY 9.4   KENYANS FOR KENYA CAMPAIGN

In 2011, Kenya was experiencing its worst drought in six decades, with 3.5 million Kenyans staring at imminent starvation and death. The Kenyans for Kenya campaign brought together corporate Kenya and the media to raise at least $5.9 million over four weeks for famine relief. Key partners included the Safaricom Foundation, KCB Foundation, and leading media operating under the umbrella of the Media Owners Association (MOA). The Kenya Red Cross Society was responsible for delivering the relief to the affected communities.

The money raised through the Kenyans for Kenya campaign was not just for short-term relief, it was also meant to ensure adequate food supplies for the long term. Short-term interventions included the purchase of feeds such as Unimix, a nutritious precooked meal, for the affected populations. It was also used to buy and transport water from existing water sources. Medium-term interventions entailed the provision of clean drinking water through the rehabilitation or sinking of boreholes (the result of industrial drilling). It also supported the construction of greenhouses in schools and development of drip irrigation.

The campaign surpassed its goal, raising nearly $8 million in cash. In-kind products valued at $336,615 were donated with a further $2,962,500 donated in in-kind services. Even after the campaign was officially concluded, money continued to pour in.

A third of this money came from individuals giving anywhere from 12 cents to thousands of dollars. The mobile money payment platforms such as MPESA, Air Money, and YuCash all played a key role. It is estimated that a quarter of the funds raised were through mobile phones. The media was also instrumental in rallying Kenyans toward the cause. Facebook and Twitter were catalysts for awareness and support for the campaign.

Kenyans for Kenya raised more money for relief efforts than ever before. Though previous campaigns led by the president raised as much for causes such as women and youth through harambees, they were political in nature. Kenyans for Kenya demonstrated the power and appeal a coordinated campaign can have.

South Africa

South Africa is Africa's economic powerhouse. It's therefore not surprising that its nonprofit sector is not only large but very diverse. There may be as many as 150,000 NGOs in South Africa, depending on how the term *nonprofit* is applied, but no one really knows the actual number.

As of 2011, South Africa's population was estimated at 50.8 million. Fifty-two percent or 26 million of the population was female with the remaining 24.5 million being male. About one-third of the population (29.7 percent) is less than 14 years of age, 65 percent are aged between 15 and 64 years, and only 5.3 percent of the population is over 65 years, most of them women. The life expectancy at birth is 43.7 years, which is rather low for a middle-income country of its stature.

Africans comprise the majority of the population at 40.2 million or 79.5 percent of the total population. Caucasians and other ethnicities are both estimated at 4.5 million each (9 percent) and the Indian–Asian population estimated at 1.3 million (2.5 percent). Though all have good philanthropic traditions, the Caucasian and Indian populations tend to have more disposal incomes than their African counterparts. There have been major steps conducted under the Black Empowerment Program (BEE) to improve the living standards of this marginalized population.

South Africa is located at the southern tip of Africa and shares borders with Namibia, Botswana, Mozambique, and Zimbabwe. It has 1,553 miles of coastline that extends from the Atlantic Ocean to the Indian Ocean. It is 745,645 square miles, making it twice the size of France and three times that of Germany. Much of the country is semi-arid but mineral rich. Its strategic location gives it relatively easy access to Europe, Asia, and the Americas. Its large markets, superior infrastructure, and abundant resources make it a favorite destination for foreign direct investment. Its location also gives it access to a large market in Southern Africa that has helped build its wealth. Its wealth has helped make it Africa's most philanthropic country.

South Africa has three capitals: Cape Town, Bloemfontein, and Pretoria. Cape Town is the legislative capital and home of parliament. Bloemfontein is the judicial capital, home to the Supreme Court of Appeal. Pretoria is the administrative parliament and the main capital. Johannesburg is the largest city and informally considered the economic capital. This distribution of power has helped spread development. South Africa has a federal structure and one of the best constitutions in the world as far as human rights are concerned. The African National Congress (ANC) is the largest and the ruling party. The country continues to attract significant sources of both foreign aid and foreign direct investment that help address the lingering effects of apartheid.

South Africa is the richest country in Africa. It has resources of gold, diamonds, uranium, and coal. South Africa is a leading tourism country with great wildlife and beautiful cities such as Cape Town. It has a strong agricultural sector famous for its wines. The country also produces cereals, dairy products, and fruits. All this abundance has supported the development of a strong philanthropic culture.

The overwhelming majority of South Africans or 79.8 percent are Christian while 1.5 percent of the population is Muslim, and nearly the same proportion as Hindus at 1.4 percent. These religions also have strong philanthropic traditions. Fifteen percent of the population have no religion.

South Africa's Nonprofit Sector

The nonprofit sector in South Africa is large and diverse. There are substantial differences between organizations in mission, funding sources, and strategies, budget size, geographical coverage, organizational culture, and operational systems. The NGOs range from big registered organizations with substantial incomes to small informal ones. Types of NGOs include Section 21 Companies that are not for profit. These companies need to have share capital and cannot distribute shares but instead are "limited by guarantee." They may be established for the promotion of religion, sciences, education, arts, charity, recreation, or any other cultural or social activity. They were registered under the Companies Act (no. 61 of 1973) which was replaced by a new Companies Act in 2008.

All considered, the sector may have as many as 150,000 organizations. NGOs are involved in HIV and AIDS, housing, human rights, gender issues, lobbying and advocacy, access to justice, land issues, entrepreneurship, environment, education, job training, capacity building, community development, animal rights, child welfare, conflict resolution, crime prevention and rehabilitation, counseling, psychosocial rehabilitation, economic development, research, infrastructure development, culture, media, voluntarism, philanthropy, and participatory democracy.

The sector here was worth $1.57 billion (Rand 13.2 billion) in 1998 with cash and in-kind factored in. Four hundred million dollars was raised from the private sector and $550 million was earned income. Voluntary labor was priced at $610 million.[3] A 1999 Johns Hopkins survey showed nonprofit sector employment of 645,316 full-time workers or 7.6 percent of the total nonagricultural workforce. Half of the nonprofit workforce was voluntary.

Income generated through grants, donations, sales, membership dues, service fees, and interest in 2007 exceeded $2.3 million and $431 million was contributed through corporate social investment. More than 2 million people volunteered their time and expertise in 2007, at an estimated value of $733 million.

Regulation

NGOs in South Africa can be registered as:

- Voluntary organizations (Universitas) under common law.
- As Section 21 Companies (Companies Registrar, Department of Trade and Industry, DTI). Section 21 Companies are registered under the Companies Act 1973.
- Trusts (under the District Master of the Court Office under the Department of Justice). Trusts are registered under the Trust Property Control Act 1957.

These organizations can also register as NGOs with the NPO Directorate under the Nonprofit Organizations (NPO) Act 71 of 1997.

The Nonprofit Organizations Act mandates the Department of Social Development (DSD) to contribute to an environment where NGOs can flourish. It also exists to encourage NGOs to maintain and improve standards of governance, transparency, and accountability. The NPO Directorate currently has approximately 85,000 NGOs in

---

[3] Swilling and Russel, *The Size and Scope of the Non-Profit Sector in South Africa* (Johannesburg: School of Public and Development Management, Durban; Centre for Civil Society, 2002).

its database. Registration as an NPO is voluntary. Registration gives an NGO some legitimacy and increases its chances of securing funding from the government or other funding organizations.

Organizations seeking tax exemption have to register as Public Benefit Organizations (PBO) with the Tax Exemption Unit of the South African Revenue Service. Public benefit organizations are registered under the Income Tax Act of 1996.

The key regulators of the civil society in South Africa are:

- The NPO Directorate, Department of Social Development
- Companies Registrar, Department of Trade and Industry
- District Master of Court Office, Department for Justice, South African Revenue Service
- Tax Exemption Unit

The Nonprofit Organizations Act requires organizations registered with the NPO Directorate to submit annual reports and accounts. The reports must follow standard formats, which are available from the directorate's website. The annual reports and accounts must be filed within nine months of the end of the financial year. Organizations that fail to do so are deregistered. Section 21 companies are required to submit accounts and reports to the Companies Registrar on an annual basis. Public Benefit Organizations, on the other hand, are required to submit accounts and reports to the revenue department for tax-exemption purposes.

With more funds being channeled to the government through bilateral and multilateral agreements, NGO funding is under threat. Large professional NGOs with greater resource mobilization capacity are likely to come out ahead of smaller nonprofits.

Influences in Giving

South Africa did not have organized welfare services before the twentieth century. Individuals and families cared for their own. A national conference held in 1916 recommended the coordination of private welfare services, leading to the establishment of a number of National Welfare Councils in the 1920s. The Carnegie Poor White Investigation report recommended the creation of a State Bureau of Social Welfare to coordinate the welfare activities of state departments in cooperation with voluntary organizations and churches. In 1937, a Department of Social Welfare was established and a decade later, the

Welfare Organizations Act No. 40 of 1947 was passed to regulate public donations.

National and regional welfare boards were established following the legislation of the National Welfare Act 79 of 1975. The Van Rooyen Commission of Inquiry into the Collection of Voluntary Financial Contributions from the Public then led to the Fundraising Act No. 107 of 1978.

Religious organizations were the driving force behind community projects from the 1950s to 1970s. This changed with the emergence of NGOs and CBOs in the 1970s. Huge inflows of funding from donors in the 1980s supported the growth of NGOs, gradually eclipsing the dominance of religious organizations. Nevertheless, Ubuntu continues to play a key role in philanthropy in South Africa and its citizens are considered among the most generous people in the world.

Infrastructure

Organizations have to register as public benefit organizations (PBO) with the Tax Exemption Unit of the South African Revenue Service if they want tax exemption. An organization does not have to be registered as a nonprofit organization to register as a PBO.

It is estimated that there are 85,000 formally registered organizations with the NPO directorate in the Department of Social Development. However, only 10,000 of these have a PBO number signifying approval of the SA Revenue Service (SARS) as public benefit organizations. Once approved by SARS, the organization is exempted from income tax, donations tax, estate duty, and other fiscal levies. A few organizations are also exempt from charging VAT as well as reclaiming VAT paid on their supplies.

NGOs seeking exemptions from dividend tax were required to register with the SARS before April 1, 2012. Exemption from the new dividends tax is not automatic and organizations need to take the required steps to notify either the companies in which they hold shares or a regulated intermediary, like their asset manager, or their tax-exempt status prior to the dates on which these companies declare dividends. Dividends tax will only impact those organizations that hold shares in public or private companies. Many organizations have investments in public and private entities as part of their long-term sustainability strategy.

Umbrella Organizations

NGOs regulate themselves through the South African NGO Coalition or SANGOCO. It has developed a code of ethics to support good governance.

Other umbrella organizations working within the Civil Society include:

- The Non-Profit Consortium, building the capacity of South African NGOs.
- Charities Aid Foundation (CAF) Southern Africa, promoting effective social investment.
- SANGOnet, improving communication and information on South African NGOs.

There are many other sector- and region-specific umbrella organizations especially in the area of HIV and AIDS.

Philanthropy and Other Support in South Africa
Individuals

South Africans are second only to Americans as the most generous people in the world according to the *2010 Barclay's Culture of Philanthropy* report.[4] The Bank of England Private Clients Survey showed that 93 percent of the HNWIs in South Africa have given to charity. A 2003 survey showed that giving was not just the domain of the rich. Ordinary South Africans gave $1.2 billion per month. This represented 2.2 percent of the government's national expenditure on wages. It was also second only to the state in terms of its contribution to poverty alleviation and development.

South Africans top the list of African philanthropists. Examples of such individuals include:

- Francois van Niekerk who in 2010 gave $170 million, 70 percent equity of his company, Mertech Group, to the Mergon Foundation that he had established with his wife. The foundation supports education, HIV and AIDS, enterprise development, and recycling projects.

---

[4] www.barclayswealth.com/insights/global-giving-and-the-culture-of-philanthropy.htm#.

- Allan Gray bestowed $150 million on the Allan Gray Orbis Foundation. The foundation supports education activities.
- Donald Gordon donated $50 million to charities including the Donald Gordon Teaching Medical Centre at the University of Witwatersrand and to British nonprofits, the Royal Opera House, and Wales Millennium Centre. He is the founder of the Donald Gordon Foundation.
- Mark Shuttleworth, famed for his $20 million trip to space, spent $25 million in support of Ubuntu, a free open source software. He is a founder of the Shuttleworth Foundation, to which he has committed $20 million. The foundation supports social change projects.

Successful black businesspeople like Cyril Ramaphosa, Tokyo Sexwale, and Patrice Motsepe have all established foundations through which they give to charity. Others who have given away substantial funds include Jay Naidoo. There are also initiatives like the Plough-Back Trust that facilitate giving by black businesspeople and professionals.

A CAF study estimated the value of individual and corporate giving in South Africa to be $1.9 billion. There are several examples that show this as well as point to the potential that still exists. These include:

- Greenpeace: In October 2008, with five full-time people under a new energetic fundraising director, the organization began recruiting individual donors through face-to-face, mainly in shopping malls and streets in Johannesburg and Cape Town. It recruited more than 10,000 monthly donors in a period of six months. According to Michael McTernan, Greenpeace fundraising director, "We managed to sign up more people in South Africa in a less time than in other countries where we are more established."
- MSF. In 2008, MSF raised $300,000, mainly through individuals recruited via direct mail and SMS, and it had only opened its office in Johannesburg in 2007. MSF is very active on HIV and AIDS issues in partnership with the Mandela Foundation.
- SOS Children's Villages. SOS has been operating in South Africa since they were established in 1980. They have 130,000 donors who contribute 25 percent through monthly and

incidental giving of gross income annually. Once SOS decided to target this market, it grew the donor list to more than 100,000 people in less than eight years.

* UNICEF: UNICEF launched its first ever e-appeal in December 2007. It raised more than $300,000 in eight months. The Super Sports Let's Play a Million Campaign raised $160,000 in just one day through SMS with the help of five national radio stations.

Foundations

There are many foundations active in South Africa, including the Charles Stewart Mott Foundation, the GM Foundation, and the Foundation for Human Rights of South Africa. International foundations with a local presence include the Hans Seidel Foundation, Open Society Foundation for South Africa, and the Bill and Melinda Gates Foundation. The local arms of these international foundations usually have their own development objectives supporting the overall vision and mission of the mother foundation. Their local staffs keep them attuned to local needs.

Corporations

National and multinational companies in South Africa take corporate social responsibility and investment seriously. A 2005 survey by Trialoge of more than 100 stock exchange listed companies in South Africa showed 73.5 percent wholeheartedly embraced corporate citizenship and 24.5 percent considered it an important part of doing business. The Johannesburg Stock Exchange (JSE) has standards for the CSR sector and the JSE Socially Responsible Investment Index, published annually, has set the foundation for this.

CSI in South Africa goes back to the apartheid era when companies investing in South Africa realized that the poor living conditions of the black majority were undermining economic development. At the time the state was not interested in supporting this marginalized group.

It was with this in mind that the Urban Foundation (now known as the *National Business Initiative*) was established in 1976 with the goal of improving the quality of life of black communities. With the enactment of the Black Economic Empowerment Act of 2003, CSI programs have become more structured and funds have been invested in the training of workers and professionals to help meet the objectives of

BEE. The CSI guidelines contained in BEE advised on what companies were expected to do, thus playing a big role in the development
of CSI initiatives.

The HIV/AIDS crisis has also encouraged corporate investment in
the health sector. Overall, CSI activities have evolved from charitable
programs to strategic investment in social development over the past
two decades.

Large companies plan their giving initiatives, measure their progress, and publish the results. It is all part of business. CSI accounted
for $360 million in 2007, an increase over the $242 million in 2003.
While company support was just half of what international donors
were providing for similar social projects, it was only a tenth of what
the state invested.

Government

South Africa is not a welfare state. As elsewhere, it is the family and
the community, not the state, that are expected to help individuals in
need in the spirit of Ubuntu.

Over the past 10 years the government has come to consider NGOs
as essential partners in the delivery of services to communities on
behalf of the state. Public-private partnerships have seen consortiums
of NGOs tendering for specific public service delivery initiatives. It
has also seen them work with national and local governments and donors
in addressing poverty, HIV and AIDS, and housing and environment
programs. Many government development agencies work with NGOs
and the private sector to support service delivery and social development.

The government is a significant source of support for many nonprofits. The study conducted by Mark Swilling and Bev Russel as a
part of the Johns Hopkins University global project measuring the
nonprofit sector[5] shows that in general charities in South Africa are
funded mainly through the government (42 percent), fees (29 percent), and private sector/philanthropy (25 percent). See Figure 9.1.

NGOs can also get development and support services from the government through the Provincial Department of Social Development.

---

[5]M. Swilling and B. Russell, *The Size and Scope of the Non-Profit Sector in
South Africa* (Johannesburg: School of Public and Development Management;
Durban: Centre for Civil Society, 2002).

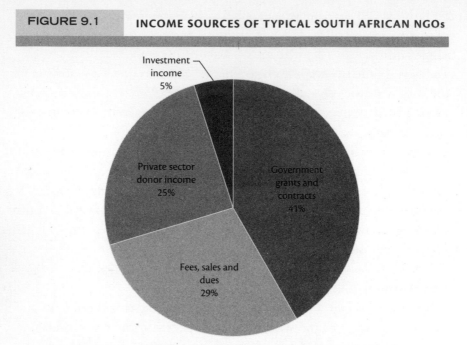

FIGURE 9.1   INCOME SOURCES OF TYPICAL SOUTH AFRICAN NGOs

Investment income
5%

Private sector donor income
25%

Government grants and contracts
41%

Fees, sales and dues
29%

Source: M. Swilling and B. Russell, *The Size and Scope of the Non-Profit-Sector in South Africa*, (Johannesburg: School of Public and Development Management; Durban: Centre for Civil Society, 2002).

The government recognizes that some of the NGOs that it funds need support themselves, especially in regard to capacity building. Other NGOs or private sector companies are contracted to provide the capacity building support to these organizations.

Fundraising Practices

Raising money is getting more challenging in South Africa, just as is the case in many other parts of the world. The financial crisis in developed countries has resulted in less funds for South Africa. As noted earlier, NGOs have had to turn their attention to local resource mobilization. Local donors, however, are demanding more accountability and transparency value for their money.

As is elsewhere the case on the continent, resource mobilization in South Africa has been dominated by foreign donor sources. Donors were eager to bring about change during the days of apartheid. Little was required in terms of accounting because NGOs avoided the risks involved with engaging with the then current government. With the birth of a new democracy, things began to change. Donors want more accountability and the greater numbers of NGOs must compete for the limited resources available. This has necessitated the learning of new fundraising skills like effective proposal writing and donor relations.

Fundraising strategies mirror what is used in other African countries. Strategies have included:

- Proposals to institutional donors such as bilateral, foundations, and trusts
- Special events such as golf tournaments and walks
- Social enterprise and investments

Greater attention is also being paid to business models that can help generate funds. Better management practices, like developing a financial reserve, is also now being considered important for sustaining operations during difficult times.

Challenges and Innovation in South Africa

South African NGOs are facing major challenges just like NGOs in other African countries. In 2010 the total income of NGOs was reduced by $360 million due to the global financial crisis and other factors. As a middle-income country, donors no longer see South Africa as a first priority. The inadequate expenditure of the South African government on social development has not helped things either.

Lack of capacity plagues South African nonprofits. Increasing operational costs had left many NGOs in an unsustainable position. A dearth of financial and management expertise discourages potential donors. Unstable and underfunded, NGOs can offer their staff little in terms of job security and the state and the for-profit private sector poach their skilled staff. Facilities are often basic and sometimes downright inadequate. This makes it difficult for staff to resist the temptations of better job prospects from the state or business. Welfare-oriented NGOs have the least sustainability.

Funds that once went to NGOs are now going to government. Donors such as the European Union, United States International Development Agency, United Nations Development Programs, Swedish International Development Agency, and the Danish Development

Agency are increasingly channeling their funds through the state. Some donors have reduced or stopped funding NGOs altogether, preferring to fund initiatives with the government. NGOs appealing for assistance are often redirected to the government.

Many NGOs think that social enterprise is the answer. The use of more business-like models is gaining currency, even among organizations that were once opposed to it. Although social enterprise is not the solution to funding challenges, it can help reduce reliance on just a few donors, a dependency that undermines organizational sustainability. In the medium or even the long term, however, it is unlikely to replace other key sources for funding.

Many organizations that are unable to mobilize resources locally or internationally may have to either significantly downscale operations or close down completely. The survivors will be those that maintain strong relationships with and are accountable to their donors and demonstrate value for money. Some will have diversified sources of income that reduce their dependency on any single source.

Even though some organizations will not be able to sustain themselves, the number of nonprofits in South Africa will probably continue to grow. Only time will tell if there are sufficient philanthropic resources in the economy to sustain them all.

Conclusion

The changing economic fortunes of the continent will have a significant impact on philanthropy in Africa. Even while the economies of the West tumbled an average of 2 percent in the meltdown of 2009, sub-Saharan Africa grew 3.5 percent. As Wolfgang Fengler stated:

> On a macroeconomic level, the new African momentum has also been evident. Africa has weathered both the global financial crisis, and the turbulence in the Euro zone. According to World Bank's latest economic outlook, Sub-Saharan Africa is projected to grow above five percent in 2012 and 2013. This would be higher than the average of developing countries (excluding China), and substantially, above growth in high-income countries. This means that at some point in this decade, Africa could grow above the levels of Asia. A few years ago, it would not have been possible for economic observers to consider such a scenario. Once Africa becomes the fastest growing continent in the world, this will also be the true turning

point for Africa's global perception . . . today the EAC (East African Cooperation), is one of the fastest growing regions in the world. If Rwanda, Tanzania, and Uganda maintain their ongoing growth momentum and if Kenya accelerates, all four countries will reach middle-income status within the next 10 years. For the first time since independence, sustainable development appears possible for East Africa, even for countries that started off from very difficult positions.

With stronger infrastructure—telecommunications and electricity—coupled with discovery of new sources of oil, gas, coal, gold, titanium, methane, niobium, and other minerals, East Africa's prospects are excellent. The same can be said about several Southern and West African countries. The growth of democracy in the North is also raising the prospects of the region.

There are ongoing talks for the establishment of a Cape to Cairo free trade zone within three years. The zone, which will combine the current economic/trading blocks of SADC (Southern Africa Development Cooperation), COMESA (Common Market for East and Southern Africa), and EAC (East African Cooperation), will bring together 26 countries and 525 million people and will have a $1 trillion market.

There is increasing trade in goods, services, music, and even art. "Nollywood," Nigeria's film industry, produces 20 films a week. It is now the world's third-largest film industry and employs 200,000 people. Its movies are now watched in theaters and at home in many African countries—unimaginable a few years ago.

Although Africa's future promises a better-educated workforce, wealthier countries, and individuals with more disposable income, it also faces declining flows from its traditional donors. Philanthropy can and will play a bigger role in the development of the continent.

IN SUMMARY

Africa, including the major players of Kenya and South Africa profiled here, is showing itself to be a rising star in philanthropy. Some of the continent's traditions, like harambees, might be successfully adapted for a Western environment. As far as special event fundraising goes, Africa has no peer.

CHAPTER 10

Middle East and North Africa (MENA)

TARIQ H. CHEEMA

Persistent societal problems and wealth creation in the Middle East and North Africa are driving a new generation of actors to commit their resources for the greater public welfare. The John D. Gerhart Center for Philanthropy and Civic Engagement at American University Cairo in its landmark study *From Charity to Social Change: Trends in Arab Philanthropy* provides a preliminary overview of Arab philanthropy in eight countries of the region including Egypt, the Hashemite Kingdom of Jordan, Lebanon, Palestine, the United Arab Emirates, Qatar, the Kingdom of Saudi Arabia, and Kuwait. The results of the study indicate that institutionalized philanthropy is rapidly growing in the region. Traditional religious motivations for giving remain strong, and both modest and wealthy citizens contribute to the welfare of those who are in need. Governments are recognizing the potential in allowing greater civic participation, and more leaders from the private sector see the importance of socially investing their wealth. This study forms the first attempt to offer a mapping of the landscape of private giving in the Arab region.

For centuries, philanthropy in the Arab region—that is spread across the Middle East and North Africa (MENA)—was driven mostly by faith. This meant that giving, which is deeply embedded in Arab cultures, was essentially conducted through faith-based structures and within the three monotheistic religions—Islam, Christianity, and Judaism—that hold sway in the MENA region.

But things have changed over the past few decades in general and the past decade, in particular. In their excellent essay, "Arab Region: The Case of the Arab Foundations Forum and John D. Gerhart Center for Philanthropy and Civic Engagement," focusing on philanthropy in the Arab region, authors Atallah Kuttab and Dina H. Sherif explain how the culture of giving in that region over past decades can largely be described as charitable in nature with individual giving, as opposed to institutional giving, being at the forefront.[1] But, they add, in a shift from the past, there has been a rise in citizen activism among successful and affluent business leaders, who are introducing both innovation and entrepreneurship to their giving. A simple fact seems to have been understood and appears to be clearly manifested in the new mind-set exhibited by Arab business leaders: They not only want to share their wealth and contribute to their societies in a meaningful way, they also want to ensure the sustainability of their own businesses. The fact that businesses cannot thrive if the communities around them are falling apart is no longer contested. To that end, the authors say, a growing number of business leaders are investing their money socially as aggressively as they do financially. To add to this, there has been a consistent increase in the number of foundations established in the region over the past decade, whether they are family, corporate, or community foundations. Those who used to give large amounts of money on an individual basis are now choosing to institutionalize their giving in the form of a foundation that is sustainable and that is strategically tackling a specific problem in society in both a transparent and responsible manner.

That means that there are now numerous grant-making foundations operating across the Arab and Muslim world, established by the rich and powerful of those countries, mostly the royals and private sector leaders. These foundations give huge sums of money to support schools, hospitals, orphanages, and faith-based institutions both in their home countries and abroad. However, these foundations generally operate in isolation, and rarely pool human or financial resources with other grant-making entities.[2] But, while the growth of endowment funds and

---

[1] Atallah Kuttab and Dina H. Sherif, "Global Philanthropy (2010): Arab Region: The Case of the Arab Foundations Forum and the John D. Gerhart Center for Philanthropy and Civic Engagement." London: MF Publishing.

[2] Tariq H. Cheema, "Muslim Philanthropy: The Current Status and Future Outlook," in *Global Islamic Finance Report* (London, 2012).

community foundations is quite slow, there is a growing class of professionally run family, corporate, or state-backed foundations, whose grantmaking is development-oriented and strategic in nature. Additionally, humanitarian aid and development organizations dominate the philanthropic landscape of the region. They are competent and resourceful, and actively raise funds from their communities.

THE CURRENT LANDSCAPE

Beyond the small pockets of extreme wealth and stability, the region is facing challenges like poverty, unemployment, long-standing regional conflicts, and political unrest. Recent events in North Africa and the Middle East lend urgency to this conversation about the future role of philanthropy in the region.

The philanthropic sector has a historic opportunity to encourage movement away from greed and self-appropriation toward a world governed by the objectives of long-term value creation and sustainability. This progress can only occur through a carefully drawn new social compact among states, the private sector, and the philanthropic sector. Regardless of how current upheavals play out throughout the region, the serious economic, social, and political challenges will not be addressed without a long-term vision for social justice and active participation among the different sectors.

History has shown that uprisings fueled by frustration can often generate enough pressure to force immediate political reforms. But they do not necessarily guarantee long-term, transformational social change. Therefore, the current situation of the region requires a well-coordinated strategic response by the public, private, and philanthropic sectors.

Individual governments across the region, excluding the Gulf Cooperation Council (GCC),[3] are falling behind in providing social safety nets to their citizens, hence forcing the philanthropic and private sectors to carry increasing responsibility for meeting basic human needs. This trend, coupled with a global financial and sovereign debt

---

[3]Formed in 1981, GCC is a political and economic union of the Arab states that border the Persian Gulf and are located on or near the Arabian Peninsula. These countries are Bahrain, Kuwait, Oman, Qatar, Saudi Arabia, and the United Arab Emirates.

crisis that further limits government capacity, could have disastrous consequences for the millions living across the region.

Although basic corporate social responsibility interventions are gradually gaining attention, corporate social strategy and corporate philanthropy are still largely alien concepts. Given the sizeable economy of the region, this is an underutilization of resources and a general wasting of opportunities to bring positive social change. Against the backdrop of a high youth unemployment rate and increasing political activism across the Middle East and North Africa, corporations must look at value creation and not just concentrate on making profits, which is likely to make corporations more vulnerable than powerful.

The region is among the largest recipients of foreign and philanthropic grants from sovereign governments, donor agencies, and grant-making foundations. Civil society, which is intended to play a key role in addressing a range of social challenges, is generally limited by skill sets, training, and development. There is a shortage of qualified, experienced experts, which reduces the value and impact of each dollar that is donated.

The majority of regional giving is fragmented and, thus, less effective, and gears toward poverty alleviation through consumption instead of investment and development. There also is a lack of clarity on how to best meet the demand for giving and supply for philanthropic funds. The philanthropic sector, therefore, is dealing with the challenges of the waste of precious funds because of subscale initiatives, limited investment in delivery capacity, and generally underdeveloped civil society. Addressing this challenge requires significant improvements on two main frontiers: enhancing the institutionalization of philanthropic spending and increasing the professionalism of philanthropic institutions.

Crucially, the growth of the philanthropic sector in the MENA region also depends very much on how governments act. States are required to make incentive-based policies for donors, establish effective monitoring systems to ensure transparency in charitable operations, and regulate the collection and disbursement of *zakat*, the mandatory alms giving for Muslims. In general, though, it is apparent that the public, private, and philanthropic sectors lack harmony, and their development strategies are not properly aligned. Further, the policy-making process or service delivery is often influenced by political or corporate interests and not necessarily driven by ground realities.

Also, according to Kuttab and Sherif, while it is clear that the institutionalized philanthropic sector is growing, it remains restricted on the whole because current legal frameworks in the Arab region continue to act as a barrier to more rapid growth. Philanthropists are challenged by a registration process for private foundations that is so complex and rigid, it discourages registering at all, or encourages registering the foundation outside the region. Other problems abound: The lack of existing NGOs with a credible track record acts as an obstacle to the growth of the philanthropic sector. Many philanthropists remain skeptical of NGOs because of the common perception that civil society in the Arab region has been known to be corrupt and unprofessional. Although this may be changing with many NGOs becoming more professional and more transparent, for some, this change is not happening at a fast enough rate, causing a number of foundations to take the path of becoming operational as opposed to grant giving. Despite all these obstacles, however, the philanthropic sector continues to grow slowly but surely.

HISTORICAL CONTEXT

Arab philanthropy is rich in history and contemporary complexity, write Barbara Ibrahim and Dina Sherif in a 2008 study. An entire book has been written about a single charitable endowment in thirteenth-century Jerusalem that continues to feed the poor to this day. Eighteen thousand comparable *waqf* endowments persist and increase across the region, while registered *mo'assasat* (asset-bearing foundations) in just one country (Egypt) now number more than 40,000. Clearly, with such deep traditions of giving, any initial attempt to cover contemporary trends in the Arab region must be in some respects incomplete.

Perhaps the new shape that giving is assuming in this region is the reason why, in this study published by the John D. Gerhart Center for Philanthropy and Civic Engagement, this current time of change is called "a vibrant time for Arab philanthropy."[4]

---

[4] Barbara Ibrahim and Dina Sherif, *From Charity to Social Change: Trends in Arab Philanthropy* (Cairo: AUC Press, 2008).

In that seminal study, the authors explore the concept of philanthropy and conclude that the idea of philanthropy does not have a single accepted definition but instead is expressed through many terms around the Arab region. And yet, the meaning underlying the concept easily understood by everyone, it holds positive valence regardless of class, gender, education, or place of residence. Giving of one's material wealth to benefit those in need is a fundamental tenet of both Islam and Christianity. Studies consistently find that this form of giving is widely practiced at all levels of society and in countries across the region. Some of the difficulty springs from the lack of a single equivalent word in Arabic. A literal translation of the Greek root—love of humanity—is unhelpful.

The idea of philanthropic giving is closely linked to the Arabic concept of *takaful* or social solidarity. For Christian Arabs, *ushur* is the practice of giving a tenth of one's wealth or income to those less fortunate in the community. This is often accompanied by giving of time for voluntary service to others. For Muslim Arabs, *zakat* and *sadaqah* (charity) is the practice that most closely encompasses their understanding of giving as both a spiritual and social obligation. For the region's Jews, charity is *tzedakah*, acts of justice and righteousness, and is considered a duty.

What is novel in the current period, the authors say, are the ways in which some actors are structuring and targeting their giving. These include revamping older forms like the centuries-old waqf endowment model, creative uses of religiously mandated donations (zakat and ushur), and a variety of other modalities such as social investing, corporate philanthropy, and the establishment of modern grant-making foundations. Another promising trend is toward regional funding institutions, based in one country but governed by a truly pan-Arab board of directors.

Faith-Based Giving

In a region where philanthropy is predominantly faith-inspired, the resolution of long-standing religious and geopolitical conflicts is critical to the peace and prosperity of the region and its neighboring lands.

The overwhelming majority of the region's population is comprised of Muslims whose giving is deeply inspired by faith. Although zakat is one of the most fundamental tenets of Islam, it is just one aspect of Muslim philanthropy, which is a broad and diverse phenomenon reflecting centuries of change in very different cultural, social, and economic contexts around the world.

The principle of zakat, the annual tax of purification of wealth, is one of the five pillars of Islam, and is obligatory for all Muslims who own any substantial amount of wealth and are capable of paying. One portion of the zakat is used as a public welfare system, providing support to poor members of the community, and was always, therefore, part of a Muslim's communal duties. It was, and is, also a spiritual act: Giving allows one to purify oneself of material selfishness, while the recipient is purified from envy and jealousy.

The practice of zakat is not just intended to temporarily alleviate suffering. By demonstrating an example of virtue and duty, granting zakat encourages all members of society to work harder, to be compassionate, and to improve the lot of the community. Zakat is, therefore, both spiritual and profoundly social.

Another is sadaqah. Unlike zakat, this is discretionary, and is the personal choice of each individual Muslim. It is also not necessarily monetary in nature. Sadaqah is in fact a broad term, and may mean anything from a kind word, to voluntary service, to clothing and feeding the poor.

Another aspect of Islamic philanthropy is the contribution of donations for building mosques, schools, and hospitals by establishing one of the strongest social manifestations of Muslim giving, waqf. The word originally meant a religious endowment, but over time the word has shifted meaning, and is now more likely to simply mean a *foundation*.

Through these different forms of giving, philanthropy binds Muslim communities together, and serves as both a demonstration of faith and of community spirit. It is religious as well as social, and it illustrates the idea that in Islam, it is not the sole responsibility of the government to help the disadvantaged members of society—it is the responsibility of all Muslims, as members of the community. That is why Islam legislated zakat, an annual tax levied by the government, and sadaqah, charity, given voluntarily to whomever we see fit; priority is given to family members and relatives.

Today, in most Muslim countries, zakat is collected through a decentralized and voluntary system, where eligible Muslims are expected to pay zakat at their own will. Under this voluntary system, zakat committees are established often at local mosques, which are tasked with the collection and distribution of zakat funds. Due to lack of awareness, and perhaps lack of trust, the number of zakat givers is much lower than it should be. In a handful of Muslim countries—including Saudi Arabia and Pakistan—zakat is obligatory, and is collected in a centralized manner by the state. In many other countries zakat is regulated by the state, but contributions are voluntary. In recent years, plenty of research is available on centralized zakat management systems adopted by the governments of Indonesia and Malaysia. These studies indicate a serious effort being put toward making zakat management more efficient, effective, and replicable.

The main objective of zakat is to achieve equitable distribution of income in the society so that the income gap can be narrowed. Therefore, managing zakat funds under a zakat institution becomes very significantly crucial and strategic for the welfare of the Muslim world. Even though the management of zakat collection is getting better from year to year, the zakat distribution mechanism is facing multiple challenges. The difficulty with the distribution methods and persistent poverty are among the issues that have hindered the performance and achievement of the zakat institution itself. The issue with zakat distribution is crucial to address because it might cause dissatisfaction among zakat givers and lead them to pay zakat directly to the needy, bypassing institutionalized channels. Such a trend will compromise both the transparency and the effectiveness of zakat.

To achieve the strategic impact of zakat, centralizing zakat management seems to be the only policy option, according to researchers. By having it centralized, coordination between the national zakat institution and the fiscal policy maker might be implemented more easily. The zakat concept can also be incorporated into the fiscal policy formulated by the government. An efficient zakat management system with a strategic distribution approach would appear to be the right vehicle for converting zakat recipients into zakat givers. Conventional practices are less likely to bring the change that zakat guarantees.

CASE STUDY 10.1   HASANAH TRUST FUND

The Hasanah Trust Fund is the result of a partnership between the World Congress of Muslim Philanthropists (WCMP) and the Islamic Solidarity Fund for Development (ISFD). Created to implement social development programs, the Hasanah Trust Fund links the global reach of the WCMP with the expertise and credibility of the ISFD to provide philanthropists, foundations, corporations, and governments with an effective platform to support innovative programs in developing countries.

Designed to focus on three key elements of social uplift, the Hasanah Fund focuses on projects that support investing in livelihoods, promote sustainable social enterprise, and improve governance and civic participation. By investing in ventures that create new and effective ways for poor people to access economic opportunities and help in shaping public policies that contribute to their long-term well-being, the Hasanah Fund lays special attention on harnessing the potential of Islamic finance for supporting positive social change.

Investments channeled through the WCMP leverage a 25 percent matching contribution from the ISFD, enabling the Hasanah Trust Fund to allow investors to promote effective solutions and to evaluate the impact of their support. Efforts undertaken by sovereign Muslim states, the Organization of the Islamic Conference (OIC) and the Islamic Development Bank (IDB) are complemented by the pooled fund while a board comprising WCMP and ISFD representatives, as well as major benefactors, governs the Hasanah Trust Fund.

In its first phase, the Fund will initiate programs in Asian and sub-Saharan countries. The Hasanah Trust Fund is presently capped at $20 million.

THE PARADIGM SHIFT

A heartening sign, according to Kuttab and Sherif, is that there has been a consistent increase in the number of foundations established in the MENA region over the past decade. The trend appears to have shifted for those who used to prefer giving large amounts of money on an individual basis: They now choose to institutionalize their giving in the form of a foundation that is sustainable and that is strategically tackling a specific problem in both a transparent and responsible manner.

This means that several broad categories of foundations can now be found in the Arab world: family foundations, where bequests are from personal assets and management may stay at least partially among family members; community foundations, that enable multiple small donors to pool their financial resources together for a common purpose, often directed to a geographic locale; a partner or membership foundation, which includes a group of individuals who pledge funding and/or annual amounts to a foundation and serve on its board of trustees; and, public-private partnership foundations, which involve the collection of funds from both citizens and the private sector that are also matched by the state or a public official.

Three independent foundations, all emerging within the past five years, demonstrate the positive change that has occurred in the regional culture of giving in the Middle East and North Africa. All three have been formed in response to specific needs and all three have assumed considerable significance within their spheres of operation in a reasonably short span of time.

THE MOHAMMED BIN RASHID AL MAKTOUM FOUNDATION

His Highness Sheikh Mohammed bin Rashid Al Maktoum, vice president and prime minister of the United Arab Emirates and ruler of Dubai, chose to announce the establishment of the Mohammed bin Rashid Al Maktoum Foundation at the World Economic Forum for the Middle East that was held in Jordan in 2007. In his keynote speech, he also announced a personal endowment of AED 37 billion ($10 billion) for the Foundation, which has been mandated to empower future generations to come up with indigenous solutions to the challenges faced by the Arab World.

The creation of this foundation is a positive move from a leader with a clearly defined vision. With its focus on education, the Al Maktoum Foundation intends, according to its mission statement, to "provide Arabs with opportunities to guide the region toward a knowledge economy through promoting entrepreneurship, research and innovation, enhancing access to quality education and professional development; and supporting the production, acquisition, and dissemination of Arab knowledge sources."

During an exhaustive and inspirational speech at the Knowledge Conference in Dubai where he announced the actual launch of the Foundation, Sheikh Al Maktoum explained why he deemed it necessary to create the foundation. "There is no doubt that the Arab state of affairs is not free from thorns and pitfalls. This is our reality. We have no choice but to work through that reality, resolved to overcome obstacles, realizing that the worth of man is not measured by his adaptation to reality, however it may be, and not by his skill in managing that reality. It is, rather, his ability to develop reality and change it to the better that matters."

THE ARAB FOUNDATIONS FORUM

The founding of a network of Arab foundations stemmed from the need, write Kuttab and Sherif, to create an infrastructure for philanthropy that would support sustainable solutions to the chronic problems of the region. So the Arab Foundations Forum (AFF) was founded with the aim of strengthening the capacity of Arab philanthropy by promoting dialogue, networking, learning, and collaboration among foundations and with partners within the Arab region and beyond.

The absence of Arab philanthropic organizations was first felt at the European Foundation Centre (EFC) meeting in Budapest in May 2005. But there were three other Arab organizations present: the Arab Fund for Human Rights, the Universal Education Foundation, and the Welfare Organization. These three organizations agreed in Budapest that it would be a good idea to convene a meeting of Arab organizations to discuss the possibility of forming a network. The Welfare Organization took the lead by creating a network of foundations and committed to hosting the forum in its early stages—this was made possible by a grant from the Ford Foundation that included the cost of a part-time coordinator and basic activities.

This eventually led to the inaugural meeting of the AFF, which took place in Jordan in 2006, a year after Budapest, as an initiative of the Welfare Organization. After that first meeting in Jordan, and with seed money from the Ford Foundation, seven more meetings took place between 2006 and 2009. During that time, the AFF was able to draft and adapt its bylaws, elect a Board of Directors, articulate a mission, vision, and strategic objectives, as well as establish a strong membership base.

THE WORLD CONGRESS OF MUSLIM PHILANTHROPISTS

The following idea was first introduced in 2006 by Chicago-based physician Tariq H. Cheema:

> In an era where, all too often, Muslims are depicted in a negative light—usually due to unresolved geopolitical conflicts and extremist elements within—it is critical to have a joint forum and a common voice that safeguards and promotes Muslim benevolence. Further, in the wake of increasing natural and man-made calamities, the need arose for an intense and determined action to better address these crises through collaborations that go beyond the lines of faith, race, and geography.

This calling led to the formation of the World Congress of Muslim Philanthropists (WCMP) in 2007, as a pioneer effort of making Muslim giving more efficient and strategic. Today, the WCMP is a strong network of affluent individuals, grant-making foundations, and socially responsible corporations, and serves as a unique catalyst for partnership across the public, private, and social sectors, offering information and resources to link donors with social investment opportunities. As a trusted broker of collaborative relationships, WCMP mobilizes financial and human resources to confront social needs and advance strategic philanthropy.

Once a year, the World Congress of Muslim Philanthropists convenes donors, social investors, government and business leaders, experts, and visionaries from across the world to offer pragmatic insight and constructive responses to pressing social challenges. The annual forum serves as a marketplace for ideas, a platform for sharing knowledge and forging partnerships, and a launching pad for high-impact collaborative activities. In addition, the annual convening of WCMP is widely recognized as the premier worldwide forum on Muslim philanthropy where issues unique to Muslim giving are debated in a safe space.

By virtue of being the first initiative of its kind, the WCMP has become a platform for a unified voice and collective action to safeguard and strengthen Muslim philanthropy. The network has engaged

world leaders and donors at the highest levels. It has built strong partnerships across sectors as it moves increasingly from a convening role
into a catalyst for social investment. The WCMP has been working
with a number of reputable institutions such as the United Nations,
the Organization of Islamic Conference, the Islamic Development
Bank, Islamic Solidarity Fund for Development, World Zakat
Organization, and the World Bank.

The World Congress of Muslim Philanthropists follows a simple
philosophy that is driven by the compassion that is intrinsic in Islamic
values. The WCMP believes that Muslims, across the board, should
reach out to the destitute and the oppressed, irrespective of gender,
ethnicity, or religious belief.

The WCMP's strategic focus is on effective and accountable giving;
strategic social investment; endowment (waqf) revitalization; entrepreneurial advancements; knowledge ecosystem; next generation philanthropists; public policy and advocacy, and environmental stewardship.

CASE STUDY 10.2   MOHAMMED ABDUL LATIF JAMEEL

Mohammed Abdul Latif Jameel, a resident of Dubai, exemplifies in
many ways the sophistication and broad concerns of wealthy Middle
Eastern philanthropists.

He is president of ALJ Group of Saudi Arabia and Chairman of
International Business Leaders Forum for the Middle East. He is an
MIT graduate with interests in research and poverty. His worth is
estimated to be $4 billion.

His wealth came from his father, who passed onto him control of
the Group. ALJ's core business is Toyota's largest world dealership.

Jameel committed $75 million in support of the MIT Poverty
Action Lab. This endows a professorship, fellowships, and a research/
teaching fund in poverty alleviation and development economics.
Beyond this prestigious project he has a number of other strands to
his philanthropy. Specifically he:

- Developed a series of community programs to promote
  opportunities for young Saudis (i.e., building a cadre of local
  taxi owners/drivers by making auto finance loans more
  accessible).

(Continued)

- Combined microfinance-style loans with training to improve the skill sets of women in the Arab labor market. The goal is to create more than 16,000 new job opportunities.
- Partnered with Muhammed Yunis to form the Grameen-Jameel Pan Arab initiative that has targeted the creation of 1 million jobs through a micro-credit program by 2011.
- Sponsors "1001 Inventions: The Enduring Legacy of Muslim Civilization," a leading and award-winning international science and cultural heritage brand reaching more than 50 million people around the world. 1001 Inventions uncovers a thousand years of scientific and cultural achievements from Muslim civilization from the seventh century onward through award-winning educational programs, books, blockbuster exhibitions, live shows, films, and learning products.
- Founded the Coexist Foundation, which, since 2006, has been working to promote better understanding among Jews, Christians, and Muslims, and between these communities and others, through education, dialogue, and research.

In Summary

The countries of the Middle East and North Africa will continue to fascinate and concern the rest of the world. With two-thirds of the world's known petroleum reserves, the region's economic and political importance far outweighs its population size. Yet, its demographic trends—especially the rapidly growing youth population—are beginning to attract notice as well. Rapid population growth rates—second only to sub-Saharan Africa—will propel its total to 700 million by 2050, exceeding the population of Europe in that year. This continuing growth is complicating the region's capacity to adapt to social change, economic strains, and sometimes wrenching political transformations.

Philanthropy indeed has a positive and immensely important role to play in the region, and it needs to become both strategic and sustainable. The challenge of the current time, in which the root causes of social and economic injustices span beyond families, villages, cities, regions, and even nations, poses a new mandate for which organized efforts are ever more crucial.

Philanthropy in the MENA region, despite facing a complex set of external and internal challenges, is bound to grow both in its maturity and effectiveness. However, without the application of research and innovation, conventional giving models will continue to be ineffective. Further, in a region where philanthropy is predominantly faith-inspired, the resolution of long-standing religious and geopolitical conflicts is critical to the peace and prosperity of the region and its neighboring lands.

CHAPTER 11

Asia

YOUNGWOO CHOI AND USHA MENON, WITH AN INTRODUCTION BY BERNARD ROSS

Everyone knows about the success of the major Asian economies and their impressive growth rates. But Asian philanthropy and fundraising is one of the less known success stories of the global giving world—at least until now.

This chapter explores the incredible diversity of giving in this vast region where truly, as the famous proverb has it, "1,000 blossoms contend." We explore especially two aspects of giving in different countries and cultures—the major donor phenomenon and the individual giver.

If you do know anything about Asian fundraising, chances are it's about *major* giving. But although the name *Bill Gates* is on many lips worldwide, in Asia there are other names that should be just as well known and probably as celebrated. Looking just at Southeast Asia, for example, there are HNWIs making a massive difference across the region. For instance, here are five outstanding philanthropists you probably haven't heard of that *Forbes* recently highlighted (July 2012) as an aspect of the Asian Philanthropic Tiger:

- Quek Leng Chan, Malaysia: Quek Leng Chan is head of the Hong Leong Group and chair of the company's associated foundation. Over the past 25 years the foundation has built up to distributing $1.6 million annually on a range of educational projects from scholarships for disabled students to school building projects.
- Gunawan Jusuf, Indonesia: Gunawan Jusuf owns the Sugar Group, and provides free education, free meals, uniforms, shoes,

and backpacks to almost 2,000 children of his employees, many of whom work in the company's sugarcane fields. And these are not are "basic" schools, but have Internet access and even air-conditioning.

- Mercedes Zobel, Philippines: Mercedes Zobel, who runs furniture and design businesses throughout the region, donates nearly $500,000 a year to projects in education, health, and culture. There's also a focus on underprivileged women and children— especially where there's an inspirational leader in place and a track record of practical action and results.

- Tan Passakornnatee, Thailand: Tan Passakornnatee is the founder of Ichitan. Despite his own factory being damaged in the middle of the 2012 floods, Tan donated $2.3 million in various forms for survivor-aid kits—containing everything from tea to boats. He has now reopened the factory with a free museum of tea history and environmental conservation.

- Oei Hong Leong, Singapore: Oei Hong Leong, property tycoon, has an eclectic and wide-ranging philanthropic agenda. In recent years this has included giving $5 million to the Lee Kuan Yew School of Public Policy and sending $1.5 million to those impacted by the 2008 Sichuan earthquake. His other causes range from Singapore's oldest school to an encyclopedia about Singapore's biodiversity.

These five philanthropists are great examples to give you a sense of the kinds of major donor philanthropy taking place in Asia currently. Notice that their giving is often focused on basic civil society needs like child education, survival from disaster, and disability issues. Much of Asian major donor philanthropy is focused on areas that in a Western setting might be seen as a "governmental" responsibility. But the role of the state in Asia can be different, so philanthropists step in to meet need.

Although there is great individual wealth in Asia, there is also considerable developing philanthropy there at a "lower" level as the middle class grows and disposable incomes increase. Interestingly the development in this lower-level philanthropy is partly being driven by the market entry of the larger INGOs—Médecins Sans Frontières/Doctors Without Borders (MSF), UNICEF, Greenpeace, Habitat for Humanity International, and World Vision rather than domestic NGOs. (Though there are exceptions to this general rule—the Philippines Red Cross, under the leadership of the dynamic Gwen Pang, runs an extraordinary range of fundraising activities and shines as a beacon of good practice in the Red Cross and Red Crescent Movement.) But it is the old-world giants of the charity world who have all invested heavily in Asian markets in recent years—mostly through direct marketing.

But there's a focus on one particular kind of direct marketing. Individuals giving in the West are used to a variety of channels including direct mail, face-to-face, telemarketing, online, SMS, DRTV, and the press, for example.

In Asian markets, however, the number of channels used is currently more limited—partly due to the relative infancy of fundraising from individuals in these markets—and partly because in some nations certain kinds of infrastructure such as a reliable postal service don't exist. However, there is one direct marketing channel that appears to be the preferred choice of nonprofits, wherever the market is—face-to-face.

Global implementation of face-to-face and direct mail in emerging markets was first pioneered by Greenpeace and UNICEF in the 1990s, followed by Amnesty and others. Today, nearly all of the top INGOs are doing some kind of direct marketing in Asian countries—with South Korea and Indonesia proving magnets, and the Philippines and Hong Kong not far behind. It is by far the primary new monthly donor recruitment tool for hundreds of nonprofit organizations.

In a second wave of development we can see global charities with local affiliates such as HelpAge International, Transparency International, and International Planned Parenthood Federation beginning to encourage their local partners to adopt these techniques as a way to build sustainability—and reduce dependence. The advantage that many of these global charities bring is capital to set up programs where the payback may be three years or more—and expertise in how to set up programs and manage them. The results so far are impressive and considerable sums are being committed to these Asian initiatives.

If success continues we might then see a third wave of direct marketing development in Asia with genuinely local NGOs creating large-scale regular giving programs. It will be interesting in coming years to see if this "imported blossom" continues to thrive or some new domestic flower emerges.

Following are profiles of two Asian countries:

1. Korea, where individual giving is really taking off.
2. Singapore, a global center for innovation in the public and corporate sectors, which is now applying its many resources to developing its nonprofit sector so that it, too, will become exemplary.

KOREA BY YOUNGWOO CHOI

The Korean tiger economy has propelled the country to a prominent place among developed nations. While its economic prowess is common knowledge, less known is its success in philanthropy. Following is a description of how this success came about and the challenges that the Korean nonprofit sector must meet in order to continue in its upward trajectory.

A Dynamic Transformation in Korean Philanthropy

"Imitation to innovation" is the best phrase to explain Korean progress. In the four decades since the Korean War (1950–1953), which destroyed almost everything in Korea, the Korean people built their country up again to be one of the top 10 world trading countries. The secrets behind that rapid economic growth are strong zeal and effective strategy for "active technological learning." Korean manufacturing industries are classical examples of successful technology learning. The imitation to innovation phenomenon is vivid in the semiconductor, electronic appliance, mobile, automobile, and shipbuilding industries.

As late as 1961, Korea suffered from almost all the difficulties that most poor countries today face. Korea's per capita gross national product (GNP) was less than that of Sudan and less than one-third that of Mexico in 1961.[1]

After 36 years of Japanese colonial rule (1919–1945) and the Korean War, Korea received $1.3 billion in foreign aid from 1945 to 1995. Korea's GNP per capita in current prices rose at a phenomenal growth rate—from $87 in 1962 to $20,165 in 2010, which is more than 12 times that of Sudan and 2.2 times that of Mexico. During this time of accelerated economic growth, Korea transformed from a receiving country to a giving country.[2]

---

[1] Linsu Kim, 1997.

[2] Korea entered the OECD (Organisation for Economic Co-operation and Development) as its 29th member in 1996 and OECD DAC (Development Assistance Committee) as its 24th member in 2010.

They discovered that imitation to innovation can also be applied to philanthropy. The following examples clearly illustrate Korea's rapid transition to a country of dynamic philanthropy.

- Severance Hospital, one of the leading university hospitals in Korea, was named after Mr. Severance, who donated $40,000 to build the first Western hospital in Korea in 1885. Severance Hospital's 2011 annual budget is $1.3 billion and it cares for 4 million patients every year. It has expanded its medical system into Mongolia in the past 20 years by building hospitals and training more than 100 medical doctors.
- UNICEF Korea started its work here caring for war orphans. They had been the key foreign aid agency for the Korean poor people before 1993. By then, the Korean economic transformation was underway, and UNICEF tried to withdraw from Korea because foreign support was no longer needed. But, realizing the growing fundraising potential of their former aid recipient, they switched their strategy from withdrawal to remaking UNICEF Korea into a fundraising center for international programs. UNICEF Korea raised $60 million in 2011.

What caused that rapid growth of Korean philanthropy?

- Meaningful economic size: Korea has sufficient resources to support both domestic and international causes. The total population of Korea is 50,004,000 and the per capita GNI was $22,489 in 2011. Korea is one of seven countries in the world with more than 50 million residents and more than $20,000 above per capita GNI. According to Merrill Lynch, Korea had 127,000 HNWIs in 2009 (Merrill Lynch 2011). Korea had 14 Fortune Global 500 companies in 2011. Korea has more companies at that level than Canada or Italy.
- Dynamic sociopolitical development: Korea is one of the few countries that has succeeded in accomplishing both democratization and industrialization in the past four decades due to both external and internal influences.

    The Korean peninsula is surrounded by four world powers (United States, China, Japan, and Russia), which has caused a rather dramatic historical development. Korea's awakening took place in the late nineteenth and early twentieth centuries when it became open and willing to learn from Western civilization. It was then that Christianity began to play its critical role in educational and medical development. Twenty-six years of Japanese colonial rule (1919–1945) caused prolonged active fundraising for the resistance movement for independence.

Internal influences have also shaped Korea's sociopolitical development. The Korean War and the division of Korea into North and South stimulated nonprofit activity in Korea. World Vision was founded because of the Korean War. The citizens' successful resistance against dictatorship and military rule and struggle for democracy and human rights laid a strong foundation for the dramatic growth of advocacy NGOs in the late twentieth century. Korea's extraordinary economic growth has encouraged corporations to invest in corporate social responsibility (CSR).

- Religious and historical readiness for philanthropy: Possessing one of the world's longest histories as an independent nation, Korea also has a long tradition of its own philanthropy. Korea was a unified, independent state for more than 1,200–years since the Silla dynasty (BC 57–AD 935). Buddhism, Confucianism, and Christianity were introduced to Korea, in that order, forming rich cultural layers.

When Koreans talk about *noblesse oblige*, they refer to the ancient "Kyungju Rich Family Choi's Code of Conduct":[3]

---

[3]Choi Guk-seon, the 19th generation descendant of Choi Chi-won, a famed scholar, succeeded his father Choi Dong-ryang, who had accumulated wealth through land development. Choi Guk-seon advanced his fortune in owning fields yielding 10,000 seok of rice, thanks to his diligent efforts and thriftiness. After that, however, Choi no longer sought to increase his fortune. He instead began to look after his neighbors. In 1671, the third year of King Hyun-jong's reign, the nation was plagued by severe crop failure. Choi installed a large cauldron to boil rice every day in his yard and opened a storehouse in order to feed and clothe the impoverished. This is just one example of the virtues of Choi Chi-won that are much admired in Korea. Based on his values in life, Choi created the six principles as the family code of conduct. Source: http://world.kbs.co.kr/english/program/program_koreanstory_detail.htm??lang=e&current_page=4&No=34149.

- Apply for *gwageo*,[4] but do not take the official rank higher than Jinsa.[5]
- Return to society any possession over 10,000 seok.[6]
- Don't expand land during a time of famine.
- Welcome guests with hospitality.
- Do not allow anyone starve to death within 100 li[7] from you.
- Have a newly wedded daughter-in-law wear cotton clothes for three years.

Korea's Nonprofit Sector

Accurate data on Korean philanthropy is not available yet. There are several academic studies[8] underway to uncover the general features of Korean philanthropy, but still there is no comprehensive philanthropy data similar to that of Giving USA.

One of the most recent studies on philanthropy by the Korea Institute of Public Finance (KIPF 2010) shows that (see Table 11.1):

- Judging by tax-deductible donation data, the total donation (2008) to NGOs (including religious organization) is around $8 billion. Considering that the tax deduction procedure is rather

---

[4]The highest-level state examination to recruit ranking officials during the Goryeo and Joseon Dynasty.

[5]A person who only passed the first exam for an official.

[6]Seok (Seom): A Korean unit of volume, approximately equal to 180 liters (144 kg of rice).

[7]Li: A Korean unit of length, approximately equal to 400 meters.

[8]Key prior researches are:

Statistics Korea, *Result of Social Survey in 2011* (Philanthropy Culture), 2011.

The Center on Philanthropy at the Beautiful Foundation, *Giving Korea 2010*, Beautiful book, 2010.

The Center on Philanthropy at the Beautiful Foundation, *Giving Korea 2008*, Beautiful book, 2008.

The Center on Philanthropy at the Beautiful Foundation, *Giving Korea 2006*, Beautiful book, 2006.

Tae-Kyu Park and Ku-Hyun Jung, "Size Estimation of Nonprofit Sector of Korea and its Structure," *Korea NPO Study 2002*, no. 1: 3–31.

| TABLE 11.1 | KOREAN ANNUAL DONATIONS (TAX-DEDUCTIBLE) BY INDIVIDUALS AND CORPORATIONS |

	1999	2001	2003	2005	2007	2008
Donations	$2,763,768	$4,391,891	$5,547,059	$6,705,585	$6,148,209	$8,373,768
Individual	$836,823	2,803,328	$3,517,121	$4,079,385	$5,028,247	$5,197,422
Percentage	29.3%	63.8%	63.4%	60.9%	61.7%	62.1%
Corporations	$1,926,945	$1,588,563	$2,029,938	$2,622,539	$1,119,962	$3,176,346
Percentage	70.7%	36.2%	36.6%	39%	28.3%	37.9%

Source: KIPF, 2010, 9.

complex and many NGOs do not have tax-deductible status, it may be much more than that.

- Since 2000, the ratio of individual giving has been higher than that of corporate giving. Proactive fundraising activities of NGOs, a positive atmosphere toward individual philanthropy, and legal improvement caused the rapid growth of individual giving.

The Federation of Korea Industry's (FKI) Corporate Community Relationships White Book 2010 (FKI 2010) also shows the general features of corporate giving (see Figure 11.1):

- The 220 companies replying to FKI's survey on corporate giving donated $2.6 million ($2.9 trillion KRW) in 2010. Their average giving was $12 million.
- Their average ratio of CSR spending out of turnover is 0.24 percent. They are contributing an average of 3.2 percent of their ordinary profit to social cause.
- On the question of global corporate responsibility, 66.7 percent of the FKI member corporations replying were participating in CSR programs outside of Korea. The 32.9 percent of corporations replying that did not have a global CSR program have a plan to develop one.

Fundraising Practices in Korea

Social Welfare and Development Charity

The Korean chapters of international relief organizations were the first movers of Korean philanthropy. They are UNICEF, World Vision,

FIGURE 11.1	GAP BETWEEN INDIVIDUAL AND CORPORATE GIVING

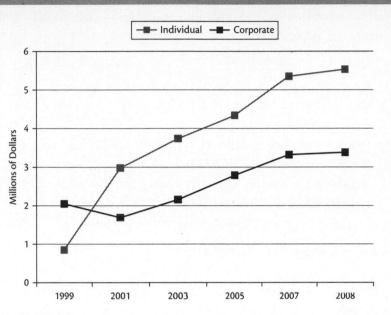

Source: KIPF, 2010, 10.

Child Fund, Salvation Army, Save the Children, Food for the Hungry, and so on. Their main role in Korea was distribution of foreign aid and building the domestic social welfare sector in Korea prior to the late 1980s. During the late 1980s and early 1990s, they either transformed their role from recipient to fundraisier and outward distributor of funds, or they withdrew from Korea. UNICEF and World Vision decided to transform its role and Compassion decided to withdraw.

UNICEF, Child Fund, World Vision, and Food for the Hungry introduced aggressive fundraising methodologies like direct mail, DRTV, telemarketing, corporate fundraising, walkathons, media-sponsored campaigns, and merchandising. This was possible because their headquarters had the willingness to guide the effort and to invest in Korea.

The Community Chest of Korea was raising annually more than $300 million in 2011. World Vision ($125 million), UNICEF ($60 million), and Food for the Hungry ($47 million) were also raising more than $50 million annually.

Recently some leading INGOs that had left Korea or had not previously fundraised proactively in Korea are now showing strong interest in raising resources there. Some are returning to raise money and are meeting with success.

- Save the Children: It has been in Korea since 1953, but did not fundraise before 2004. After a successful merger with Child Protection Foundation, a local NGO, it became one of the most dynamic fundraising stars.
- Compassion Korea: It supported 100,000 Korean children after the Korean War (1953–1993) before leaving the country. The organization returned to raise money in Korea for developing countries in 2003. In 2011 it raised $41 million.

Universities and Educational Institutions

Historically, Korea is famed for its strong commitment to education and scholarship. There are more than 400 universities and colleges in Korea. Among them are 50 public institutions. The number of scholarship foundations has increased steadily since the Korean War. Most university donations were for scholarships before the early 1990s. It was in the 1990s that university fundraising, which was passive and unorganized, changed. Korea University, Yonsei University, Ewha Women's University, and many others introduced a proactive fundraising system. They have achieved varying levels of success. Some of the credit for progress belongs to the many pioneering university presidents of the 1990s and 2000s, who are now recognized as fundraising heroes and heroines, including:

- Dr. Yoon Dae Euh (former president of Korea University, 2003–2006)
- Dr. KyungSook Lee (former president of Sook Myung Women's University, 1994–2008)
- Dr. Song Ja (former president of Yonsei University, 1992–1996)

From 2006 to 2010, Seoul National University successfully designed and managed the first Western-style capital campaign in Korea. Seoul National University raised $340 million under the leadership of former president JangMoo Lee. The Seoul National University capital campaign raised the level of expectation among Korean high education society.

Health Care

The most effective and best practices of Korean Universities' fundraising have been transferred to their affiliated academic hospitals. Severance Hospital (Yonsei University hospital), Seoul National University Hospital, and Catholic Hospital took the leading role in health care fundraising.

The majority of academic hospitals, excepting 11 national university hospitals, are heavily dependent on service fees for their financial sustainability. The leadership of leading hospitals is, however, realizing the power and potential of fundraising. These hospitals enthusiastically established fundraising departments and some are planning comprehensive capital campaigns.

Traditional health care fundraising in Korea was limited to the area of "linking poor patients with support from grateful patients." But now fundraisers are realizing the potential of private donations for medical research, the pursuit of medical excellence, and foreign aid.

Civic Organizations

The YMCA (founded in 1903) and the YWCA (founded in 1922) have been leaders in civic organizational fundraising in Korea. Both have a strong membership culture. When they recruit members, they are also recruiting volunteers and donors.

The 1980s and 1990s was a period of explosive growth for the advocacy movement in Korea. The Korea Federation for Environment Movement (KFEM), one of the biggest environmental organizations in Asia, was started in 1982 by Mr. Yul Choi. KFEM opened a new era of advocacy in Korea and showed the possibilities of raising money for the advocacy movement. Mr. WonSoon Park, the present mayor of Seoul City (2012–), brought new energy and creativity to advocacy since he founded the People's Solidarity for Participatory Democracy in 1994. Some of the other key organizations are:

- Consumers Korea, 1982
- Korea Women Link, 1987
- CEMK (Christian Ethic Movement in Korea), 1987
- CCEJ (Citizens' Coalition for Economic Justice), 1989

The fundraising efforts of advocacy organizations have taken one step forward, one step back, over the past 10 years, but now, undeniably, they have progressed to adapting integrated fundraising strategies.

- Amnesty Korea invested aggressively to recruit donors using face-to-face in the streets. Since 2005, they have recruited (and retained) more than 15,000 monthly donors.
- Many advocacy organizations realize the importance of integrating interaction with various constituencies: management of volunteers, campaign participants, and donors.
- INGOs are coming to Korea. Greenpeace and MSF are already here. Many others are considering entry. INGOs' aggressive and organized fundraising will undoubtedly draw local NGOs into the fundraising race.

Arts and Culture

The Korean arts and cultural communities are not adequately funded by either the government or the private sector. National and local governments have been steadily increasing their spending in this area (Ministry of Culture, Sports, and Tourism 2012),[9] but the arts community always cries for more support. Their outcries will intensify, because the social demand for art and culture are on the upswing because of corresponding personal income growth. Also there are plenty of artists desperate to share their creative ideas and talent with the public and nonprofit arts organizations wanting money to fund their projects and show their work.

Philanthropic development for the arts and culture is slow compared to that of education and health care. The Korean Business Council for the Arts (Maecenas Korea) was founded in 1994. It play an active role linking art with business. The Korea Arts Council (ARKO), which is a major supporting agency for art, is looking for ways to boost philanthropy for art and culture. In 2010, the Korea Arts Management Service, which is newly established by the government, conducted a national fundraising workshop for art organization that was resoundingly applauded by many art organizations. It will take some time for art organizations to be equipped with a viable

---

[9]In 2012, the Korean government increased the budget for arts and culture 11.5 percent (1.6 trillion KRW or $1.4 billion) compared to over that of 2011.

fundraising capacity in Korea. But it is just a matter of time and it will not be long.

Challenges in Korean Philanthropy

My 10 years of fundraising consulting experience, in a nation that has one of the most actively engaged in learning societies in the world, has enabled me to see that what really shapes philanthropy are proactive NGOs. So when we talk about health care philanthropy, we should look at the attitudes of leading hospitals toward fundraising. Let me share just some of the proactive approaches to mass fundraising, major gifts, and CSR being employed in Korea. I will also point out some challenges in each area for the future development.

Breakthroughs in Mass Marketing

- **Korean nonprofits are stepping up investment in street fundraising for recruiting monthly donors**. Amnesty International, UNICEF, Save the Children, UNHCR, Help Age Korea, and Green Korea United, were among the first to embrace the methodology. Part of the appeal of the method is that it can be difficult to get lists for donor acquisition in Korea. Meeting people in the street is a wonderful way to overcome that limitation.
- **Integrating fundraising with Korean "do-it-yourself" spirit**. Save the Children's mass campaign, "Let's Knit a Hat for an African Child," has produced unbelievable results. Knitting is a forgotten skill in Korea, but the campaign's nostalgic appeal excited the public. The initial demand for participation was huge and is growing every year.[10] Engaging knitters in the cause in this way cultivates participants to become regular donors to Save the Children. In 2011, they raised $20 million.
- **Using fundraising programs for educational purposes**. World Vision, UNICEF, and Good Neighbors are pioneers in introducing global citizenship programs to schools. Beautiful Store is one of the resale shop leaders, even providing chances

---

[10]There have been more than 140,000 participants and 560,000 hats gathered in the campaign from 2007 to June 2012.

for children to sell their used goods for charity. Many thousands of kids participate in this way and young donors easily persuade their parents to donate as well.

- **Cultivating HNWI society for mass fundraising**. Compassion Korea has invited key high-net leaders capable of inspiring and influencing others to lead their fundraising endeavors. Among them are church leaders, who open their congregations to Compassion, as well as celebrities, who were inspired by the values and vision of Compassion to transform their way of life, and to reach out to their fans. These celebrities are powerful magnets for some donors. Compassion Korea has also engaged and challenged business leaders to personal sacrifice.
- **Integrating mass fundraising channels (online, media purchase, DRTV, telemarketing) for better results**. Several NGOs made a group purchase of several days of time on public television to recruit monthly donors for their international programs.

Challenges in Mass Marketing

- **The gap between rich and poor organizations is widening**. Rich organizations have (1) a commitment to finding the best methodologies, (2) resources to invest, and (3) a leadership that understands its role in ensuring adequate financial resources. Start-ups and small NGOs do not have these advantages. They are easily pushed here and there by the latest opportunity and the most recent crisis.
- **Many advocacy organizations do not really align fundraising with their core values**. They fail to understand the philosophical value of fundraising or to communicate that understanding internally and externally.
- **Many organizations are not ready to steward donors properly or to provide meaningful participation**. This is critical for donor retention.

Breakthroughs in Major Gifts

- **Capital campaigns work in Korea**. Seoul National University and Severence Hospital's success in capital campaigns shows that key principles of major gift fundraising can be perfectly applied in Korea. These organizations discovered in the process that fundraising is more than just money. Volunteer-driven fundraising has a far-reaching positive impact on organizations and can provide valuable constituent feedback and rekindle dormant relationships. Seoul National University and Severance leaderships saw that they could learn a lot from donors. Their success underscored the importance of volunteer leadership for strategic development.

- **University and hospital active engagement in major gift fundraising deepened understanding of donor relationships**. Both NGOs and donors are more interested in naming opportunities, gift acceptance policies, and ethical concerns around the same time. NGOs became more circumspect in every respect concerning donor relationships.
- **Interest in giving societies is growing**. The Community Chest of Korea founded a giving club named *Honors Club*. This select group only invites donors of at least $100,000.[11]
- **The government is very interested in providing legal support for annuity trusts** and this reflects the great potential of legacy giving in Korea. Baby boomers, who benefited from exponential Korean economic growth from the 1960s to 1990s, have the resources to give in this way and are being encouraged to do so by NGOs.

Challenges in Major Gifts

- **Demand for better governance**. An open and dynamic board is crucial for successful major gift fundraising. The majority of nonprofit boards in Korea do not take their responsibility to fundraise seriously. Many boards do not have clear rotation rules. More proactive board development and adaptation of global best practices of governance will be critical for sustainable growth of major gift fundraising in Korea.

---

[11] The Honor Society was established in December 2007. Since June 2012, 117 members have joined (6 members in 2008, 9 members in 2009, 27 members in 2010, and 45 members in 2011).

- **Need to institutionalize major gift fundraising**. The fundraising performance of many nonprofits is fluctuating seriously. These ups and downs are dependent upon the capability of the chief leader of the organization. The usual tenure of a Korean university president is four years. Deans of colleges and heads of cultural organizations usually serve less than that. This lack of stability makes it difficult to plan and implement a long-term fundraising campaign. Not only that, it has been difficult to find professional fundraising directors to lead fundraising departments in universities and hospitals. The professional fundraising community needs to develop within key NGOs.

Development and Challenges of CSR in Korea

Korean corporations are spending serious amounts of money on CSR and their practices are maturing. Leading Korean businesses are integrating CSR into their corporate cultures and core business strategies. See Table 11.2.

Corporations are seeing the value of employee volunteerism and giving. Many companies provide their employee's family members and customers with opportunities to join their volunteer programs. These are good opportunities for NGOs to recruit donors using CSR.

Financial companies are developing "donor consulting systems" for their clients to find the best recipient organizations. Leading NGOs need to cooperate with banks for planned giving opportunities.

TABLE 11.2   **DEVELOPMENT OF CSR PRACTICE IN LARGE KOREAN CORPORATIONS**

CSR Activity	2000	2010
We have designated personnel for CSR.	25.9%	95.5%
We have a budget system for CSR.	27.5	89.9
We have a formal written declaration and policy for CSR.	22.3	81.9
We have a matching gift policy for employee donations.	NA	78.4
We have a formal CSR committee.	6/7	65.8
We have a company-wide formal volunteer organization.	NA	86.3
We allow our employees to volunteer using their working days.	4.7	60.9

Source: FKI, 2010: 80–81, paraphrasing.

Challenges for CSR Development

- **Social polarization issues are getting more serious in Korea**. People are asking for justice and ethical practice from corporations on top of their charitable work. The demand for creative capitalism will be a challenge for corporations in designing CSR for the near future.

- **Comparing the global CSR of Korean companies with those of companies in other countries, Korean companies' global CSR is less visible**. The major obstacle for Korean companies' international programs is that it is difficult to find appropriate local partner organizations and professionals.

- **A significant portion of Korean companies' CSR is used for their own programs**. There are growing concerns around that trend. The business community's excuse is that they face difficulties in finding reliable NGO partners. Businesses need to invest more aggressively in the capability of building in the NPO sector.

SINGAPORE BY USHA MENON

Singapore has a highly developed and successful free-market economy. It enjoys a per capita GDP higher than that of most developed countries.

Homeowners constitute 87 percent of households. Reflecting the rising affluence of the population, the size of Singaporean residences has grown over the past decade. A Boston Consulting Group report indicated that Singapore had the highest concentration of millionaire (in U.S. dollars) households in the world, with 11.4 percent of families owning investable assets valued at seven figures or higher.

The total population of Singapore was 5.18 million at the end of June 2011. This includes 3.26 million Singapore citizens, 0.53 million permanent residents, and 1.39 million foreigners working, studying, or living in Singapore. There were more females than males in Singapore's resident population—the ratio was 972 males to 1,000 females in 2011.

As Singapore transforms into one of the world's richest societies, the idea of sharing wealth beyond one's immediate clan or community is gaining broader support. There are also more women with higher education and purchasing power choosing to remain single to build their careers and pursue their passions in life, including philanthropy.

Singapore is a regional leader in many areas, including philanthropy. Singapore's multiracial and multicultural demographics have made it a hub for Asian diaspora communities. It has provided thought and practice leadership in the region in governance, policy making, and implementation — leveraging its intellectual capital so that governments, businesses, and academia can access information and knowledge on regional and global trends. Given the role that Singapore plays as a hub for the region, there is a growing interest among the more enlightened Singapore residents to enhance their involvement and impact across the region through their volunteer and philanthropic efforts.

Tax policies, however, lag behind these regional aspirations, as there are no tax incentives for philanthropic contributions for causes outside of Singapore. Despite the lack of incentives, in 2011 there were 94 fundraising permits granted by the Commissioner of Charities, which totaled S$42.9 million (US$34.4 million) being raised for overseas causes. Of these, 36 permits were granted in response to international natural disasters. This was in addition to unofficial support for regional causes by individuals.

Asian traditions and religions like Confucianism, Buddhism, Hinduism, among others, give tend to prize humility, and many are averse to public displays of generosity. Many donors anonymously give millions, and this is not reflected in the reports compiled by various researchers. At the same time there are those who are keen on visible acknowledgment of their contributions in terms of naming rights, awards, and other accolades.

Many wealthy Asians, who made their fortune within this generation through their entrepreneurial talents, want to invest their wealth and skills in driving social change. Venture philanthropy is emerging as a promising tool to support enterprise solutions while generating both financial and social or environmental returns.

Organizations that focus on the venture philanthropy community across the Asia Pacific region are growing. The Asian Venture Philanthropy Network[12] (AVPN) is one such entity. It provides specific networking and learning opportunities for its members.

---

[12] www.avpn.asia/.

Asia is also leading the growth of social capital markets and organizations have sprung up to support this growth. Singapore-based Impact Investment Exchange Asia (IIX) is Asia's first private and public platform for social enterprises to raise capital efficiently. The Association of Social Enterprise is an umbrella organization promoting social entrepreneurship. The SEHub was established to invest in and incubate social enterprise, the Social Innovations Park provides retail space for up-and-coming social enterprises. National University of Singapore's Centre for Social Entrepreneurship and Philanthropy and others focus on building a viable social enterprise ecosystem in Singapore.

Singapore's Nonprofit Sector

The Commissioner of Charities annual report[13] for year ended December 2011 showed the total income of the charity sector (which includes fees for services rendered, donations, and government grants) amounted to $8.58 billion. Of the 2,093 registered charities in Singapore, there were 112 large charities with annual income of more than $8 million, up from 104 charities the previous year. These large organizations garner 85 percent of the total income of the sector.

The types of registered charities include 568 Institutions of Public Character (IPCs)—a status conferred onto a nonprofit organization serving the needs of Singapore communities, which currently allows the issuance of 250 percent tax-deductibility to the donor for (local causes only) donations made until the end of 2015. Nonprofits registered in Singapore raising funds for programs outside of Singapore are not conferred the IPC status.

The total value of the tax deductible donations received in 2011 was about $718 million, which is approximately an increase of 15 percent from the amount received in 2010. Of the $718 million tax-deductible donations to IPCs raised,[14] corporate contributions constituted the largest portion of the donation pie.[15]

---

[13] www.charities.gov.sg/charity/index.do/.

[14] An IPC is a nonprofit charity, institution, or fund meeting certain qualifications and approved by the government of Singapore.

[15] Commissioner of Charities Singapore 2011 Annual Report.

This anomaly in Singapore is mainly due to the fact that individual philanthropists use their private corporate vehicles to make the gifts. In Singapore, as in many other countries in Asia, business families and individual philanthropists view corporate responsibility initiatives as extensions of their own or family giving.

To encourage giving, the Singapore government is matching donations to key causes such as universities and charities providing long-term care for the elderly.

Philanthropy in Singapore

Major Donors

Major gift giving is growing, especially from HNWIs. Although traditional individual support to meet the immediate short-term needs of charities is prevalent, more contributions are being strategically focused on long-term systemic changes and ensuring effectiveness in meeting nonprofit missions. Education has been especially successful in mobilizing exceptionally large, multiyear major gifts from local donors and foundations, more so than in the social services.

The rich are incorporating philanthropy into their wealth management plans, in part because of an increased use of the philanthropic advisory services provided by wealth management institutions. Also the concept of *giving while living* is gaining popularity with the new philanthropists.

In the 2011 UBS-INSEAD study *Family Philanthropy in Asia*, the number one reason for engaging in philanthropy, cited by 42 percent of the people and organizations surveyed, was "ensuring the continuity of family values or creating a lasting legacy."

Individuals

As for raising funds from the general populace, most nonprofits in Singapore are focused on special events as their main fundraising activity. These include mass events like walkathons and flag day (street collections) as well as niche events like gala dinners and charity golf tournaments. Mega-events like the Standard Chartered Marathon in Singapore have provided viable platforms, both on-site and online, for nonprofits and individuals to raise funds for various causes. Another such event on the fundraising calendar in Singapore is the SGX Bull

Charge that has raised more than $13.5 million since its 2004 inception. Five thousand participants from listed companies and the financial community joined in the effort in support of selected charities in 2011. As the novelty and the efficiency of raising funds solely through special events diminishes, however, interest in other kinds of fundraising grows.

Corporations

As indicated earlier, the corporate sector is an important source of fundraising dollars through outright donations, grants, sponsorship, and cause-related marketing. Additionally businesses are recognizing the value of CSR in establishing brand recognition, enhancing corporate reputation, increasing trust among stakeholders and as part of recruitment and retention strategy. Although the differences between CSR and philanthropy are still confused, some corporations are rolling out CSR initiatives that focus on environment and climate change challenges and community development.

Professor Eugene K. B. Tan, in his 2011 research paper *State of Play of CSR in Singapore*,[16] commissioned by the Lien Centre for Social Innovation, identified four key drivers of CSR in Singapore. These drivers work interdependently to help shape the direction and emphasis of the CSR movement in Singapore. The key drivers are:

- The government as the agenda-setter, agenda-manager, practitioner, and promoter.
- CSR as a strategic differentiator in the economic realm.
- The reality and imperative of Singapore's export economy, which nurtures and drives concerns that CSR could, in time, operate as a trade barrier and eat into Singapore's export competitiveness.
- Use of CSR as a catalyst for regulation (in particular, self-regulation) and setting as well as reinforcing the norms in governance and regulation, especially in the business realm. In this regard, the utility of CSR as *soft law*, if properly developed, can translate to soft power for a country so dependent on foreign trade and investments.

---

[16] www.lcsi.smu.edu.sg/downloads/TheStateOfPlayOfCSRinSingapore.pdf.

Singapore is rising to prominence as a global hub for business, with finance and banking moving operations to Singapore from Europe and with more international companies listing on the Singapore Exchange. With this comes the responsibility to ensure that companies operating in Singapore are world class in every sense, including CSR.

In May 2012, the Monetary Authority of Singapore (MAS) issued a revised Code of Corporate Governance. The revised code requires corporate boards to consider sustainability issues, such as environmental and social factors, as part of its strategic formulation. Corporations must broaden their strategic priorities to include sustainability and ethical standards for operating in the community.

Foundations

A study[17] done by the National University of Singapore in January 2011 showed that there is a growing group of grant-making entities in Singapore. A grant-maker, or grant-making organization, is a registered entity whose primary purpose is to make grants to unrelated institutions or individuals in pursuit of its charitable objectives (such as poverty relief, education advancement, and religious advancement, among others).

In this study, based on secondary sources of data, each grant-making entity in Singapore was classified into one of the following 13 categories:

1. Private foundations
2. Charitable trusts
3. Corporate foundations
4. Corporate funds
5. Ethnic self-help organizations
6. Chinese clan associations
7. Religious organizations and affiliated foundations
8. Health-care-related funds
9. Politically affiliated foundations
10. Government-run grant-making entities
11. Government-run funds
12. Tertiary education–related funds
13. Social interest and advocacy groups

---

[17] www.worldfuturefound.org/uploads/media/doc/GrantmakingEntitiesIn SingaporeJanuary2011.pdf.

Fundraising Practices

In 2010, I tracked the fundraising performance of 20 locally active nonprofits in Singapore. Figure 11.2 shows how they ranked their fundraising by methodology. Nearly 70 percent of these organizations sought corporate donations. More than 40 percent of the 20 organizations indicated that securing corporate donations was their top ranking methodology. Special events (both mass and niche events) were the next most used methodology. Although direct mail is also popular, unlike mature fundraising markets, most of it is implemented in-house, because there are few vendors and suppliers focused on the charity sector. More than 60 percent had begun incorporating online technology to raise funds, although the amounts raised by individual organizations were not significant.

Another study conducted in 2011 looked at the use of social media and Web 2.0 technology by nonprofits in Singapore. This study,

FIGURE 11.2

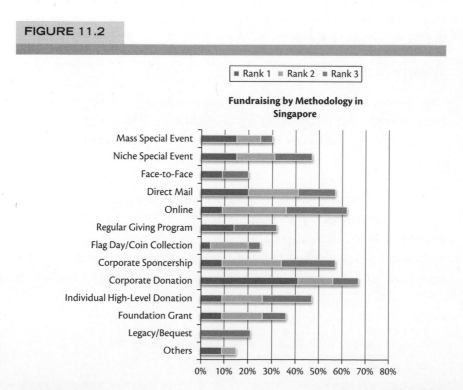

Source: Usha Menon.

commissioned by the Infocomm Development Authorities (IDA), identified two top reasons nonprofits were not fully leveraging technology for their fundraising and community engagement efforts:

- Lack of knowledge of the range of Web 2.0 tools and solutions.
- Lack of savvy personnel to efficiently use the tools available.

The People Sector Infocomm Resource Centre (PSIRC) is an online initiative of Nanyang Polytechnic, supported by IDA, to address some of the barriers identified in IDA's study. This resource center will accomplish this by providing information and examples on use of social media by nonprofits.[18]

Singapore Gives (SgGives) is an online donation portal for Singapore-registered charities. SgGives is an initiative of the National Volunteer & Philanthropy Centre.[19] The portal saw a 46 percent increase in total donations in 2011 as compared to 2010. Between February 2010 and 2012, the portal raised more than $7.9 million.

GIVE.sg is another Singapore-based peer-to-peer fundraising portal for local charities. It is a community-driven website conceptualized by social entrepreneurs and run by young and passionate volunteers from the GIVEfellows program.[20]

Singapore as a Hub for INGOs

The Singapore Economic Development Board (EDB) set up its International Organizations Program Office in 2007. It is a government effort to facilitate the relocation of international nonprofit organization to Singapore. The government is also supporting INGO infrastructure through resources such as the Tanglin International Centre for clustering and shared services for such organizations. There has been a growth of international organizations conducting their regional work from Singapore.

In late 2011, I tracked the fundraising performance of 12 INGOs registered in Singapore. The study was done through an online

---

[18] www.psirc.sg/resources/social-media-for-the-people-sector/.

[19] www.sggives.org/.

[20] www.give.sg.

questionnaire followed by an in-person or phone interview. The following patterns were found:

- All 12 INGOs focused 70 to 80 percent of their community development efforts on regional programs.
- Of the 12 INGOs, two focused 90 to 95 percent of their efforts in Singapore to raise funds locally for overseas programs through private supporters. Another six INGOs focused between 50 and 89 percent of their efforts in Singapore on fundraising for overseas causes.
- Other aspects of overseas-focused development, besides fundraising, included volunteer mobilization, regional program planning, and regional advocacy programs, including those related to disaster response and community development.

INGOs focus their Singapore fundraising on private supporters, as fundraising regulations do not encourage public fundraising for causes outside of Singapore. Likewise, there are no tax incentives for donors contributing to causes beyond its borders.

Organizations wishing to appeal for funds for any foreign charitable purpose[21] must apply to the office of the Commissioner of Charities for a permit. The application must be submitted not less than 30 days before the date on which the fundraising appeal commences. If the funds are raised from the public, the applicant has to utilize at least 80 percent of the net proceeds of the funds raised within Singapore. This 80/20 rule is waived for private donations or for appeals to aid major disaster relief. The Commissioner of Charities has the discretion to allow a lower percentage to be applied within Singapore.

Despite this limiting policy environment, the 2011 UBS-INSEAD study *Family Philanthropy in Asia* found that Singapore had the highest levels, 33 percent, of "Nondomestic Giving by Philanthropists." Hong Kong came next, with 23 percent.

Conclusion

Singapore is a model for how a city can leverage its unique strengths and build its value as a global center for innovation in the public and corporate spheres. Its nonprofit sector needs to do the same.

---

[21] www.charities.gov.sg/charity/charity/ffrPreRequisites.do.

Innovation requires the discipline of process and the courage of the entrepreneur. If nonprofit leaders could take a more creative approach fundraising processes, they might dare to move away from transactional activities where the donor is not drawn closer to the charity, the cause, or the community served.

Like Singapore the nation, the fundraisers in Singapore must learn to do more with less. We need to toss out stale methodologies that have passed their "use-by" date. They must come to understand the changes needed in fundraising—and to draw on the rich array of resources available from within the organization (board, staff, volunteers, donors) and from the community at large—if Singapore is to have robust and sustainable nonprofits.

Five areas that would help bring about some of these changes in fundraising:

1. Co-creation: With the creation of new wealth and more individuals interested in becoming strategic philanthropists and impact investors rather than mere check-writers, nonprofits should learn to co-create with them the desired future for the community.
2. More than money: Given the strong base of the corporate sector in Singapore, nonprofits need to increase their understanding of the way the corporate sector works and thereby access a whole gamut of possible collaborations in gifts, grants, marketing deals, and volunteer resources.
3. Leverage peer power: It is important that nonprofits are not the sole voice promoting a cause. The ability to influence others through peer-to-peer strategies and crowdsourcing should be part of any fundraiser's skill set.
4. Sharing and learning: In my 25 years in the sector, one quality that I have found in exceptional fundraisers is that they are willing to share—knowledge, time, and encouragement— to motivate others to be as passionate as they are themselves. Make the donation pie bigger so that all benefit instead of worrying about who will get the largest share. I urge fundraisers to join local, regional, and international forums that provide the opportunity to share, compare, and learn from other professionals.

5. Culture that innovates: An organization as a whole—the board and all staff—must be committed to innovation, and not delegate it to just a few individuals. And although many nonprofits excel in this area, they are not as good at committing themselves to full implementation of ideas, and good ones just fizzle out. Nonprofits could engage with the government, private sector, or foundations to stimulate innovation in fundraising for Singapore and beyond.

In Summary

Asia, including the major players of Korea and Singapore profiled here, is a force to be reckoned with. Its present successes and ambitions for the future will position them to achieve even more and to serve as leaders in charitable giving and the world will look to the example they set.

CHAPTER 12

India

USHA MENON AND ANUP TIWARI

The three opening words of ancient scripture Isha Upanishad are *tena tyaktena bhunjita*, "By renouncing it, enjoy it."

More than 80 percent of Indians practice Hinduism. The Hindu spiritual books (the shastras) do not require tithing to any temple or religious institution.

Despite the noncongregational nature of Hinduism and its purely voluntary ethos, this way of life has attracted people from many different cultures and the resources needed to sustain its religious and social activities.

At the same time, charitable donations do not necessarily win social recognition in Indian society. It may even be avoided, as recognition of one's charitable giving is detrimental to the process of salvation—*moksha*—as conceived by the Hindus.

THE DEMOGRAPHICS OF INDIA

By 2030 the population of India will reach 1.6 billion, making it the most populous country in the world.[1] India is also set to become the largest contributor to the global workforce. Its population in the 15 to 59 age group is likely to swell from 749 million to 962 million over 2010 to 2030.[2] According to Charities Aid Foundation's *World Giving Index 2011*, 28 percent of the Indian population gives—*336 million individuals*. This is more than the entire current population of

---

[1] "World Population Prospects," the 2008 Revision; United Nations Department of Economic and Social Affairs/Population Division.

[2] "Skilling India," 2010, Centre for Economic Research, CRISIL Ltd.

the United States, the leading market in the survey. In other words, India has the biggest potential donor population in the world.

India not only has the largest population, it is the seventh biggest country in the world in terms of area. It has more than 50 cities with a population of 1 million people or more.[3] These cities are dispersed across the country. Since the urban population is so widely spread, fundraising is not limited to certain metropolitan areas. And while some parts of India experience extreme summer heat, overall the climate is suited for every type of outdoor fundraising.

India gained independence from the British Empire in 1947. During the colonial era it was known as the *jewel in the crown*. The founding fathers of independent India declared it a secular republic and it continues to be world's largest democracy.

According to the 2001 Census, Hinduism accounted for 80.5 percent of the population of India. Islam (13.4 percent), Christianity (2.3 percent), Sikhism (1.9 percent), Buddhism (0.8 percent), and Jainism (0.4 percent) are the other major religions followed by the people of India.

The Tirumala Tirupati Devasthanam, considered the richest Hindu temple in the world, has an annual income of INR 170 million[4] ($377 million). Faith-based giving, significant for other religions too, has accustomed people to giving, and many of the traditional charitable concerns of religion have easily transferred to modern philanthropy.[5]

Hindi is the official language of India. According to the 2001 Census, 30 languages are spoken by more than a million native speakers and 122 by more than 10,000. However, English, an inheritance from the British era, is widely used. So much so that in 2004, India's English-speaking population was larger than the United States and United Kingdom together.[6] English is the unifying language for communication about giving across the country.

---

[3] http://en.wikipedia.org/wiki/List_of_million-plus_agglomerations_in_India.

[4] www.indiatvnews.com/news/India/Huge-Amount-Of-Black-Money -Pours-Into-Tirupati-Shirdi-Shrines-15496.html.

[5] Sanjay Agarwal, "Daan and Other Giving Traditions in India," *The Forgotten Pot of Gold* (Account Aid India, 2010).

[6] Rishi Majumder, "The Trouble with English," *Tehelka Magazine* 7, no. 13, April 3, 2010. www.tehelka.com/story_main44.asp?filename=hub030410the_ trouble.asp.

India ranks number three in the world in terms of gross domestic product (GDP) based on purchasing-power-parity (PPP) valuation,[7] and has high potential breeding for philanthropic growth. See Table 12.1.

THE NONPROFIT SECTOR IN INDIA

A study commissioned by the government puts the number of nonprofit institutions in India at 3.3 million. The nonprofit sector is one of the largest institutional sectors in India.[8] The main statutory laws governing the various types of registered nonprofit organizations are:

- Nonprofit organizations created for the larger public good
  - The Societies Registration Act, 1860
  - The Indian Trusts Act, 1882
  - Public Trust Act, 1950
  - The Indian Companies Act (Section 25), 1956
- Religious nonprofit organizations
  - Religious Endowments Act, 1863
  - The Charitable and Religious Trust Act, 1920
  - Mussalman Wakf Act, 1923
  - Wakf Act, 1954
  - Public Wakfs (Extension of Limitation) Act, 1959

While the government has begun studying the economy of the sector in the second phase of the aforementioned survey, estimates from within the sector suggest that NGOs, or *NPIs* as nonprofits are known in India, raise anywhere between $8.3 billion and $17 billion annually. The government has been the biggest donor to the sector—$3.75 billion was set aside in the XI Plan. The second largest source of funds for the sector are foreign contributors ($2 billion in 2007 to 2008). Individual donors, however, are emerging as the most promising new source of funds and may well become the largest single source.

---

[7] "World Economic Database," April 2012, International Monetary Fund.

[8] "Compilation of Accounts for Non Profit Institutions in India in the framework of System of National Accounts"; National Accounts Division; Central Statistical Organization; Ministry of Statistics and Programme Implementation; Government of India; 2009.

TABLE 12.1   POTENTIAL FUNDRAISING SOURCES

Stream	Approximate Size as a Percent of Total Market	Current Status of Stream	Potential for Growth
Individuals Small Donations by Individuals	The middle class numbers some 50 million people (2007). By 2025 it will have expanded dramatically to 583 million people—some 41 percent of the population.	*India Philanthropy Report 2010* by Bain & Company grouped charitable donations across three classes in urban India defined by income and education: middle, high, and upper. The high class, which is ranked one level below the "upper class" on the income and education scale, donates 2.1 percent to charity. The middle class gives 1.9 percent of household income to charity.	Sampradaan Indian Centre for Philanthropy (SICP) reported that 96 percent of upper- and middle-class households in urban areas donate for a charitable purpose. However, promoting giving must address all forms of wealth, as giving money is not the only form. For instance, community grain banks offer a solution to development projects.
Individuals Major Donors	India had 162,000 millionaire households in 2011.[9] It as one of the fastest-growing HNWI populations in the world. This demographic group grew by 21 percent in India between 2009 and 2010. In India, the wealthiest 1 percent of the population controls about 16 percent of national wealth.	According to 2010 report by Bain, India's wealthiest have the lowest level of giving compared to other economic classes surveyed by Bain, just 1.6 percent of household income. The Indian Diaspora has been one of the larger global migrant movements in the world, an estimated 20 million persons. Remittances in 2005 were $21.7 billion, four times higher than India's Foreign Direct Investment.	By 2025, there will be 9.5 million Indians in this class and their spending power will hit $253 billion or 20 percent of total Indian consumption.
Corporations and Corporate Foundations	Corporate and business donations in 2008 may have amounted to $180 million to $215 million, judging by the tax loss figures in the annual budget as reported by PRIA (Participatory Research in Asia).	Only 10 percent of charitable income is from individuals and corporations. Among the top 40 business groups, nearly 70 percent are family-owned/controlled enterprises. Some families and individuals view corporate responsibility initiatives as extensions of their own giving and less likely to make personal donations according to the 2010 Bain report.	As the growth of wealthy individuals continues to accelerate and more foundations are created, foundations may come to play a greater role in meeting community needs. Most Indian companies donate in the range of $200,000–$1 million annually.

Foundations Including Family Foundations	Institutional giving by foundations is difficult to assess. $180 million is a generous estimate of total disbursements.	Jamshedji Tata is considered as the father of modern Indian philanthropy. The J. N. Tata Endowment Scheme was launched in 1892, much before the first major foundation was formed in the United States. The Tata trusts currently disburses around $36 million. The Tata trusts today control 65.8 percent of the shares of Tata Sons, the holding company of the group. The Ratan Tata Foundation, Birla Foundations, Nanndi, Reddy, Godrej, Azim Premji Foundation, Infosys Foundation, Bajaj trusts, Bharti Foundation are other major foundations operating in India.	Just three publicly listed firms, Reliance Industries, Jindal Steel & Power, and Jaiprakash Associates donated more than $5.5 million each for the year ended March 31, 2009.
Community Trusts and Foundations		In recent years foundations have been established by groups of community leaders. Examples of such trusts are National Foundation for India (NFI), Rashtriya Gramin Vikas Nidhi, Rajiv Gandhi Foundation, Helpage India, Diwaliben, and Mohanlal Mehta Charitable Trust. These foundations have their own resources and are involved in extensive grant-making. There are also community foundations like the Bombay Public Trust.	The lines may be blurred between personal giving and corporate social responsibility initiatives because much of corporate India is run by family-owned groups.
State or Statutory	65 percent of income to voluntary sector comes from the government and foreign organizations.	There are government-sponsored foundations like the Council for Advancement of People's Action and Rural Technology (CAPART).	

Source: Online domain study in India done by Usha Menon, 2010.

[9]Global Wealth 2012 by Boston Consulting Group. www.bcg.com/expertise_impact/publications/PublicationDetails.aspx?id=tcm:12-1070818&mid=tcm:12-107011.

How much could individual giving grow? According to an internal study by a leading U.K.-based NGO, donations by individuals are expected to have grown from $460 million in 2005 to $1.7 billion by a conservative estimate, and to $4.4 billion by more liberal estimates.[10] An even more optimistic study in 2006 estimated the total giving in India as 0.6 percent of GDP[11] or $5 billion. At this rate giving could double to $10 billion in 2011.

In 2010, all private charitable contributions (individuals, corporations, foundations, and trusts; both domestic and foreign) stood at 0.3 percent to 0.4 percent of GDP—up from about 0.2 percent in 2006. Corporate giving is estimated at $1.5 billion in 2010, up more than five times since 2006. Only 26 percent of private charity contributions were from individual donors,[12] which works out to somewhere between $1.3 and $1.6 billion in 2010.

Infrastructure

NGOs are required to register under Section 12A of the Indian Income Tax Act. This provides tax exemption on their income, but the exemption does not apply to activities deemed of a business or commercial nature. The leading NGOs in India—WWF and CRY (Child Rights and You)—have now formed separate for-profit companies to sell merchandise.[13]

If an NGO registers under Section 80G, their donors can deduct 50 percent from taxable income. The Central Government approves certain NGOs that are eligible for project or schemes for the purposes of Section 35AC. If a NGO succeeds in getting such an approval for its projects then it stands a good chance of mobilizing funds from the

---

[10]Archana Shukla, "First Official Estimate: An NGO for Every 400 People In India," *Indian Express* (New Delhi), Wednesday, July 7, 2010. www.indianexpress.com/news/first-official-estimate-an-ngo-for-every-400-people-in-india/643302/0.

[11]"India Philanthropy Report 2011," Bain & Company.

[12]Ibid.

[13]"Charities Face Tax Troubles over Calendars, Greeting Cards"; Anupama Chandrasekaran, June 19, 2009. www.livemint.com/2009/06/19232856/Charities-face-tax-troubles-ov.html.

corporate and the business sector. Businesses making contributions to such approved projects are allowed to deduct such contributions as expenditure.[14]

SAFRG (South Asian Fund Raising Group) is a think tank that promotes fundraising and philanthropy in South Asia. SAFRG also acts like an association of fundraisers, conducting research and advocating on issues impacting fundraising.[15] The Resource Alliance, a global fundraising and philanthropy capacity building organization, has an office in India. Both of these organizations conduct courses and workshops for NGOs on fundraising and other relevant issues. SAFRG organizes an annual summit and workshop around New Delhi that attracts grassroots organizations as well as leading NGOs. The SAFRG Institute of Fund Raising organizes courses of up to three weeks duration for beginners and intermediary fundraisers. Courses on philanthropy and fundraising are also slowly finding a place in graduate level educational programs for business and social work.

Technological infrastructure for the nonprofit sector exists, but has challenges. There are some database vendors and prospect list brokers, but the quality of the information they provide is questionable. The postal services are also not reliable. There are several agencies that raise funds through telefacing,[16] a hybrid of telemarketing and face-to-face. India also has a couple of established face-to-face agencies that raise funds for leading NGOs. Digital media agencies are in abundance but not many of them have fundraising experience. Direct debit via bank accounts and credit cards is increasingly popular.

Significant Nonprofits

The leading nonprofits in India include the following nonprofits, CRY, HelpAge India, and Give India.

CRY—Child Rights and You
CRY—Child Rights and You is the leading NGO in terms of gross income from local fundraising. In the financial year April 2010 to March 2011, CRY raised $10.7 million and 94 percent of it came from individual donors.

---

[14] www.incometaxforngos.org.

[15] www.safrg.org.

[16] www.telefacing.net.

Unlike many older NGOs of comparable size encumbered by years of dated fundraising practices, 30-year-old CRY had a clean slate to begin with. Quite early on it raised funds through merchandising and special events, both of which have contributed to a highly visible brand. CRY has invested in expertise, consistently hiring professional fundraising staff as well as outside help. In 2002 CRY started face-to-face fundraising using an outsourced agency, long before other NGOs did. CRY also outsourced its merchandise business to a leading Indian company, Archies Greetings and Gifts.

CRY makes use of a wide variety of technological tools. In 1993 CRY got a grant from Norad and Stromme Memorial Foundation, Norway, to support fundraising through direct mail. On January 26, 2005, Indian Republic Day, a seven-hour CRY telethon was organized on Sony TV. It was India's first-ever, interactive social responsibility show, where celebrities and personalities appealed to audiences to contribute time or money toward changing children's lives. CRY is active in the digital fundraising domain, using both conventional and less traditional tools, like email marketing and social media marketing.[17] CRY was the first NGO to use telefacing, a hybrid of telephone and face-to-face fundraising, which is now popular with many other NGOs in India.

CRY partners with many homegrown and multinational companies. One of its biggest corporate partners is P&G, with whom they have a multiyear program called *Project Siksha* that promotes education of underprivileged children.

HelpAge India

HelpAge India[18] is another leading NGO in terms of gross income from local funds. It works to improve the welfare of the elderly in India and is part of the HelpAge International network. In the financial year April 2010 to March 2011 it raised $10.4 million.[19] More than 85 percent of its resources come from individual donors.

---

[17] www.cry.org.

[18] HelpAge India, though part of an international network, is being separately considered from INGOs as it has been raising funds for a long time before the INGO fundraising trend caught up in India.

[19] Annual Report 2010–2011; www.helpageindia.org.

HelpAge India, like CRY, has a long history of fundraising. Generations of Indians have been touched by its still very successful school fundraising program. It still succeeds using direct mail for acquisition. Digital media fundraising does not play a large role in HelpAge's strategies. It mostly uses email marketing and Google AdWords. It is moving, however, toward newer methodologies. Four years ago it started raising funds using an outsourced face-to-face fundraising agency.

HelpAge India was supported by around 50 corporations in the year 2011 to 2012. That year HelpAge forged one of the biggest ever partnerships between a nonprofit and corporation in India. The ONGC (Oil and Natural Gas Company) supported HelpAge India in launching a pan-India health-care program for the elderly called VaristhajanSwasthya Seva Abhiyaan. HelpAge was the first NGO in India to partner with Archies Greetings and Gifts to sell HelpAge-branded merchandise on receipt of royalty.

HelpAge India's brand is strong due to its presence in schools and its merchandising. Its brand also stands out because there are fewer NGOs working with than there are those involved with children, education, health, and environment, and so on. Therefore, despite adopting face-to-face fundraising much later than CRY, it has almost caught up in this area in terms of gross income.

Give India

Give India promotes efficient and effective giving linking donors to a catalog of causes. In 2011 to 2012 it channeled funds totaling $4.4 million to 270 NGOs and 91 percent of it was raised within India. Give India operates an online portal that allows donors to directly donate to causes of their choice. Another area of its focus is an automatic payroll giving system that allows corporate employees to contribute to projects of choice. In 2011, 16,500 employees and 21 new corporations joined this program, bringing the total number of payroll givers to 30,000.

Give India also helps corporations, institutions, and high-net-worth individuals in directing their giving to identified causes and supports the monitoring of their gifts.[20]

Give India is also behind the Joy of Giving Week (JGW), a "festival of philanthropy." JGW is celebrated around October 2, Mahatma Gandhi's

---

[20] Annual Report 2010–2011; www.giveindia.org.

birthday. It encourages people to engage in giving money, time, resources, and skills. The target audience includes corporations, NGOs, government, schools, colleges, and the general public. It also organizes "Giving Challenges" as part of this week. Give India has a HNWI donors group, a First Givers Club that had more than 100 members enrolled in 2011.

Experimentation with various concepts and channels of giving has contributed to Give India's success over the past 11 years of its existence. It succeeded with payroll giving when most of the other fundraising NGOs were struggling with it. Its ability to give donors choices in terms of causes to support is also a distinct advantage to raise funds.

Other leading nonprofits similar to Give India are CAF (Charities Aid Foundation) India and United Way.

INGOs

There are two phases in the growth of INGOs in India. The first phase started at the turn of twenty-first century when World Vision and Greenpeace began to raise funds in India in a big way. World Vision started recruiting child sponsors using direct mail while Greenpeace used face-to-face fundraising to acquire monthly donors. CAF (Charities Aid Foundation), an intermediary organization, Action Aid, and SOS Children's Village's also started fundraising around the same time.

The second phase of INGO fundraising started after 2005, when organizations like UNICEF, Save the Children, Oxfam, and Plan International became active in local fundraising. WWF India, which had been selling merchandise in India for a long time, also started toying with the idea of raising funds locally.

More recently, Sight Savers, PETA and Amnesty International have been raising local funds. The INGOs brought in three new things to the Indian fundraising market—investment funds, monthly giving, and a whole lot of aggressiveness. Accompanying this was a growing demand for trained and experienced fundraisers, something that continues today.

In 2010 to 2011, World Vision India raised $4.7 million from local sources. In the same period Save the Children India (Bal Raksha Bharat) raised $4.3 million; SOS Children Villages $3.2 million; Plan International $52.7 million; and Oxfam $1.8 million. UNICEF India raised \$3.7 million from private sources and Greenpeace India raised \$41.7 million locally in 2010.[21] Save the Children has invested a lot in the market and caught up with others, despite a late start.

CASE STUDY 12.1 | **BUILDING SUSTAINABLE ROI THROUGH TELEPHONE—BETTER IN-HOUSE OR OUTSOURCED?**

Save the Children India (SCI) has invested in building in-house telephone fundraising teams, rather than only using external agencies. In the short term, it's a nightmare: employing so many people, training, and retaining them. Add to that the cost of office space and other infrastructure involved.

But SCI thinks this has some distinct advantages—the primary one being that in-house teams offer a sustained growth and a higher long-term ROI. Besides, a second advantage is that it offers greater control over quality and testing possibilities. The in-house teams assist in closing leads generated by a gamut of sources—DRTV, awareness campaigns, and online activities.

SCI India has realized that in-house teams also are handy during emergency fundraising. For example, when the town of Leh in India was hit with flash floods, SCI was able to rapidly train and equip in-house teams for responding to in-bound calls resulting from TV news tickers scrolling at the bottom of the TV screen. Moreover, they were able to quickly call both existing donors and new prospects.

But SCI has not gone for an either/or approach. It also uses external agencies to meet increased need and avoid the challenges of recruitment, space, supervision, and so on, they would otherwise encounter if they rapidly scaled up with staff alone. It has set up outbound and inbound telephone fundraising hubs in Mumbai, Delhi, Kolkata, Chennai, Bangalore, and Hyderabad from where calls are made to more than 40 locations across India.

Although outsourcing in some circumstances is preferred, outside suppliers can be erratic and expensive. SCI's in-house teams are there to deliver long-term objectives, including higher ROI, and the fact that SCI manages its own teams puts the nonprofit in a strong position when negotiating costs with agencies.

---

[21] Annual reports for each organization, as available on respective websites.

There are also benefits to using outside expertise. Syrex Infoservices, a telefacing agency that raises funds for 10 leading NGOs, believes it brings to the table fundraising expertise and shared costs, since not every NGO can invest in setting up and running its own call center.

All this augurs well for NGOs. With successful examples in both in-house and outsourced telephone fundraising, they can choose what fits their particular situation.

Profile of Fundraising by INGOs in India

The following are insights into fundraising in India based on a study I conducted of eight INGOs raising funds in India. This study was done by in late 2010. The five key insights revealed in the study are:

1. Raising unrestricted income is the main focus of all their fundraising efforts.
2. Hence the focus is on mass-marketing methodologies.
3. Major donor fundraising is conspicuous by its absence in the fundraising mix.
4. Grant-writing (restricted) fundraising is outside of the fundraising departments, responsibility.
5. Those successful in local fundraising have made substantial investments to develop the fundraising capabilities of their India operations, and this is entirely funded by the headquarters of the respective INGOs.

These insights are based on the following 13 findings:

1. The main objective of local fundraising by INGOs in India is to raise unrestricted income. Mass-marketing (face-to-face, telemarketing, telefacing, and/or direct mail) methodologies are used by all of the eight INGOs studied. Their international offices' strategy is to develop the local fundraising structure (in-house and/or outsourced).
2. Only three of the eight INGOs focus on corporate donors. The rest focus on mass-marketing techniques such as face-to-face, telemarketing, and to a lesser extent, direct mail. In seven out of eight cases, mass-marketing techniques bring in more than 50 to 90 percent of their local income.

3. With the exception of two, all the INGOs in the study have outsourced their face-to-face and telemarketing functions. All INGOs in the study started out with the outsourced model. One of the INGOs now conducts its face-to-face fundraising with a 250-strong staff force. Another INGO is in the process of reducing their dependency on external agencies/mass marketing service providers and has been investing heavily in developing their in-house staff/consultant team since 2009.[22]

4. Although one INGO depends mostly on one-off donations of average $18, others have regular donors give in the range of $1.80 to $9 per month. Most of these INGOs have an average individual donor retention rate of 25 percent.

5. The ratio of restricted/unrestricted income is consistent across the INGOs studied. In most cases local grant/restricted income (government and institutional) raised by the fundraising department is below 10 percent.[23]

6. In most cases grant fundraising was handled by program staff together with the international office, rather than by the local fundraising staff. The latter focused mainly on raising unrestricted income from individuals through mass-marketing methodologies

---

[22] The three reasons why the INGOs have chosen to set up their face-to-face fundraising infrastructure in-house include:

1. Few professional agencies with expertise in mass-market fundraising.
2. Agencies unable to recruit monthly/regular donors—overly commercial practices, unskilled solicitors, and high-pressure tactics did not engage prospective donors.
3. Quality issues and ethical issues:

Instances of misrepresentation and fabrication.

Agencies shifting people from one NGO to another as soon as they get new, more lucrative business—without informing existing clients.

Unreasonably high costs, sometimes double that of in-house costs.

[23] This differs drastically from the "traditional" profile of fundraising by NGOs where grant income (government, institutional, and foreign funders) makes up most of the income sources to date. However, this trend is also emerging in the local NGO space—with some key local NGOs investing to raise unrestricted funds.

(face-to-face, telemarketing, direct mail, payroll giving) and corporate donation, sponsorships, and special events where relevant.

7. Seven out of the eight INGOs studied have based their national office and fundraising and marketing in the Delhi area.

8. New Delhi and Mumbai were identified as the best markets (although one also identified Bangalore and Hyderabad as their best markets).[24]

9. Most of the INGOs studied started their local fundraising with funding from the international office's fundraising investment fund ranging from $50,000 to almost $1 million.

10. The ratio of restricted to unrestricted is consistent across the INGOs studied. In most cases local grant-restricted income (government and institutional) raised by the fundraising department is below 10 percent.[25]

11. The annual fundraising expenditure is an average of 25 percent of funds raised locally. One INGO counts the 10 percent of income that comes from their international office funding toward their India fundraising income, but most of the other INGOs studied did not.

12. The international offices of all the INGOs studied provided the following capacity-building assistance:

    a. Skill-share sessions, including workshops, discussion, and exchanges in developing the tools needed to be better fundraisers and communicators.

    b. In-house conference where subject matter experts on fundraising talked about best practices in the fundraising profession and looked at future trends that will affect fundraising in the future.

    c. Consultant to coach and advice Indian fundraising teams.

    d. Exposure trips to countries with advanced fundraising experience.

---

[24] The proximity and attention given to the city that the headquarters is based on may be a factor in Delhi's better returns.

[25] This differs drastically from the "traditional" profile of fundraising by NGOs in India, where grants make a bulk of the income today. However, this trend is also being picked up locally, with some key local NGOs investing to raise unrestricted funds.

e. Visits by international office experts in specific methodologies.

f. Internship of Indian staff with advanced fundraising affiliates.

g. Regular email, calls, and handholding by International office fundraising staff.

13. There is no major gift fundraising strategy in place at this time to develop the pool of high-net-worth local donors.[26]

India Philanthropy Report 2012[27] reports that of the 400 HNWIs and emerging HNWIs in Delhi, Mumbai, Hyderabad, and Pune surveyed:

- More than 70 percent of the donors have less than three years of philanthropic experience. The majority were 40 years old or younger.
- Among families who participate in philanthropy, 76 percent have younger relatives who have assumed an active role in choosing charities, while 69 percent say young members shape or spearhead the family's charitable mission.

Hence the current profile of the HNWI philanthropists in India differs drastically from the profile of philanthropists in mature fundraising markets.

Philanthropy in India

Billionaire business founders are among the many new HNWIs, and they are creating influential new foundations as part of their philanthropy. At the same time, Indian fundraisers are successfully wedding new and old methodologies to reach the general populace.

Donors

India is home to one of the fastest-growing HNWI populations in the world. This particular demographic group grew by 21 percent in India between 2009 and 2010, compared with just 12 percent in China, 8 percent in the United States, and 6 percent in Brazil. The level of giving of these HNWIs has been growing and is expected to

---

[26]There is a likelihood of major donor fundraising becoming a key income source in the coming years as relationships are built and enhanced.

[27]www.bain.com/publications/articles/india-philanthropy-report-2012.aspx.

grow further.[28] The private foundations of the newly rich are going to play an increasing role in philanthropy's near future.

Indian businesspeople have traditionally set up foundations to contribute to various charitable causes. Tata group, the consumer goods to steel conglomerate, has three major trusts: JN Tata Endowment; Sir Dorabji Tata and Allied Trusts; and Sir Ratan Tata and Navjibhai Tata Trust. The earliest one was formed in 1892. The Tata founders bequeathed most of their personal wealth to the trusts they created for the greater good of India and its people. Today the Tata trusts control 66 percent of the shares of Tata Sons, the holding Tata Company. The wealth that accrues from this asset supports an assortment of causes, institutions, and individuals in a wide variety of areas.[29]

Similarly other business founders also created trusts: Numerous Birla trusts (Birla Group); Jamnalal Kaniram Bajaj Trust founded in 1963 (Bajaj Group); and several Modi trusts (Modi Group).

Billionaire businesspeople of a more recent vintage are also establishing foundations. In 2010, the top 10 philanthropic commitments in India added up to a whopping $2.5 billion. These were in the form of multiyear grants to their foundations and trusts.

Azim Premji, chairperson of $5.7 billion Wipro Group, founded Azim Premji Foundation in 2001. The foundation has identified education as its primary domain of work.[30] Shiv Nadar, founder of HCL, a $6 billion global technology and IT enterprise employing more than 82,000 employees across 31 countries, established Shiv Nadar Foundation with a personal contribution of $122 million.[31] Bharti Foundation, the philanthropic arm of Bharti Enterprises, was established in 2000 to help underprivileged children and young people with a corpus $42 million.[32] The list can go on.

---

[28] India Philanthropy Report 2012, Bain & Co.

[29] www.tata.com/ourcommitment/sub_index.aspx?sectid=i6eUTkvtRos=.

[30] www.azimpremjifoundation.org.

[31] http://articles.economictimes.indiatimes.com/2010-09-29/news/27586896_1_richest-people-wealth-shiv-nadar-foundation; www.shivnadarfoundation.org.

[32] http://articles.economictimes.indiatimes.com/keyword/bharti-foundation; www.bhartifoundation.org.

Individuals

Telefacing is a unique feature of Indian fundraising, a hybrid of tele-marketing and face-to-face joining the major donor process with cold solicitation. This is how it works: A telephone caller makes a brief pitch to a prospect, asking for a meeting with a field executive, who would make a presentation to the prospect at home or at work.[33] Another name for it is *fundraising by appointment*.[34]

It is successful in India, even effectively used to acquire and retain committed givers, as well as single gifts. Today most of the major NGOs raise funds using telefacing. These include CRY, UNICEF, Plan, Save the Children, Oxfam, Action Aid, SOS Children's Villages, Greenpeace, Sight Savers, World Vision, and several others. Some organizations use agencies for this, others have created in-house teams.

Figure 12.1 explains the cyclic process of telefacing. It is a cycle, because donors are not only acquired but also retained through this method.

FIGURE 12.1	THE CYCLIC PROCESS OF TELEFACING

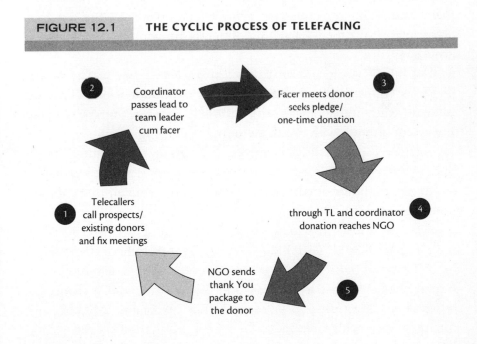

2 — Coordinator passes lead to team leader cum facer

3 — Facer meets donor seeks pledge/ one-time donation

1 — Telecallers call prospects/ existing donors and fix meetings

4 — through TL and coordinator donation reaches NGO

NGO sends thank You package to the donor

5

---

[33] www.sofii.org/node/187.

[34] Becky Slack, "Fundraising by Appointment," *Professional Fundraising* (United Kingdom), December 2007.

Telefacing is an approach tailored for Indian markets[35] but it can be also used in countries that have similar cost structures to India. It could be applicable for small and midsize organizations anywhere in the world. Smaller organizations operating locally can keep travel costs low, as fundraisers may visit the donor nearby. It can be useful to larger ones in the Western world, too, but that still needs to be tested; the cost might be too high.

Telefacing is also being used to convert leads generated through the various online and social media campaigns. Since telefacing's two-step approach has an advantage over cold-call telemarketing in India, some NGOs have already started using it, calling it web-telefacing.

A combination of several tools—website, email, social media, search engines, and web banner display advertisements on popular websites—are increasingly finding a place in the Indian fundraiser's repertoire. However, email or telephone remains the best for follow-up and all the leading NGOs in India use these. World Vision has been using online campaigns to recruit new sponsors consistently for the past four to five years. Save the Children uses Internet banners and search engine advertising.

Most NGOs, large and small, have blogs, Facebook, LinkedIn, and Twitter accounts, and use social media for communication. These are low cost, easily implemented, and accessible, but few are able to raise money consistently with just these means.

Greenpeace consistently integrates its advocacy campaigns with its fundraising appeals. Their fundraisers not only ask people to give, but also to sign petitions or take other action, and in general, to spread the word. See Figure 12.2.

IndiaGive, India's donation portal, raises almost 30 percent of its funds. In March 2011, Give India was selected as the official charity partner of Twestival India 2011. It is a one-day meet-up of Twitter followers in more than 100 cities across the world. Each city chooses a charity for its donations. The cities of Bangalore, Cochin, Hyderabad, Mumbai, and Pune partnered with Give India. Give India also ran a matching challenge that furthered the competition between the cities. See Figure 12.3.

---

[35] Hanna Gannangé-Stewart, "On Tour," *Fundraiser* (United Kingdom), December 12, 2011.

FIGURE 12.2   GREENPEACE FUNDRAISING VIDEO

Source: Greenpeace.

Corporations and Corporate Social Responsibility (CSR)

In India, CSR has evolved to encompass employees, customers, stake-holders, and notions of sustainable development or corporate citizenship.[36] As CSR grows, so has corporate philanthropy, which has increased fivefold since 2006.

CSR is not driving business decisions at present and only 16 percent of the top companies in India have a CSR strategy in place. It is, however, getting more attention in the boardroom. There is a growing trend of including CSR initiatives in annual reports and/or on the company website. The CSR agenda for most companies encompasses education, health care, HIV/AIDS, and community development.[37]

---

[36] "The Challenge of Corporate Social Responsibility in India," John Quigley, *EurAsia Bulletin* 10, no. 11, 12, November–December 2006; www.eias.org/bulletin.html.

[37] Corporate Responsibility Survey 2011, KPMG India.

FIGURE 12.3	GIVE INDIA'S MATCHING CHALLENGE ON CRY.ORG WEBSITE

Source: Give India.

Coupled with CSR is a growing demand for employee engagement and volunteering.[38]

Indian consumers want to buy from socially conscious companies. They are aware that CSR is less about community and more about reputation management, but nevertheless see its value. Product brands associated with positive social impact are the ones that are more memorable in the buyer's mind.[39]

---

[38] "Changing Trends in Business NGO Relationships in India; SOS Children's Villages." The Partnering Initiative & International Business Leaders Forum, 2011.

[39] "CSR Examined, What People Want." The Lowe Lintas-MSN-Cross-Tab.

Some corporations are forming foundations to look after their CSR. Prominent examples include Infosys Foundation (IT), ICICI Foundation (banking), Max India Foundation (health care), and Times Foundation (media). Even multinational companies have registered foundations in India—Amway, Coca-Cola, and Shell among them.

Some would even like to make CSR a legal requirement of doing business in India. A bill was proposed to make CSR spending mandatory even for private companies, but it was vehemently opposed by the corporate world. Although it is not mandatory, Clause 135 of the Companies Bill of 2011 stipulates that every company with a net worth of $90 million or turnover of $180 million or more, or a net profit of $895,000 or more in a financial year, must have a CSR committee consisting of three or more directors, of which at least one should be an independent director.[40]

CSR is mandatory for the Public Sector Enterprises (PSE) and non-adherence to the guidelines can result in penal action.[41] For PSEs with profit ranging between $21 million and $41 million, CSR expenditure should be 2 to 3 percent of the net profit of the previous fiscal year and a minimum of $625,000. PSEs making more than $41 million in the prior year must spend 0.5 to 2 percent.[42]

The new CSR guidelines are expected to make corporate giving a part of the culture over time.

Challenges in India's Philanthropy

Poor Infrastructure for Fundraising

The quality of prospective donor databases in India is not consistent. The delivery rates of postal services also leave much wanting. There is a wide gap between demand and supply of fundraisers, besides a lack of specialized full-service fundraising agencies in India.

---

[40] www.business-standard.com/india/news/csr-not-mandatory-for-pvt-firms-moily/155653/on.

[41] Ibid.

[42] www.indianexpress.com/news/govt-directs-psus-to-spend-up-to-5-pc-of-pro/607137/.

Loss of Telephone Access to Prospects

Prior to 2011 NGOs could call people who were on the "do not call" list. Then this critical privilege was withdrawn.[43] Since most NGOs depend heavily on telephone to communicate with donors, this has dampened fundraising efforts. NGOs still raise close to $21 million using the telephone.

Inadequate Tax Incentives for Giving

There is 50 percent tax exemption and selected projects are 100 percent exempt, but only up to 10 percent of a donor's annual income.[44]

A 2008 income tax amendment narrowed the definition of charitable activity exempted from tax. What was included was mostly service-oriented work, leaving out all other fields, including advocacy and human rights.[45]

Lack of Capacity Building

Poor focus on fundraising capacity building and lack of budgets for supporting such activities hampers nonprofit development.

IN SUMMARY

The parable of the blind men and the elephant that originated in India has been used the world over to provide insights into relativism and to illustrate the behavior of experts in fields where there is a deficit or inaccessibility of information. This parable aptly demonstrates the situation when advising on fundraising in India. Any broad generalization about its fundraising market is bound to be incorrect.

However, it will help nonprofits and social purpose organizations raising funds in India to keep these five points in mind:

1. The country: India is like a kaleidoscope. It depends on which angle you are looking at it. It is important to be able to identify the segment of the population that an organization would like to focus on and then develop the methodology and messaging

---

[43] www.nccptrai.gov.in/nccpregistry/.

[44] www.incometaxforngos.org.

[45] http://business-standard.com/india/news/ngos-cry-witch-hunt-after-tax-notices/465292/.

that works for it. The examples of CRY and HelpAge show that substantial funds can be raised from Indian middle classes by adapting channels relevant with time, transitioning from direct mail to face-to-face fundraising. In the past decade some leading INGOs have also witnessed success in their fundraising efforts.

2. The people: India's diversity is both an asset and a challenge. There are very wealthy individuals in rural India, just as there are many of the urban poor. The large size of middle class as well as the corporate sector across the country presents a sizeable opportunity for NGOs to raise resources. At the same time the growing number of HNWIs and family businesses are leveraging local tax breaks to institute foundations and create social enterprise systems parallel to NGOs. Thus in some sense they are in direct competition to the traditional role of the NGOs and thus its ability to mobilize resources.

3. The process: The multinational corporation as well as the many INGOs raising funds in India have learned the hard way that their "global strategy" does not necessarily translate well in India but "made for India" strategies work extremely well. For example, fundraisers and nonprofit leaders in mature fundraising markets may not have heard of telefacing, a made in India practice that is showing good fundraising results. NGOs still do not focus on stewarding their donors to higher levels and continue to be focused on raising the lower-level gifts.

4. The ethos: Indian donors are exceptionally value-conscious. Programs that were previously generously funded by international aid and approved by personnel without any real local connections and insight into the community may have their fundraising efforts met with skepticism. Local supporters want innovative programs that make good use of funds. This is another reason why major donor fundraising has not yet taken off as expected, given the growing HNWI population.

5. The future: The reemergence of India is being called the *Asian Century*. The country's growing importance in philanthropy compels fundraisers to adapt and experiment to succeed in this culture. Nonprofit practitioners need to also build their fundraising skills to make the most of a growing trend toward local institutional and individual donors who want to see program impact and a sustainable nonprofit business model.

Overall Topics in Giving

CHAPTER 13

Major Donors

ANGELA CLUFF AND PAULA GUILLET DE MONTHOUX

We live in times of economic insecurity. One downturn seems to follow the other. Doom-laden headlines have relentlessly tracked a global economic crisis that has lurched from sector to sector—financial, housing, and banking—and from region to region—the United States, Japan, and Europe. Writing about global wealth against such a backdrop may seem like a gloomy venture.

But in fact, the world has never been richer than today. Total global private financial wealth exceeds precrisis levels and is estimated to be a mind-boggling $122.8 billion in 2011.[1] That is a lot of zeros! So the world is getting richer, and there is more money for NGOs and INGOs to tap into. This chapter is about where and how that can be done.

GLOBAL WEALTH

First we need to recognize that **wealth is unevenly spread**. So let's look at where to find it by "following the money." This seems like an obvious imperative and the starting point for any fundraiser. Only someone with money enough to give can be a potential donor. So fundraisers need to look at where in the world people have enough money to give some of it away. Sounds easy. But in practice it is more complex.

What countries host the best prospective pool of wealthy donors differs depending on exactly what we are after.

---

[1]BCG Global Wealth Report 2012.

WHERE ARE THE RICH PEOPLE?

There are formal definitions of wealth.[2] The two primary distinctions are: HNWI and Ultra-High-Net-Worth Individual (UHNWI). These two definitions have specific meanings, drawn from the financial industry.

- HNW–At least $1 million in financial assets.
- UHNW—At least $30 million in financial assets.

There are 12.6 million HNW households worldwide by the end of 2011, 175,000 more than the year before.[3]

The "old world" economy, specifically the United States, Japan, and Europe, showed a decline in the number of millionaires as a result of the economic crisis. At the same time, emerging markets—especially those in Asia Pacific—showed strong growth. And as a result China, Singapore, and India enjoyed the largest increases in millionaire numbers. Specifically "millionaire households" grew:

- In China 16 percent to 1.43 million.
- In Singapore 14 percent to 188,000.
- In India 21 percent to 162,000.

This shift is expected to continue. Asia-Pacific, excluding Japan, saw an 11 percent increase in total wealth to $23.7 trillion in 2012. If that rate is maintained Asia Pacific will overtake private wealth in Europe in the next five years. The implication is that the region may reach $40 trillion by 2016. Private wealth in China and India will increase by 15 percent and 19 percent a year respectively through 2016, with the richest Chinese more than $10 trillion better off by the end of the period.

Density of Millionaires

If you look for a place with a high relative number of rich people, in other words a high likelihood of bumping into a millionaire, you should go to Singapore, Qatar, or Kuwait, all of which host more than 10 percent HNWIs in the population. And in fourth place was Switzerland with 9.5 percent. Note, though, that Switzerland was

---

[2]These definitions of wealth exclude investors' own businesses, residences, and luxury goods.
[3]BCG Global Wealth Report 2012.

top ranked for the proportion of households with more than $100 million—11 households per 100,000 had this significant sum tucked away. Singapore was a little behind on this metric with 10 and, perhaps surprisingly, Austria was number eight.

And if you're looking for billionaire households, Hong Kong is your top spot with more billionaire households there as a percentage than anywhere else.

And in Latin America a small number of wealthy individuals, concentrated in Brazil and Mexico especially, saw an increase of almost 11 percent in their total disposable assets in 2012. Carlos Slim, for example, continues to vie for top spot as the world's richest man.

Total Number of Wealthy Households

If instead you look at the *absolute* number of millionaires, the top 10 looks quite different:

- The United States hosts by far the highest number of wealthy with 5,134,000 millionaire and 2,928 UHNW households.
- The top three countries alone, the United States, Japan, and China, account for well more than 50 percent of the world's millionaires.

Looking at the UHNW households, the old-world economies still dominate, with the United States, United Kingdom, and Germany still at the top in the global number 1, 2, and 3 spots.

The Wealth of the Global Middle Class

We may also choose to look at this through a slightly different lens and see which countries have the highest average wealth. This perspective, offered by *Credit Suisse Global Wealth Report 2010,* lists some of the typical INGO current top fundraising markets with the United Kingdom, the United States, France, Italy, Switzerland, Australia, and Scandinavian countries all among the top 10. Such wealthy middle classes contribute the lion's share of many NGOs, and INGOs, fundraising income.[4]

---

[4]=mc INGO benchmarking from 2010 lists the United States, Canada, United Kingdom, Australia, Netherlands, Germany, Switzerland, Spain, Italy, France, Norway, Sweden, Denmark, and Japan as the current top fundraising markets of leading INGOs.

Looking ahead there are dramatic shifts happening also within this broader global donor target group:[5]

- Globally the middle class is booming and expected to reach 4.8 billion people by 2030, growing from 1.8 billion in 2009.
- By 2020 more than 50 percent of world's middle class will be in Asia.
- The middle class of Europe and the United States stays constant in absolute numbers with around 1 billion people.

The world's wealth is experiencing a dramatic shift toward the East, with Asia gaining enormously in importance. Interestingly with the middle class figures figured in, the growth of wealth is expected to be flat in Europe and North America. This means that fundraisers could carry on doing what they have done for decades, addressing the same audiences and expecting similar results, without really registering the change the world is going through. They would simply miss the Asian train!

WHO GIVES?

There is a no correlation between wealth and philanthropy—some people of modest means are very generous and some very wealthy people are notoriously reluctant to be generous toward good causes.

A first attempt was recently made to measure generosity across the world's population and create a global comparison between countries.[6] Three different expressions of generosity were included:

1. Charitable giving
2. Volunteering
3. Helping a stranger in need

The three scores were balanced to an overall generosity index with the following countries ranking top 10:

Australia
New Zealand

---

[5] OECD, "The Emerging Middle Class in Developing Countries 2010." Middle class refers to the number of people living in middle class households using an absolute definition, ranging from $10 to $100 in purchasing power parity per capita per day to characterize middle class households.

[6] *CAF World Giving Index 2010*, survey by CAF and Gallup.

Ireland
Canada
Switzerland
United States
Netherlands
United Kingdom
Sri Lanka
Austria

Some of the top countries reappear in the wealth lists earlier, suggesting that indeed wealth could be an indicator that supports giving. But the study revealed a perhaps more surprising correlation: that between giving and happiness.

The survey asked people about satisfaction with life today. And the correlation between happiness and giving is stronger than the correlation between wealth and giving.

So seek the happy and the rich—this is the perfect donor profile.

Why Do the Wealthy Give?

So why do people make major gifts? The reasons are varied and complex, but are the same for the donor who gives a few dollars as it is for those who give millions. It's helpful to consider four different dimensions:

1. Philanthropy: Perhaps this is the most obvious. From either a religious or other moral base, many people have a desire to improve the situation for other people or for the world they live in. They want little in return, gaining satisfaction by giving something back.
2. Affinity: Here there is a direct, personal connection to the cause. It is typical for medical causes where what happens to a family member or friend can be the catalyst for a deep and lasting interest in the cure or prevention of a medical condition, based on a direct personal experience. Sometimes the affinity may be a long-standing family tradition.
3. Exchange: In some circumstances a gift is about a transaction— perhaps a naming opportunity, a seat at a prestigious event, a coveted place on a leadership board, a related business opportunity.
4. Social: Here a gift may be motivated simply by who asks or by how the donor's community standing might be enhanced

by the gift. And some people like doing good through their social lives. These are social motivations.

These categories do not describe groups of people. Rather they are the dimensions that will have differing degrees of importance to people making a decision about a particular gift. The same individual will have different reasons for why they support different causes. There will be differing motivations behind gifts made by the same person to a favorite organization depending on the project, who asks for the gift, what is being offered "in exchange" for the gift, and what is going on in the life of the donor at the time. So why does all of this matter? Understanding donor motivations are key to securing gifts—and to maximizing the size of the gift that can be secured.

An attempt to cluster donors by motivations linked to age, beliefs, and source of wealth was made by Barclays Wealth in 2010. Their study included 500 high-net-worth donors in the United Kingdom and the United States and identified six different donor typologies:

1. Privileged youth—Motivated by a desire to engage.

   Typically younger, with inherited wealth, the privileged youth tend to give their time and energy to charity as a means of offsetting some guilt for their comfortable lifestyles. Raised to help the less fortunate, they also give to set an example to their own children. Seeing themselves as citizens of the world they typically support global social causes.

2. Eco givers—Motivated to save the planet.

   Typically younger and of all groups, most likely to be female. They earned their wealth and do not believe that children should inherit large amounts of money. Eco givers mainly support environmental charities but also give to disaster relief, children's, and social welfare charities.

3. Altruistic entrepreneurs—Motivated by duty to give back.

   Typically middle-age self-made business owners, the altruistic entrepreneur is motivated by religion and a sense of duty for the wealthy to give back to society. This generous group sets few demands on the charities they support and are not motivated by public recognition. They invest their money and their time into their communities and they donate across causes such as education, social welfare, and environment and are also active fundraisers themselves.

4. Reactive donors—Motivated by peer pressure.

Predominantly male, high-earning executives, this group typically holds low engagement and little time commitment to the causes they support. They give because of expectations by their peers. They are most likely to support health and medical charities, and want public recognition for their donations.

5. Cultured inheritors—Motivated by legacy.

Cultured inheritors are in their late fifties and sixties, often in semi-retirement, and with young grandchildren. Besides their own success, they have typically inherited wealth and want to hand much if it over to the next generations. Personal values and moral beliefs motivate the cultured inheritors who volunteer, fundraise, and give to immediate family and community causes as well as to the arts.

6. Professional philanthropists—Religious and political motivations.

Professional philanthropists are typically older donors who have built their own wealth. They are demanding of charities and want to be shown the impact that will result from their often very large gifts. They donate to education and religious causes, and are less likely to support global or environmental organizations.

Why Should NGOs and INGOs Target the Wealthy?

There are many reasons why NGOs and INGOs are keen to secure support from major donors—especially HNWI and UHNWI:

- With a single gift a wealthy donor can transform a charity's ability to deliver a program or achieve a vital mission goal.
- A major donor can lend significant credibility to an agency, giving others the confidence to contribute.
- A major donor often has powerful networks and can open doors to other donors.
- A major donor is typically an accomplished professional within his or her field and can be a source of valuable expertise and experience on a board or committee.

- Experienced major donors may have valuable insights into program areas they have focused on. For instance, the Bill and Melinda Gates Foundation has learned a great deal about global health concerns.

But these kinds of donors can bring challenges. Today's major donors are more proactive and demanding than ever. They may think that their business success naturally guarantees success in another area, but this may not necessarily be true.

For example:

- Their desire to restrict funds may mean that unpopular but important programs are ignored.
- There may be a conflict of interest if donors start to interfere with the governance and policy of an agency.
- Overdependence on one or a few donors can jeopardize the financial stability that a broad donor base provides.

You may assume that, given the obvious benefits, that every nonprofit is eagerly seeking major donors. In fact not all INGOs/NGOs do. Some organizations choose to not accept donations over a certain amount. For example, Avaaz has a policy of not accepting contributions over $5,000. The reasoning behind this is to protect its independence, in the same way as many NGOs refuse to accept donations from certain or all corporations, and others not accepting government contributions.

How Do NGOs and INGOs Go About It?

The United States and the United Kingdom have long and strong traditions of major donors. Some of them funded the very cornerstones of British and American societies: museums, libraries, hospitals, and universities. But major donor fundraising in other parts of the world, including mainland Europe, can be traced far back in history, for example, in the building of cathedrals, but was then somewhat forgotten by professional fundraisers only to come back as a much more recent phenomenon. Individual giving in Europe has a stronger tradition in grassroot memberships and broad-based collections, and subsequently nonprofits have developed fundraising skills in the areas of mass marketing and public campaigning.

In recent years, many international organizations are getting serious about major gifts and investing in dedicated teams of major gift fundraisers. No longer is this limited to higher education as in the past. Nor is it something that only the United States branches of international organizations are involved in. Only in the past few years we have seen the establishment of new professional functions and global strategy development among many of the leading INGOs including Amnesty, Greenpeace, SOS Children's Villages, UNHCR, UNICEF, and WWF. We should expect to see much more happening over the coming years.

Major donor fundraising is a systematic process, requiring an attractive case for support and the time needed to develop strong individual relationships.

A commonly used framework for such a donor development process is the Seven Steps Approach:

1. Identify: Find the right prospects by evaluating their capacity to give, their affinity with the cause, and the links you have to them.

2. Research: Prepare yourself by investigating the interests, donation history, and motivations of the potential donors.

3. Plan: Every donor is unique. You need a customized plan for each of them, to know when to systematically move them closer to the cause and to making a gift to your organization.

4. Involve (and cultivate): Engage the donor in the cause, communicate, invite to events to show the needs and the work of your organization.

5. Ask: A successful ask is done at the right time, by the right person, and for the right amount.

6. Close: Once the donor said yes, make sure that you agree on the details—lump sum or staggered payment, tax restrictions, recognition, and so on, and you need to be clear to avoid future complications.

7. Stewardship: The first gift is only the beginning. If you get it right, it starts the journey of building a long-term relationship with the donor, providing thanks, recognition, further engagement opportunities to build loyalty, future donations, and introductions to other donors.

On an organizational level, there are two key strategies deployed by NGOs and INGOs to secure major gifts.

1. Campaigns
2. Products

Campaigns

Campaigns are about creating time-bound objectives and inviting donors to join in to reach those. The targets set need to be inspiring and challenging yet realistic to be achieved. The best campaigns have targets that are expressed in terms of mission delivery change as well as financial goal. Whatever the starting point, mission, or financial goal, it can require hard work to translate one target to the other.

Considerations in Campaigns

- Campaign initiation: Our wider experience suggests that successful campaigns can be initiated by staff, donors, board members, partners, suppliers, or external entrepreneurs.[7] The importance is not where the idea comes from, but rather is it appealing and relevant. Which markets to target: A campaign can be constructed to appeal to a certain market, but similarly a campaign can be created out of pure need and necessity to later find its appropriate markets.
- Cultural differences: Some parts may work across borders, others won't. That in itself is not a reason for not running an international campaign. The trick is about testing and identifying the global common core components and then leaving the other parts for local adaptation and implementation.
- Campaign management: Internal communication and coordination, expectations and delivery, including the crucial link between fundraising and mission delivery; that is, making sure that the fundraisers raise the resources that are needed and that

---

[7]We need to note a difference here between U.S. fundraising and models developed elsewhere in the world. The U.S. model uses boards extensively—and although this model is also used elsewhere, there are many cases where staff-led initiatives have been successful.

the program staff deliver the expected impact. This can be handled by a global manager, or a management team with representatives from different functions and regions.

- Reporting: What updates and information will the donor need, when? Some of this can be streamlined and used to all donors, to keep expenses down; others will need individual tailoring.
- Targets and goals: It is important to be ready for both successes and failures in terms of meeting financial targets and programmatic goals. Both scenarios can be turned into powerful messages, if well prepared and reasoned.
- Donor stewardship: Possibly the most important to consider is how contacts with the donors are managed, ranging from day-to-day queries to the strategic, and deliberate steps to developing long-term mutually valuable relationships.

CASE STUDY 13.1 **HABITAT FOR HUMANITY GLOBAL CAMPAIGN**

Habitat for Humanity International is a Christian organization that seeks to eliminate homelessness from the world—put simply, it works for simple, decent, affordable housing for all.

At the time of this writing it is midway through an enterprise-wide campaign to raise $3.9 billion. The campaign was launched in 2010 and now is at least on track to reach four specific goals:

1. Raise $3.9 billion for program expansion. At the halfway point the fundraising goal is just ahead of target.
2. Serve more than 100,000 families annually by the end of the campaign (more than double that of 2010). This goal will be reached a year ahead of plan.
3. Mobilize 1 million volunteers annually. This goal has been reached.
4. Engage 250,000 advocates of affordable housing. This goal is on track to achieve target.

Habitat is a federated organization—with 85 national offices globally and 1,500 U.S. affiliates. The campaign was an opportunity for these independent organizations to unite behind a global theme. Habitat for Humanity International provides both opportunities and practical tools, but it is for each part of the highly decentralized organization to decide to join the campaign—or not.

(Continued)

The target is a combination of "business as usual" annual figures and a significant incremental target. One learning is that the headline number is so large that it has been hard to maintain the momentum for the incremental aspect of the target, other than in a few markets.

The timing for the campaign has been crucial. The global feasibility study was carried out in 2007, when the trend was for campaigns with big headline numbers. Of course since then the economic situation has deteriorated, with 2009 being particularly tough. This global trend has been especially true for traditional U.S. donors and in the very industry—property—that typically supports Habitat. Some offices and affiliates have successfully responded to these environmental challenges by launching short, specific mini-campaigns that can help maintain momentum.

The campaign has a traditional volunteer/leadership-based approach. There is a global campaign cabinet and success has tended to follow the recruitment of regional champions. For example in the Philippines a localized case and branding connected to the global approach has been successful.

Key Lessons

- It is hard to succeed in a highly decentralized organization where each national office or affiliate can decide whether or not to take part. The issue how to achieve alignment is key.
- A very large headline campaign target means that it is hard to maintain momentum to achieve the incremental part of the target. Smaller, specific campaigns may be necessary and help engage donor and affiliates.
- Habitat is very committed to the volunteer leadership campaign model. And this has proved successful in some places. But it will take a long time to move from 35 years of small sum giving to a genuine depth of major donor giving. To achieve a real shift will need more major, long term campaigns.
- Changes in staff leadership can mean it is very difficult to sustain a five years or longer campaign duration. There is also a serious lack of practitioners at the right level—as staff or consultants—to support global campaigns.

Products

Products are about packaging and pricing the organization's mission delivery in attractive and separate chunks that deliver benefits to beneficiaries and at the same time satisfy a donor's want and needs. Some type of mission delivery is more immediately suited for such product packaging like building houses, or a distinct research project. Other causes, such as environmentalists or other kinds of organizations that advocate for policy change, are often more challenged to identify separate communicable parts of their work that they can put a price tag on and present to donors. But there are creative and successful examples from different sectors. Examples include:

- SOS Children's Villages have individual prominent donors funding the building of a whole new children's village. For instance, Henning Mankell, the Swedish author and creator of the Inspector Wallander character, has funded a village for 100 orphans in his second home country Mozambique.
- An art museum often gets donations for the acquisition of specific art. The discreet Danish philanthropist Jytte Dresing in 2011 donated eight major works to create the Damien Hirst room at the Arken Gallery in Copenhagen.

Even online fundraising initiatives that mainly target the broad masses of smaller donors may include some high value offers for potential major donors. The UNICEF Inspired Gifts campaign lists a Jeep for a little over $32,000 on its website. And on the British Red Cross site you can make gifts of up to $450,000.

The two approaches of campaigns and products are interrelated and can be successfully combined.

For example, many universities successfully set an overall campaign target and then create products for donors to support separate building blocks, for example, specific research projects or endowments of chairs.

CASE STUDY 13.2 | PETER KRÄMER

Peter Krämer from Hamburg, Germany, dreams of saving the world,[8] or at least making it a little bit better. This dream started one Christmas when he was a teenager and saw that the presents overflowing the gift table for him and his siblings were far beyond their needs or what they could reasonably expect to use. He started his own Christmas fundraising campaigns for the less privileged. The sensitivity to injustice and the dream of saving the world stayed with him. He became a wealthy and accomplished shipping magnate and initiated a partnership with the Nelson Mandela Foundation and UNICEF in order to tackle one of the world's biggest challenges: education. Guided by the Millennium Development Goal 2, to achieve universal education, the Schools for Africa campaign was launched in early 2005.

The Schools for Africa fundraising initiative successfully combines a campaign dynamic, using the iconic inspiration by Nelson Mandela and the networks of Mr. Krämer, with an approach of tangible high value fundraising products. Program delivery is broken down in communicable and attractive items, such as the construction and equipment of a classroom in Niger for $14,000.

The campaign successfully met its first target of $50 million to benefit 4 million children in 6 countries and expanded into new countries and higher goals, and raising $90 million. Part of the lead gift of $5 million, made by Mr. Krämer himself, was to match all donations made by the German public. Since then contributions have been received by many individual and corporate donors from around the world joining Mr. Krämer in his dream.

THE RICH WILL SAVE US ALL—PHILANTHROCAPITALISM

A powerful movement to encourage major donor giving has been labeled *philanthrocapitalism*. The name comes from an influential book of the same title published in 2008 and an associated website. Two

---

[8]"Ein bisschen die Welt verbessern." Interview with Peter Krämer in *Die Zeit* September 16, 2011, and Schools for Africa.org.

journalists working for the *Economist* magazine, Matthew Bishop and Michael Green, wrote the book.

The philanthrocapitalism argument is simple and in many ways compelling, especially in our current economic situation:

- There's a need for a "leadership force" to tackle the *big* social issues of our time . . . poverty, climate change, health inequality, and so on.
- In the past century we have expected our governments, by and large, to tackle these challenges either directly or through social programs and policies.
- Sadly governments seem to have had mixed success at tackling many of these issues—even those that see it as a fundamental part of their work.
- The continuing financial challenges in many parts of the world means that social budgets are diminishing and governments are scaling back activity.
- Entrepreneurs have a track record of applying efficient thinking to solving challenges—and these skills could be applied elsewhere.
- An innovative partnership approach to solving problems is possible, where governments business and nonprofits can collaborate in new ways.

So far so good . . . and now the interesting bit:

A number of wealthy entrepreneurs and business leaders are taking the lead in creating those new solutions and partnerships to solve social challenges. They are putting more than just ideas into it; they are backing it with money and asking NGOs and governments to join with them. Bill Gates is the obvious example, but there are others from Arpad Busson in the United Kingdom to the Tata family in India and Jet Li in China.

Bishop and Greene note that implicit in the philanthrocapitalism thesis are two key ideas that to some extent confound previous thinking on the rich and businesspeople in particular:

- One is a rejection of the idea that business is exclusively about profits with little concern for the consequences to society or environment.
- Second is the belief that "the winners" from our economic system *should* give back and that business can "do well by doing good."

Philanthrocapitalism has some powerful champions endorsing the broad concept, among them Bill Gates, Bill Clinton, George Soros, and Richard Branson. The Giving Pledge, for example, contains many of the philanthrocapitalist ideas.

And the philanthrocapitalism revolution, if it takes off, will have huge implications. As governments cut back their spending on social causes, it may prove to be a significant force for change in society.

But philanthrocapitalism is not universally admired. There are criticisms that the philanthrocapitalists are naive and underestimate the complexity of the social problems they seek to resolve. Or that they have no mandate. Or that they pick and choose issues that appeal to them and not those that are most urgent.

There are even those who worry that Gates, specifically, may achieve "market domination" in global health issues the way his company Microsoft was once the lord and master over the software and computer industry. The concern here would be that his funds draw skills and expertise to the issues that he believes are important rather than those that are most pressing. Critics also worry about Gates' legitimacy in terms of a power base. He can and does negotiate directly with governments. In this setting who is he accountable to? And there have been criticisms that some of his initiatives—for example, that the Global Fund has been no more efficient than governmental or NGO efforts.

Despite these concerns Gates and the other philanthrocapitalists continue to attract a great deal of interest.

CASE STUDY 13.3   BILL AND MELINDA GATES

Bill Gates made his money by building up Microsoft over 20 years. In 2008 he stepped down from operational control. He and his wife, an active partner, now give almost all of their time to looking after the work of the Bill and Melinda Gates Foundation. The foundation has spent $26.2 billion since its inception in 1994. It has a number of programs, some domestic to the United States. But it is best known for its focus on eradicating infectious diseases in the developing world.

By setting up and promoting the foundation, he has inspired other rich people to join him in the Giving Pledge.

Gates knows than even his vast wealth cannot solve the challenges that he is keen to tackle, so he has set up a number of projects and agencies. As well as the work of the foundation, Gates has supported two major initiatives: the Global Fund and GAVI.

(Continued)

Gates launched the Global Fund to Fight AIDS, Tuberculosis, and Malaria in 2002. He saw the elimination of these three diseases as essential to raising the level of health among less-developed societies to that of the developed ones. Importantly, he leverages his gifts to motivate others to contribute or to other action. The partnership model, with governments, NGOs, businesses, and even other philanthropists, is a core part of his strategy. As an example the Malaria No More initiative—involving governments, multilaterals, NGOs, and companies—pledged $3 billion to reduce malarial death to near zero by 2015. Malaria currently kills more than 1 million people a year, mostly in Africa.

In 2000 he launched the Global Alliance for Vaccines and Immunization (GAVI) with $750 million. The goal was to boost aid spending to prevent deaths from communicable but eradicable diseases. The single simple step of getting children in developing countries vaccinated has had an impact—GAVI says it has already saved more than 3 million lives. It cannot, however, claim victory entirely as its own—other initiatives are effective as well, notably the Rotary International campaign to eliminate polio, which in 2012 announced it had seen in India the last case of polio.

About the Giving Pledge

The Giving Pledge is a movement of HNWIs and UHNWIs who are publicly committed to giving away the bulk of their wealth to good causes. (The website of the Giving Pledge states that it's "an effort to invite the wealthiest individuals and families in the United States to commit to giving the majority of their wealth to philanthropy.") Although formally based in the United States, the campaign has sought in recent years to spread its philosophy internationally with mixed results.

One attractive aspect of the Pledge is its flexibility. The donation can happen during the lifetime *or* after the death of the philanthropist. Another feature that appeals to potential Pledge signers is that the Pledge is a moral commitment to give, not a legal contract (although as of yet no one has reneged).

Almost 100 U.S. billionaires have joined this campaign and pledged to give 50 percent or more of their wealth to charity. At least $125 billion total had been promised from the first 40 donors based on their aggregate wealth as of August 2010. Despite the recession the number of pledgers and the amounts pledged is growing.

Philanthropist Warren Buffett, one of the early signers, was an admirer of the Gates Foundation and its goals and so saw it as a channel for his philanthropic intentions. Buffett committed much of his wealth to the Gates Foundation. (See Case Study 13.3.)

In 2006 Buffett and Gates began discussing how to encourage other wealthy entrepreneurs to commit their resources to philanthropy. They decided to host a series of dinners bringing together some famous names, including Michael Bloomberg, Oprah Winfrey, and Ted Turner, and asked others to do so as well.

At one of these dinners Marguerite Lenfest, one of the invitees, proposed, "The rich should sit down, decide how much money they and their progeny need, and figure out what to do with the rest of it." This statement was the inspiration for the Pledge.

In June 2010 the campaign for the Giving Pledge was formally announced. Gates and Buffett announced that they would be proactively contacting potential signatories.

The two philanthropists then declared that they would travel to meet wealthy individuals in Europe, India, and China to talk about philanthropy and the idea of the Pledge. The idea was not universally well received. German and French millionaires met with Gates, but only a small number signed up to the Pledge. French billionaires Arnaud Lagardère and Liliane Bettencourt were approached directly by Buffett, but they refused to commit to the Pledge.

Some of the most strident criticism of the Pledge approach came from Germany. In an interview with *Der Spiegel* magazine, Peter Krämer, the Hamburg shipping millionaire who has donated millions to UNICEF to support schools in Africa, criticized the tax advantages U.S. philanthropists had that elsewhere did not exist. His argument? "The rich [in the United States] make a choice: Would I rather donate or pay taxes? The donors are taking the place of the state. That's unacceptable."

In China and India there was polite interest, but no real commitment as there had been in the United States. Buffett and Gates tried to be sensitive to this. They wrote an open letter to the official Xinhua news agency:

"We know that the Giving Pledge is just one approach to philanthropy, and we do not know if it's the right path forward for China. Some people have wondered if we're coming to China to pressure people to give. Not at all."

They continued: "Our trip is fundamentally about learning, listening, and responding to those who express an interest in our own experiences. China's circumstances are unique, and so its approach to philanthropy will be, as well."

There has been some success with this more diplomatic approach. Xinhua subsequently reported that Chinese millionaire Chen Guangbiao will leave his entire fortune—some $440 million—to charity after his death. He also claims that he has convinced more than 100 other industrialists to give away their personal wealth. Guangbiao has said, "Although the pledge makers do not want to be exposed to the media, I give my sincere respect to their charity spirit."[9]

There are still questions about how much influence the Pledge will ultimately have outside the United States.[10]

A recent discussion triggered by the Giving Pledge is that of impact investment. The buzzword as reported in the *Economist* in May 2012[11] was the hottest topic at the second Giving Pledge meeting, organized to share experiences and improve giving. The meeting was held

---

[9]The 2009 *Hurun Rich List* reported there were 130 U.S. dollar billionaires in China. Yu Pengnian, 88, became the first Chinese philanthropist to break the billion-dollar barrier when he announced that he had donated his remaining fortune amounting to $470 million of cash and property assets into the Yu Pengnian Foundation, increasing the value of the Foundation up to $1.2 billion.

[10]From the documentary *Das Milliardenversprechen/The Giving Pledge*. Broadcast in 2012 on German/French TV. The film contains interviews with a number of key protagonists in the debate on the Pledge: Warren Buffett; Bill and Melinda Gates; Nicolas Berggruen—the only major European philanthropist to have signed the Giving Pledge; the eighth-generation member of the banking firm Ariane de Rothschild; Hasso Plattner, cofounder of software company SAP and a university donor; and Peter Krämer, significant contributor to UNICEF's Schools for Africa program.

[11]"Spreading Gospels of Wealth," *Economist*, May 19, 2012.

behind closed doors in order to create a safe environment for investors to share giving experiences, including failures. The term *impact investment* remains a loose one, and a new meeting will be dedicated to investigate it more fully. But the fundamental idea of following through and paying attention to the effects of investments can both be read as a criticism of the Giving Pledge and an extension of it—a criticism because it points out the limitations of the Pledge's focus on the amounts and share of wealth donated rather than on what the money actually does. It raises the question of the measurable effect of the donation, what is changed by the transfer of wealth.

It can also be read more positively as a way of expanding the Giving Pledge by involving the wealthy not just in philanthropic giving, which is bound to involve just a share of their wealth, but in their overall wealth creation and management. What we have seen so far may only have been a soft start of what the world's rich can do to save the world.

CASE STUDY 13.4   OXFORD THINKING

One of the most exciting and challenging major capital campaigns of the last decade was the *Oxford Thinking* campaign based around Oxford University. The campaign originally aimed to raise $2 billion, a target achieved four years after its launch in June 2008.

The campaign was impressive for its ambition. It was also impressive because it dispelled popular myths about fundraising.

- Myth 1: You can't raise money in a crisis. The campaign was launched more or less at the same time as the global financial meltdown, including the failure of Lehman Brothers bank—even in the middle of the biggest economic crisis ever there are still wealthy individuals, and they are still prepared to be generous.
- Myth 2: Only alumni give to universities. Many of the donors were not alumni of the university. Oxford alumni tend to relate to the colleges rather than the entire university. Oxford fundraisers had to look for outside donors more than is the usual case.
- Myth 3: It takes a long time to build up a major capital campaign. The Oxford campaign was originally led by the visionary

(Continued)

> Sue Cunningham, director of development, who built up the
> development department to the necessary levels for a cam-
> paign of this magnitude in less than a year.

Among the major donors was Lev Blavatnick, a Russian-American industrialist. He immigrated to the United States from Russia in 1978, Blavatnick is the chairman of Access Industries, a global company based around natural resources, telecommunications, and chemicals.

His $75 million gift is designed to fund Europe's first School of Government—a rival to the Kennedy School of Government at Harvard. It will give 120 students a year the opportunity to study for a master's degree covering topics from humanities to law, and social science to finance, via energy, technology, and security policy.

His donation was the largest individual campaign gift to Oxford and, indeed, one of the largest individual donations to a specific university and he has indicated he may invest more to ensure the success of the project.

Apart from Cambridge, Harvard, and Tel Aviv Universities he has also invested in a number of British cultural flagships such as the Tate Gallery and the Royal Opera House.

In Summary

In this chapter we looked at the phenomenal growth in worldwide wealth and the implications this has for fundraisers. The motivations for giving were considered and ways of approaching these individuals were outlined. Philanthrocapitalism, an increasingly prominent vehicle for major donor philanthropy, was examined.

Next up is a chapter in which the transformative power of social media is discussed.

CHAPTER 14

Globarity—The Impact of Social Media on Global Solidarity

MARCELO IÑARRA IRAEGUI AND
ASHLEY BALDWIN

The director of the nonprofit awoke from his sleep with a nagging worry in the back of his mind. He ate a light breakfast while reading the day's news on his tablet from the kitchen table. Nothing grabbed his attention.

He hadn't been able to sleep at all that night and had laid in bed, tossing and turning, worrying about the meeting that he was due to attend that morning with the members of his NGO. The fate of the organization rested on the decisions that were about to be made.

His coffee had gone cold but he gulped it down anyway. He was going to need all the caffeine he could get. He took a deep breath and walked over to his desk, past the electric mirror that had replaced the old system decades earlier with a thin layer of silver nitrate. "You might want to sort your hair out first," said the voice in the mirror, referring to some rebellious strands that had ventured onto his forehead, breaking the symmetric algorithm of his face. He paused, brushed the strands that were bothering the mirror back behind his ears and walked into his office. His computer screen lit up automatically and his assistant on the West Coast greeted him with a smile. "Is everyone ready for the meeting?" he asked. "Yes," she replied. "One thousand two hundred and thirty-five people have confirmed their attendance: 343 in India, 244 in China, 140 in the United States,

115 in Brazil, 72 in the United Kingdom, 52 in Australia, 48 in Switzerland, 47 in Germany, 15 in France, and representatives from another 65 countries." He didn't have to ask whether the organization's troublemaker would be attending. He knew that the guy would already be logged on from his home in Tuvalu, a tiny island located between Hawaii and Australia, ready and waiting to ask some difficult questions.

With just five minutes to go before the meeting commenced, the director sat down and made himself comfortable in his chair. It was incredible to think that such a small NGO could have such significant reach. Who could've imagined years ago that 1,235 members, donors, and volunteers from all over the world would become so active in the fight to preserve the cultural heritage of Elvis Presley, an almost mythical "King of Rock" figure from the twentieth century!

The meeting began, dividing the screen into 1,235 little squares, each showing a very different face. A lady from India began the debate, proposing that the average ask be increased to 25 Social-dollars from 15, as the effects of global inflation were already being felt just 48 hours after the Russian elections. "While it remains the strongest global currency, even Social-dollars are being hit by these elections and we really need to react immediately," she insisted in her strong accent, which everyone recognized as being from Bhubaneswar in the Orissa province of East India.

Once the issue of the ask had been settled, the conversation changed course: an Elvis fan from New Amsterdam, Indiana, lamenting the end of the glory days of rock and roll, proposed a campaign to relaunch the idea of "vintage" concerts (the kind where people actually got together to listen to a band perform). The current trend was for people to buy access to 300 cameras that gave them a personalized view of a performance direct to their mobile phones. It wasn't so much the personalized view that had enabled this trend to take off, but the free beer included in the price of the ticket, delivered straight to your door an hour before the concert! The idea was warmly received by members all over the world and the virtual billboard being used for the meeting quickly filled up with ideas and proposals. Even the troublemaker from Tuvalu was getting involved. It wasn't long before the time arrived for virtual voting to take place to settle the issue of the campaign, the increase in donations, and a couple of other issues that had arisen during the meeting.

We think that this science fiction-esque glimpse at the possible future of our work in NGOs you just read serves to put the title of this chapter in a bit more context.

In this chapter we reflect on our vision for the future of the social sector, based on our experience gained over 16 years of work with international organizations, many times as protagonists of this digital story and other times as members of the global community. However, our main objective in this chapter is to analyze current trends and provide our strategic vision for the next few years to come. Although we aim to do this by providing general concepts and supporting them with good causes, the primary focus will be on the *we* without borders.

The "We" without Borders

The first thing we must do before we focus in on this new paradigm is to redefine the word *we*.

The relationship between *we* and its possessive pronoun, *our* and *ours*, is the first challenge in changing vision during this new, digital era. In its beginnings, the Internet provided us with a basic, one-directional form of communication: an organization spoke to its community and the community responded according to the channels established by the organization; online channels such as email; and offline channels such as the telephone, fax, or traditional (snail) mail. However, in the middle of the first decade of the twenty-first century, when social networks really began to take off, the members of social organizations started to say, "I'd like to get together with other members of the organization that live nearby," and "I've got a great idea for a campaign that I'd like to share with you." And it was this verb *share* that really began to change the rules of the game:

> If I am part of a social organization, why can't I do something for that organization when it is convenient to me rather than having to wait for the organization to ask me?

And during the workshops and seminars that we gave to social sector staff, they began to ask us questions like "How can I control or moderate uncomfortable questions if I open up my network to donors . . . or to people who haven't even donated yet?"

So the wall of *we* began to crumble and, in much the same way as when the Berlin wall came down in 1989, history started to change. See Figure 14.1.

FIGURE 14.1   MYCHARITY: WATER ENABLES SUPPORTERS TO FUND SPECIFIC PROJECTS OF THEIR CHOICE AND FOLLOW THE DEVELOPMENT OF THOSE PROJECTS THROUGH TO COMPLETION

Source: mycharitywater.org.

The inside and outside of social organizations got mixed up . . . irreparably! Staff, board members, volunteers all had to listen to (and manage) the things that the "organization's immigrants" wanted to say and see.

An interesting example of this occurred when Greenpeace International developed the first "leading social network" with the aim of opening the organization up to a further 30,000 "employees" that would work voluntarily, each developing their own campaign to save the whales. It was one of the authors of this chapter, Marcelo Iñarra Iraegui, who in 2006 created and directed this global experiment, "I Go—Defending the Whales." To put this endeavor in a bit more context, in 2006 Facebook had only just begun and Myspace was still the most popular social network in the world. Even so, networks such as

Care2 in the United States and MyActionAid in the United Kingdom had already started to tear down the wall of *we* within the social sector.

We'd like to take this opportunity to state that when building a social network from scratch, one of the most sensible things to do would be to establish boundaries. "I Go," however, was left totally open. People could do whatever they wanted, wherever they wanted, so long as the focus was on saving whales. The only criterion established was that the community would be self-regulating and any abuses would be reported to Greenpeace. The community would set its own rules. Marvelous!

After a few weeks, there were a few intercultural clashes that had to be moderated. When it comes to issues of gender equality for example, the perception of a Swede can be very different from that of a Brazilian!

Without restricting creative freedom, the network began to focus on actions that would enable Greenpeace to achieve its political objective: to encourage more countries to vote in favor of a ban on whale hunting at the International Whaling Commission. These actions would also mean that the organization could achieve objectives in countries where there wasn't even a Greenpeace office, such as Colombia . . . all thanks to its own community. So just like that, the wall came tumbling down!

Toward the end of the campaign, the final remaining bricks in the wall of *we* started to collapse: One of the 30,000 campaign volunteers was Anne-Mari Van Hees, a mother from Queensland, Australia, who set up her own campaign on the I Go website with her son. She responded to an international brainstorming to generate ideas for a global march that would take place at the meeting of the International Whaling Commission in Anchorage, Alaska, on May 27, 2007. Her idea was simple—to organize a public gathering in cities and towns where everyone would come wearing a blue shirt. Simple, yet brilliant! This gathering would be called the *Big Blue March*.[1] Now before we go on, let's just take a step back: Greenpeace International, with its head office in Amsterdam, more than 1,000 employees all over the world, 2.7 million members, and a global budget of around 200 million Euros, was allowing Anne and her son to lead its communications! The wall had disappeared. The Big Blue March took place in 50 countries, presenting

---

[1]"The Big Blue March," http://prismwebcastnews.com/2007/05/23/big-blue-march-for-whales/.

significant organizational challenges for Greenpeace. After all, what do you do when members of your organization get together to arrange a blue march in the organization's name but without its control? Well, the head office in Holland ended up co-organizing the campaign along-side members of the I Go community and other offices, such as Mexico, were completely overwhelmed by a 500-strong march organized in Mexico City's main plaza. The I Go community headquarters was inun-dated with emails and the phone rang off the hook. How on earth do we cope with this reaction from the other side of the wall?

I Go—Defending the Whales from Greenpeace International, was the first example of mass participation from an NGO, and established a new paradigm for the social sector as a whole: decentralizing power and creativity and providing a clear framework for action is part of the solution. This new definition of the word "we" and its implications of mass participation has opened up the game to a whole new genera-tion of social participants, much in the same way that the Wikimedia Foundation has opened up the sharing of knowledge with its online encyclopedia, Wikipedia. But there is still a long way to go before we can find ways that this new paradigm can be used to help solve the many problems that exist on planet earth.

THE INDIVIDUAL AS KING OF THE CROWD EMPIRE: IS CROWDFUNDING A THREAT TO NGOS OR AN OPPORTUNITY?

The massive growth experienced by Facebook from 2007 to 2012 has completely changed the rules of the game for NGOs, as well as for all other businesses and organizations that need to communicate with their audiences. This growth reached a peak in March 2009 when the Nielsen Company announced that the amount of time that users spend on social networks had exceeded the amount of time that users spend online doing other things, such as emailing or browsing other sites. The amount of time that users were spending on Facebook, particularly, had also increased by 566 percent in just one year, reaching a total of 20.5 billion minutes.[2]

Individuals now require ever more involvement in their social organizations of choice. They are no longer willing to donate online

---

[2]David Kirkpatrick, *The Facebook Effect*, 2010.

Social Trysumers: People who wish to try out the experience of a social organization, and determine its effectiveness, before deciding whether or not to become a donor or to remain a nonfinancial, digital supporter.[3]

and await a thank-you email from the NGO for their kind action. They want to be the protagonists, the social heroes. And what's more, they want to become Social Trysumers and get their first experience of a social organization for free!

The pioneering actions of the few thousand early adopters that participated in actions such as these, has now been multiplied by millions. And those same early adopters are now even beginning to question the existence of large, costly bureaucratic structures when one individual can mobilize millions of people for a cause and fundraise on a global scale using crowdsourcing, crowdfunding, or whatever the next big crowd thing turns out to be. The new generation of twentysomething, potential supporters are (quite rightly) asking themselves, "Why should I finance the white elephants that are large NGOs?" Little by little, peer-to-peer fundraising platforms such as Justgiving and Crowdrise are continuing to gain space and effectiveness, developing functions such as mobile giving and integration with social networks to name but a few. And that's without mentioning groundbreaking sites such as Kickstarter and its many clones.

But before we decide whether these websites are a threat to NGOs or an opportunity, let's look at a precise definition of the concept of crowdsourcing.

After studying more than 40 definitions of crowdsourcing, we propose a new integrating definition:

Crowdsourcing is a type of participative online activity in which an individual, an institution, a nonprofit organization, or a company

---

[3] This definition established by Marcelo Iniarra and Alfredo Botti, "Social 'Trysumers," Chapter 10 in Ted Hart et al. (eds.), *Internet Management for Nonprofits Management*" (Hoboken, NJ: John Wiley & Sons, 2010).

proposes to a group of individuals of varying knowledge, heterogeneity, and number, via a flexible open call, the voluntary undertaking of a task. The undertaking of the task, or variable complexity and modularity and in which the crowd should participate bringing their work, money, knowledge, and/or experience, always entails mutual benefit. The user will receive the satisfaction of a given type of need, be it economic, social recognition, self-esteem, or the development of individual skills, while the crowdsourcer will obtain and utilize to their advantage that which the user has brought to the venture, whose form will depend on the type of activity undertaken.[4]

Heraclitus' quote, "The only thing permanent is change," is a difficult concept for mature NGOs with large structures to assimilate. Approval procedures and other factors implied by this kind of organization means that change can take years. But even so, we believe that this shift is a great opportunity for NGOs to harness the power of the community in a collective and collaborative way. This will be more challenging for social organizations that focus on raising awareness and changing public or private behaviors (whether that be in the field of human rights or the environment), than it will be for organizations that focus on more tangible field work, such as providing drinking water to remote areas in Africa. Even so, we believe that if these organizations innovate and experiment with involving their supporters in their work, listening to them, and then acting in accordance with the interests and behaviors of this community, then change *is* achievable.

NGOs can still have control over why a community should act, but the community needs to have more control over the *how* and *what should we do* aspects.

In Eric Von Hippel's book, *Democratizing Innovation*, he presents a possible resolution to this challenge using his open source innovation model: In order for X organization to achieve change, it opens up the challenge to its community. Ideas are generated and these ideas are listened to. The organization then meets with lead activists virtually and a campaign toolkit is prepared and dispersed among the community

---

[4] Enrique Estelles and Fernando Gonzales, 2012, www.crowdsourcing-blog.org /wp-content/uploads/2012/02/Towards-an-integrated-crowdsourcing -definition-Estell%C3%A9s-Gonz%C3%A1lez.pdf.

for action and to spread the word.[5] There are an infinite number of ways that organizations can experiment along these lines of innovation.

One organization that is already harnessing the power of crowd-funding is charity: water, which uses this model to finance its projects within the organization's community, assuring donors that 100 percent of funds will go directly to the projects. As a result of this method, charity: water has an ever-growing community of active and mobi-lized members. According to Chris Anderson's Long Tail Theory[6] this community is part of a very specific niche of people interested in supporting projects that increase access to clean water. These people are able to sponsor projects with donations ranging from $5 to $5,000 and, just like with any other crowdfunding platform, can create their own profile and raise funds within their own community. The team in the field then provides the transparency and assurance that the donors require by uploading photos of the projects being funded, in real time, using a geolocation platform. This kind of internal crowdfund-ing model is a great opportunity for NGOs to finance specific projects using the power of the crowd. See Figure 14.1.

No More Sweeping Things under the Rug

The growth of the digital universe has provoked a return to a pre-Columbus era. The world has, once again, become flat! (Don't worry, this is just a metaphor. We haven't gone *completely* mad!)

When we talk about global solidarity, issues that are close to us geo-graphically are just as relevant as those taking place 10,000 miles away. The Arab Spring not only grabbed the attention of the countries in which it was taking place, but people all over the world were follow-ing the issue and choosing their position in relation to human rights and the freedom of expression online. The international face of the Arab Spring, the person who showed us all exactly what was being swept under the rug, was none other than the Regional Head of Mar-keting for Google Middle East and North Africa, Wael Ghonim. In

---

[5]Eric Von Hippel, *Democratizing Innovation* (Cambridge, MA: MIT Press, 2005).

[6]Chris Anderson, *The Long Tail* (New York: Hyperion, 2006).

FIGURE 14.2   **WE ARE ALL PART OF THE NGO: COMMUNICATIONS, FUNDRAISING, POLICY, PROGRAMS, FIELD WORKERS, SUPPORTERS, AMBASSADORS, DIRECTORS, ETC.**

© copyright 2010 marceloiniarra.com

2010, Ghonim started the Facebook page, "We are all Khaled Said," supporting a young Egyptian man who was tortured to death by police. This page mobilized and organized the anti-government protests of the January 25 revolution. Ghonim became an international figure, provoking pro-democracy demonstrations in Egypt following his 11-day secret incarceration by the Egyptian police, during which time he was interrogated over his role as administrator of the Facebook page. He later became one of *Time* magazine's "100 most influential people of 2011."

If we look at it from a more extreme point of view, even social networks are unable to save themselves from their own impact as there is nothing that can be swept under the rug. Everything that was previously invisible has become massive and public. So when Greenpeace International began a campaign against Facebook for using carbon-based fuel to power its data center, where did the organization choose to implement this campaign? That's right, Facebook!

In his article for *Wired* magazine, journalist Eric Smalley wrote, "The activist environmental organization declared victory in its nearly two-year campaign to pressure Facebook to reduce the environmental impact of its data centers. The social media giant's data centers house a colossal arsenal of servers that supports the friendships and marketing campaigns of 800 million people across the globe."

Most of the electricity that powers Facebook's data centers—and most other data centers—comes from coal-fired power plants. Greenpeace's Facebook campaign, dubbed *Unfriend Coal* and centered on a Facebook page, gathered 700,000 supporters, according to the organization. The campaign also garnered a Guinness world record for most Facebook comments in a 24-hour period.[7]

But how can NGOs reveal what is under the rug and tell relevant stories in a compelling way that involves their supporters?

We think that one of the fundamental elements in the creation of a campaign that empowers people on a digital level is the development of a Public Mobilization Concept (PMC).

In our experience, there are two models that can be used to develop a digital campaign concept:

1. Reactive PMC (opportunistic model)
2. Proactive PMC (established by social organizations)

Reactive PMC

This model is driven by opportunities presented by the market: News that shocked a society, a presidential election, or any other event that an organization can take advantage of in order to establish a digital campaign within a matter of hours. At first glance, this is not an easy model to include in a marketing plan but it does require a new kind of management that should be included within a strategic plan: rapid digital response management.

This model differs somewhat from the traditional rapid response model that has been used following catastrophes, accidents, or terrorist attacks, where people push organizations to act. In this reactive or

---

[7]Eric Smalley, "Greenpeace Declares Victory Over Facebook Data Centers," *Wired*, December 2011.

opportunistic model, the organization bases its action on a theme or issue brought to the forefront by external actors and develops a campaign around this issue.

We don't want to go into further detail about this model as it requires an organization to have reached a higher state of digital maturity. Campaign organizations such as Avaaz, Greenpeace, and Amnesty all use this model effectively to select campaign concepts.

Proactive PMC

This model is a traditional model where the organization establishes the theme or issue of a digital campaign for society. There is a vast bibliography surrounding this model with many recipes! In our experience, we would suggest adhering to the 10 following principles to select a campaign theme:

1. Simple to understand

   If you can't explain the core objectives of a digital campaign in a Facebook comment or SMS, it is too complex.

2. Easy to share, easy to love

   The theme of the digital campaign should be easy to share among ordinary, digital users, both Internet and mobile users. People want to share the fact that they are social heroes.

3. Emotional

   Human beings are emotional animals. A general audience reacts to themes that touch their hearts.

4. Relevant

   Real political change is a key factor. Throughout our careers we have seen many digital campaigns that are driven by cool tactics but which didn't imply any real social change. Integrated planning with program managers is the only way to select a relevant campaign theme. First, we must establish the political target that we wish to achieve and then establish the tactics we must use to obtain that goal. This goal could include political or financial change, or even a change to social behavior.

5. Remarkable

   Seth Godin, author of *The Big Moo* and other marketing bestsellers, established this concept. People want to participate in a campaign that provides them with a unique and unforgettable experience.

6. Personal

People want to take an active digital role. They want to be the social heroes as well as the organization. A campaign theme therefore needs to take into consideration the fact that supporters want to play a key role in achieving campaign goals together.

7. Positive

If you are a social hero, you want to feel positive about it. As a result, the themes of social organization campaigns are shifting from guilt provoking to engaging and positive.

8. Sticky

Many authors talk about *stickiness* when it comes to campaign themes. Why is a campaign successful? Why has it gone viral? It takes a combination of factors to make a *sticky* campaign: understand both the market and the audience; intuit that a theme will work; have no fear of failing; and test a variety of messages and offers.

9. Instant win: Personal reward

Long-term objectives do not work for anxious users who remain on a website for just a few seconds. The life cycle of a campaign should mimic that of a fly . . . short!

10. A good bad guy

Alfred Hitchcock once said, "Give me a bad guy and I will build a great story." Storytelling is crucial for building a good digital campaign. Selecting a bad guy to fight against in order to change political objectives, raise funds, and obtain new supporters is a particular challenge for organizations such as UNICEF. However, positive and creative approaches toward asserting pressure on key actors could be a great way to engage supporters.

The Social Speed of Light

The ways through which ideas can be spread and the speed at which this takes place is something completely new in the history of communication. A previously unknown participant on a reality show such as *American Idol* (or one of its many local versions) can acquire hundreds of thousands of fans on their Facebook and Twitter accounts in a matter of hours. Using these platforms, an individual or small group of people can achieve amazing results with minimal financing, diffusing their message among millions of users who have the potential to become active members of their organizations.

In March 2006, Jack Dorsey (@jack) scribbled a quick note to himself about an idea that would enable an individual to communicate with a small group of people using an SMS service. It didn't take long for this idea to be developed into Twitter, king of real-time communication.

In 2007, Twitter began to take off and we started to open Twitter accounts to look for new ways to involve our supporters. At first, it was difficult to see how the platform differed from more traditional, SMS. However, the tipping point occurred with the increase in use of smart phones, and suddenly people from all corners of the globe began to share their thoughts in 140 characters. Now, according to Twitter's blog, the platform boasts 140 million unique users, sending around 340 million tweets per day!

Among these 340 million tweets per day are plenty of "Going out to eat sushi with my friend Mary #Sushi" and even a few "So I've been told by a reputable person that Osama Bin Laden has been killed. Hot damn!" But Twitter was also the first place to report that President Obama was about to address the nation on an issue of national security. This happened at 10:25 EST, when Keith Urbahn, former chief of staff for Bush's Defense Secretary, Donald Rumsfeld, broke the news.[8] Then less than an hour later at 11:35, Obama made the official announcement.

And this is why Twitter is the best example of the social speed of light!

Activist organizations have learned to move at the speed required to manage campaigns and programs at this pace, quickly positioning themselves on this social network to accompany actions and generate awareness and activism. Other organizations, such as charity: water

---

[8] "Twitter Just Had Its CNN Moment," www.businessinsider.com/twitter-just-had-its-cnn-moment-2011-5#ixzz1w0weJLfH.

effectively utilized Twitter for fundraising in 2009 with innovative and successful social media campaigns such as the Twitter festival, Twestival, which raised $250,000.[9]

But even though Twitter is king as far as speed of light social networking is concerned, Facebook has certainly not been left behind. In the controversial case of Kony 2012, developed by the organization, Invisible Children, Facebook was used very well indeed. In an interesting analysis of the campaign on his website,[10] Chris Rose comments on the speed at which the Kony 2012 video documentary was diffused:

> Social Flow noted that its 100 million views on YouTube in only six days was the fastest campaign after Susan Boyle did it in nine, and Lady Gaga's Bad Romance took 18 days. The video was heavily viewed from mobile phones and is most popular with 13–17-year-old females and 18–24-year-old males.[11]

Facebook, as well as other communities created by Invisible Children were a key factor in achieving rapid dissemination of this campaign or, better said by Rose, an excellent exercise in video marketing.

In their book, *The Dragonfly Effect*, Aaker and Smith reveal four useful tips to guide organizations in the development of "at the speed of light" campaigns.

But how must social organizations adapt in order to make the most of the opportunities provided by social networks? Should they exchange their analogue or web 1.0 structures that focus on content generation for more dynamic teams that empower communities on social networks? And finally, should approval protocols be radically changed in order to save time?

Answering these questions would surely take up an entire book but we are convinced that the social organizations that are able to answer them (and act accordingly) are the ones that will lead social change.

---

[9] www.charitywater.org/twestival.

[10] www.campaignstrategy.org.

[11] Chris Rose, *Exploring Konyism*, http://threeworlds.campaignstrategy.org/?p=71.

THE DRAGONFLY EFFECT

Focus + GET

The Dragonfly Effect relies on four distinct wings. When they work together, they achieve remarkable results.

1. Focus. Identify a single concrete and measurable goal.
2. Grab attention. Make someone look. Cut through the noise of social media with something personal, unexpected, visceral, and visual.
3. Engage. Create a personal connection, accessing high emotions through deep empathy, authenticity, and storytelling. Engaging is about empowering the audience enough to do something themselves.
4. Take action. Enable and empower others to take action. To make this easy you must prototype, develop, and continuously tweak tools, templates, and programs designed to move audience members from being customers to becoming team members—in other words, furthering the cause and the change beyond themselves.

Source: Aaker, Jennifer and Smith, Andy. The Dragonfly Effect. Jossey-Bass, 2010.

TRANSCENDING SPACE: CONNECTING THE GLOBAL COMMUNITY

The digital revolution is no longer limited to our homes and offices. Now, we can access an international community of potential supporters with the ability to act for the social causes that interest them, in real time, wherever they may be; on the bus, at a café, even on the treadmill at the gym.

"Today, everyone is carrying around a wormhole in their pocket," claims Amber Case, San Francisco–based Cyborg Anthropologist, currently being hailed as one of the world's most influential women in technology.[12] Not wormholes in the traditional sense of the

---

[12]Amber Case, "We Are All Cyborgs Now," *TEDWomen*, Washington, DC, December 2010.

word—intergalactic, vacuous tunnels that transport us to weird and won-derful new universes—but wormholes that allow us to virtually transport ourselves to a completely different location with just one click of a but-ton. Yes, you've guessed it—she's talking about the smart phone.

And with the sale of smart phones continuing to skyrocket in most markets, reliance on this technology has begun to filter into most aspects of our daily lives: We use them for social networking (with more than half of Facebook users accessing the platform via their mobile phones, it won't be long before almost all of us are access-ing social media in this way). We use them to chat, send instant mes-sages via SMS or applications such as Whatsapp, and even video-chat via Skype. We use them to make payments, to alert friends as to our whereabouts, to play games, watch movies, listen to music, and, most importantly, to interact with the causes and social organizations that interest us the most.

This new kind of real-time interaction with human beings from all corners of the globe has become so popular that it has even provoked an anthropological revolution: Whereas anthropologists traditionally studied human beings and the tools they used to expand their physi-cal selves, cyborg anthropology focuses on the study of how human beings are using new technology such as mobile phones, tablets, and ever-more transportable computers to expand their mental selves.[13]

"It's not that machines are taking over," insists Case. "They're help-ing us to connect with each other regardless of geography, helping us to increase our humanness."

For fundraisers, this technological revolution implies a massive shift in the way we communicate. As we mentioned earlier, our potential supporters are no longer content to simply read about our causes on a website or see them on a YouTube video. They want to experience and contribute to the work of social organizations beyond making a financial donation. By ignoring the potential of new, cyborg tools such as mobile phones, social networks, apps, gaming, and location-based platforms, not only are we ignoring the tools of globarity, but we are also missing out on a wealth of potential supporters simply by refusing to speak their language.

---

[13] Ashley Baldwin, "Welcome to the Wormhole," *Innophoric Watch*, June 2011.

Livestreaming

One of the primary communication methods to have emerged in recent years, with the potential to unite supporters from across the globe, is livestreaming. Leaving YouTube trailing behind as far as the number of video hours uploaded is concerned, and now posing a threat to traditional television networks, livestream services are online platforms that enable users to record and public content to a live, worldwide audience . . . for free!

According to the CEO of Skype, Josh Silverman, "People have shared meaning through language for hundreds of thousands of years, evolving from oral to visual and, for the past few thousand years, written. However, until the twentieth century, true conversations were tied to a shared place and time. But video conferencing and livestreaming is changing all of that, combining oral, visual, and written traditions into virtual presence." This technology is a real opportunity for social organizations as a whole to open up communication channels with their supporters and potential supporters, providing them with a very real insight into our work and also finding out what they want from us.

This kind of technology is already being adopted by some organizations. UNHCR used livestreaming to broadcast from refugee camps during World Refugee Day live, breaking down the barriers of globarity and enabling donors and potential supporters to interact with recipients, from their living rooms, offices, and cafés all over the world. Even so, the potential of this technology for basic fundraising, for example, remains untapped. We must not forget that asking supporters for a financial donation to help resolve a problem that is occurring thousands of miles away and affecting a population or an environment that they cannot see, hear, or speak to, with consequences that they cannot fathom, is asking them to make a huge leap of faith. But the technology now exists to show potential supporters the cause via a tablet in their local high street or shopping mall and enable them to really see, hear, and even interact with the recipient of their donation.

Livestreaming also has the potential to be used as an add-on to crowd-funding platforms. With a simple camera or smart phone, staff, members, and supporters of an organization can broadcast their work, campaigns, and fundraising activities to a global audience on a massive scale. This could include anything from a simple sponsored run, to a large-scale act of environmental or political activism, not only enabling supporters to become social heroes, but also enabling organizations themselves to provide a further element of transparency to their activities.

Augmented reality is another technology that has the potential to give supporters a real experience of a social organization or cause using virtual technology. Put simply, augmented reality works using interactive, fictional layers that can be downloaded online and then observed within the context of one's immediate reality using a computer or the camera viewfinder on a smart phone.

This technology was implemented wonderfully by WWF China in its award-winning campaign, "Wildlife's Fate is in Your Hands."[14] This campaign used augmented reality to show supporters how displaced wildlife copes outside of its natural habitat. This was a great example of Social Trysumerism, providing supporters with a real experience of an organization and its cause before asking for a financial commitment, and was also a great example of how social organizations can provide this type of experience to potential supporters all over the world irrespective of their location. Two weeks after launching the campaign, WWF China's membership rates doubled and hits to the organization's website reached more than 535,000.

While researching this kind of technology and its potential implication for the social sector, one of the authors of this chapter, Ashley Baldwin, interviewed spatial computing expert, Albert Hwang.[15] According to Hwang, "There is a lot of technology available to give people the sense of an environment without actually being there. Augmented reality can give people a sense of the size and the scale of a place and what sorts of activities are being done there, all from the comfort of their own homes."

While the implementation of campaigns that involve cutting edge technology is certainly not the most tried-and-tested method, it is vital that social organizations continue to experiment in these areas. Campaigns such as "Wildlife's Fate Is in Your Hands," show that done

---

[14] www.wwfchina.org/aboutwwf/miniwebsite/fateinhand/en/.

[15] Albert Hwang, 3D information artist, www.albert-hwang.com.

well, the potential globarity on the Go: the potential impact of this kind of campaign can be massive.

Globarity on the Go

As well as enabling us to connect and communicate with each other irrespective of our global location, the proliferation of smart phone and tablet technology also means that we no longer have to participate in a physical march, rally, or flash mob in order to act for a cause. Nor is our virtual participation (including making donations) limited to our homes and offices.

We have become a society of technological nomads, booking our holidays in the dentist's waiting room while waiting for a root canal, doing our weekly supermarket shopping on the bus, and catching up with our friend in Norway while we chill out on the beach in Brazil. Although many still lament the "good old days" of the 1960s and 1970s, when participating in a cause meant marching on the street, handcuffing oneself to railings, or various other forms of physical participation, this shift in the way that people take part in social causes means that, in theory, our supporters and potential supporters should be easier to reach than ever given that they are increasingly more connected. On the other hand this presents us with a challenge: how do we distract our supporters and appeal to them to act wherever they may be, whether at work at their local coffee shop, or browsing the web in the bathtub?

Over the past couple of years, this shift in the way that people protest, act, and even donate, toward a more technology-led participation, has provoked increasing debate on *slacktivists*, donors whose feel-good giving has little impact on the causes they support, and their role within social organizations.

Certainly in our more digital and innovation-focused consultancy, we disagree with many elements of this definition, especially the claim that these digital actions have little or no practical effect. We prefer to call these so-called slacktivists (people who participate in social organizations digitally by "liking" a Facebook page, signing an online petition, forwarding an interesting video to their friends, etc.) as a new generation of living-room, or digital activists. And the great thing about digital activists is that there are millions of them willing to act if only we appeal to them in the right way.

Whatever your position regarding the Kony 2012 video and the organization behind it, this video was viewed more than 100 million times in just six days and is a great lesson in the kind of digital impact that digital activists can have on our causes if we just learn to speak their language. At a time when we buy our products online, work online, book our travel online, and even find a date online, it is a little naive for us to expect our supporters to put their mobile phones and tablets to one side and get their bums off their seats to act for a cause. It is up to us to look at these new ways of behaving and modify the ask accordingly. Give your digital activists a call, send them a video, invite them to participate on your social media platforms, and see what an impact they can have. Stop complaining about them and start using them!

The technology at the forefront of nomad activism, and one that pushes the boundaries of global solidarity is location-based services (LBS). LBS are platforms that enable users to connect with others based on their current location and obtain information, interact with other users, and check in to the businesses and places they visit, using nothing more than a smart phone. These services incorporate the best of social media but with a GPS dimension, allowing users to connect physically as well as virtually. This is great news for the social sector, where combining online and offline campaign elements is usually a recipe for success. Although there are hundreds of location-based platforms to choose from, the two predominant services include Facebook places, which has more than 30 million users (and counting) and Foursquare, which has grown by more than 3,400 percent from 2010 to 2011.

Many businesses have adopted LBS to reward customer loyalty. For example, some platforms reward users for checking in the most to certain locations. This reward can either be a title (for example, mayor of a particular location on Foursquare) or a discount or freebie. One of the benefits of LBS for social organizations is that global supporters can follow an offline action, online. In 2010, Greenpeace Argentina used Foursquare to campaign against Duracell refusing to recycle its batteries. The organization asked its cyberactivists to check in to the local branch of Procter & Gamble using this location-based social network and leave a message asking the company to take environmental responsibility for its batteries. Every time people checked in, their followers and contacts on Foursquare and Facebook (which can be integrated with Foursquare) were able to view this action, thus diffusing the campaign way beyond Procter & Gamble's Argentina office. It wasn't long before Greenpeace Argentina became "Mayor" of Procter & Gamble on Foursquare!

Weight Watchers in partnership with Action against Hunger also harnessed the power of location-based platforms with its Lose-a-Palooza campaign. As part of this campaign, Weight Watchers donated $1 to Action against Hunger every time someone checked in to a participating Weight Watchers venue. In total, the company raised $75,000 in just one day!

Although these traditional uses of LBS hold vast potential for the sector, what would happen if we ran a global campaign where users could check in to a virtual location and protest without leaving their seats?

Fun Activism and Fundraising

Gaming is another media that companies and organizations can use in order to break down borders and reach a wider, global audience. Although to some it might seem a bit frivolous to introduce "fun" elements into serious causes, there is actually significant research to suggest that this isn't such a crazy idea after all! Individuals now spend more money on video games than any other form of entertainment, including DVDs, recorded music, and even cinema tickets.

According to Tom Chatfield in his book *Fun Inc.*,[16] "The benefit that games have over any other medium is that they provide experiential learning." So while your friends and family may be somewhat justified in getting a bit annoyed at the amount of time you've been spending constructing chicken coops and planting crops online, you aren't *completely* wasting your time: You've actually been learning something and you probably didn't even realize it. You were too busy having fun! This theory is supported by Jane McGonigal, Head of Game R&D at the Institute for the Future. In her presentation for TED Long Beach in 2010, McGonigal highlighted online gaming as vitally important in the creation of a future generation equipped with the four primary skills necessary to change the world: Urgent

---

[16]Tom Chatfield, Fun Inc.: Why Games Are the 21st Century's Most Serious Business (Virgin Books, 2011.)

optimism, social fabric, blissful productivity, and epic meaning. Gaming allows us to experience something firsthand in a controlled environment and, if applied to social organizations, this can include issues such as deforestation, famine, poverty, and human rights abuses. It can also teach us about what we can do to help fight for these causes wherever we may be in the world—a virtual, and fun, call to action.

Volkswagen's Fun Theory is a particularly good example of how behavior can be changed for the better by making something fun, and has been successfully applied to hard-hitting issues such as recycling and complying with speed limits, simply by introducing gaming elements into these activities.

Although several NGOs have been quick to jump onboard this bandwagon by including gaming elements in their programs, many have been lacking in the most vital element of this medium . . . fun! Instead, concentrating on lengthy, text-heavy games obviously aimed at directly educating potential supporters. Other games, however, have been more successful: MSF Australia's Swat Malaria Mosquitoes game is simple, catchy, and fun and its strategic placement on a landing page full of information about malaria transmission and prevention makes it difficult to avoid learning about the issue while you play. More sophisticated games include the World Bank–sponsored Evoke, which describes itself as a "crash course in changing the world," challenging players to solve real-world issues and offering real-world prizes for their efforts, including mentorships and scholarships.[17]

Another great game that successfully combines the idea of acting for a social cause while doing something fun is the iPhone application, "Commons." This app, which won the Real World Games for Change Award, encourages citizens in New York City to act for social causes in their local area. As part of the game, players walk around their city, identifying social and environmental problems using GPS integration and suggesting ways that these issues can be overcome.

Perhaps the most compelling app of recent months, however, affirming our belief that simple, fun, digital actions can have a massive impact on our programs, was DePaul United Kingdom's "iHobo."[18]

---

[17] Ibid.

[18] Ibid.

This cheaply produced app invites iPhone users to download a virtual homeless person who lives in their phones for three days. The aim of the app is to give people a real, interactive experience of the complexities surrounding homelessness and the work of the organization. And it certainly paid off: With a budget of just $9,400, iHobo has been downloaded more than 600,000 times and monthly traffic to DePaul's website has increased by almost 60 percent. Estimates suggest that the combined media value of this campaign has reached more than $1.88 million.[19]

In Summary

This chapter discussed the following equation:

"Global" plus "Solidarity" equals "Globarity."

"Are you sure these photos are from Iraq?" was the first question to meet Marcelo Iñarra Iraegui, as he walked into the office on a May morning in 2005 during Greenpeace's "Non Whaling Virtual March"; the campaign mentioned at the beginning of this chapter.

And sure enough, there on the computer screen were two photos of children holding signs in Korean that read, "Please don't hunt whales," taken in Iraq. In the middle of a war, with bombs going off and gunshots sounding, there were two children that still considered Greenpeace's campaign to be *their* campaign. The two photos from Iraq joined the other 31,000 from 151 other countries.

Since the beginnings of the digital era, NGOs have approached the issue of globarity or global solidarity with caution. There are still significant barriers to achieving this in the structures of both national and international NGOs, and even more when we start talking about fundraising.

Initiatives such as Global Giving and Kiva.org are leading the way, with some international NGOs also making attempts to break down these barriers with varying levels of success. But how much farther can we go?

One of the biggest barriers in terms of globarity is the analogue logic that many NGOs still use in their administration and management. We often hear questions such as "What happens if a donor in

---

[19] www.depauluk.org/newsandresources/ihobo-wins-three-marketing
-excellence/.

country X makes a donation in country Y or on the organization's international website? Who manages supporter services for that person, country X or the international headquarters?" "What happens if an international headquarters launches a mass campaign that captures the audiences of national offices that are competing for resources and attention?" "If am a supporter in X country, what happens if I am interested in a campaign being run by Y country and want to receive the information that they are sending to their supporters?" "Who is responsible for managing a global campaign in 15 languages that must be adapted for various local markets?" "When should NGOs use new technology to expand beyond their national boundaries to a global audience?"

We still have a long way to go, and lots of disruptive changes to be made before we can make the most of the opportunities that a global society offers. The science fiction story with which we opened this chapter plays with a wide range of possibilities that could occur within the framework of globarity. But how many of our readers would like to branch out into this terrain? Whoever does is sure to reap the fruits of globarity.

CHAPTER 15

Innovation—The Only Competitive Advantage

BERNARD ROSS WITH RESEARCH FROM SUDESHNA MUKHERJEE

Innovation matters. It matters in the commercial world, where marketing guru Philip Kotler[1] calls it "the only sustainable competitive advantage." But from =mc's research and consulting work it is also becoming increasingly important in charities, NGOs, and NPOs worldwide, especially in their fundraising.

This chapter explores this issue and identifies:

- Why innovation has become important to fundraisers
- Which are regarded as the most innovative charities—and why?
- What processes can help drive innovation
- What cultural or organizational issues can help or hinder innovation

In this chapter we also profile three notable charities working to be more innovative. Internationally, UNICEF and Greenpeace, once seen as sleeping fundraising giants, now are reinventing themselves through innovation programs. In the United Kingdom, Cancer Research UK, already the largest European charity by some way, has worked hard to maintain its competitive edge through innovation.

---

[1]Kotler, Philip. *Marketing Insights From A-Z: 80 Concepts Every Manager Needs To Know*. John Wiley & Sons, Inc, 2003.

These organizations are not just working on innovation as an added extra, but are putting it at the very center of their strategies. They want to be innovative 24/7 rather than simply chase one good new idea for a quick fix, or pick up on the latest trends. It is this approach—making innovation a core competence—that seems to drive success.

WHY IS INNOVATION SO IMPORTANT?

Why has fundraising innovation acquired such importance in recent years? From our work, and our interviews and research with directors of development/fundraising worldwide, we've established five commonly mentioned key drivers for fundraising innovation:

1. Challenging economies: Worldwide charities are having to compete with each other, and with other's "social" concerns for donors such as paying for education or health care. The same old approaches simply won't cut it in that context and charities are increasingly looking for new ways to raise more money.

2. Supporter apathy: There is some evidence that supporters are becoming blasé about a great deal of "me, too" or commodity fundraising—where they are unable to distinguish the difference between causes and their propositions. Differentiation is a key issue in the sector and innovation is a way to differentiate yourself.

3. Beneficiary need: Sadly the world is in many ways becoming less comfortable and more difficult for many disadvantaged individuals and groups as climate change, domestic violence, war leading to displacement, and so on, take their toll. Charities, it is clear, need more money to do their work, not less. And may even need new ways to communicate need.

4. Culture: Some approaches apparently work everywhere in the world—for example, the peer-to-peer approach for major donors. But some other approaches such as telephone fundraising seem to be more culturally specific—they need to be adapted to specific cultural or national context. So charities need to be innovative to adapt ideas and make them work.

5. Technology: A great deal of innovation is driven by the growth in disruptive technologies. There is enormous interest in, for example, online fundraising using mobiles. Interestingly many

African nations such as Kenya are farther ahead in this than many so-called developed nations.[2] Many charities are looking for faster/cheaper technologies.

In our research no one driver emerged as overwhelmingly important. But almost all of the charities studied mentioned one or more of these drivers as being important and driving a desire for innovation among boards and senior managers.

Yet, although almost everyone—in both the commercial and charitable worlds—agrees that innovation is important, our research suggests that only a small number of charities worldwide are really embracing it in a systematic way. In fact, the benchmarking data in Fig. 15.1 suggests that even the top 10 innovative charities in the United Kingdom and the United States are not seen as being *very* innovative.

One encouraging note, however. Our research suggests that you don't have to have as big an investment budget as Greenpeace, or have to be as attractive a brand as the Red Cross/Red Crescent, or have as loyal a supporter base as Amnesty to succeed in innovation. Many small organizations are successfully innovating.

Who Is Innovative?

There is no universally accepted definition of innovative. The word itself derives from the Latin *innovatus*, which is the noun from the verb *innovare* (to renew or change). That verb itself is based on two further words: *in* (into) plus *novus* (new). Wikipedia defines *innovation* as "the creation of better or more effective products, processes, services, technologies, or ideas that are accepted by markets, governments, and society." In fundraising, this definition also applies—so innovation can mean a new method of fundraising, or a new way to engage donors, or use of a new technology to reach supporters, or even a new kind of proposition, like micro-loans rather than donations.

---

[2]We have consciously avoided focusing on the technological side of innovation here. This is partly because there is another whole chapter devoted to the use of social media and cell-phone technology. And partly because many of the senior figures we interviewed were less sure that technology offered a new way to fundraise directly but rather to enhance supporter engagement.

Which charities are seen as being most innovative? Figure 15.1 shows the results of a poll carried out by =mc at the annual AFP International conference among U.S. directors of development and fundraising. This graph combines data collected over the three years of 2010 to 2012 to provide an average result. In the online poll participants were asked to rate a number of U.S.-based charities on their perceived level of innovation. (Note that this result is simply based on opinions though it is perception among credible and knowledgeable peers.)[3]

The results—excluding any charity that scored less than 30/100—are illustrated in Figure 15.1. So World Vision, Greenpeace, WWF Amnesty, UNICEF, Habitat, Save the Children, and Feed the Children were all seen as scoring more than 50/100 on a score of innovation. What's immediately noticeable is that even relatively low scorers such as Red Cross, Salvation Army, and United Way are still in the top 10.

FIGURE 15.1   **INNOVATION RANKING OF TOP NONPROFITS**

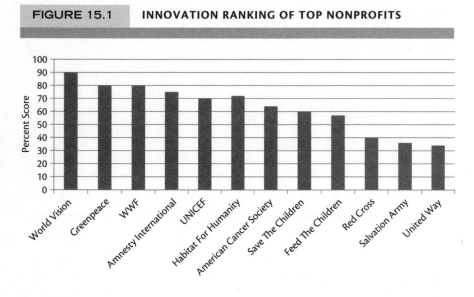

Source: =mc.

---

[3]The survey was administered to 100-plus senior development professionals and they were asked to rank a number of charities on a scale of 1 to 5. The results have been converted to a percentage.

We repeated the same survey among U.K. charities. The survey produced similar results, with many of the same brand names appearing— Red Cross, World Vision, UNICEF, and Amnesty. In this case, however, a number of U.K.-based charities scored highly such as Oxfam, Cancer Research and the National Society for the Prevention of Cruelty to Children (NSPCC). The highest scoring was Comic Relief—seen as consistently innovative especially in terms of events and social media. See Figure 15.2.

Our further research among respondents in both surveys suggested that in forming their judgment about innovation, these senior fundraisers had three main measures for the usefulness of innovation: supporter responsiveness, use of social media, and speed of response to events.

If you visit the websites of many of the organizations you can see these characteristics in action with links to topical events, a range of ways to engage with the agency or the cause, and an ability to track and adapt to donor/supporter interests. Respondents also tended to mention specific programs or initiatives that they admired—so, for example, UNICEF's Inspired Gifts where you can "buy" a cow or

FIGURE 15.2   **U.K. INNOVATION RANKING OF TOP NONPROFITS**

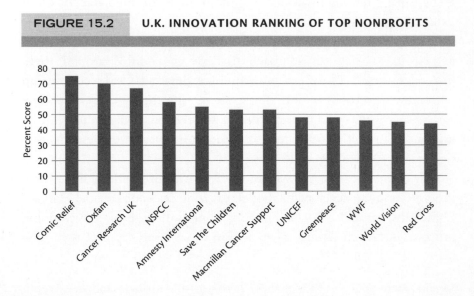

Source: =mc.

similar for a loved one, or NSPCC's Letter to Santa where through a donation you can arrange for a child to receive a personalized letter from Santa Claus.[4]

However, it's interesting that these adaptive issues are the key metrics rather than the introduction of radical new approaches. It's also interesting that while some causes such as charity: water are lauded as being innovative by those outside the industry for their business model, they are not seen as being fundamentally innovative in what they do. (Also note that respondents did not introduce or rank some social enterprises such as Tom's Shoes or Kiva.)

So these results, although not part of a precise quantified survey, do provide interesting insights into who is seen as long-term systematically innovative and who not.

HOW DO CHARITIES BECOME INNOVATIVE?

Again, our research and consulting work suggests that one key challenge to innovative fundraising is that few organizations have a systematic process to create, integrate, and exploit innovation. Mostly innovation is a random, happenstance phenomenon—led perhaps by a charismatic development director or through the involvement of an external consultant.

Those agencies that do succeed long term, like the examples earlier, seem to share an approach that we've codified around three linked processes. These processes involve devising ideas—coming up with new approaches—developing them—to the point where they can be successful—and then delivering the result, usually an increase in income as a result of new ideas. It is this combination of elements that signals success. See Figure 15.3.

Our company =mc has worked on how organizations use these three processes and we developed a model, drawing on some original Harvard University research that argues that innovation is a value-adding process with seven distinct stages within these three key processes. The

---

[4]Again interestingly neither of these programs is actually brand new—both are adaptations of programs dreamed up by other agencies. What is new is the ability to drive it at scale.

FIGURE 15.3	DEVISE DEVELOP DELIVER

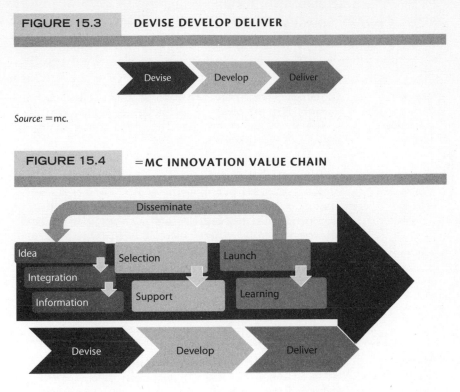

Source: =mc.

FIGURE 15.4	=MC INNOVATION VALUE CHAIN

Source: =mc.

value adding approach suggests that organizations likely to succeed systematically need to apply a development model to a number of ideas over a period of time rather than seeking the one-off success.

Figure 15.4 illustrates these three processes expanded across six operational and two review elements.

At each stage in the process, a fundraising organization can be strong or weak. Figure 15.5 asks *questions* relevant to each stage to help you assess yourself in terms of the challenges you face and the *consequences*—or symptoms—if you are less than effective in that stage.

As indicated in Figure 15.5, at each stage in the overall innovation process, an organization can be strong or weak. You may want to assess your own effectiveness and we have provided a link to an online survey.[5]

---

[5] =mc has developed an online tool that allows staff members to complete a confidential questionnaire to assess themselves against each stage in this process. To access this tool visit the book's wiki site at http://globalfundraising .wikispaces.com or write to d.segal@managementcentre.co.uk.

FIGURE 15.5	INNOVATION CHALLENGES AND CONSEQUENCES

Stage	Challenges and Consequences
1. Ideation: Coming up with specific ideas internally	Do you come up with enough new fundraising ideas and approaches internally? Does your organizational culture support this approach or are ideas formed outside often valued more? You need lots of ideas to develop real creative momentum.
	If you don't have a process to create ideas you'll always be running to catch up with other agencies.
2. Integration: Cross-pollination of ideas across functions	Are ideas exchanged between branches or departments or HQ and regions? Do you have systematic processes to ensure this happens? Do supporters feel that they are dealing with one organization or a series of functions—DM, face-to-face, bequests, and so on?
3. Information: External sourcing of inspiration and ideas	Do you consistently scan the environment—commercial and noncommercial—for new fundraising approaches and ideas you can adapt? Is there a "not-invented here" syndrome at work that ignores stimulus from outside?
	Are you allowing others to gain and exploit first mover advantage by not paying enough attention to developments and competitor activity?
4. Selection: Identifying ideas with potential and rejecting others	Do you have a systematic and transparent process for identifying high-potential/high-payoff ideas? Is this process rigorous and well understood? Does the process have a track record of success?
	Otherwise you may be developing ideas but not choosing the potential high pay-offs or only choosing ones that fit with current thinking and so missing out on some real breakthrough opportunities.
5. Support: Developing and nurturing ideas with potential	How are ideas assessed and progressed? What metrics do you use to establish what has real fundraising potential and what isn't going to make it?
	If you don't have a rigorous development process you may waste time and energy on low pay-off initiatives. Or you may not put enough energy into potential high flyers.
6. Launch: Diffusion of outputs and securing returns	How well are ideas rolled out to donors and supporters? What expectations of financial return do you have? And over what period? If you have too short-term an approach, ideas will never succeed.
	If you expect results too soon you may pull the plug on an initiative that needs a longer development period. You also need to ensure that the initiative goes out at scale.
7. Learning: Establishing what can be improved to maximize results	How clearly are successes and failures recognized? Are the people who come up with successes acknowledged? How is learning captured and shared across the organization?
	If you don't evaluate and review your innovation process you may be doomed to make the same mistakes again or not to learn to apply lessons.

Source: =mc.

Using this value chain model =mc has developed a series of benchmarks[6] for fundraising charities organized by broad geographical location. These are listed in Figure 15.6—for Africa, for the United Kingdom, and for the United States. There is also a specific benchmark for INGOs such as Greenpeace, UNICEF, WWF, and so on. Figure 15.6 shows the latest data we have available.

These results suggest that, in terms of fundraising innovation, fundraising charities/NGOs:

- Are weak as ideas/projects work though the value chain overall—most score around 60 percent in coming up with ideas stages 1 to 3. But they are weaker at actually developing the ideas and market-launching those ideas.
- INGOs, perhaps not surprisingly, score lower at initiatives based on working effectively together. But they see themselves as good at studying competitors and adapting or adopting their ideas.
- African NGOs also score low in this competitor stage, perhaps reflecting their relative isolation from many of the main fundraising forums such as the IFC or AFP. They also see themselves as struggling to support new ideas—perhaps reflecting a lack of capital.
- Worryingly, organizations see themselves as weak at learning—suggesting that they are unable to build systematic innovation processes. This reflects our understanding that knowledge management is often weak in charitable organizations.

We at =mc are continuing to develop this framework with a number of national and international agencies—including a number in the top 10 of each national table. And some organizations such as UNICEF adopted the model and undertook a global survey to establish their innovation process.

---

[6]These benchmarks are based on online self-assessment undertaken by directors of fundraising/directors of development.

FIGURE 15.6   INNOVATION BENCHMARKS

Stage	1. Ideation	2. Integration	3. Information	4. Selection	5. Support	6. Launch	7. Learning
U.K. NGO Benchmark	62%	50%	54%	44%	51%	43%	46%
International NGO Benchmark	64	43	76	62	45	46	50
African NGO Benchmark	60	65	41	55	36	34	39
U.S. Nonprofit Benchmark	61	57	61	59	57	43	51
Meaning	Low scores potentially indicate a devising-poor organization			Low scores potentially indicated a development-poor organization		Low scores potentially indicate a delivery-poor organization	

Source: =mc.

Obviously there is no one right structure for innovation. Apple relies on a small number of influential designers whereas Procter & Gamble use open source ideas. Both are successful companies. But their culture dictates different approaches.

The following text shows a framework, developed by =mc, with seven structural approaches used by various charities to drive innovation. You can probably identify how one or more might apply to you. Each structure is followed by the description of its general characteristics.

No one approach is ideal for any organization. And an organization might go through a series of these approaches as it develops its approach.

Structure: Pirates

Create a small team that works away from the headquarters to develop high-risk/high-potential projects. The team acts like pirates, taking ideas from anywhere without having to report back to headquarters. It returns when it's come up with "loot"—any idea that might work.

Structure: Skunk Works

Organize time-limited, cross-functional project teams to generate ideas in response to specific challenges, and work them through. As a part of this, it's common to bring in outsiders to stimulate thinking. So an organization's new strategic plan is being developed, for example, over three weekends by a group of 50 percent insiders and 50 percent outsiders.

Structure: Revolutionaries

Train a small group in innovation techniques. Members return to their normal roles empowered to stimulate innovation among others. The United Kingdom's NSPCC (National Society for the Prevention of Cruelty to Children) chose a team of 50 creativity coaches who had been trained in creativity and innovation techniques to encourage others to have great ideas. (They're not innovators themselves, but people who help others to be innovators.)

(Continued)

STRUCTURE: PRODIGIES

Encourage ideas from everywhere through prizes and awards that anyone can apply for. This approach involves reducing bureaucracy and avoiding the dreaded *ideas committee*. (Doesn't that term just seem like an oxymoron?) One person assesses the ideas, and there are various levels of prizes and awards to stimulate participation. Prizes involve time off to develop your idea. The United Kingdom's Royal National Institute for the Blind developed such a program to stimulate ideas from throughout the organization.

STRUCTURE: DRAGONS' DEN

Create a formal *American Idol*-style system to select ideas. A group that has an investment budget assesses innovations. The Dragons' Den involves staff bringing ideas into the fierce heat of critical thinking. The dragons' job is to weed out ideas that won't make it. (You need a process to stimulate ideas to this stage. And make it clear it's tough!) You need to be careful with this approach though—UNICEF international tried this but then found few of the ideas actually made it through the tough process. Some ideas need nurture first.

STRUCTURE: OPEN SOURCE

Pose problems online, and ask users, donors, supporters, and customers to solve them. This is the newest of the innovation approaches. It is used by major corporations such as Procter & Gamble to develop new projects. They essentially laid off 1,600 in-house scientists and instead asked scientists worldwide to suggest product improvements that they could be paid for. This approach was adopted by Greenpeace to ask supporters *how* to raise funds.

STRUCTURE: FUNCTIONALIZE

Create a team whose job is to come up with innovative ideas. Sometimes you need to create a team of people whose sole focus is generating ideas and then selling them to another part of the organization to deliver—more like a conventional research-and-development operation. At Cancer Research UK the team focuses on high-value ideas that will create more than $10 million a year.

You might like to reflect on which of these approaches would fit most neatly in your organizational culture.

How to Improve Innovation?

Using this value chain framework allows you to identify where you need to improve. The following are some simple, practical strategies used by organizations to improve performance in each area.

Stage 1. Ideation: Idea Generation

- Have stimulating or even "weird away days" for team members— UNICEF hired an arts center to get staff involved in using theater and art to stimulate their fundraising ideas.
- Create a stimulating environment in the office—RNIB, a U.K. charity, created a donor corner where staff could go and sit at the dressing table for a typical donor—a 55-year-old woman.

Stage 2. Integration: Cross-Pollination

- Invite people from different departments to work together. So Royal Society for the Protection of Birds (RSPB) held workshops with mixtures of people from different departments to help reengineer the department structure in a more donor-friendly way.
- Organize workshops between different departments and teams based around the supporter/donor journey showing the key touch points and decision structures. Put this journey up on a wall for everyone to see.

Stage 3. Information: External Sourcing

- Visit commercial companies you admire, and see what you can learn from them. So a North of England–based theater company visited the local soccer team to learn about creating "fans."
- Benchmark yourself against other charities and see how you can learn from them in terms of improving your process. As a starting point you may want to take =mc's innovation benchmark test referred to earlier.

Stage 4. Selection: Identifying Ideas

- Organize an *American Idol/Dragons' Den*–type contest with external judges for the ideas presented. UNICEF did this and even put the ideas up on YouTube so that others could vote on the ideas as well as the judges.

- Develop a set of clear and specific metrics for success—and failure. Think about creating a return on innovation (ROI) measure. Be clear on what period you need to succeed. The NSPCC changed its innovation program as a result of reviewing its ROI.

Stage 5. Support: Developing Ideas

- Create a central team that acts as *gardeners* or *developers* who nurture ideas to launch. These people should not have their own ideas that compete but should have an interest in developing others. The RNIB innovation team adopted this approach.
- Create a wiki or web structure to help nurture innovation. UNICEF and the Federation of Red Cross and Red Crescent both created interactive web structures to allow their international teams to collaborate on developing ideas virtually.

Stage 6. Launch: Diffusion and Returns

- Create a separate internal "launch" team that acts as salespeople for ideas it didn't invent. NSPCC created a specially trained group of 50 innovation coaches who worked to help get ideas out to market quickly.
- Create a special budget, which allows ideas to be properly developed and launched. (This may mean that you have fewer ideas supported—but those that are more likely to succeed.) Cancer Research UK adopted this approach but focussed on supporting projects that were worth $8M or more.

Stage 7. Learning: Identify and Integrate Learning

- Have a wash-up event to identify what worked and didn't as a result of your innovation initiative. The Red Cross/Red Crescent are outstandingly good at reviewing their work and being innovative. They have recently developed a global online forum for staff and volunteers to drive this process.
- You can train people in innovation: Water Aid undertook a significant program of training for their innovation team to make sure that they were fully up to speed in techniques and able to evaluate why projects had succeeded or failed.

Given some thought, most can easily come up with additional ideas that will be useful. But remember, the key is to focus where you need to improve—that's where the innovation-chain approach and bench-marking are useful.

In Summary

Innovation matters, not just to help you deal with the crunch/crisis/catastrophe, but to help you thrive as you come up with new ideas in fundraising, to persuade existing supporters, staff, and even board members that you're committed to really stepping up to the mark. And it also matters if you are to attract good, new people—staff and donors—to your cause.

It's not an added extra now, it's a survival strategy. As Bill Gates said, in his book *Business @ the Speed of Thought*, "In three years, every product my company makes will be obsolete. The only question is whether we'll make them obsolete or if someone else will."

Now, *that's* a commitment to innovation!

CHAPTER 16

The Charity Giants

REBECCA MAUGER

Who are the charity giants? One important factor is size. International organizations raising more than $1 billion a year in 2011 include: International Red Cross and Red Crescent Movement; UNICEF; United Nations' World Food Programme; World Vision International; Office of the United Nations High Commissioner for Refugees (UNHCR); Save the Children; and SOS Children's Villages. These organizations typically have a global head office and then national offices; for example, the American Red Cross is part of the International Red Cross and Red Crescent Movement, and World Vision USA is part of World Vision International. The aforementioned $1 billion comes from consolidating income from across all the national organizations and their global office.

But size is not the only determinant. According to the top 200 largest U.S. charities (*Forbes*) there are also many U.S. organizations, some global organizations, or a national office of a global organization as well as some that concentrate their efforts at home, that raise more than $1 billion in the United States alone—American Red Cross, Boy Scouts of America, and Boys & Girls Clubs of America, Catholic Charities USA, Salvation Army, United Way of America, World Vision USA, and YMCA International, to name a few. For our purposes we consider charity giants as those that are intentionally structured to raise money all over the world.

The origins of charity giants vary. The Red Cross and Red Crescent Movement, founded by Swiss businessman Jean-Henri Dunant, set up the International Committee of the Red Cross and Red

Crescent in 1863 and national organizations in Belgium, Denmark, France, and Spain followed in 1864, after the adoption of the first Geneva Convention (a conference establishing the standards of international law for the humanitarian treatment of the victims of war).

Many other giants were founded at the end of specific significant conflicts. The U.K. founders of Save the Children were moved by the plight of children on the losing side of World War I. The end of World War II resulted in the formation of the United Nations that created UNICEF in December 1946 to provide food, clothing, and health care for European children facing famine and disease after World War II. UNHCR was established in 1950 by the United Nations General Assembly to help Europeans displaced by World War II. SOS Children's Villages was founded in 1949 in Austria and the first village was built in Imst, Austria in that year. World Vision was founded in 1950 in the United States and its child sponsorship program began in 1953 in response to the needs of hundreds of thousands of orphans at the end of the Korean War. Though not yet a $1 billion organization, Doctors Without Borders/Médecins Sans Frontières (MSF), promises to grow into a charity giant. It was founded in 1971 by a group of French doctors and journalists who, following Nigeria's civil war, were moved to speak out about the plight of victims, and who sought an independent, impartial way to provide care where they saw the greatest need. BRAC (Bangladesh Rural Advancement Committee) was established in 1972 following Bangladesh's War of Liberation and has grown significantly, now having offices in 11 countries and more than 115,000 employees.

Globalization has influenced the operations of these large charities and their fundraising efforts. Some, such as Save the Children International, have completely restructured their entire organizations to respond to the changing global environment (the impact of this organizational change on Save the Children's fundraising has yet to be realized). For others, such as the Red Cross and Red Crescent Movement, it has been a driving force in their fundraising strategy. Many have capitalized on the changes in the distribution of wealth created by globalization and a growing middle class in many new markets such as the BRIC countries (Brazil, Russia, India, and China). They have already become significant new sources of income growth.

It may be helpful for comparison to look at what is happening in the commercial world, where there are four main drivers for globalization.[1] These drivers apply to charities as well as businesses, and are important factors in the expansion into new markets.

MARKET DRIVERS

Some companies have needed to identify new markets to increase profit because their existing markets were no longer delivering the level of return expected by shareholders. This decline in returns from existing markets can be due to saturation of these traditional markets, or new technological advances making products defunct.

Many charities are also experiencing increased competition in their traditional markets and are seeing declining returns from their investment in fundraising in these markets.

The worldwide change in wealth patterns are also resulting in new market opportunities. Growth in the middle class means more people have the disposable income to donate to charity. Having so recently experienced poverty firsthand, some in this growing middle class feels responsible for those less fortunate. For some large nonprofits, these attractive new markets are providing higher returns than the traditional markets. As shown, there are both push and pull market drivers that are encouraging charities to grow fundraising in new markets.

COMPETITIVE DRIVERS

Increased internal competition from traditional competitors or new competitors entering the home market of companies from overseas have compelled some companies to go outside of their traditional markets.

In a more globally interconnected world, both companies and charities know there are great benefits in having a strong and well-recognized global brand. Donors have to trust that the organization will spend their money wisely and a strong charity brand helps to build this trust. Strength of brand in one market helps build a reputation in a new market.

---

[1] George S. Yip, "Global Strategy . . . in a World of Nations," *Sloan Management Review* 31, no. 1 (Fall 1989): 29–41.

Cost Drivers

Due to technological and logistical advances in the 1990s many companies recognized that the differences in cost of living around the world provided opportunities to employ cheap labor and produce products more cheaply in new and different markets. Efficiencies could also be gained through streamlining some central functions and outsourcing some operations.

There are fundraising cost benefits to large organizations. Expertise in growing particular income streams, such as regular bank deductions/pledge/committed giving can be shared across markets. Successful fundraising products can be adapted and launched without needing the staff or agency investment in fundraising product development that new domestic organizations would experience. The success of this relies on good organizational learning and many INGOs invest in different skill-sharing forums and in creating technical expert roles in their global head offices for this purpose. Most recognize that cultural factors do make a difference and some products need to be modified to work effectively in some new markets.

Government Drivers

Some governments have proactively welcomed new businesses from outside through beneficial tax breaks and others have proactively encouraged and supported companies within their countries to globalize.

The governments that form part of the Organization for Economic Co-operation and Development's (OECD) Development Assistance Committee (DAC), which meet to define and monitor global standards in key areas of development, are significant funders of INGOs. Decisions about which countries are identified as priorities for funding by these governments significantly impact the operational presence of the charity giants. Government decisions about the tax benefits and investments in infrastructure needed for efficient fundraising, such as encouraging a banking system that allows regular bank deductions or the promotion of a culture of giving, are important.

The following case studies show the journey of a few of the charity giants; specifically, what is driving them to expand and the challenges they are facing in this expansion.

As the largest humanitarian network, the Red Cross and Red Crescent Movement operates in 188 countries (e.g., from Iranian Red Crescent to the Italian Red Cross). It is the largest in terms of income at an estimated $30 billion a year and the oldest; the International Committee of the Red Cross (ICRC) was founded in 1863. Though a significant segment of this income comes from private fundraising (individuals, companies, foundations), it is estimated that more than 50 percent of the income is earned. For example, the American Red Cross runs a blood service, both the German and Japanese Red Cross run a number of hospitals and many national organizations, called *National Societies*, run ambulance services.

The Red Cross and Red Crescent is a federation of national organizations. Each National Society has a special auxiliary status with its government, defined in the Geneva Convention, which gives them a role in times of war. Its core focus is to fulfill this and a broader domestic agenda, that is, emergencies, and health or social crisis within their own country. As such, many National Societies can also receive major domestic funding from their own government, although the degree of this income stream varies across countries. The Red Cross Movement was founded on the principle of *sono tutti fratelli*—they are all brothers—and so in addition to having a domestic remit, many National Societies also fundraise for the international work, and support sister organizations all over the world.

At an international level, activities of the National Societies have been coordinated through the Secretariat of the International Federation of Red Cross and Red Crescent National Societies (IFRC) since 1919. With the Secretariat based in Geneva and delegations across the world, they are responsible for supporting and coordinating the fundraising of National Societies from government and private income sources. This second International body (the *ICRC*) is also headquartered in Geneva: As the custodian of the Geneva Conventions, the ICRC has a permanent mandate to undertake humanitarian activities during armed conflicts—much of this activity done in partnership with the relevant National Societies. Most funding for ICRC comes from government. Many National Societies fund the work of ICRC and ICRC also has its own private fundraising department.

(Continued)

In 2011 the Red Cross approved its first global fundraising strategy, covering both private and government income of the IFRC (National Societies and its Secretariat). As an organization that sees itself more as a federation of domestic organizations, rather than as a global or international charity, this was a landmark moment. A number of internal and external factors drove the creation of this strategy. From an external perspective there were concerns about the potential decline of government funding, especially from the traditional DAC countries. There was also a concern about the politicization of aid that makes it difficult to operate independently and therefore it always accepts funds available. National Societies were all seeing significant competition from INGOs that were investing in long-term and emergency fundraising. New technologies were creating new ways to interact with donors. Finally there was recognition that some new emerging markets would be critical for the future growth of the Red Cross and Red Crescent movement.

Internally there was recognition that many National Societies did not have the funds they needed. Some donors, especially companies, wanted global engagement with the Red Cross and there was a need to change the way the Red Cross worked with these donors. There was recognition that there was already huge expertise in resource mobilization (both private income and government) in National Societies, but systems for learning from each other and sharing best practices needed improvement. Another key challenge was that there were some markets that had great potential for generating income, but activities were hampered by the lack of available funds within that National Society to invest in growing fundraising.

The new strategy was developed in partnership with some of the major income-generating National Societies and the Secretariat, and the implementation has been designed to build on this model. Expertise in some major private income streams, such as individuals and companies, sits with National Societies. These National Societies are being tasked with showing global leadership by creating forums where this expertise can be shared. The strategy also recommends the creation of an investment fund for fundraising growth. This is a critical tool to support the growth of emerging income-generating markets; money that can be loaned strategically to those National Societies with the potential for greatest return on investment. The structure of the fund has not yet been established and

(Continued)

research is currently being undertaken into how the fund will be financed. As this book is being finalized, the new global strategy is in its early implementation stages. The big question is: Will the creation of this first global fundraising strategy wake up the International Red Cross and Red Crescent Movement, known by other charity giants as the *sleeping giant*?

CASE STUDY 16.2   WORLD VISION INTERNATIONAL

World Vision got its start in the United States, but it is now as much of an international success story as an American one (see also Case Study 6.1 in Chapter 6). It raised an estimated $2.6 billion in 2011 with 60 percent of this raised outside of the United States. Between 2004 and 2011 it has grown on average 5 percent each year. Private income-generating activities happen in around 40 markets, with the number of markets where they are raising more than $1 million from private income increasing from 17 in 2004 to 29 in 2011.

Aki Temisevä, Partnership Leader-Global Marketing, based in the London head office, shared the World Vision growth story.

World Vision initially started its expansion into new fundraising markets organically—the U.S. office helped start the Canadian office, which in turn helped Australia start, and new offices were opened as the internal energy around the cause spread like wildfire. However, since 2000, World Vision's new market strategy has been more intentional with the organization identifying gaps in markets with great income-generating opportunities. The expansion is driven by the organizational vision—they want to help 150 million of the most vulnerable children. To do this, they need more money. Aki Temisevä shared his feeling that as an organization, and certainly as a marketing team they are likely to always feel that there will always be more children in need, and so the drive to raise more money to help them will not end. World Vision does not have a global revenue target as of yet, but they are working on a portfolio approach, which outlines key new markets entries as well as future products for those markets.

(Continued)

Decisions on investing in new markets or scaling up existing fundraising markets are made by estimating the income growth opportunity for each, using factors such as the wealth in the country and also looking at the general national propensity to give, which can be influenced by historical and cultural factors. World Vision has found some correlation between a nation's background in Christianity and the propensity to give to World Vision, but they recognize that country specific factors (i.e., high taxation) can have a significant impact on philanthropy. Other factors that are considered are the competition in the market and the public perception of the needs in their own country—fundraising for work overseas may be more challenging in a country where there is high public perception about domestic needs, especially if World Vision offers little local programming. As they do local programming in many markets, however, this is not always an issue. Internal factors also matter in the decision. Leadership needs to be fully committed to investment in growing fundraising and enthusiastic about the role they need to play in supporting income growth. Then there is a need for skilled fundraisers, either in country or those willing to transfer and having the requisite language skills and cultural sensitivity.

Unlike organizations such as the Red Cross and the UN agencies that already have significant government funding and so are vulnerable to a potential decline in this income stream, World Vision derives 80 percent of its income from private sources. There is in fact internal pressure to increase government grants that are seen as an untapped potential income stream. Aki Temisevä recognizes that World Vision relies heavily on child sponsorship, and that they would benefit from diversifying their funding sources to include more from governments, foundations, and companies. However, because the operation is set up to report on child sponsorship, it is not always easy for their field offices to additionally incorporate the different reporting systems needed for grants. This is work in progress.

Many of the challenges facing World Vision as they look to continue to grow internationally are shared with many other both domestic and international organizations. Aki Temisevä says he's kept up at night worrying about how he can help World Vision keep the child sponsorship offer fresh and exciting for donors. Many charities, including World Vision, are experiencing a trend with donors wanting more from their relationship with a charity and to feel closer to the impact their gift is making. He worries about donors becoming fatigued—overwhelmed with the relentless media bombardment of crises everywhere. World Vision tries to counter this

(Continued)

by focusing on positive messages, by demonstrating progress, and by otherwise inspiring hope in donors. In more competitive developed markets, some charities are offering to save the world for just $2.40 a month, and he is really concerned that these kinds of unrealistic claims will erode donor trust in all charities.

Temisevä faces internal challenges as well. It is sometimes hard to make sure that the national offices are raising as much funding as they can in their market. The recession is significantly affecting some markets, but he wonders if some fundraisers may be hiding behind this as an excuse. His peers in other INGOs report that they are experiencing significant growth in some of the same markets that World Vision fundraisers are struggling.

Although World Vision has an investment fund for fundraising, Aki Temisevä estimates that it is typically only able to support 30 to 40 percent of the requests it gets for investment from its national offices. World Vision has had to establish clear guidelines about what type of activities and markets will be priorities for investment just to help manage the internal desire for growth. Leadership at the top support investment in fundraising, but as is the case with many organizations, there are always competing priorities, like programming. There is never enough investment to do everything.

WORLD VISION KOREA'S 60TH ANNIVERSARY

In 2010 World Vision celebrated its 60th anniversary in South Korea, attracting considerable media attention. Kevin Jenkins, president of World Vision International, speaking on the occasion said, "Just as South Korea has developed, so has World Vision, which started in Korea, started as a small seed and has grown into a mighty tree. From that tiny seed of $25 a month that Bob Pierce committed here every month, you now raise $124 billion won annually [more than 100 million dollars]." A video was produced that highlighted the story of World Vision Korea (World Vision 60th Anniversary Commemorative Film 2010), and how in 1991 World Vision Korea moved from being a recipient country to a supporting country.

World Vision Korea started raising funds with a small plastic *love loaf*—a donation piggy bank that allowed people to collect money to help provide food aid in other countries. It was phenomenally successful. They have had telethons and 24-hour famine events. Korean child sponsors now support more than 300,000 children around the world.

From its start as a limited relief operation in 1972 in a remote village of Bangladesh, BRAC has turned into one of the largest development organizations in the world. Organizing the poor using communities' own human and material resources, it catalyzes lasting change, creating an ecosystem in which the poor have the chance to seize control of their own lives. They do this with a holistic development approach geared toward inclusion, using tools like microfinance, education, health care, legal services, community empowerment, and more. Their work now touches the lives of an estimated 126 million people, with staff and BRAC-trained entrepreneurs numbering in the hundreds of thousands, a global movement bringing change to 10 countries in Asia, Africa, and the Caribbean: Bangladesh, Afghanistan, Uganda, Tanzania, Pakistan, Sierra Leone, South Sudan, Liberia, Sri Lanka, and Haiti. Operations in the Philippines were launched in 2012.

BRAC has been a social innovator in many areas, including microfinance, health care, and education. The concept of microfinance was originally conceived in the mid-1970s in Bangladesh. Banks had previously not provided financial services such as loans, saving accounts, and insurance to poor people—the banks had believed that the transaction costs were prohibitive and with no assets to use as collateral for loans, the risk of default was too high. The poor were therefore left to borrow from lenders who often charged usurious interest rates. Organizations like Grameen Bank and BRAC proved that it was possible to successfully lend to the poor. Giving people access to loans, savings, and insurance encouraged entrepreneurship, and allowed people to take advantage of opportunities to increase their income and help them cope more effectively with personal emergencies such as ill health or unexpected costs. These early organizations showed that focusing on women and lending through a group delivers the highest repayment rate and supports economic development.

BRAC works by using village organizations, where groups of 30 to 40 women members meet regularly. These groups provide members with emotional support, access to financial, legal, and health information and training, and access to microfinance, which BRAC believes is a vital tool. BRAC believes in a holistic approach and incorporates health, education, and empowerment practices as

(Continued)

part of its support. Additionally BRAC runs a series of enterprises that help to link its borrowers and other poor farmers to domestic or international markets as well as earning a profit that can be used to fund the development programs. The businesses include Aarong (retail handicraft chain stores), poultry hatcheries and feed mills, a vegetable export program, and many more.

Many have called this combination of services *microfinance plus*, with a portion of program costs funded through the returns from microfinance. BRAC also runs a massive health-care delivery network, driven largely by self-employed community health workers numbering 97,000 worldwide; BRAC's health program reaches more than 110 million in Bangladesh alone. With 38,000 primary and preprimary schools worldwide and 1.1 million enrolled students as of December 2011, BRAC is also the world's largest private, secular educational system. These schools offer a second chance to students who have been left behind by formal schooling systems due to poverty, displacement, and discrimination. In Bangladesh, donor funding accounts for less than 30 percent of BRAC's 2012 budget; however, outside Bangladesh funding is still largely donor-driven with the majority coming from government and large foundations.

BRAC is an interesting example of a charity globalizing from the southern hemisphere to other countries in the south, unlike the majority of the charity giants that originated from either the UN system, Europe, or the United States. It first expanded into Afghanistan in 2002. Seeing a situation there that closely resembled the postwar environment, in which BRAC began work with refugees in Bangladesh,[2] they also saw that shared cultural and religious affinities between the two countries would help to ensure success.

BRAC explains the motivations behind its expansion into other countries as a mixture of opportunity and need. It could make a social difference as well as fill a gap in the market with the *microfinance plus* model. Following the 2004 Tsunami, BRAC expanded into Sri Lanka, initially with a focus on disaster relief and rehabilitation, but it decided to stay on when a gap in the microfinance market was identified. BRAC is focused on replicating its success in terms of its management approach, the focus on capacity development and

---

[2] Naomi Hossain and Anasuya Sengupta, "Thinking Big, Going Global: The Challenge of BRAC's Global Expansion." Institute of Development Studies Working Paper no. 339 (December 2009).

(Continued)

strong training programs for staff and constant program innovation. BRAC has additionally set up offices in both the United Kingdom and the United States with a primary focus on raising funds and its international profile.

The internationalization strategy of BRAC has been about taking the microfinance plus model into new countries, some of them particularly welcoming to BRAC because of its southern origins. BRAC may not have developed the microfinance concept, but it has been able to build on its success and apply it in new markets

COMMON THEMES FROM THE CASE STUDIES IN THIS CHAPTER

The case studies of Red Cross and Red Crescent, World Vision International, and BRAC offer a useful comparison of three charity giants. As shown, some charities like World Vision have a global product offering, child sponsorship, which has been a key driver of growth. Others like the Red Cross have a more generic offer or an offer that varies significantly from country to country. BRAC has taken an innovative model and has applied it in environments where it is likely to succeed.

In Table 16.1, some of the fundraising products that have been particularly successful in driving the income growth of INGOs have been highlighted (please note that the majority of these organizations has a diverse portfolio of income-generating activities). The table illustrates fundraising products or mechanisms, which have a particularly significant impact.

Charity giants are currently debating if and how the exponential growth of income generation online will compel them to develop a clearer global offering. Increased cross border visibility in the digital and social media world may require organizations to standardize their fundraising across channels and to more firmly maintain the consistency of the brand. It is too early to draw conclusions, but this and other technological developments are high on the agenda of many international fundraising directors, especially in nontraditional markets like South America and Asia. Many are positioning themselves to capitalize on these changes as opportunities.

TABLE 16.1	SUMMARY OF FUNDRAISING PRODUCTS DRIVING INCOME GROWTH

Fundraising Products	Organization Where Product Is Employed
Child or animal sponsorship	Action Aid International, ChildFund International, Plan International, SOS Children's Village, World Vision
More generic regular giving (supporting the organization as a whole)	Greenpeace International, MSF, Save the Children, UNICEF, WaterAid, WSPA (World Society for the Protection of Animals)
Membership	Amnesty International
Emergency appeals	Oxfam, Red Cross and Red Crescent Movement, UNHCR, UNICEF
Microfinance	BRAC, Grameen Bank, KIVA

Changes in the distribution of wealth in the world will continue. If charities want to raise more funds for their missions, they are going to need to invest in fundraising in new countries. The International Monetary Fund (IMF)'s *World Economic Outlook (WEO) Database, April 2012 Edition*[3] suggests that by 2050 China will be the world's largest economy followed by the United States and then India, Eurozone, Brazil, Russia, Japan, Mexico, Indonesia, and the United Kingdom. This is quite a different picture than that of 2010, when the United States ranked as the largest economy followed by the Eurozone, China, Japan, Germany, France, United Kingdom, Brazil, Italy, and Canada. Although some INGOs leaders were quick to adapt to new realities, others are just beginning to pay attention to the long-term implications of this change in the order of national monetary power. If the IMF's prediction does come true, having a strong fundraising operation in China, India, Brazil, Russia, Mexico, and Indonesia will be as important as in the more traditional North American and European fundraising markets. There is no certainty that the IMF forecast for 2050 will be realized, but it is a brave or maybe foolhardy INGO that ignores the winds of change.

---

[3] www.gfmag.com/tools/global-database/economic-data/2368-the-world-as -you-have-never-seen-before.html#axzz1y2T9URSY.

Moving into new markets is no easy thing. In some of the newer markets, such as Brazil, many INGOs are experiencing challenges in implementing traditional regular giving programs because the banking systems cannot easily accommodate direct debit giving. Other markets face a deficit of suppliers to implement face-to-face fundraising. In some, legislation is making it difficult to fundraise.

Not all the challenges are external. The ability to invest in these new markets varies across different organizations. There can be understandable internal conflict around how much should be spent now to tackle immediate needs against how much should be spent in anticipation of future needs. The importance of investment funds is highlighted in the Red Cross and Red Crescent Movement case study (see Case Study 16.1)—most of the charity giants have a mechanism to support this investment, from having the richest/strongest national members investing directly in markets with growth potential, to allocating an established amount to the annual budget.

As identified earlier, the INGOs that have mechanisms to encourage learning between fundraisers enjoy a competitive advantage and increased efficiency. Although cultural differences matter and one size does not fit all, those that have long-established skill-sharing mechanisms are confident that it makes a difference. A common mechanism is having at least one annual meeting where all the organization's fundraisers gather and share both their successes and their mistakes. Some organizations also have income-stream specific groups that communicate more regularly throughout the year to continue this sharing and learning process. Some create dedicated roles in either their global teams to address skill sharing or have a high-performing office mentor a newer one.

Another issue for many INGOs is the challenge of finding the right people, with the right fundraising or transferable skills—and then retaining them. There are lots of markets where fundraising is not yet seen as a profession and this is another reason why skill-sharing programs, like those highlighted above are so important.

In Summary

The charity giants know they have much in common, facing similar issues and challenges, and having the same opportunities that come with globalization. Fundraisers in the charity giants are the same as those in any mission-driven organization—possessing a real passion for the cause of their organization and a desire to raise as much as they can in the pursuit of mission.

Their distinct advantages—the strength of their brands, being able to share fundraising expertise across their organization and across markets, their investment capacity—can make them formidable fundraising machines. It is always worth paying particular attention if any of these charity giants enter your market.

About the Editors

Penelope Cagney, CFRE, president of the **Cagney Company**, has consulted on fundraising and nonprofit management for more than 20 years in North America, Europe, and North Africa. She has worked with the National Cultural Centre of Egypt, the Joffrey Ballet of Chicago, CFRE International, VA, and the Charities Aid Foundation, London. She began her management career at one of the largest nonprofit organizations in Chicago, Rush Medical Center. Penelope is the author of *Nonprofit Consulting Essentials* (John Wiley & Sons, 2010).

Bernard Ross is a director of the **Management Centre (=mc)**. He has consulted for many of the world's leading INGOs from Amnesty to Oxfam and from the Red Cross and Red Crescent to Greenpeace. He is an expert on change innovation and strategy. He is the author, with Clare Segal, of two books: *Breakthrough Thinking* (John Wiley & Sons, 2001) and *The Influential Fundraiser* (John Wiley & Sons, 2010).

About the Contributors

Ashley Baldwin has worked in innovation and communications at www.marceloiniarra.com since 2008 and has participated in consultancy projects for a number of organizations including Amnesty International, Médecins Sans Frontières, and Greenpeace. She is the editor of *Innophoric Watch*, an innovations trend-watching platform for the social sector. Ashley is also the communications director for AnyBody.org in Argentina and is currently leading a body-image campaign for the organization in Latin America. Prior to this position Ashley worked as a journalist for a number of international publications, including the *Times, Diplo*, and *Lonely Planet*.

Lu Bo is the managing director of **World Future Foundation Ltd.**, a charitable foundation incorporated in Singapore. Before that, he had worked with several international NGOs operating in China for more than 15 years. Lu Bo has a bachelor of arts and a master of economics. He is currently pursuing his doctoral degree at Beijing Normal University, and is among China's first PhD candidates in nonprofit management. Lu Bo is active in the international nonprofit community as a board member, consultant, speaker, and author on topics related to philanthropic development, corporate social responsibility, nonprofit management, and fundraising.

Mair Bosworth is a director of the fundraising research consultancy **Giving Insight** and is a specialist in major gifts fundraising and is a research expert. Prior to establishing the company, Mair was research and information manager at the international development charity ActionAid, and has worked as a senior research consultant at fundraising research consultancy Factary, where she worked with a wide range of charities, arts, and heritage organizations, universities, and schools, helping them identify, approach, and retain high-value donors. Mair specializes in using research to inform fundraising strategy and to help organizations engage with high-net-worth individuals, companies, trusts, and foundations. She is passionate about helping nonprofit organizations to work better and win funding through knowledge sharing and improved knowledge management. She works with charities to help them understand philanthropic trends and develop strong relationships with their donors.

In addition to her work with Giving Insight, Mair puts her love of research, writing, and interviewing to other uses, making radio documentaries and podcasts for the BBC and arts organizations.

Tariq H. Cheema, MD, CEO, **World Congress of Muslim Philanthropists**, is a renowned social innovator and philanthropist who has devoted his life to making the world a peaceful, equitable, and sustainable place for all. He is the founder of the World Congress of Muslim Philanthropists, a global network of affluent individuals, foundations, and socially conscious corporations dedicated to advance efficient and accountable giving. He ranks among the 500 most influential Muslims impacting the world today.

YoungWoo Choi is the CEO of **Doum & Nanum Co. Inc**., a fundraising consulting company based in Seoul, Korea. He worked for Habitat for Humanity Korea as founding staff and the managing director for seven years before he started Doum & Nanum in 2001. His company is covering services from capital campaign design and management for universities to face-to-face services for INGOs. Among his clients are leading universities, hospitals, and INGOs.

Angela Cluff's early career was in commercial advertising and market research. She joined the voluntary sector more than 15 years ago to set up a corporate fundraising for British Heart Foundation. She then moved to NSPCC as head of major donors and was promoted to joint campaign director for the NSPCC's groundbreaking Full Stop Appeal and then to deputy director of fundraising. Angela became a consultant in 2002 after the birth of her first child. Since then she has advised a number of international agencies from Care International to WWF and recently finished a global unrestricted income strategy for UNICEF International. She is a director at the **Management Centre (=mc)**.

Nan Fang has worked for **Save the Children China** since 2006. She led the national campaigns of child rights governance and is responsible for building organizational partnerships with key stake-holders. She has been a freelance consultant since 2011 and has advised a number of international agencies such as UNICEF, Sweden Center of Child Rights and Corporate Social Responsibility, and Save the Children China. She began her career as a policy analyst of Beijing Municipal Government. She has a master's degree in public adminis-tration and public policy from University of York (United Kingdom) and is pursuing her PhD in the School of Social Development and Public Policy, Beijing Normal University.

Norma Galafassi is co-director and founder of **n2action.net**, Fundraising & Communication for Nonprofits. She has more than 22 years' experience in marketing and for the past 19 years has focused on fundraising and marketing for the nonprofit sector. She has worked in more than 30 countries helping different organizations with fund-raising and marketing strategies, training, consultancy, direct response implementation, and campaigns. She was the first fundraising manager for UNICEF Argentina, where she was in charge of developing the annual national telethon, as well as many successful corporate alliances and a proactive direct marketing campaign among other activities. She comes from the private sector originally and holds a degree in indus-trial engineering. She is founding member and has chaired the Argen-tinean Fundraisers Association (AEDROS), board member at the Resource Alliance (United Kingdom), and she is an invited speaker at congresses all over the world.

Paula Guillet de Monthoux is currently based in Denmark. She was at **UNICEF** for 15 years, working in different regions from Zurich to Geneva. She spent much of her time at UNICEF developing fun-draising strategies, working in national roles, and then an advisory role—her final task being to oversee the development of the global innovation strategy. As principal international fundraising consultant at the **Management Centre (=mc)** she is currently working with OECD, running workshops to help transform its fundraising capabilities and supporting a national branch of an INGO on its innovation strategy. She is also excited to be working toward a PhD.

Matt Ide is the managing director of fundraising research consul-tancy **Giving Insight** and is one of the United Kingdom's leading fundraising research experts. A specialist in global fundraising market research, competitor analysis, HNWIs, and global foundations, Matt's passion for knowledge sharing and research intelligence has seen him launch numerous websites, but he is perhaps best known for creating the world's first global fundraising resources website (fResource). He is a member of the Institute of Fundraising and serves on its committee, the Researchers in Fundraising (RiF) Special Interest Group. He is also a member of the Association of Professional Researchers for Advancement (APRA) in America. Matt has a degree (BA Hons) in economics and a master's (MRes) in development research.

Marcelo Iñarra Iraegui currently leads his own international creative consultancy, www.marceloiniarra.com, providing social marketing and public mobilization strategies powered by innovation to social sector organizations like Amnesty, Greenpeace, UNICEF, UNHCR, Action Aid, Médecins Sans Frontières, and SOS Kinderdorf. He was one of the global pioneers of digital mobilization within the social sector, leading the design and implementation of cyberactivism and fundraising at Greenpeace International. He is also the cofounder of www.chaxcha.com, a digital advertising agency for social causes. Marcelo has been an environmental activist for more than 20 years, constantly striving to take an original and groundbreaking approach to his work. He is constantly on the move, both mentally and physically, giving workshops and presentations all over the world.

Rebecca Mauger has more than 12 years' fundraising experience at the Children's Society, Action for Children, and has been at **British Red Cross** since 2003. Her current role is head of high value giving (major donors; companies, trusts, and government grants; and via prestige events). During 2010 to 2011 Rebecca jointly led the development of the first global fundraising strategy for IFRC (Red Cross and Red Crescent National Societies and its Secretariat), the first in its 150-year history. Through the development of this strategy Rebecca has been involved in forums and benchmarking exercises with other charity giants.

Andrea MacManus, CFRE, is president of the Calgary-based **Development Group**. She is a recognized leader in Canada's charitable and nonprofit sector. As the current president of AFP International she is also working globally to promote the cause of philanthropy and ethical fundraising. With more than 22 years' experience in fund development, communications, media, public relations, and marketing, Andrea has particular expertise in environments where major changes, restructuring, or transition require innovation, leadership, creativity, and an entrepreneurial attitude.

Usha Menon has worked, volunteered, and consulted in the social purpose sectors for 25 years and has held leadership positions at national and international organizations. For the past four years, she has been a consultant for nonprofits in the areas of leadership, management, and fundraising. She has developed Asian-market entry strategies for INGOs, built national and regional fundraising strategies to engage diaspora communities, major donors, and the corporate sector. She has also orchestrated community-based fundraising and advised on the use of social media. As a volunteer, she is building a strong philanthropic Asia through her roles with the Resource Alliance, having been chair of its international board; the organizing committee of the Philanthropy in Asia Summit 2012 in Singapore; the editorial advisory board for the Fundraising & Philanthropy Australiasia; and others. She regularly shares her "Asian Insights on Nonprofit Leadership" through her blog: www.ushamenon-blog.org.

Mike Naholi Muchilwa is a social entrepreneur, development catalyst, and strategic thinker. He runs **Innovative Concepts**, a development consultancy that focuses on resource mobilization, strategic planning, business planning, organization development, project formulation and evaluation, enterprise development and fair trade. He is the chair of the **Kenya Association of Fundraising Professionals** and is one of Africa's leading fundraisers with more than 18 years' experience. He has trained boards, senior management, fundraisers, students, and beneficiaries. He has also run nonprofits and been on the board of others as well as founding managing a social enterprise. He has developed the course curriculum offered by the Eastern Africa Resource Mobilization Workshop that brings together fundraisers from 14 countries globally. He holds a degree in economics from the University of Nairobi and has written two previous books. He is currently working on a book on social enterprise.

Sudeshna Mukherjee, Atlas Corps fellow from India, currently serves with **GlobalGiving**'s project team in Washington, DC, where she supports its open access initiative to devise strategies for better engagement of social entrepreneurs who host projects and raise funds through the website. With a master's in social work from TISS (Mumbai) and nearly seven years of experience in program management and resource mobilization, Sudeshna has worked with Indian and global nonprofits. During her last assignment at Oxfam India she focused on corporate fundraising. Sudeshna also represents the fundraising innovation website SOFII as its ambassador for India.

R. F. Shangraw Jr. is the chief executive officer of the **ASU Foundation for A New American University**. Prior to joining the foundation in November 2011, he served as ASU's senior vice president for knowledge enterprise development and director of the Global Institute of Sustainability. Rick was responsible for ASU's growing annual $350 million research portfolio, which placed ASU among the top 20 research institutions in the country without a medical school. Before joining ASU, Rick was the founder and CEO of Project Performance Corporation, a research and technology consulting firm specializing in environmental, energy, and information management issues. He has a bachelor of arts, magna cum laude, in political science and a certificate in environmental studies from Dickinson College in Pennsylvania; a master of public administration from the Maxwell School at Syracuse University; and a doctorate from the Maxwell School with a specialization in technology and information policy and organization design. Rick also currently holds a professor of practice appointment with ASU's School of Public Affairs within the College of Public Programs and the School of Sustainability.

Anup Tiwari is honorary chair of **SAFRG**, a think tank on fundraising. He also heads Asia-wide fundraising and communications for a leading INGO. In the past, he has raised funds for UNICEF, Child Rights and You, CAF, HelpAge, and has worked in commercial marketing for Macmillan and Reed Elsevier Group. Anup speaks internationally on fundraising and blogs on www.fundraisingasia.org.

Sean Triner, the copywriting mathematician, has been a fundraiser since leaving school, working in events, corporate, and grant fundraising; direct marketing including introducing direct dialogue (face-to-face) at the U.K. charity Action Medical Research in the early 1990s, one of the first charities to embrace this method. His final job before crossing to the agency side was marketing and communications director at a U.K. mental health charity, Mind. In 2002 his team, Leeds United, was doing badly so he fled to Australia, set up a full-service charity marketing agency (**Pareto Fundraising**) and soon after that set up a charity telemarketing agency with a friend. The agency works with around 50 Australian, New Zealand, and Hong Kong charities doing direct mail, digital fundraising, bequest marketing, training, and data analysis. Pareto's reputation is built around its data knowledge.

Masataka Uo is CEO and cofounder of the **Japan Fundraising Association** and president of **FUNDREX. Co. Ltd.**, a fundraising consulting company. He is one of the top leaders in Japan's fundraising sector. Previously he worked in the international development field and in supporting the capacity of CSOs in developing counties for 15 years. He led the launch of the Certified Fundraiser (CFR) program in Japan, and published the first annual giving report in Japan, *Giving Japan*, to promote philanthropic giving.

Anca Zaharia, after completing graduate studies in humanitarian law in Geneva, has been working in the humanitarian field for six years in Romania and Switzerland. Part of the team of the Romanian Red Cross HQ, she has been in charge of communication and relationships with corporate donors, cooperation within the International Red Cross Movement, and has managed different educational EU-funded projects. She has thus coordinated several major fundraising events, the brand awareness campaign "Be the Red Cross" and reached more than 10,000 young people through their humanitarian values sessions. For the past couple of years she has been involved in coordinating a Red Cross European network of specialists focused on EU funding—European Funding Practitioners' Group.

Index